THE AMERICAN FAMILY

THE AMERICAN FAMILY
A Sociological Interpretation

BERT N. ADAMS
University of Wisconsin

MARKHAM PUBLISHING COMPANY / Chicago

MARKHAM SOCIOLOGY SERIES
Robert W. Hodge, Editor

Adams, *Kinship in an Urban Setting*
Adams, *The American Family: A Sociological Interpretation*
Appelbaum, *Theories of Social Change*
Farley, *Growth of the Black Population: A Study of Demographic Trends*
Filstead, ed., *Qualitative Methodology: Firsthand Involvement with the Social World*
Laumann, Siegel, and Hodge, eds., *The Logic of Social Hierarchies*
Zeitlin, ed., *American Society, Inc.: Studies of the Social Structure and Political Economy of the United States*

Copyright © 1971 by Markham Publishing Company
All rights reserved
Printed in the United States of America
Library of Congress Catalog Card Number: 74–122303
Standard Book Number: 8410–4004–2

To my socializing agents:
Beulah R. and William W. Adams

Preface

For several years, the author has taught courses focussing on the family in the United States—supplementing his lectures with summary textbooks, research monographs, and books of readings. These reading materials have, with rare exception, been descriptive, without presenting any particular framework through which to view the family in its U.S. variety. The author has therefore found it necessary to develop his own framework, distributing it to the class by means of lectures and handouts. This volume is a result of the conviction that there is need, not for just another summary text on the family, but for a text that presents analytic frameworks and theoretical conceptions for organizing and interpreting the great mass of information now available on the U.S. family.

The purpose of the book is admittedly ambitious. It is an *introductory text*, in the sense that the reader is introduced to all the traditional subjects relating to the family: socialization, dating and mate selection, marital roles, kinship, divorce, and so on. These subjects are introduced, however, not exhausted; the author has selected and presented those materials he believes to be most useful in understanding the family in the contemporary United States. The book is also a *theoretical monograph.* The cross-cultural and historical backgrounds form the foundation for the development of propositions regarding the U.S. family and the continua on which the characteristics of this or any other family system may be located. These propositions and continua are the basis for the entire work, focussing as it does on one specific family system. In addition, this volume is in many ways a *series of essays,* or working papers, on the family. Chapters such as "Family Subcultures and Subsocieties in the United States," "Love and Mate Selection in the United States," and "Family Response to Change and Challenge," can stand alone—furnishing their own subframeworks for organizing the data presented therein. If an issue is an open one, as in the case of factors in mate selection, it is treated as such by the author. The major concern throughout is that the student confront interpretations to think about, react to, argue with, and expand—not just facts to memorize.

It may be instructive to indicate what the book is not as well as what it is. It is not a book of suggestions on how to be happily married, how to get along with kin, or how to rear children. As the subtitle asserts, this is a "Sociological Interpretation" of the U.S. family for the purpose of understanding it; whatever suggestions the reader finds within its pages must and should be derived by inference from the findings reported and the conclusions drawn. Nor is this an encyclopedic summary of all the literature on the family —it is not a "compendium of all knowledge." We have tried to avoid as much mediocre material as possible, rather than reviewing all the extant research results. Furthermore, we are confident that supplementary readings can be obtained as desired. The need, we feel, is for interpretation rather than for another descriptive compilation. Finally, this book is clearly not a set of final answers regarding the family in the United States. Hopefully, many of our interpretations and conclusions will stand the test of time, but the state of family study is such that the drawing of anything but *tentative* conclusions would be presumptuous at this juncture.

Aside from the many authors whose works and insights proved of value in the writing of this book, the author would be remiss if he did not acknowledge three specific contributions. Bernard Farber and Harold Christensen read and criticized the first six chapters, and many of their suggestions were gratefully adopted. Any errors which remain are, of course, the author's responsibility. In addition, the process of moving toward a finished product was aided immeasurably by the careful editing of Peggy Nenno, of Markham Publishing Company.

The writing of this volume has been an exciting experience; it is hoped that some of the excitement will be conveyed to the reader as he peruses its pages. If a few readers determine that the testing of the conclusions and interpretations presented herein would be a worthwhile endeavor, and if many readers better understand the family system of U.S. society, then the book will have served a useful purpose.

Madison, Wisconsin
June, 1970

B.A.

Contents

PREFACE   vii

I.   INTRODUCTION TO FAMILY STUDY   1

     Section One. The History of Family Study   4
         1860–1890: *Social Darwinism*   4
         1890–1920: *Social Reform*   5
         1920–1950: *Scientific Study*   5
         1950–Present: *Attention to Family Theory*   6
     Section Two. Studying the Family   12

II.   FAMILY STRUCTURES AND VARIETIES   15

     Section One. Family Structural Principles   15
         Marriage Arrangements and Types   16
         Household Arrangements   18
         Residential Clustering and Location   21

     Section Two. Selected Cultural Distinctions and the Use of Types   22
         Descent and Inheritance   22
         Authority   24
         Types of Nuclear Families   24
         The Use of Types   25

     Section Three. Family Structure and the Incest Taboo   26
         Incest Motivation and Structure: An Interpretation   31

III.   FAMILY VARIETIES EXEMPLIFIED: NAYAR, PAPAGO, CHINESE   35

     Section One. The Nayar of South India   36
         Is the Family Universal?   39

	Section Two. Papago Family and Kinship	40
	The Workability and Value of Normative Practices	42
	Section Three. The Chinese Family in Historical Perspective	43
	Section Four. Summary of Chapters II and III	52
IV.	ANTECEDENTS OF THE MODERN AMERICAN FAMILY	55
	Section One. Pre-colonial Influences	55
	Section Two. Family Life in the American Colonies, 1611–1800	59
	Section Three. Changes in the American Family, 1800–1970	64
	Section Four. Summary and Conclusions	75
V.	THE FAMILY IN A DIFFERENTIATED SOCIETY: TOWARD A THEORETICAL PERSPECTIVE	79
	Section One. Universal Family Functions	81
	Section Two. The Family and Its Changing Functions: Three Views	83
	Section Three. Division of Labor and the Family: Extensions and Clarifications	85
	Section Four. Quasi-theoretical Propositions about the U.S. Family	93
	Section Five. Family System Characteristics: Five Continua	96
VI.	FAMILY SUBCULTURES AND SUBSOCIETIES IN THE UNITED STATES	102
	Section One. Middle-class and Lower-class Family Models	103
	Section Two. The Religious Subculture and Subsociety	107

Section Three. The Ethnic Subculture and Subsociety 113

Section Four. Racial Groups: The Black American Family 115
    History of the Afro-American 116
    The Black American Family Today 120

VII. THE SOCIALIZATION PROCESS 134

Section One. Some Principles of Socialization 137
    Conscience and Guilt 138
    Ego Struggle 139
    Identification 140
    Personality Integration 142

Section Two. Socialization in the United States 143
    The Principles Applied 143
    Middle-class and Lower-class Styles of Socialization Compared 147
    Rearing by the Book 153

VIII. ADOLESCENCE 157

Section One. The Adolescent As an Ideal-type 159

Section Two. Adolescents, Parents, and Peers 161
    Emancipation 161
    Youth Culture 163
    Conflict with Parents and the Generation Gap 167

Section Three. The College Adolescent 170

Section Four. Socialization and Adolescents: Summary and Conclusions 172

IX. PREMARITAL RELATIONSHIPS IN THE UNITED STATES 176

Section One. The Nature and Functions of Dating 178
    The Dating Continuum 178
    General Functions of Dating 180
    Stages and Specific Functions of the Dating Continuum 181

	Section Two. Problematic Aspects of Dating	184
	Parental Influence	184
	Intergroup or Heterogeneous Dating	185
	Physical Attractiveness	186
	Social Awkwardness	187
	Insincerity	187
	Section Three. Premarital Sexual Relations	188
	Extent and Significance of Premarital Sex in the United States	189
	Value Positions on Premarital Sex	193
	Premarital Sex As a Cultural Alternative	195
	Section Four. Conclusions	199
X.	LOVE AND MATE SELECTION IN THE UNITED STATES	203
	Love, Kin Group, and Mate Selection	203
	Section One. Negative Factors in Mate Selection	206
	Incest Taboos	206
	Propinquity	207
	Homogamy in Mate Selection	208
	Section Two. Positive Factors in Mate Selection	212
	Values in Mate Selection	212
	Common Interests	213
	Complementary Needs	214
	Other Psychological Factors in Mate Selection	215
	Section Three. Mate Selection As Process	218
	Section Four. Critique and Tentative Conclusions	221
	Section Five. Racial Homogamy: A Case in Nonuniversal Availability	224
	Norms Governing Black-White Intermarriage	252
	Intermarriage Laws	226
	Black-White Intermarriage: How Many and Who?	226
	Motives for Racial Intermarriage in the United States	229

XI.	MARRIAGE: PROCESSES AND ROLES	234
	Section One. Marriage As A Process	234
	Section Two. Marriage As Changing Roles	240
	Role Differentiation	240
	Role Blurring	242
	Role Choice and Conflict	244
	Section Three. Husband-Father Role Choices	246
	The "Feminization" of Occupations	246
	Home versus Community	247
	Husband and Father	248
	Section Four. Wife-Mother Role Choices	249
	Role Censensus	251
	Motives	251
	Social Class, Wife's Work Status, and Marital Adjustment	252
	Wife's Work Status and Child Adjustment	253
	Conclusion	254
XII.	MARRIAGE: INTERACTIONS AND ADJUSTMENTS	259
	Section One. Husband-Wife Interaction: Running the Household	259
	Decision-making and Power	259
	The Sexual Division of Labor	262
	Section Two. Financial and Sexual Adjustments in Marriage	264
	Financial Adjustment	265
	Sexual Adjustment	266
	Section Three. A Summary of Marriage: Predicaments, Communication, and Choice	268
	Marital Predicaments	269
	Communication in Marriage	271
	Summary and the Value of Choice	272
XIII.	KINSHIP RELATIONS	277
	Section One. Kin Functions in Cross-cultural Perspective	278

Section Two. Some Issues in Kinship Analysis 281
    Kin Terms 281
    Kinsman As a Person 284
    Kin "Distance" 285
    Unimportance, Isolation, and Consistency 286

Section Three. Categories of U.S. Kin and Their Characteristics 288
    Parents and Adult Offspring 288
    Adult Sibling Relations 289
    Secondary Kinship 291
    In-law Relations 292

XIV. AGING AND THE FAMILY IN THE UNITED STATES 299

Section One. Disengagement Theory and Its Critics 300

Section Two. Socialization: The Decisions of the Aged 304

Section Three. The Social Network and Age Segregation 306
    Kin Relations of the Elderly 307
    Non-kin and Age-grading 309

Section Four. Husband-Wife Relations in Old Age 311

Section Five. Summary and Conclusions 313

XV. RESPONSE OF THE FAMILY TO CHANGE AND CHALLENGE 319

Section One. A Framework for Analyzing Challenges and Family Responses to Them 320
    (1) *Expected or Unexpected Challenges* 325
    (2) *External Versus Internal Origin* 325
    (3) *Family Structure in Its Network* 326
    (4) *Internal Family Organization* 326
    (5) *Definition, or Perception, of the Stressor* 327

Section Two. Four Changes and Challenges Briefly Considered 328
    Illegitimacy 328
    Economics, Employment, and the Family 329

		Divorce in the United States	331
		Death and the Family	341
	Section Three. Conclusions		343
XVI.	THE FAMILY IN THE UNITED STATES: RETROSPECT AND PROSPECT		348
	Section One. The Contemporary United States Family: A Review		349
	Section Two. The Future Prospects for the U.S. Family		353

INDEX 361

1

Introduction to Family Study

This book is about one of man's basic institutions, the family. At some time or another most Americans have been told that the three great institutions of the community are the home, the church, and the school—with the word "institution" left undefined. An *institution* may be defined as an organized aspect of man's social existence which is established and perpetuated by various norms or rules. Family and kinship; the economy; political, legal, educational, religious, and scientific structures—these are some of the more important institutions or organized aspects of modern society.

In many ways the family is the most remarkable of these. The state or political structure concerns itself with social control and mobilization; economic institutions regulate the production and distribution of goods and services; religious organizations seek to relate man to the supernatural and to ultimate values. Yet, basic to these types of social organization *historically* has been the family, that institution pertaining to sexual relations, marriage, reproduction and child-bearing, socialization or child training, and the relating of the individual to the other institutionalized aspects of society.

The key word in the previous sentence is "historically." Is the family in modern industrial society still of central importance? Is it dominant; is it specializing and adapting to the contemporary world; or is it disintegrating? This complex question lies at the heart of current preoccupation with the family, which is reflected in Margaret Mead's statement that the "American family is at the center of American concern at the present time; its strengths and weaknesses, its past and its future are being subjected to every kind of scrutiny, pessimistic and optimistic."[1]

The interpreters of and commentators on the American family are as varied in their assumptions and views as they are numerous. To some it is the object of serious *criticism*. The radical may claim that the contemporary family is the greatest single hurdle to be overcome before social equality, personal freedom, and self-realization can be achieved. In 1884 Friedrich Engels expressed it thus: "The modern individual family is founded on the open or concealed domestic slavery of the wife, and modern society is a mass composed of these individual families as its molecules."[2] Radicals are not, however, alone in their criticism of today's family. Edmund Leach, a British social anthropologist and provost of King's College, has asserted that "far from being the basis of the good society, the family with its narrow privacy and tawdry secrets is the source of all our discontents."[3]

Many of those more favorably disposed toward the family nevertheless find it a source of *dismay*. Individuals from Carle Zimmerman and Pitirim Sorokin, sociologists, to Ann Landers, a newspaper columnist, observe with concern the practice of marriage at an early age, the high divorce rate, the prevalence of premarital sex, and the generation gap. The inference often drawn is that the institution of the family is decaying and, with it, the nation. Among the pessimistic are those who feel that, far from being the *source* of discontent, the family is an unwitting victim of rapid social-cultural-technological change, having little control over its own destiny.

A large number of practitioners address themselves to the family as an object for *advice*. A few of the indicative book titles are: *Making the Most of Marriage, Understanding Your Teenagers, Growing with Your Children, The Art of Dating,* and *The Macmillan Guide to Family Finance*. The advice directed at the modern family virtually ranges from the advocation of complete sexual freedom to that of a return to the family farm as the panacea for individual and family problems.

Preoccupation with the family is manifested in at least two other ways among Americans. Because one of the means by which men cope with strains and tensions is humor, the relations between family members are often handled in this fashion. *Jokes* about the mother-in-law and the henpecked husband are ubiquitous in the family humor of American society. Finally, in addition to criticism, dismay, advice, and humor, the family is currently the focus of serious and substantial efforts to describe and *understand* it. Research studies with authors' interpretations comprise a large segment of the literature on the contemporary family. Seeking to avoid any judgment as to the "goodness" or "badness" of the family in its contemporary form, these writers attempt to report what the family is like and how it functions.

There are, therefore, several bodies of materials on the family which are available to the text writer. There are *factual materials*, drawn from empirical studies of various sorts. Sometimes their results reinforce each other, while at other times they appear to be contradictory. Second, there are *interpretations and explanations* of the facts. How, why, and to what extent has the family changed? What is the larger significance of the family's characteristics? How can the differences between research results be resolved? Several of the best available sociological texts on the family assemble vast amounts of research findings but explicitly avoid taking interpretive positions on the open issues.[4] In fact, the scientific study of the family is currently long on data and short on interpretation and explanation. A third type of material available consists of *social criticisms or critiques* by such insightful writers as Paul Goodman, Barrington Moore, and Edgar Friedenberg, as well as by Karl Marx and Sigmund Freud and their followers. Finally, there are abundant *suggestions* for family improvement and change which have been articulated by both professionals and non-professionals concerned about today's family.

The majority of twentieth century family texts have focussed upon either factual materials or suggestions. The reasons for the dominance of these two approaches will become more apparent as we briefly review the history of family study. We have, however, determined to emphasize *interpretation*, using suggestion and criticism quite selectively, and introducing those research studies that seem most useful for understanding the contemporary family. These interpretations should not be accepted as absolutes; the reader will find himself agreeing with some and disagreeing with others. The purpose is to get you to think *sociologically and interpretively* about the American family in its historical and cross-cultural context.

SECTION ONE

THE HISTORY OF FAMILY STUDY

Systematic study of the family did not begin until after the middle of the nineteenth century. Until then, interest in the family had been expressed by means of folklore, proverbs, moralisms, and laws. Its importance in the structure of society was affirmed in much of the early wisdom literature of China, India, and the pre-exilic Hebrews. The beginning of the movement toward systematic understanding rather than folklore can be traced roughly to the time of the appearance of Charles Darwin's *Origin of the Species* in 1859. The years from 1860 to 1950 may be profitably divided into three thirty-year periods, each one characterized by a particular emphasis with respect to the family.[5]

1860–1890: Social Darwinism

From 1860 to 1890 the attempt was made by numerous writers to apply Darwin's biological evolutionary scheme to the course of human history. Discussions of origins, coupled with notions of evolution and progress, were found in the writings of Lewis Henry Morgan, Friedrich Engels, J. J. Bachofen, Edward Westermarck, and others. Did the family begin in a primitive horde? Was marriage originally by capture? What is the origin of monogamy, and what will be its fate? These sorts of questions interested the social darwinists when they wrote about the family. Their treatises were macrocosmic, or large-scale, and cross-cultural, attempting to devise universally applicable laws of societal development. Their scholarly techniques were often intuitive, involving the somewhat unscientific approach of drawing a conclusion or developing a theory and then mustering evidence from diverse sources to support it. Yet, despite the inadequacy of some of their methods, the writings of the darwinists aroused the kind of interest in family and kinship which eventually gave rise to efforts to empirically investigate families in relation to their societies.

During this period there were exceptions to the eclectic, large-scale approach to family analysis, a prime example being the work of Frederic Le Play, a Frenchman. The methods he used to study the families of European workingmen foreshadowed later developments in the use of both the interview and participant observation in data collection. He lived in many workingmen's homes, and took notes on his observations as he participated in family activity. Le Play can thus be viewed as a forerunner of later attempts at scientific study of the family.

1890–1920: Social Reform

The second period, especially in America, was dominated by an urgent concern with social problems and reform. Industrialization and urbanization had resulted in a heightened awareness of poverty, child labor, illegitimacy, and other problematic or problem-producing aspects of family life. The Chicago school of sociology, with its journal, *The American Journal of Sociology*, founded in 1894, became a spokesman for reform. The underlying assumption, though not always expressed, was that "we understand both the family and the effects of urban and industrial developments; what we must do is solve the resulting problems and strengthen the family." However, the problem- and reform-orientation gave rise in the early 1900's to another viewpoint, to the effect that "maybe we don't know as much as we need to about the conditions and characteristics of the modern family." This school of thought also had its focal point in Chicago.

1920–1950: Scientific Study

The 30 years from 1920 to 1950 are best characterized as the years of scientific study of the family. In the early years of this century, even while reform movements held sway, statistical techniques were being developed and social psychologists such as W. I. Thomas and Charles H. Cooley were focussing on individual personality adjustment. Both Thomas and Cooley were influential at the University of Chicago, but it was under the leadership of Ernest Burgess that the study of the family became a major sociological endeavor. Burgess conceived of the family as a "unity of interacting personalities," as he stated in an article published in 1926; through Burgess and his students, the study of the family became more than a speculation about origins or a plea for social improvement. He fostered efforts to understand the factors involved in choosing a mate in the U.S., the various forms of interaction between family members, divorce and breakup, the position of the aged, and so on. By 1950, and perhaps before, it was proper to speak of a body of scientific facts about the family.

1950–Present: Attention to Family Theory

Since 1950 there have been renewed attempts to explain the family and its forms and changes—attempts beyond mere description. Harold Christensen, in his *Handbook of Marriage and the Family*, labels this the period of systematic theory building.[6] This label, however, appears a bit presumptuous. Instead, the present period might best be described as the period of summarization of findings and conceptual frameworks, of complaint about lack of a comprehensive theory, and of substantial theorizing. Currently, much synthesizing and macro-research is being done in an attempt to bring sociology of the family into the mainstream of the sociological discipline. Men such as William J. Goode, Reuben Hill, Robert Winch, and Ira Reiss are in the forefront of present attempts at theory building.

Christensen reports seven dominant trends in family study from its beginning to the present: (1) There is increasing acceptance of the scientific viewpoint. (2) The field is increasingly respectable within sociology. (3) More attention is paid to personal adjustment within the family context—a result of Ernest Burgess' influence. (4) Substantive reports or empirical studies are proliferating. (5) There has been an elaboration of organization programs concerned with the family. Of special importance is the National Council on Family Relations (NCFR), of which the *Journal of Marriage and the Family* has been the official publication, with the *Family Life Coordinator* added recently. (6) Research methodology is being increasingly refined. (7) There is much concern over theory building. This last trend Christensen uses to characterize the period from 1950 to the present.

Three of these trends require extended comment before we close our brief history of family study. The first two, acceptance of the scientific viewpoint and increasing respectability, are closely related. As we have said, the study of the family in the U.S. in the early years of the twentieth century was problem- and reform-oriented. Many professionals were involved: lawyers, doctors, psychologists, clergymen, and others were seeking to cope with the effects of urban life upon the family. Gradually, the impact of scientific thinking resulted in a separation between the practitioners and the researchers, as a result of the consolidation of practitioners, first into a sub-field and then into the separate discipline of social work. Today there is a form of family course that is consistent with the approach of each of the major parties to this separation. First, there is the problem-oriented, or "how to" course, sometimes called the *functional* course. This type of course ordinarily uses a suggestion-centered textbook; is often taught through the home economics or social work department; and may explain how to rear well-adjusted children, how to plan and maintain a family budget, or perhaps the mechanics of an adequate sexual adjustment. The extreme *sociological* family course, oriented toward factual materials, may simply catalogue the findings of sociological researchers, without espousing a particular stance with respect to family values and often with little interpretation of the facts.

Since sociology as a discipline seeks to be objective and scientific, you perhaps can see why Christensen's first two trends are closely linked. The more that students of the family have espoused a scientific orientation, the more respectable family study has become among sociologists in general, since they regard themselves as trying to be scientific. However, it must be added that, as long as practitioners of various sorts see the family as good and important, it is hardly likely that the problem-orientation will ever be completely dominated by the scientific approach. The National Council on Family Relations well illustrates the dual orientation of family study up to the present. Its statement of purpose, found inside the front cover of the *Journal of Marriage and the Family*, reads as follows: "Its purpose is to advance the cultural values now principally secured through family relations for personality development and the strength of the nation. It seeks to unite in one common objective persons working in all the different fields of family research, teaching, and welfare." On the same page is found a description of the *Journal* and its contents: "The *Journal of Marriage and the Family* is a medium for the presentation of orginal theory, research interpretation, and critical discussion of materials related to marriage and the family. The *Journal* does not assume any responsibility for the written content of articles." This is, of course, the typical disclaimer found in media presenting fact and opinion. Recently, the NCFR's division of labor has resulted in its sponsorship of two journals; the aforementioned *Journal of Marriage and the Family*, which emphasizes scholarly work, and the *Family Coordinator*, which is more action-oriented.

The point is simply that, although the trend toward scientific study of the family has increased the respectability of the field, it is unlikely that the family, at least in the foreseeable future, will become strictly a subject of scientific investigation. Personal and societal values will continue to support a particular form of family system. The present volume seeks to avoid the extremes of the numerous suggestions of the practitioner on the one hand and the stultifying effects of fact without interpretation on the other hand.

Let us now look at Christensen's seventh trend, theory building, which he uses to characterize the period since 1950. Granting that there is great current concern with understanding the family and its relation to man's social existence, it is readily obvious that the theoretical inroads in the family field have been limited to date. Reuben Hill and Donald Hansen, for example, perceive the family field as currently being a considerable distance from an adequate theoretical synthesis, but as being at the stage of employing several definable *conceptual frameworks*.[7] These frameworks are not theories or explanations, but are viewpoints from which to analyze and describe family structure and behavior. An analogy from the physical sciences might make clear what Hill and Hansen mean by a conceptual framework. Suppose a scientist were to decide to study the common earthworm. He might investigate it in any of several ways: (1) its chemical properties; (2) its internal structure; (3) its reaction, as a nervous system, to stimuli; (4) its relation to the phyla, orders, families, genera, and species of the animal kingdom; or (5) its position in both the organic and inorganic environment. Each of these approaches would provide a *description* of the earthworm from one perspective—whether that of the biochemist, biologist, taxonomist, or animal ecologist. A theory, however, might *explain* how the earthworm acquired its characteristics or the nature of its significance within the animal kingdom. Conceptual frameworks, in summary, are descriptive standpoints from which to view reality; they are not theories.

According to Hill and Hansen, there are five clearly definable frameworks being utilized by students of the family. The *interactional* approach focusses upon family members in intimate contact. Because it is concerned with the relation between individual and family group, it is a social psychological approach. Beginning especially in the work of Burgess, its emphases include psychological and interpersonal adjustment in the family, the roles that the family members play, and the kinds of relationships that develop in a family setting.

A second approach, the *structure-functional*, is found in the work of William J. Goode, Meyer Nimkoff, and Robert Winch. What different sorts of family structures are there? How does the family system articulate with other societal institutions, such as the economic, educational, and religious? What functions does the family perform on behalf of the individual or his society? This is an a-historical approach that assumes that at any given point in time the various structures of a society tend to be coherent, consistent, and to perform specific functions. A problem with this approach is the "ideal-real," or normative-actual, fallacy, which will be referred to in Chapter II.

The *situational* approach is concerned with adaptation and problem-solving in a family context. How do individuals and the family unit respond to different circumstances and situations that arise, such as the marriage of a daughter, the death of a family member, or even the eating of a meal together? James H. S. Bossard has used this approach to examine family ritual, and much of the literature on family crises revolves around the problem of adaptation.

A fourth framework for viewing the family is called the *institutional* by Hill and Hansen. Like the structure-functional, this approach is concerned with the relation of the family institution to the rest of the society, but it is overtly historical in nature. The family in a particular society is described as it changes over time. This approach is exemplified in a history of the American family, written by John Sirjamaki in 1953, in which he records its current characteristics and the ways in which it has changed in recent history.[8] The focus of this approach is not upon the individual in the family, but upon the family in the society over time.

Finally, the *developmental* framework is simply a technique for observing changes occurring, not in the society but in the family life of the individual as he is born, grows up, marries, raises his family, and dies. The time span is the life cycle of any nuclear family, and the units of analysis are the stages—childhood, adolescence, marriage, adulthood, and old age—which can be demarcated within the life of an individual and his family. Most textbooks on the family utilize this framework at least to some extent, and ours will be no exception.[9]

Because family-kin units face both ways, toward the individual and toward society, Hill and Hansen's five conceptual frameworks can be dichotomized on the basis of their directional orientation. The structure-functional and institutional are concerned with the family-in-society, the former being a-historical and the latter historical. The other three frameworks are oriented toward individuals-in-families, the developmental being historical with respect to the individual's life span, the situational being historical within the span of a particular occurrence, and the interactional being a-historical regarding any particular family unit.

There is nothing immutable about the number of conceptual frameworks identified by Hill and Hansen. Others have discovered more frameworks, such as the economic, psychoanalytic, and anthropological, or have felt that the five can be subsumed under a smaller number of types.[10] The important thing to note is the fact that these various approaches, taken independently, tend to describe only a portion of the reality of the family. In this work, the chapters on cross-cultural variations and on the relation between the family and society, take an approach that is primarily structure-functional. In examining the historical antecedents of the American family, an institutional stance is employed. Much of the material on the modern American family, with its parental roles and husband-wife interaction, is concerned with adjustment—an interactional issue. The bulk of the volume will follow a developmental outline, beginning with the early socialization of the child and carrying him through adolescence, mate selection, adulthood, and old age. Finally, specific problems, such as the crises discussed in Chapter XV, are viewed from a situational perspective. These, we are saying, are not theories of the family, but are simply viewpoints from which to try to describe reality.

According to Hill and Hansen, the family field is currently long on conceptual frameworks and short on theory. A major purpose of the present volume is to supplement summaries of research results with explanation and interpretation. The setting for the interpretations includes the various types of family *structures* found around the world, the *functions* performed within family and kinship units, and the other internal aspects of *family culture*. Family systems—and families within the same system—vary in terms of their structures, including marital linkages, household members, and residential location *vis-à-vis* kin. The issue of family functions, or what the family does on behalf of the individual and of the society, has also been analyzed by scholars interested in the family institution. Other aspects of family-kin culture include descent and inheritance, husband-wife authority and roles, approaches to mate selection, and the cultural emphases in child-rearing. While all of these are important in preparing the reader to understand the American family, this treatment of the family in the United States will focus upon the last three issues: husband-wife relations, mate selection, and child-rearing.

Within the setting of the structural types, functions, and other internal culture, two basic concepts will be employed to help the reader understand the family against an historical and cross-cultural background. These concepts, *institutional embeddedness* and *personnel embeddedness*, mirror the two orientations of family and kinship: toward society and toward the individual. The first idea, that of institutional embeddedness, is well expressed in the following quotation from David Schneider:

> In many primitive and peasant societies a large number of kinds of institutions are organized and built *as parts of the kinship system itself*. Thus the major social units of the society may be kin groups—lineages perhaps. These same kin groups may be property-owning units, the political units, the religious units, and so on. Thus, whatever a man does in such a society he does as a kinsman of one kind or another.[11] (Italics added.)

In such societies, the other institutions are "embedded" in the kinship system, so that economic productive, political, religious, medical, and other activities take place within, and as aspects of, the kinship organization of the society. Thus, the head of the kin line may also be political ruler, performer of religious ritual, the primary educator, and the leader of the kin division of labor. A second form of institutional embeddedness is present if a "nuclear" unit (a set of parents and their children) is the seat of multiple societal activities, but is emancipated from the larger kin group. One of the key questions toward which this volume is directed concerns the extent to which other institutions have become differentiated from (are no longer embedded in) either the kin groups or nuclear families of the contemporary United States.

Personnel embeddedness, or the relation of family and kin to the individual, is a second major focus of this book. There are societies in which individuals and nuclear families are embedded in, and serve the needs of, the kinship system. Personnel embeddedness involves interaction patterns, solidarity, and values. If, for example, a conflict between the wife and her mother-in-law is resolved by sending the wife away, this would seem to indicate that the husband-wife unit is of secondary importance to the kin group. In some societies the nuclear family unit has been little distinguished from other forms of kin solidarity or in terms of interaction. In these societies, the major emphasis in child-rearing is that one develop into a good kin-community member. There are actually two levels of personnel embeddedness: (1) The individual and nuclear family are interactionally embedded in, and of secondary importance to, the kin community, or (2) the family unit of parents and children may be emancipated from kin dominance but the individual may still be subservient to, and operate primarily within, the nuclear family. If the alternative to institutional embeddedness is institutional differentiation, the alternative to personnel embeddedness is individualism. Therefore, a second key question in the present volume involves the extent to which the individual is still embedded in the nuclear family, and the family within the kin group, in modern U.S. society.

This introduction of the institutional and personnel embeddedness concepts has been both brief and somewhat premature, for the understanding of these concepts requires a level of cross-cultural and definitional sophistication that the reader may not have yet attained. The author, however, has felt it important to introduce these concepts early; they should become increasingly clear as the reader moves through the cross-cultural and historical materials of Chapters II through V. Particularly in Chapter V will these and other theoretical issues in family study be confronted directly. It is this author's conviction that explanation and interpretation, however tentative, is preferable to simple fact-gathering. The reader must judge the outcome for himself.

SECTION TWO

STUDYING THE FAMILY

Studying the family in one's own society, it may be well to note, is different in one crucial way from the study of theoretical astrophysics, the classical background of English literature, or multivariate analysis in social research. This difference is due to the fact that most readers are familiar in their daily lives with, and thus to some extent experts on, the phenomenon we call "family." This familiarity and expertise in family relations can be both a help and a hindrance to the sociological study of this institution. It is a help because a certain amount of understanding can be assumed. When one reads the word "family" he will think of two parents and one or more children whom they are rearing. Seeing the term "marriage," one thinks of two individuals of different sexes, legally joined together for the sake of sexual access, procreation, and the sharing of a common residence location—though perhaps not in these terms. "Divorce" the reader understands to be the legal separation of these two individuals. When one mentions "courtship," the sharing of time and activities with a member of the opposite sex comes to mind, perhaps in terms of dating or going steady.

Yet this very familiarity may likewise stand in the way of an attempt to step back and consider the family either objectively or in terms of generalities. The majority of families in the United States may or may not closely resemble one's own. However, even if the reader's family is rather typical, it is important to be aware of the tendency to feel that the way one's own family does things is the only, or at least the best, way. It would be improper to condemn such feelings; it is quite proper to be aware of them. In order to gain some sense of perspective and objectivity, this discussion shall begin with some examples that illustrate the great diversity of family systems throughout the world.

A generation ago, Robert MacIver defined the family as "a sex relationship sufficiently precise and enduring to provide for the procreation and upbringing of children."[12] This definition, while descriptive of essential elements in the family, is inadequate for use in this volume. Our purpose is to interpret family experience within the context of American society. This study will concern itself with the rearing of children, the adolescent experience, and the premarital relations between the sexes, as well as with marriage itself. The subject is the American family, its history and change over time, its relation to the society of which it is a part, its formation and dissolution, and its internal relationships. The foundation for this superstructure includes cross-cultural and historical variations in structure, functions, and internal culture. This setting or foundation is the focal point of the next four chapters, beginning in Chapter II with structural principles and types and certain other aspects of kin-family culture.

NOTES

[1] Margaret Mead, "The American Family," in Huston Smith, ed., *The Search for America* (Englewood Cliffs, N.J.: Prentice-Hall, 1959), p. 116.

[2] Frederick Engels, *The Origin of the Family, Private Property, and the State* (New York: International Publishers, 1942), p. 65.

[3] *Wisconsin State Journal*, November 27, 1967.

[4] One of the very best empirically based, but non-interpretive, sociological family texts is Gerald Leslie, *The Family in Social Context* (New York: Oxford University Press, 1967). An exception is Bernard Farber's *Family: Organization and Interaction* (San Francisco: Chandler, 1964), in which the author posits two types of family systems and interprets data on the modern family according to these types.

[5] For a discussion of the history of the family field that uses a somewhat different temporal framework, see Harold T. Christensen, ed., *Handbook of Marriage and the Family* (Chicago: Rand McNally, 1964), pp. 3–32.

[6] *Ibid.*

[7] Reuben Hill and Donald A. Hansen, "The Identification of Conceptual Frameworks Utilized in Family Study," *Marriage and Family Living*, 22 (1960), 299–311.

[8] John Sirjamaki, *The American Family in the Twentieth Century* (Cambridge, Mass.: Harvard University Press, 1953).

[9] For an example of a cross-cultural application of the developmental framework, see Kiyomi Morioka, "Life Cycle Patterns in Japan, China, and the United States," *Journal of Marriage and the Family*, 29 (1967), 595–606.

[10] See F. Ivan Nye and Felix M. Berardo, *Emerging Conceptual Frameworks in Family Analysis* (New York: Macmillan, 1966).

[11] David M. Schneider, *American Kinship: A Cultural Account* (Englewood Cliffs, N.J.: Prentice-Hall, 1968), p. v.

[12] Robert MacIver, *Society: Its Structure and Changes* (New York: Ray Long & Richard R. Smith, 1931), p. 112.

II

Family Structures and Varieties

THE DIFFERENT TYPES OF FAMILY STRUCTURES WHICH HAVE EXISTED IN VARIOUS SOCIETIES, AND THE PRINCIPLES WHICH UNDERLIE THEM, ARE ALMOST INNUMERABLE. IN THIS CHAPTER THE MOST IMPORTANT STRUCTURAL PRINCIPLES, AND THE TYPES PRODUCED THEREBY, ARE INTRODUCED. THESE PRINCIPLES INCLUDE MARITAL AND BLOOD LINKAGES AND RESIDENTIAL CLUSTERING. IN ADDITION, OTHER FACTORS USEFUL FOR DISTINGUISHING FAMILY SYSTEMS ARE INTRODUCED: DESCENT AND INHERITANCE, FAMILY AUTHORITY, AND TYPES OF NUCLEAR FAMILIES. SPECIAL ATTENTION IS GIVEN TO THREE PROBLEMS IN FAMILY STUDY: (1) THE DIFFERENCE BETWEEN NORMS OR EXPECTATIONS AND ACTUAL BEHAVIOR IN A FAMILY SYSTEM; (2) TYPES OR TYPOLOGIES AND THEIR USE; AND (3) AN EXPLANATION OF THE INCEST TABOO AND ITS RELATION TO SOCIAL STRUCTURE.

SECTION ONE

FAMILY STRUCTURAL PRINCIPLES[1]

In United States society a young male and female decide to marry. His name is added to her maiden name, and they affirm that their marriage is for as long as they both shall live. If possible, they move into a dwelling separate from both sets of parents, and they begin to plan for the coming of children. Their parents and other kin are interested in them and help them when the need arises, but the young couple is generally expected to be independent, to go it alone. In an introductory textbook written in the Western world, the word "family" is likely to signify what we have just described. Technically, this unit is called the *monogamous nuclear family,* consisting of a male, a female, and their offspring, and is, of course, the prevalent and legalized form of family in the contemporary United States. Common residence, which is typical for this unit, facilitates the sexual access of the married couple, care for the offspring, and a familial division of labor. A distinction is made in everyday speech between this unit and one's kin; when an American says "I want you to meet my family," he ordinarily means the unit of parents, brothers, and sisters, or else (if he is one of the parents) the unit consisting of his spouse and children.

This, then, is the type of family with which Americans are most familiar. Yet, when family structures are viewed cross-culturally, the variations from this pattern are seen to be enormously great. These variations are based upon such structural issues as the number of persons of each sex who are allowed to marry; the expected household composition, including both marital units and blood kin; and the pattern of residential clustering of kin. An understanding of these structural principles, and of the types of kin-family systems produced by them, should give the reader a better sense of the United States family system as but one type among many. In addition, we shall try to make it clear that expectations and reality often diverge—that the way people expect to, desire to, and say they behave, and the way they actually behave,. are not necessarily the same. This latter point, while drawn in this chapter from cross-cultural illustrations, will be seen to be important when husband-wife decision-making, treatment of the aged, the position of the working wife, and other issues in the U.S. family are confronted. The first structural principle to be introduced concerns marital arrangements and types.

Marriage Arrangements and Types

Marriage in the United States is monogamous, meaning that only one male and one female are allowed to be married to each other. Though it is quite natural for the individual without cross-cultural experience to assume that this is the way marriage "should" be, when compared with other times and places, monogamy is seen to be but one type among others. The other possibilities, all involving more than one member of one or both sexes, are together called by the term "polygamy," or multiple marriage. The polygamous possibilities are three. There may be two or more females married to one male; the term *polygyny*, or "many wives," refers to this. Or two or more males could be married to one female, in which case the term *polyandry*, or "many husbands," is used. Theoretically, two or more males might be married to two or more females, which would be *group marriage*. Therefore, polygyny + polyandry + group marriage = polygamy, as distinguished from monogamy.

The frequency with which these four types of marital arrangements occur normatively, i.e., as expectations or desires, in various societies is interesting because of the light it sheds on man's sexual and economic nature. In a world sample of 554 societies, George P. Murdock finds polygyny to be normative in 415 of them, monogamy in 135, polyandry in 4, and no instances of group marriage.[2] A thesis proposed to account for the prevalence of polygyny is that men are generally governed by internal sex drives and disposed toward sexual variety to a much greater extent than are women. If this is so, then men are subjected to a greater strain in monogamous marriages than women are.

Two cautions should be added regarding the prevalence of polygamous marriages. A distinction must be made between the normative marital arrangement in a society, or that dictated by its ideology, and the frequency with which specific arrangements occur empirically. In some societies, such as the United States, monogamy is required and multiple partners prohibited. Yet in many, if not all, of the 415 societies in which polygyny is normative, monogamy in fact predominates numerically. Suppose, for example, that in a normatively polygynous society each male married but two females. If the sex ratio (the number of males per 100 females in a population) of the society were approximately 100, half the males would have to remain unmarried. Only if the sex ratio were quite low or if extremely large numbers of males were killed in warfare would there be any possibility of most males in the society marrying more than one female.[3] It is well to note at this juncture that some of the early anthropologists, who visited exotic places and asked informants how things were done there, came away with the normative rather than the actual structural arrangements. The resultant difference is comparable to that between the impression a visitor from Mars would receive if he accepted our account of what families are like in the U.S., and his impression if he went into our houses to observe those living there. We shall return again to this normative-actual distinction.

There is more than a logical-statistical reason why monogamy predominates in many societies that ideologically favor, or are dominated by, the polygyny principle. Most men in a polygynous society are simply too poor to afford more than one wife. The important or high-ranking male takes additional wives to validate his superior status and to aid him in the care of the fields, the raising of cows, or other economic ventures. He must, however, be able to afford the bride price, the cost of purchasing her from her parents. In such societies, wives are considered economic and sta-

18 THE AMERICAN FAMILY

tus assets if they can be afforded, with sexual access being a secondary motivation for polygyny, if it is a motive at all. Polygyny is normative, therefore, for what it signifies, but it is far from behaviorally dominant in the 415 societies.

Household Arrangements

In the United States, a couple, following marriage, may live for a time with the parents of one of them. This arrangement is usually temporary, for the desires and expectations of the pair are ordinarily for housing apart from all other kin. The nuclear family is not, however, the normative household unit in all societies. On the contrary, the number of nuclear units may be compounded, as indicated above, by the addition of marital partners and their children in the various forms of polygamy. The household may also be compounded by the addition of other blood (consanguineal) kin. Perhaps the two best-known examples of consanguineal household extension are the three-generation extended family and the joint family. These may be compared with the monogamous nuclear family by means of Figure 1.

Each of the three parts of Figure 1 depicts a household type based upon blood ties. Type I is, of course, the typical household in the United States, consisting of a parent of each sex and their children. Type II shows a joint family composed of three brothers,

FIGURE 1

Three Types of Household Arrangements Based on Consanguineal Ties

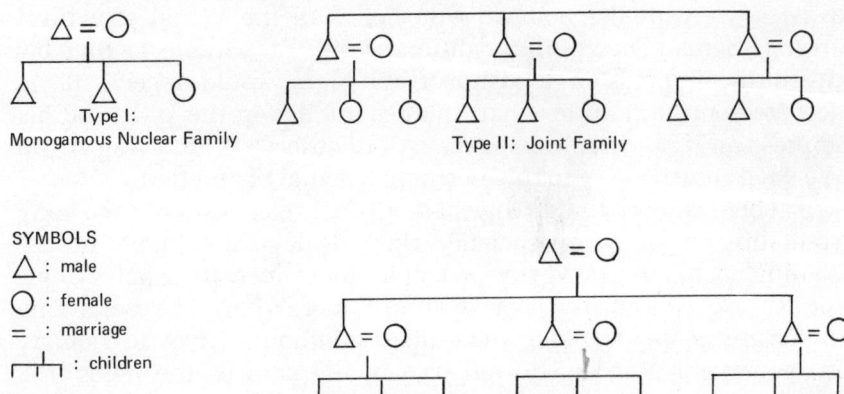

their wives, and their children living together. The best-known example of such a family pattern is the traditional Hindu family of India. Type III depicts the extended, or three-generation extended, family. Here the aging parents live with their sons, the sons' wives and children. Classical China is frequently used as an example of a society in which the extended household pattern was prevalent.

Once again, two qualifications should be added to the delineation of normative household arrangements according to consanguineal ties. First, it will be noted that both the extended and joint family were diagrammed with the brothers living together and their sisters presumably having married into other such units and having left home. There is no logical reason why the diagram should not have shown sisters living together with their husbands and children, with their brothers having married and moved out. The only reason for depicting these consanguineal arrangements as we have is a statistical one: the pattern in which brothers live together after marriage is normative in a larger number of societies than is that in which sisters live together.

Second, the important distinction between norms or expectations and actuality or behavioral variety can be profitably reinforced in this connection. In classical China, the ideal in the upper echelons of society was for the aged patriarch to keep his family together and continue to wield authority over them as long as he lived. As in the case of normative polygyny, however, extended-family households were in the minority. Historical data indicate that in reality the great majority of pre-Communist Chinese households were rather small, averaging about five persons. The family ideology, especially among the *literati,* and actual family patterns are again found to be divergent.

A study of an Arab village, reported by Henry Rosenfeld, may illustrate and help to explain the great disparity between normative and actual family structures. Upon entering this community, the researcher asked what sort of family system they had. The uniform response was that they were an extended-family village. Then, rather than stopping with the verbal expression of norms, he went from door to door to see the household composition himself. Here is what he found:

17 complete extended families, consisting of grandparents, their sons and their wives and children;
27 partial extended families, one or more brothers having left;
15 joint families with the grandparents deceased;

11 unmarried brothers living alone or with their mothers, their fathers being deceased;

205 nuclear family households, consisting of a male, female, and their children.

Are the 205 nuclear families unhappy and longing for the norm or cultural ideal? The answer is simply no. If anything, the tendency is for more of those involved in extended or joint households to desire the nuclear arrangement than vice versa.

What, then, keeps some of the extended and joint families together? The religio-cultural norm of filial piety or obligation to parents is still quite strong and influential. However, the primary reasons for the continuation of extended and joint households appear to be economic. Extended, partial extended, and joint families are most prevalent under two opposing conditions. First, if the family is economically *prosperous,* the aging father may attempt to keep his family together for reasons of prestige and authority and for reasons of economy—to help him do the work. The male offspring, on their part, may be willing to accept this subordinate position during the father's lifetime for the sake of the inheritance that will eventually come their way. At the other extreme, the *poor* are likely to stay together out of economic necessity. They must pool their resources in order to survive. Unquestionably, the overall movement in the village is toward more nuclear households, though the people, when asked, will still express the traditional extended-family ideology.[4]

It is necessary, we are suggesting, to examine both the cultural ideal and the variations and direction of change when studying the family system of a given society. The fact is that there may even be different ideals operating within the same culture. Some of Rosenfeld's villagers desire, for very good reasons, to preserve the traditional extended-family household and economic unit, while others, for what they consider to be equally good reasons, prefer the monogamous nuclear family. When we turn to the family in the United States, we shall once again see multiple normative principles at work, and will be concerned to discover the direction and speed of change.

The monogamous nuclear family, polygamous marriage, and composite consanguineal unit—these are three basic structural distinctions among marriage-family-household types. One further word regarding these distinctions is instructive. Meyer Nimkoff, as well as several other writers, in making the same general threefold distinction (see note 1), simply uses the term "nuclear family" to refer to the monogamous nuclear family. Our purpose in adding the word "monogamous" is to indicate that there are nuclear units within each of the structural types. The monogamous nuclear family has but one nuclear unit, consisting of two parents and their children. In a polygynous family, a man who has three wives is a member of three nuclear units simultaneously, each consisting of himself, a wife, and their children. Likewise, in a composite consanguineal household, there are multiple nuclear units under the same roof. The classical Chinese ideal, for example, might comprise four nuclear units: the grandparents and their sons being one, and each of the sons and his wife and children being another nuclear family. Thus, if the term "nuclear family" is used to describe the first structural type, it is not mutually exclusive from the two composite types. But the addition of the marital designation "monogamous" makes the three structural categories mutually exclusive.

Residential Clustering and Location

Besides the typical marital linkages and household units described above, there are other structural principles that distinguish between family-kinship systems. One pertains to residential clustering from the perspective of the nuclear family. A man and woman, when they marry, may be expected to locate with or near his kin, her kin, both sets of kin, neither set of kin—or they may spend part of their married life near his kin and part near hers. Among the possible arrangements, the ones that occur most frequently may be reduced to five. The single most prevalent residence pattern cross-culturally is that closely related to Figure 1: settling with or near the husband's parents following marriage, a practice that is called patrilocality. Other recurrent practices include matrilocality, living near the parents and kin of the wife, and neolocality, settling apart from both sets of parents. This latter is the normative pattern in the contemporary United States. Some young couples in the U.S. may live for a time with one set of parents or the other, but this is usually due to economic or other necessity; the ideal, or desired, arrangement is a separate, or neolocal, residence not governed by the location of either set of kin. Two other patterns occur in enough societies to be worthy of mention. One is called by Murdock "bilocality," meaning that the newly married couple may choose whether to reside near the husband's or the wife's parents.

22   THE AMERICAN FAMILY

Avunculocal residence, a fifth pattern, signifies that the young couple is expected to live with or near the husband's mother's brother, his (the husband's) maternal uncle.[5]

Other aspects of residential clustering involve, not the location of the nuclear family, but persons such as aging parents, single adults, and so on. Yet the major issue here is the way in which the nuclear family is related structurally to household and kin clusters.

SECTION TWO

SELECTED CULTURAL DISTINCTIONS AND THE USE OF TYPES

Thus far we have introduced the marital, consanguineal, and residential clustering principles that help to shape the various family-kin structures. These principles, and the types of structures produced thereby, give us some sense of the U.S. family within the larger context of societal variations. At this point we shall turn to some additional cultural distinctions that are useful in defining the setting and background of the U.S. family. Rules of descent and inheritance, family authority, and types of nuclear families will be discussed.

Descent and Inheritance

Descent and inheritance are closely related, but not synonymous. Descent has to do with the formal manner in which the individual is related to his kin. Inheritance involves the property, goods, and obligations that are passed along through specified kin. The three most prevalent types of descent groupings are patrilineal, matrilineal, and bilateral. Patrilineal descent is traced through the male line; matrilineal is traced through the female line. Bilaterality signifies normative equality in affiliation with both the mother's and father's kin, although, in actuality, kin ties in a bilateral system tend to be overbalanced in favor of the preferred kin.[6] Inheritance follows the same types of patterns, but is generally more complex than the determination of descent because there tend to be multiple items to be inherited, as we shall see below. As a society, the United States is basically bilateral in descent; i.e., we trace descent through, and consider ourselves equally related to, both parental kin groups. Only in the practice of naming, with the husband's family name being added to the wife's at marriage, does U.S. society retain a vestige of patrilineal inheritance.

Although descent lines tend to be relatively clear-cut, neither descent nor inheritance ordinarily operates in either-or terms. Patrilineal descent does not mean that an individual is related to his father's male kin to the exclusion of interaction, obligation, and intimacy with the mother's kin. In fact, intimacy in a patrilineal society is often greater between an individual and his maternal kin simply because there are "no strings attached." In the case of inheritance, even more than in the case of descent, involvement with the two kin groups tends to be a matter of degree or kind rather than of exclusiveness. For example, J. B. Christensen reports that, among the Fanti of West Africa, along with membership in a matrilineal clan (matrilineal descent) goes the right of property inheritance, the use of clan land, succession to a position of political authority, and a proper funeral and burial. Thus, on first examination, this might easily be considered a matrilineal society. Yet the father's line among the Fanti is also a source of certain types of inheritance. From the patriline, the individual receives his military allegiance, the father's deity, and his soul; physically, the father is regarded as the primary donor of blood. The author concludes that the Fanti are, in fact, characterized by double descent (from our perspective—"double inheritance"), receiving certain benefits and obligations from one kin line and others from the other line.[7] While inheritance is not always as equally divided as it is among the Fanti, many of the unilineal, i.e., either patrilineal or matrilineal, systems are characterized by a secondary inheritance and by close relationships with members of the opposing kin group or line.

If an offspring desires to inherit property when his parent dies, he may be obliged to help care for that property while his parent is alive. Because of this and other socioeconomic reasons, it is not surprising that there is a fairly high correlation between residential clustering and descent-inheritance patterns as follows: patrilocality with patrilineality, matrilocality with matrilineality, and neolocality with bilaterality. These correlations are, however, far from perfect. Under certain conditions, for example, matrilocal residence may occur in combination with bilateral or patrilineal descent rather than with matrilineal. In order to understand the bases for the relation between residential clustering and descent-inheritance in a particular society, one must understand the overall societal configuration—not just the kinship system, economy, polity, religion, or geography and climate. Discussions of the Nayar, Papago, and Chinese family systems in Chapter III should make apparent both the interconnectedness of parts and the strains that are inherent in systems different from that of the United States.

Authority

Authority, status, and decision-making patterns in the family and kin group may be profitably divided into three ideal types. The most familiar pattern historically and cross-culturally is patriarchy, or father-rule. A matriarchal society is one in which the mother makes the decisions and wields the authority in the family. Equalitarianism signifies approximate similarity between the husband and wife in status, in authority or control, and in decision-making. In this pattern, equality in the latter area is effected either by coming to an agreement or by dividing areas of influence. The unilineal descent systems are usually characterized by a single, aged individual in each kin unit wielding great authority, with varying amounts of inequality between husbands and wives within the various nuclear families. One of the important effects of the emancipation of the nuclear family from the larger kin group, or its freedom from personnel embeddedness, is that, at first, the authority of the husband tends to be heightened. Thus, it is under a system of nuclear family centrality—both institutionally and in terms of personnel—that normative patriarchy within the nuclear family appears to reach its zenith. One of the topics that will engage us throughout this volume is the extent to which the typical American family has changed from a patriarchal to an equalitarian authority pattern; or whether both the patriarchal and equalitarian patterns are found in different segments of the U.S. population.

Types of Nuclear Families

The diagrammatic presentation of the patrilineal extended family in Figure 1 shows that, within this household unit, the adult son is simultaneously a member of two nuclear families. One of these involves his parents and brothers (as well as any sisters who may have married and moved away) and the other consists of his wife and their children. Several years ago W. Lloyd Warner made a valuable terminological distinction between these two types of nuclear families. "Every normal adult in every human society," Murdock asserts, referring to Warner's distinction, "belongs to at least two nuclear families—a family of *orientation,* in which he was born and reared, and which includes his father, mother, brothers, and sisters, and a family of *procreation* which he establishes by his marriage and which includes his" spouse and their children.[8] Whether the members of a nuclear unit are living together or apart is unimportant to the definition. The sisters who have married and left home (and are therefore omitted from Figure 1) are still members of the adult son's family of orientation, although the residential component may be clarified by the use of the term *"kin* of orientation" to indicate a non-domestic unit. The neolocal United States pattern means that the adult ordinarily lives with his family of procreation and apart from his family (kin) of orientation.

The Use of Types

Types of family structures based upon marriage, consanguineal ties, and residential clustering have been introduced, as have descent-inheritance links, authority patterns, and types of nuclear families. We have tried to indicate that these types are often expressed normatively in a society despite a disparity between norms and empirical behavior. The use of types, even when they depict empirical reality fairly accurately, must be within the bounds of three further qualifications. First, they are *group* identifications. When we speak of a patrilineal-patrilocal-patriarchal society with extended family households in North Africa, for example, it may or may not be true that the majority of specific kin-family units actually fit the definition of all these types. Nor can we expect our "type" to necessarily predict the character of Ahmed's or Abdul's family. The type is a construct that is not predicated on a specific example from within the group or society, but upon common denominators. While we can't guarantee that Abdul's family will fit the construct perfectly, we can expect Abdul and his friends to resemble the constructed type more closely than, say, a number of Bemba families from south central Africa.

A second qualification on the use of types is that they are *comparative* constructs: compared to the Bemba, we can say that Arab families are more likely to have the characteristics that have been defined as patrilineal and patrilocal. If Ahmed has no male offspring, his daughter and her husband may decide to live with him in order to inherit the flocks—thus exhibiting a matrilocal pattern. Although this makes their situation more like the Bemba than like their own people, our constructed type tells us that this is an exceptional situation among the Arabs.

Finally, the best way to think of types is as *reference points* on a continuum. These possible variations in human behavior are infinite. Types should be thought of as nothing more than modal (or in some cases even arbitrary) points on a continuum from one logical possibility to another. Thus, for example, the authority continuum described in the three types—patriarchal, equalitarian, and matriarchal—might look something like this:

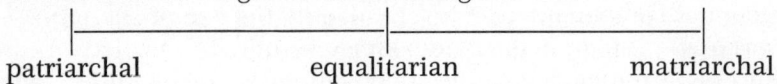

|---------------------------|---------------------------|
patriarchal   equalitarian   matriarchal

Now it would be difficult to find a society in which patriarchal authority means that, in the majority of family-kin units, females have absolutely no ability, either overt or subtle, to influence decisions and determine policies. In fact, it would be hard to find societies whose family units would uniformly fit any of the three types. There are, however, noticeable differences between societies, both in their dominant behavior patterns and in the expectations, or norms, that they express regarding structural or behavioral arrangements. These norms and behaviors can be located on an ideal-typical continuum.

In summary, it can be said that types are very useful for distinguishing the gross differences between societies or categories of people, as long as they are seen to be *group* constructs to be used *comparatively*, and as points on an ideal-typical *continuum* of either expectations or empirical reality.

SECTION THREE

FAMILY STRUCTURE AND THE INCEST TABOO

One important feature of family and kinship structure has not yet been mentioned: the incest taboo. Yet this taboo, or prohibition of sexual intercourse and marriage between specified kin, has crucial structural implications for the organization of society. Were brothers and sisters, for example, free to or expected to mate, they could continue to live in the same household with the parents of both of them. The incest taboo is, however, a virtually universal prohibition in human societies, though societies vary widely in the specific relationships covered by the taboo.

The origin of incest taboos is a subject, says J. Robin Fox, "on which too many words have been wasted already."[9] There are two reasons why discussions of the origin of incest taboos have been unproductive: (1) restrictions against sexual intercourse have not been distinguished from restrictions against marriage, and (2) the *post hoc* nature of the theories of origins have in most instances resulted either in discussions of motives for avoiding incest or of the advantages of non-incest. A brief description of some of the prevalent theories should make these two points clear.

Two of the theories of incest taboo origins relate almost exclusively to marriage prohibitions. The theory of the *biological ill-effects of inbreeding* is meant to explain why persons in the immediate family are not allowed to mate and produce offspring, but this view has gained few adherents. The notion is that inbreeding is dangerous because it perpetuates deficient genetic traits such as hemophilia, and that over a period of time all human societies have discovered these effects and have enforced regulations against inbreeding. This theory does not account for the universality of the taboo unless one admits the universal discovery of harmful effects. In turn, one must assume a universal understanding and sophistication in human societies regarding the reproductive process—an understanding that is simply not in keeping with anthropological evidence. Equally important is the fact that there is little evidence that inbreeding is uniformly biologically harmful. In fact, inbreeding methods have been used in many animal populations to produce higher quality specimens. Nor does this theory explain the wide variations from society to society in the category of kin outside the nuclear family with whom marriage is prohibited. In some cases, the prohibitions govern marriage with more distant kin, while marriage with certain kin whom we would define as closer is permitted.

The *structural confusion* theory of incest taboos is nowhere fully spelled out, but is well illustrated by Kingsley Davis' brief discussion. If brothers and sisters were allowed or expected to marry, he says, jealousy would be the result if there were two brothers and only one sister in a family. Since the number and sex of siblings is uncontrollable, institutional patterns could not be worked out that would make jealousy a support rather than a menace. Then he notes the confusion that would result when children were born of the brother-sister relationship. "The brother would be not only the child's 'father' but also his 'uncle'; the sister would be not only her child's 'mother' but also his 'aunt.' "[10]

The words "uncontrollable" and "confusion" are, however, not adequate explanations for incest taboos. Societies have been able to work out the complexities of the six marriage section system, with its two matrilineal moieties and three patrilineal descent groups,[11] and have effected alternatives to primogeniture, or inheritance by the eldest son, in cases where the family has no son. Why, therefore, is it impossible to conceive of structuring brother-sister marriage to account for various occurrences? The oldest son, for example, might hypothetically be normatively expected to marry the oldest daughter, if there is a daughter. If not, other arrangements could be made. Nor is being a child's mother and aunt simultaneously anything more than a terminological confusion caused by the use of our own culture-bound terms. The great diversity of kinship terminology systems reviewed by Murdock should make it apparent that appropriate terms can be devised for almost any social structural arrangement. Without belaboring the argument, it seems to this author that "impossible structural confusions" hardly explain the ubiquity of incest taboos in human societies.

Prohibitions of sexual intercourse (as differentiated from marriage) with designated kin have been explained by three theories of incest taboos. The first, while it could be applied to marriage taboos as well, seems more closely related to intimate sexual involvement. There is, says Robert Lowie, an *instinct* against inbreeding, a universal revulsion against sexual intimacy with close kin.[12] This theory need detain us but briefly, since it accounts neither for the scattered occurrences of incest despite the taboos, nor for the wide variety of kin relationships covered by the taboo. If there were an instinctual revulsion, it would operate quite consistently and naturally from one society to another.

Edward Westermarck proposed to account for the sexual taboo as due to the "absence of erotic feelings between persons living very closely together from childhood."[13] *Lack of interest* is transformed into a positive aversion because of the intimacy resulting from everyday contacts between these close kin. Though there is substantial evidence that close association may dull the sexual appetites even of married persons, this theory cannot—as a single-factor explanation—account for either the occurrences of incestuous relations, for the variety of kin relations implicated in the taboo, or for the strength of the sanctions brought against those violating the taboo.

The final theory, proposed by Freud, accounts for incest taboos as a result of the opposite of a cooling of interest. The taboos are a result of the *primacy of incestuous love and sex desire*. The child is sexually attracted to the parent of the opposite sex, but must repress these feelings due to the consequences that would result if the same-sex parent found out about them. It is in the repression of such feelings that the strong taboo appears, strengthening the individual in his attempts to withstand his own impulses.[14] This is, of course, a most reasonable sounding theory to Western observers, with their own history of general sex repression and guilt. However, it has some of the same difficulties as the previous theories in accounting for the variety of prohibitions.

These theories, it must be recalled, have been introduced as accounting for the origin of the incest taboo. The authors themselves, except in the case of the instinct and Freudian theories, would make no such claim. Furthermore, it appears that Freud's theory is the only one of the five which might be even a partial explanation of origins. Aided by insight gained from observation of lower animals, some writers, including Freud, have adhered to the theory that there was a stage in human development which was characterized by the strongest and largest male having sexual control over a number of females. Other males, including his offspring, who tried to encroach upon his mating territory would have had a physical struggle on their hands. The earliest prohibitions of intercourse and mating may have grown up around just such impulses and struggles.

Much human history, however, has passed between these hypothetical early developments and the current motivations for and structural ramifications of incest taboos. More profitable than the hypothetical reconstruction of origins is the attempt to explain the motivations and structures that now embody the incest taboos. Time and again we have noted that a particular single-factor theory cannot seem to account for extensions of the incest taboo, sexually and maritally, beyond the nuclear family. Two interesting discussions of incest are pertinent to the issue of structural extensions and motivations. One is by J. R. Fox, whose article focusses upon brother-sister incest prohibitions; the other, by Frank Young, notes the relation between incest taboos and general considerations of social solidarity.[15]

Using illustrative material from six societies, Fox concludes that both Freud and Westermarck are right regarding brother-sister incest taboos. In those societies (such as the Tallensi, Pondo, and the Israeli kibbutzim) in which siblings have engaged in much play and other heterosexual activity prior to puberty, the sexual appetite does in fact appear to be dulled. There is little anxiety in adulthood regarding brother-sister incest in these societies. Fox calls this the "interaction–aversion–non-temptation–non-anxiety type." In other societies, such as the Chiricahua Apache, the siblings are reared in close proximity, but by the age of six or seven close contact between them has ceased. Furthermore, they are not allowed intimate contact with other members of the opposite sex prior to puberty. The result, says Fox, is the "separation–desire–temptation–anxiety type" reaction, which resembles quite closely Freud's idea that temptation plus frustration demands strong prohibitions. Fox summarizes his bipolar theory of motivations as follows: "The more intensive the bodily interaction between opposite-sex children during sexual immaturity, the more likely the possibility that they will voluntarily abstain from sexual relations with each other after puberty."[16] The reactions will range from disgust and strong taboo when siblings have been separate prior to puberty, to virtual indifference when they have had close prepubertal contact.

Although he does not pursue in detail the ramifications of this separation-interaction theory of motivations for incest taboos, the author does note the complications that arise when it is applied to parent-offspring taboos. Though his own discussion is a bit confusing, we can discover four possibilities in the relations between parent and child: mother and son in intimate contact or separated, and father and daughter intimate or separated. Ordinarily, mother and child are in frequent and close contact prior to the puberty of the offspring. According to the theory, this should produce indifference on the offspring's part. It should, however, produce temptation and anxiety on the mother's part, since she obviously had no contact at all with the son prior to *her own* puberty (he was not yet born), and they are now in close contact. As Talcott Parsons puts it, her "regressive need system" or suppressed erotic impulses, must not be left uncontrolled.[17] The situation with respect to father and daughter should tend to produce mutual temptation and anxiety, rather than one-way as in the case of mother and son. The reason for this mutual temptation is that there is normally greater prepubertal separation-with-proximity between father and daughter, a situation that should increase both hers and her father's sexual desire for each other, according to Fox's theory. The result should be the highest incidence of incest between fathers and daughters, which is indeed the case. There is less incidence of incest between sons and mothers, which, according to Fox's view, should be due to the postpubertal indifference of the son. Furthermore, there should be virtually universal abhorrence of and strong sanction against parent-offspring incest of either kind, since both adult males and females should recognize their susceptibility to this temptation. Of course, if parent-offspring sexual intimacy is provided for by the society's structure, then abhorrence and sanction will not be present.

This last phrase brings us to Young's article, and the issue of societal variations in incest taboo extensions. Young simply claims that the incest taboos and sanctions that are developed will be consistent with the lines of solidarity within a community or society. If the nuclear family is a solidary unit, as it seems to be in most societies, Young would argue that sex and mating must be restricted to one pair within the unit, the father and mother. However, if husbands, wives, and children are discrete units with little solidarity or intimate contact (as was the case in the royal families of ancient Egypt) it is reasonable to assume that they may be positively oriented toward each other as sex and marriage partners.[18] Separation, then, is a function of non-solidarity, and is a primary basis for mate selection across lines of solidarity. It is outgroup status that makes marriage possible; ingroup status gives rise to the prohibition of incest.

Incest Motivation and Structure: An Interpretation

This writer agrees with Parsons that, in explaining incest, "a combination of sociological and psychological considerations is involved; that a theory which attempts to by-pass either of these fields will find itself in difficulties."[19] It is quite useful to add Young's emphasis upon societal definitions of solidarity, structural divisions, and "we-ness" and "they-ness" to Fox's concept of prepubertal intimacy and postpubertal taboos, in order to explain the cross-cultural variations in marital and sexual prescriptions and prohibitions.

Societies have differing residential arrangements that bring kinsmen into close proximity or keep them apart. In the patrilocal extended family, a grandparent will live with the young child, as will his paternal uncle and parallel cousin. (By parallel cousins is meant the children of brothers or sisters). Here is a structural situation in which parents, siblings, grandparents, paternal uncles, and parallel cousins all live close together. The first question to ask is whether any of these persons are expected to marry in adulthood. If the answer is no, then there are two ways, according to Fox, in which the incest taboo might work. On the one hand, these kin may be allowed intimacy or even a joking relationship during the prepubertal phase of the child's development, since this will dull the appetite, make strong taboos unnecessary, and keep these relationships within the bounds of the solidary unit. Or there may be a separation with proximity—such as a clear sexual division of labor and leisure—in which case, sexual and mating desires must be controlled by a strong incest taboo. If, however, these proximate parallel cousins are expected to marry in adulthood, proximity without intimacy may be utilized to heighten their interest in each other. The latter case is exemplified among the Arabs of Kurdistan, where parallel cousin marriage between the children of brothers is both preferred and prevalent.[20] Of course, a fourth possibility is that marriage is expected to be with someone who has not been proximate during childhood. Such exogamy, or marriage outside one's group or community, is characterized both by non-proximity and by the absence of intimacy prior to puberty, thus making the problem of intimacy and the dulling of interest irrelevant.

The application of Young's and Fox's analyses is, in summary, that strong incest taboos are developed to handle situations of postpubertal proximity with mating prohibited, when there was no intimacy prior to the puberty of the adult member or members of the pair. It is the specific structural arrangement in relation to proximity–non-intimacy–temptation which determines the extensions and strength of incest taboos in a given society. Such an explanation draws upon the psychological viewpoints of Freud and Westermarck, as well as upon the structural insights of Parsons, Young, and others.[21]

The norms of endogamy, or marriage within one's group or community, and of exogamy, or marriage outside one's group, are intertwined with these incest taboo extensions, as are the often complex rules of residence and descent.[22] But how do these rules and those governing marriage, authority, and household composition work effectively and coherently in societies that differ from Western industrial society? The answer to this question requires at least a brief description of some family-societal systems that diverge greatly from that in the United States. These illustrations, and the questions they raise and resolve, are the subject matter of Chapter III.

NOTES

[1] For a parallel but somewhat divergent treatment of family structural variations, see Meyer F. Nimkoff, *Comparative Family Systems* (Boston: Houghton Mifflin, 1965), Chap. 2. Perhaps the most insightful introduction to cross-cultural differences in family and kinship is Robin Fox's *Kinship and Marriage* (Baltimore: Penguin, 1967). Fox points out clearly how *unimportant* marriage is, in many societies, compared to various consanguineal kin linkages. In this chapter, we have treated marriage as more central than it actually is cross-culturally, because most Western readers have experience in a marriage and nuclear family-centered system. The interested reader may, however, want to move on to a book such as Fox's.

[2] George Peter Murdock, "World Ethnographic Sample," *American Anthropologist*, 59 (1957), 686.

[3] On the prevalence of polygyny in normatively polygynous societies, see Vernon Dorjahn, "The Factor of Polygyny in African Demography," in William R. Bascom and Melville J. Herskovitz, eds., *Continuity and Change in African Culture* (Chicago: University of Chicago Press, 1959), pp. 88–112.

[4] Henry Rosenfeld, "Process of Structural Change within the Arab Village Extended Family," *American Anthropologist*, 60 (1958), 1127–39.

[5] Murdock, *Social Structure* (New York: Macmillan, 1949), pp. 15–17.

[6] *Ibid.*

[7] James Boyd Christensen, *Double Descent Among the Fanti* (New Haven, Conn.: Human Relations Area Files, 1954).

[8] Murdock, *Social Structure*, p. 13.

[9] J. R. Fox, "Sibling Incest," *British Journal of Sociology*, 13 (1962), 128.

[10] Kingsley Davis, *Human Society* (New York: Macmillan, 1949), p. 404.

[11] John Layard, *Stone Men of Malekula* (London: Chatto & Windus, 1942), p. 98.

[12] Robert Lowie, *Primitive Society* (New York: Boni and Liveright, 1920). As Murdock shows, Lowie later repudiated this position on the incest taboo. See Murdock, *Social Structure*, p. 290.

[13] Edward Westermarck, *A Short History of Marriage* (New York: Macmillan, 1926), p. 80.

[14] Sigmund Freud, *A General Introduction to Psychoanalysis* (New York: Liveright, 1920), pp. 187, 294.

[15] Fox, "Sibling Incest" and Frank W. Young, "Incest Taboos and Social Solidarity," *American Journal of Sociology*, 72 (1967), 589–600.

[16] Fox, "Sibling Incest," p. 148.

[17] Talcott Parsons, "The Incest Taboo in Relation to Social Structure and the Socialization of the Child," *British Journal of Sociology*, 5 (1954), 108.

[18] Young, "Incest Taboos and Social Solidarity," p. 599. On ancient Egypt, see Russell Middleton, "Brother-Sister and Father-Daughter Marriage

in Ancient Egypt," *American Sociological Review,* 27 (1962), 603–611. Middleton is currently completing a major analysis of the incest taboo.

[19] Parsons, "The Incest Taboo," p. 101.

[20] On this, see Frederik Barth, "Father's Brother's Daughter's Marriage in Kurdistan," *Southwestern Journal of Anthropology,* 10 (1954), 167–69.

[21] Further discussion of incest taboos, joking relations, and avoidance may be found in Murdock, *Social Structure,* especially pp. 273–76, 292–303. On "role inertia" as an explanation for incest taboos, see William R. Catton, "What's in a Name? The Case for Role Inertia," *Journal of Marriage and the Family,* 31 (1969), 15–18.

[22] Fox, *Kinship and Marriage,* pp. 54–76, distinguishes quite carefully and consistently between *incest* taboos, or sexual restrictions, and *endogamy* prohibitions, or restrictions upon mating. We have not drawn this distinction quite so carefully in the preceding explanation since discussion is based upon the interwoven nature of sexual attractions and mating prescriptions.

III

Family Varieties Exemplified: Nayar, Papago, Chinese

THE FAMILY SYSTEMS OF THE NAYAR OF SOUTH INDIA, THE PAPAGO INDIANS OF SOUTHERN ARIZONA AND NORTHERN MEXICO, AND THE CHINESE OF PRE-COMMUNIST CHINA ARE DISCUSSED AND INTERPRETED. THE DISCUSSION CENTERS AROUND LENGTHY QUOTATIONS FROM KATHLEEN GOUGH, RUTH UNDERHILL, AND MAURICE FREEDMAN. THREE PROBLEMS IN FAMILY STUDY ARE HIGHLIGHTED BY THESE EXAMPLES: (1) THE UNIVERSALITY OF THE NUCLEAR FAMILY, (2) THE POPULAR QUESTION, "HOW COULD SUCH A SYSTEM WORK?" AND (3) THE USE OF HISTORICAL SOURCES.

The great variety of family structural possibilities is apparent from the structural and cultural principles discussed in the previous chapter. Family-kin systems do not, however, exist in isolation, but in complex relations with the societies in which they function. These variations and complexities may come alive for the reader as he confronts specific examples of social systems different from his own.

The family systems of three societies are described at length in the pages that follow. These societies are that of the Nayar, the Papago, and the Chinese. The Nayar is one of several sub-castes living in Kerala State, South India, and is sometimes characterized as practicing group marriage, but more often as polyandrous. The arid region of southern Arizona and northern Mexico is the rather inhospitable home of the Papago Indians, a normatively polygynous society. Chinese civilization is an ancient and proud one, traditionally viewed as patrilineal and patriarchal in family structure. None of the three has escaped change in recent centuries, but in a consideration of their "classic," or traditional organization, we may gain insight, not only into their ways, but into several crucial questions in family study.

Whether or not marriage and the family are universal depends upon how one defines the terms. The Nayar are an exceptionally valuable case study, around which, discussion of the family's universality has revolved. A second troublesome question for the beginning student of the family is "How could such a system possibly work?" The questioner may be referring to arranged marriage, exogamy, polygyny, or any other arrangement that differs greatly from his own. The Papago Indians illustrate arranged, polygynous, village exogamy (marriage outside one's home village), and may aid the reader in perceiving how such a system can "make sense" to the people who practice it. The material on the Chinese family once again points up the ideal-actual distinction, but the reason for its inclusion in this chapter is primarily to indicate the problems encountered in using historical materials, as well as to illustrate the distinction between nuclear family institutional embeddedness and personnel embeddedness (in the Chinese) and kin embeddedness (found among the Papago).

SECTION ONE

THE NAYAR OF SOUTH INDIA

The nuclear family of father, mother, and their children has been considered by Murdock and others to be virtually universal in human societies, being found without or within the composite marital and consanguineal structures referred to in Chapter II. However, under stable social conditions, at least one prime example of a family system without the father as a continuing member has been found. It is the Nayar of the Malabar coast of India, prior to British rule (before 1792). The best-known research on the Nayar is that of E. Kathleen Gough; much of the ensuing discussion is drawn from her writings.[1] (The use of the past tense indicates that the practices being described have long since been substantially altered.)

The Nayar were matrilineal and matrilocal. Between the ages of seven and twelve, or prior to puberty, Nayar girls were ritually married to a male of the appropriate sub-caste. After four days of celebration, during which defloration of the bride by the ritual husband was permitted, the husband left the house and had no further obligation to his bride.

> A bride in turn had only one further obligation to her ritual husband: at his death, she and all her children, by

whatever physiological father, must observe death-pollution for him. Death-pollution was otherwise observed only for matrilineal kin.

After the ritual marriage, the bridegroom need have no further contact with his ritual wife. If both parties were willing, however, he might enter into a sexual relationship with his ritual bride about the time of her puberty. But he had no priority over other men of the neighborhood group. . . . There appears to be no limit to the number of wives of appropriate sub-caste whom a Nayar might visit concurrently. It seems, therefore, that a woman customarily had a small but fixed number of husbands from within her neighborhood, that relationships with these men might be of long standing, but that the woman was also free to receive casual visitors of appropriate sub-caste who passed through her neighborhood in the course of military operations.

A husband visited his wife after supper at night and left before breakfast next morning. He placed his weapons at the door of his wife's room, and if others came later they were free to sleep on the verandah of the woman's house. Either party to a union might terminate it at any time without formality. A passing guest recompensed a woman with a small cash gift at each visit. But a more regular husband from within the neighborhood had certain customary obligations. At the start of the union, it was common although not essential for him to present the woman with a cloth of the kind worn as a skirt. Later he was expected to make small personal gifts to her at the three main festivals of the year. These gifts included a loin-cloth, betel-leaves and arecanuts for chewing, hair-oil and bathing-oil, and certain vegetables. Failure on the part of a husband to make such a gift was a tacit sign that he had ended the relationship. Most important, when a woman became pregnant, it was essential for one or more men of appropriate subcaste to acknowledge probable paternity. This they did by providing a fee of a cloth and some vegetables to the low-caste midwife who attended the woman in childbirth. If no man of suitable caste would consent to make this gift, it was assumed that the woman had had relations with a man of lower caste or with a Christian or a Muslim. She must then be either expelled from her lineage and caste or killed by her matrilineal kinsmen. I am uncertain of the precise fate of the child in such a case, but there is no doubt that he could not be accepted as a member of his lineage and caste.

Although he made regular gifts to her at festivals, in no sense of the term did a man maintain his wife. Her food and regular clothing she obtained from her matrilineal group.

In these circumstances, the exact physiological fatherhood of a child was often uncertain, although, of course, paternity was presumed to lie with the man or men who had paid the delivery expenses. But even when physiological paternity was known with reasonable certainty, the genitor had no economic, social, legal or ritual rights in, nor obligations to, his children after he had once paid the fees of their births. Their guardianship, care and discipline were entirely the concern of their matrilineal kinsfolk headed by their *kāranavan*, [or the oldest male of the group]. . . .

All the children of a woman called all her current husbands by the Sanskrit word *acchan* meaning "lord." They did not extend kinship terms at all to the matrilineal kin of these men. Neither the wife nor her children observed pollution at the death of a visiting husband who was not also the ritual husband of the wife.[2]

The rationale for the Nayar system, so far as it pertained to the men, was that they were employed as mercenary troops, often being absent from their village in wars against neighboring kingdoms. The family system, of which they were not expected to be permanent members, meant that their loyalties were not divided between family and military service. The women were landholders, holding land as tenants for a raja or other landlord, to whom they paid rent. Land passed from a mother to her female children; this matrilineage was buttressed by the absence of the males, since they thus made no claim on their wives' goods. Whether this system is called "group marriage," since several males and several females appear to have sexual access to each other simultaneously, or "polyandry," since the women are the permanent residents and entertain several husbands, is relatively unimportant. However, of crucial importance is the absence of the male as a permanent family member, in conjunction with the necessity of assumption of legal paternity by some male in order to legitimate the child. This latter point—legal paternity—deserves some elaboration. The term "father" may have any of three connotations. It can mean the physiological progenitor of the child, the legal father or legitimator of the child, or the socializer of the child—the one with specific responsibilities for passing along family culture. In the case of the Nayar, fatherhood is restricted to the notion of legitimation, with no implication of duty as a socializing agent and little direct connection with biological parenthood. There are other societies in which the physiological and social concepts of father must be separated, with the category of "father" being more social than physiological.[3]

Is the Family Universal?

The answer to this question must, of course, rest upon one's definition of "marriage" and "family." The *Notes and Queries* definition of marriage, published in 1951, states that "marriage is a union between a man and a woman such that children born to the woman are recognized legitimate offspring of both parents."[4] It can be seen from this definition that the family form it assumes is the nuclear family, as it was defined earlier. The Nayar are often cited as an exception to the rule that nuclear marriage and the nuclear family are universal, or are found in every human society. We emphasized in preceding pages that co-residence in marriage is normative, facilitating sexual access, child-care, and economic cooperation. The Nayar do not fit this pattern. Nor, as Ira Reiss and others have pointed out, do the Israeli kibbutzim, the matrifocal families of Jamaica, or certain other systems.

When it is claimed that the nuclear family is not universal, is this the same as saying that the family is not universal? The responses of Gough and Reiss to this question are negative. The problem is that, for cross-cultural purposes, the nuclear family cannot be thought of as synonymous with "family." Therefore, Gough suggests that marriage be defined as follows: "Marriage is a relationship established between a woman and one or more other persons, which provides that a child born to the woman under circumstances not prohibited by the rules of the relationship, is accorded full birth-status rights common to normal members of his society or social stratum."[5] For her, then, the key is not the idea of mating and common residence, but the legitimation of offspring.

Reiss notes in his article that Murdock postulated the nuclear family—functioning for socialization, reproduction, economic cooperation, and sex relations—as universal. Citing evidence, Reiss states that there are societies that do not have a family system performing these four tasks. He then posits this definition of the family: "The family institution is a small kinship structured group with the key function of nurturant socialization of the newborn."[6] Gough and Reiss, in short, are saying that, cross-culturally, marriage should be viewed as an institutionalized means of legitimating offspring, while the family is the institutionalized means of raising them.

While their insights are valuable (we shall return in Chapter V to the issue of family functions) the principle effect of these definitions is to relocate the argument regarding the universality of the family away from the nuclear unit. The difficulty with this relocation is that the posing of definitions of "family" which might be universally valid has no logical limit. One might claim that the family is "a unit involving two or more persons who share an intimate sexual relationship and a common residence," but in so doing one would be including even the homosexual liaison. The point is simply that one's decision regarding the universality of the family may easily become a function of how he personally defines it, with the debate becoming endless. Of greater value, it would seem, is the question of whether or not the *nuclear* family is universal, since the addition of this restriction provides a common denominator for discussion. Cross-cultural indications are that such a unit is not a universal phenomenon, though it is of central importance in a book that focusses primarily upon the family in the United States.

SECTION TWO

PAPAGO FAMILY AND KINSHIP

The Papago Indians of southern Arizona and northern Mexico present a noticeable contrast to both the Nayar and the U.S. family in the centrality of their kinship organization and in the extent of both institutional and personnel embeddedness in the kinship system. Until the early 1900's, they were rarely disturbed by Spaniards or by whites from the U.S. Their location was the semi-desert region spanning the Rio Grande, land that no one else seemed to want. The raising of crops on scant rainfall had resulted in close and cooperative relations among them over the years. For three or four summer months each year, the Papago lived in small thatched-roof villages of about 200, raising corn, beans, and squash. The other eight months or so they scattered to the isolated mountain springs to hunt.[7]

A Papago village consisted almost entirely of kin. In conversation, cousins were called by the same terms as one's brothers and sisters, although a terminological distinction between cousins and siblings could be made, if necessary. The father, besides being economic head of his family, was also teacher and governor. The village council, composed of the adult men, was about all the government the Papago had, there being no higher-level tribal government. The council met only in the summer when the village was occupied; leadership was more religio-ritualistic than political or jural. From time to time a person might be ostracized or cast out of a village for misbehavior, the result of which would be either death in the wilds or adoption by another village. Ordinarily, however, the council's function was to symbolize community solidarity.

Marriage was exogamous in terms of one's own village, being arranged by kin units of neighboring villages. Almost before any sexual urge arose in the child, his parents had made an appropriate pairing. What developed between couple members after marriage was loyalty, rather than what Americans would call romantic love.

At marriage the girl often showed fright, and perhaps even ran away during the ceremony. It was her mother's responsibility to bring her back if she took flight. One reason for the girl's fear—whether it was real or ritualized—was that, during most of the twenty-four hours of a day, males and females were separate. Not only in the division of labor, but even for conversation in the evenings, the sexes tended to remain apart. Thus, her contact with males had been infrequent and often fleeting, as well as authoritarian, even with her father. Now, however, she was to be sexually intimate with a male. Even more important, she knew that her marriage meant moving from her own kin village to one consisting of strangers and a few former members of her village of birth.

Polygyny was the preferred marriage form among the Papago. How, we might ask, could this work without jealousy and constant friction between wives of the same husband. For the Papago it was relatively simple. First, as we have said, the wife married into a village other than her own, and was a stranger there. Secondly, the marriage was arranged, lessening to some extent the romantic feelings which would be likely to give rise to feelings of jealousy. Thirdly, and most important, polygyny among the Papago was most often "sororal," i.e., sisters marrying the same man. Would this not, however, intensify rather than mitigate feelings of jealousy? Underhill responds to this question with the following quote from a Papago woman: "After you have slept on the same mat with your sister for ten or twelve years, of course you are glad to have her come to your new home."[8] Sisters actually appeared to get along well as co-wives—a sign that the nuclear family is quite embedded, personnel-wise, in the kin system. As noted earlier, the majority of Papago males had but one wife, but, due to the village exogamy and the clear division of activity between the sexes, the normative practice of polygyny seemed to work satisfactorily when it did occur.

Virtually the entire organization of Papago society was kin-based at the village level. Child-rearing was strict, separation between the sexes extensive, and cooperation between kin imperative for survival. This last phrase should not be interpreted to mean that the Papago were simply passive and friendly to everyone. During the course of the year the marauding Apache would steal their animals and generally pester the Papago. Therefore, about once a year, the Papago organized a raid in which they burned a few Apache huts as a reminder of who controlled the area. Maintaining the regional balance of power was as necessary for survival as was cooperation.

The Workability and Value of Normative Practices

Among the Papago, sororal polygyny seems to have worked fairly well. Is the point of this discussion, you might ask, the acentric notion that one way of organizing a society and its family system is as satisfactory to its members as another, provided that the arrangement is normative or expected? This would be an incorrect interpretation of the Papago example, and of material on normative arrangements in general. William Stephens, writing about a number of polygynous societies, states that there is often jealousy among polygynous wives. "In most known cases at least some co-wives seem to suffer rather intensely from jealousy, and a good many of the polygynous families are strife-torn."[9]

Stephens' comment indicates that the distinction between workability-acceptance and value-satisfaction should be kept in mind. It might be said that any system that is accepted as normative by a particular people is workable, whether it is polygyny, head-hunting, or the extended family. This is not, however, the same as saying that everyone who accepts a particular system as normative is consequently happy and satisfied with it and his position in it; nor that one system makes for about as many problems as another. It is in the discontent fostered by a given arrangement that is found one of the seeds of social change, of the rethinking by each new generation of the society's familial and other structural arrangements. Many different kinds of systems can and have worked, historically and cross-culturally; our task is to *understand* their rationale and workability, not to conclude that all systems are equally "good" in some absolute sense, or equally satisfying to their constituents. When we confront issues such as premarital sex in U.S. society, the question, "How can a specific system work?" will once again arise.

SECTION THREE

THE CHINESE FAMILY IN HISTORICAL PERSPECTIVE

Many writers have referred to the society of pre-Communist China as one dominated by family and kinship organization. The large family unit with the aging patriarch ruling the household has sometimes been pictured as typical of classical China. Recently, however, scholars have recognized the fact that classical China had a strong state organization and a complex, though primarily agrarian, economy, and thus should not be thought of as an example of total institutional embeddedness. A consideration of Chinese society and its family-kin system allows us to raise the issues of historical change and the use of historical sources. This consideration also allows us to ask what it means for a kinship system to be functionally central to its society. In an insightful account of the Chinese system, Maurice Freedman clarifies some of the dimensions of family and kinship and the relation between them and the political and economic realities of the larger society. In the following section, Freedman will be allowed to speak for himself at considerable length.[10]

The patrilineage was the key kin unit in classical China, however, it hardly incorporated all the other institutional activities of its society. In fact, even among high-status Chinese, it would be proper to ask whether the patrilineage dominated the state, or vice versa, or whether the two institutions were actually in a power balance. Furthermore, we might ask whether the strong patrilineage and its patriarch were characteristic of the entire Chinese population, or only of high-status persons. Let us assume, says Freedman

> that the problem is to decide what strength or potency lay in kinship relations as a whole. We may take China as it was in the last hundred years of its existence as an imperial state. The question resolves itself into an analysis of how the solidarities and values of kinship were enmeshed in a political and economic order which required of individuals that they owe allegiance to a state and participate, despite the dominance of agriculture, in a wide-ranging economic system.
> From the point of view of the state, a man's obligation to it were in fact both qualified and mediated by his

kinship relations. They were qualified in the sense that obligations springing from filial piety and mourning duties were held to modify duties owed to the state. An official who lost a parent was supposed to retire during the mourning. People related to one another in close bonds of kinship were so far regarded by the written law to require solidarity among them that the Code provided that certain relatives might legitimately conceal the offenses of one another (except in cases of high treason and rebellion), either escaping punishment altogether or suffering a penalty reduced in accordance with the closeness of the relationship; and that it was an offense generally for close kinsmen to lay even just accusations against one another. There was built into the system the principle that close patrilineal kinship set up special rights and duties standing apart from the rights and duties between man and the state. . . .

In the eyes of the state, then, a man stood posed against it in a network of primary kinship duties. But the state also regarded kinship units as part of its system of general control, so that a man's duties to it were mediated through his membership in these units. The family is the clearest case. The Confucian emphasis on complex families and the legal power vested in the head of a family to prevent its premature breakup are aspects of a total political system in which some authority is delegated from the administrative system to what, in a metaphorical sense, we may call natural units. The Confucian moralizing about the family, the stress put upon filial piety and the need for solidarity among brothers, the underlining of the importance of domestic harmony—these reflect a political view in which units standing at the base of the social pyramid are expected to control themselves in the interest of the state.

But the family is not the only case. It was morally right for men to align themselves on the basis of their common patrilineal descent and to form lineages. Lineage organization implied ancestor worship, a Confucian value of high order. It implied the promotion of schools and mutual help; in these the state could take pleasure. It implied, finally, an organization which could be used by the state for political and fiscal control. And at once we can see the dilemma faced by the state when it tried to make use of the lineage and encourage its prosperity. To be of use to the state, the lineage must be organized and strong; but strength might grow to the point at which what was once a useful adjunct of government now became a threat to it. Where the lineages grew in numbers and riches they fought with other lineages. This was objectionable enough, but clearly what frightened the central administration more than anything else was the tendency for patrilineal organization to snowball. A lineage was justified by a genealogy; people began to produce longer and wider genealogies to justify more extensive groupings, going so far—and this "excess" excited very great official indignation—that attempts were sometimes made to group together in one organization all the lineages in one area bearing a common surname. It is important to realize that genealogical rearrangement and the grouping together of lineages makes perfect sense, given the logic of the patrilineal system, and that the objections raised by officialdom, although they might be couched in terms condemning the falsification of genealogies, were essentially political. That is to say, strong nuclei of local power were being created which constituted a threat to state authority.

From the political point of view, then, kinship organization entailed a balance of forces with the state. . . .

On the role of kinship in economic life we have no systematic and large body of information on which to rely, but we can make a general argument. If we start from the assumption that kinship relations and values predominate in the conduct of economic affairs, we must expect that enterprise will take the form of what is often called the family business. Now, of course, there is plenty of evidence to show that Chinese economic enterprise has tended strongly to be organized so that people associating their capital, or capital and labor, are related by kinship or affinity. But what is the real significance of this fact? Is it that the moral imperatives of kinship impel people to seek out kinsmen with whom to work? The answer is no. Given the nature of the capital market, given a legal system which offers little protection to business, given the tendency to rely on people with whom there is some preceding tie, we should expect that kinsmen would be associating with one another in economic activities. What is really involved is that these activities are made to rest on highly personalized relationships and that a man's circle of relatives is likely to contain the greater number of individuals apt for selection. It is important to remember that, outside the family, a kinsman has few specific economic claims, that he can be approached as a landlord or creditor, and that in general we must not look to see preference being shown to a kinsman in economic matters on the grounds simply that he is a kinsman.

We have so far been concerned with the question of how far the family in "pre-modern" China can be said to have been the basic unit of society. The argument has taken the form that family and kinship together provided one method of balancing the power of the state and that kinship was not *in principle* basic to economic life. If we confined our attention to the family in the strictest sense of the term, we might be able, by noting how much of the ordinary individual's life is lived within it, to assert that we were dealing with something fundamental. But in doing this we should be ignoring the whole range of wider institutions without which the family can in fact have little meaning.

We must now turn to the inner structure of the Chinese family before modern times, placing emphasis on two things: first, the nature of the tensions inherent in it, in order to see whether they can help us in our understanding of modern developments; and second, the linkages between the family and the wider society, so that we may look for changes in the family which may correspond to changes in society at large.

It has become an accepted fact, says Freedman, that the average size of the traditional Chinese family was no more than five or six. Of greater importance currently would seem to be the question of

why it was that some families were very large and others very small, with many gradations between these extremes. Let us go back to the political point that the state looked to the family as the first unit of social control. The ideal family from this point of view was one in which large numbers of kinsmen and their wives were held under the control of a patriarch imbued with the Confucian values of propriety and order. Some families came close to this model, several generations living under one roof. They were powerful families. We may consider the power they wielded in terms both of their control of economic resources and of their command over other people. They were rich. They owned much land and other capital resources. By renting land and lending money they could exert influence over other people. They could afford to educate their sons and equip them for membership in the bureaucratic elite. They often (perhaps usually) entered into the life of this elite, making use of their ties in it to control both less fortunate families and their own subordinate members. Such a family may be looked upon as a large politico-economic corporation with much power vested in its chief member. But this corporation could not grow indefinitely in membership, for with the death of its senior generation it split along the lines laid down by the constitution of the next generation, every son having a right to an individualized share of his father's estate on that man's death. However, despite the partition which took place every generation, high status families were able to remain large. The passing of the senior generation was likely to take place at a point when the men in the next generation were themselves old enough to have descendants sufficient for complex families of their own. At this level of society fertility was relatively high, the chances of survival were higher, adoption was easy, the age of marriage was low, and plural marriage was possible.

At the other end of the social scale the family was, so to speak, scarcely Confucian. Poverty and powerlessness produced, instead of a strong patriarch, a weak father. He could rally no support from outside to dominate his sons. He had few resources to withhold from them. In fact, he might well have only one son growing to maturity. If, however, he had two or more sons reaching manhood, only one would be likely to stay with him, and perhaps even this one would leave him too. Demography, economics, and the power situation at this level of society ensured that families of simple structure were a constant feature of the landscape.

Changes in social status promoted changes in family structure. Upward social mobility was partly a matter of increasing the complexity of the family, both because changing demographic, economic, and power conditions entailed complexity and because the ideal Confucian family was a model towards which people strove when they were moving upwards. And we should note that downward social mobility brought with it a corresponding decline in complexity.

The relations between the sexes and between the generations were dependent on differences in family structure. It will be convenient to start from a feature of Chinese family life which has always attracted the attention of outsiders: the unhappy position of the daughter-in-law. She may be looked upon from three points of view: as a woman, as a member of the family by incorporation, and as a member of a junior generation. It needs no stressing that being a woman was a disadvantage. Every aspect of her society and its values left the Chinese woman in no doubt on that score. In the family into which she was born she might indeed be well and affectionately treated, but this favorable treatment rested on the paradox that she was merely a temporary member of it. Certainly, her marriage would call upon the family's resources, for it would cause her father to assert his status by sending her off in such a manner as to narrow the status gap between him and the father of the groom. But her marriage cut her off economically and as a legal person from her own family and transferred the rights in and over her to the family receiving her. In this new family she was at once a stranger and a member—the former because she was new and the latter in that, henceforth, the rights and duties in respect of her would lie with her husband's people. From the day of her marriage she must begin to think of her interests as being inevitably involved in those of her husband and the members of his family. She had no secure base outside this family from which to operate, because, while she might try to bring in support from her family of birth to moderate oppression, she could not rely on it. To a large extent physically, and in all degrees legally, she was locked within her husband's gates.

Her husband's mother was her point of contact with the new senior generation to preside over her—whence the tears, for she had to be disciplined into a new role in a new family. In fact, however, the difficulties faced by the daughter-in-law were only one aspect of a broader configuration of difficulties. Men in Confucian morality were urged to reject the claims made by their wives on their attention and their interests, and to stand by their brothers against the threat posed to fraternal solidarity by their wives. Women were troublemakers, partly because they were strangers. Her mother-in-law represented for the wife the female half of the family into which she was firmly thrust if her husband refused to come to her aid. Mother-in-law, daughter-in-law, and unmarried daughters formed a battlefield on which any one daughter-in-law must fight for herself and, later, for her children.

Now if in fact the married brothers in a family did stand together, refusing to listen to their wives' complaints, it was because they were posed against their father. And this father was a strong figure whose power rested on the economic resources he controlled and the command he could exert on the world outside the family. It will be seen, therefore, that we have been dealing with the characteristics of a family of high status. Because of riches, life might in one sense be easy for the married woman (she had servants and other luxuries), but she was distant from her husband and at the mercy of the other women in the house until she was herself senior enough to pass from the dominated to the dominators.

In a family of low status and simple structure the elemental relationships of father and son, brother and brother, and husband and wife formed a different pattern. The father's control was weak and the brothers highly individualized among themselves. Each brother stood close to his wife, so that while the wife might be made miserable by poverty and hard work, at the lower levels of society she had greater strength as an individual. Here she was far less likely to need to cope with other mature women in the house.

From this summary analysis we may conclude that the probability of tension between the generations and the sexes increased with a rise in social status, and we may look forward from this point to the attempts made in modern times to remedy what seemed to be the difficulties and injustices of the Chinese family system.[11]

The reform attempts, as Freedman summarizes them, actually involved change in the structure of high-status families, making it more similar to the historical form of the low-status Chinese family just described. That is, much effort was expended in the first half of the twentieth century (and was continued under Communism) to weaken the control of the lineage, thereby increasing the status and power of women and children in relations with males. Moreover, in matters of conflict of interest, the state must hold sway, to the extent that a parent who disregards a regulation of the state may be in danger of being reported by his own children.

The major change is therefore that the

> family now lies open to the state. It has little property to hold it together. Its ritual bond has been removed. Its head can call on few sanctions to support him in the exercise of authority—his wife can divorce him, his children defy him. The allocation of tasks in economic life is not now in any important respect a family matter. The whole range of activities once covered by the family is now reduced to a narrow field in which husband, wife, and children associate together in the interstices, so to speak, of large institutions—the work group, the dining hall, the nursery—which have taken over the functions of economic coordination, housekeeping, and the rearing and education of children. The family has become an institution for producing babies and enjoying the leisure time left over from the major pursuits of everyday life.

Now, as soon as we formulate our account of the contemporary Chinese family in this fashion—and of course the account may well be overdrawn, which in fact strengthens the argument to follow—we can no longer rely on the assumption that the family is to be destroyed. The more we look at this picture the more familiar it will seem to us, for it contains features from the Western experience of family life. For most of the inhabitants of an industrialized society the family is a small residential group from which many of the major activities of life are excluded. The factory, the office, and the school separate the members of one family for many hours of the day and provide them with different ranges of relationships and interests. What they unite for as a family is a restricted number of activities of consumption, child care, amusement, and emotional exchange. True, if we are to believe what we are told, the Chinese family in the commune has gone further in reducing the minimal functions we associate with family life, but it has not necessarily departed in principle from a pattern which we know to be intrinsic to the modern form of society.

If we begin a discussion of whether the family now exists in China with a definition of the family which lists a number of functions, it is possible that we shall deny it to present-day China, just as some people have denied it to collective settlements in Israel. If instead we look in the family for a configuration of relationships between spouses and between parents and children, a configuration standing out from other patterns of relationship in which people are involved, then we should have little difficulty in satisfying ourselves that the Chinese family has survived.

But there is more to it than that. We can argue that the family has survived not *against* the wishes of the people responsible for policy in Communist China but rather in accordance with their desire to see the institution persist and flourish. The persistence is of course on their terms, but what they may seek to perpetuate is necessary for the orderly working of their society. Marriage may be potentially fragile, but marriage there certainly is. Its purpose is to provide a locus for the raising of useful citizens. Children are not going to be produced on an assembly line; they must be linked to parents before they can be linked to society. In the early years of their control the Communists gave the appearance of waging a war on the family. Since about 1953, the war having been won to their satisfaction, they have been at pains to stress such of the value of family life as they regard as important in the institution as it now is. Old people must be looked after by their children; the young must be respectful; there must be a harmonious relationship between husband and wife.

It would appear that the form taken by the family in recent years is essentially the same as that which we have seen to have characterized the greater part of the Chinese population before any of the modern trends began. That is to say, the family is either a unit of parents and their immature children, or it includes, in addition to those people, the parents or surviving parent of the husband or the wife (of the former rather than of the latter). The "solution" produced by the Communists is in reality an old one, and in arriving at it the Communists were continuing a process of change which had started many years earlier at the higher levels of Chinese society. In fact, it could be argued that just as the Communists worked on peasant hunger for land to bind the mass of the people to them in the early days of land reform, so they commanded the allegiance of many people by playing on the stresses inherent in complex family organization. The resentment of the wife and the son, and the strains between the sexes and the generations were material on which politics could work to create opinion favorable to its general aims."[12]

What conclusion can be drawn regarding the importance of the family in classical China? What is the nature of recent changes? According to Freedman, classical China was characterized by a balance of power between strong patrilineages and state authority. The vast majority of the population, however, lived in nuclear units on the land, without the complexities of patrilineal organization being highly developed.

Much of the historical literature on China has, of course, focussed on the life of high-status people. The nucleation and weak kin linkages of the poorer segments of the population have hardly been noticed. The trend in the Chinese system toward a decrease in the importance of lineages in favor of nuclear family units has in fact been toward a pattern that was already typical of low-status families. The primary political result of the changes has been to weaken the powerful intermediate lineage structures, thereby providing state leaders with more immediate access to and control over the nuclear units.[13]

A second way of viewing the changes in Chinese society pertains to the embeddedness of the economy in either the kin group or the nuclear family. Although Freedman says little about this, it is nevertheless true that in many land-based economic systems, conjugal and kin units are important loci of productive activity. In classical China, the lower-status population has for centuries been primarily a series of nuclear units, with productivity embedded within them. The change within the higher status population has been away from lineage-based production to nuclear-based production, with the agrarian economy now centered to a great extent in nuclear units. With the increasing industrialization of modern China it is predictable that the nuclear unit will likewise give way to the individual worker as the main productive unit. However, while this latter change is under way, much of the Chinese population still consists of family units working the land.

When we turn in Chapter IV to the antecedents of the American family, the reader will notice many parallels between the histories of China and the United States. At no point in history has the *typical* Chinese pattern been a high degree of institutional and personnel embeddedness in the kin group, though a minority of high-status lineages could be thus characterized. Nor do you find in classical China a pure example of institutional embeddedness even in the nuclear family. The political organization of China has for centuries been over against the kin-family organization of the society, the link being certain powerful patriarchs playing both political and kin authority roles. The complexity of agrarian China was such that, on the one hand, the nuclear family was more important to the functioning of society than we found it to be among the Nayar, but, on the other hand, kin group and social organization could not be considered virtually synonymous as we found them to be among the Papago.

SECTION FOUR

SUMMARY OF CHAPTERS II AND III

Some of the major principles by which family and kinship structures may be distinguished include marriage patterns, consanguineal ties, and residence location. In addition, descent and inheritance and authority patterns differentiate between the family cultures of various societies. Among the most significant types produced cross-culturally by these principles are: (1) monogamous, polygynous, and polyandrous marriages; (2) monogamous nuclear, joint, and extended households; (3) patrilocality, matrilocality, neolocality, bilocality, and avunculocality; (4) patrilineal, matrilineal, and bilateral descent and inheritance; and (5) patriarchal, matriarchal, and equalitarian authority. Such types are, of course, group constructs that are useful for comparisons, but are in reality simply abstractions and points on a continuum of societal expectations and empirical reality.

The married person is simultaneously a member of two nuclear families, the one into which he was born, called his family of orientation, and the one which he establishes by means of marriage and parenthood, called his family of procreation. The incest taboo, which designates certain categories of kin as unavailable for sexual intercourse or mating, is a virtually universal aspect of human societies, though there are substantial differences from one society to another in the specific relations falling under the taboo. Even sibling and parent-child mating have been considered legitimate in certain societies.

Three societies were used to exemplify some of the problems in cross-cultural family study. The Nayar of South India, a quasi-polyandrous people, were the focal point for discussing the universality of the family. These people appear to have traditionally lacked the husband as a permanent member of the household. Thus, if the question concerns the universality of the *nuclear* family, with father, mother, and child as permanent members, the answer is probably "no." If, however, "family" is redefined as a mechanism for legitimatizing or rearing offspring, it is very likely universal.

A Western observer understands his own family system and considers it "natural." But how, he might ask, can a "totally kin-embedded" system work which includes polygyny, arranged marriage, and village exogamy as attributes? Among the Papago it seems to function fairly satisfactorily. For one thing, the majority of household units are monogamous rather than polygynous. More important, sororal polygyny, or the marriage of the male to sisters, is apparently pleasing to the Papago female who is living as a stranger in her husband's village. This does not mean that polygyny does not cause problems. Instances of jealousy between co-wives are reported in the literature. Rather, the point is that any system can function, once established; although it may include within it the seeds of discontent and eventual destruction.

Classical China was considered for many years to have consisted of a series of large family-kin households. Freedman's discussion illustrates the difficulties in using historical sources, in speaking of family-kin "importance," and in determining direction of changes over time. In the case of China the problem is that many of the authors were writing about the high-status family as if it were typical. The direction of recent changes in China toward greater nucleation of families has actually been toward the small household that characterized the poorer masses during the classical period. The kin-lineage system was important to classical China in the sense that among the wealthy it acted as a political balance against the forces of centralized state authority and as a major unit of agrarian economic production. Today the nuclear unit is the seat of agricultural production, but industrialization is even weakening this form of economic embeddedness in the family. But there is more to be said later on this last point.

NOTES

[1] E. Kathleen Gough, "The Nayars and the Definition of Marriage," *Journal of the Royal Anthropological Institute*, 89 (1959), Part 1; reprinted in Norman W. Bell and Ezra F. Vogel, eds., *The Family* (New York: Free Press, 1960), pp. 76–92. See also Gough, "Female Initiation Rites in the Malabar Coast," *Journal of the Royal Anthropological Institute*, 85 (1955), 45–80, and Gough, "A Comparison of Incest Prohibitions and Rules of Exogamy in Three Matrilineal Groups of the Malabar Coast," *International Archives of Ethnography*, 46 (1952), 82–105.
[2] Gough, "The Nayars and the Definition of Marriage," in Bell and Vogel, *The Family*, p. 80.
[3] *Ibid.*, pp. 81–83.
[4] *Notes and Queries on Anthropology*, 6th ed. (London: Routledge and Kegan Paul, 1951), p. 24.
[5] *Ibid.*, p. 90.
[6] Ira L. Reiss, "The Universality of the Family: A Conceptual Analysis," *Journal of Marriage and the Family*, 27 (1965), 449.
[7] Ruth M. Underhill, "The Papago Family," in Meyer F. Nimkoff, ed., *Comparative Family Systems*, (Boston: Houghton Mifflin, 1965), p. 149.
[8] *Ibid.*, p. 152.
[9] William N. Stephens, *The Family in Cross-Cultural Perspective* (New York: Holt, Rinehart and Winston, 1963), p. 63.
[10] Maurice Freedman, "The Family in China, Past and Present," *Pacific Affairs*, 34 (1961–1962), 323–36.
[11] *Ibid.*, pp. 328–29.
[12] *Ibid.*, pp. 333–34.
[13] For an extended treatment of the process of weakening the intermediate structures of family, kinship, and religion, so that in modern society the individual lies more open to state control, see Robert A. Nisbet, *Community and Power* (New York: Oxford University Press, Galaxy Books, 1962 ed.).

IV

Antecedents of the Modern American Family

PRE-COLONIAL INFLUENCES UPON THE FAMILY IN AMERICA INCLUDE THE BEGINNINGS OF PRIVACY; THE APPEARANCE OF A STRONG REPRESSIVE SEX CODE AND THE NOTION OF SANCTITY; INCREASED AWARENESS OF WOMEN'S LOW STATUS IN THE FAMILY; AND THE DEVELOPMENT OF THE ROMANTIC LOVE CONCEPT. THE SEX CODE AND SANCTITY CONCEPT WERE IN DIRECT CONFLICT WITH THE LOOSER NORMS OF THE LATE MIDDLE AGES. PRIOR TO AND DURING THE COLONIAL PERIOD, OTHER INSTITUTIONS WERE TO A GREAT EXTENT EMBEDDED IN THE NUCLEAR FAMILY, NOT THE KIN GROUP; ALTHOUGH AN INCREASING NUMBER OF SPECIALIZED FUNCTIONARIES WERE OPERATING OUTSIDE THE FAMILY UNIT. IN THE COLONIES, ROMANTIC LOVE BEGAN TO BE LINKED WITH MATE SELECTION. THE FAMILY WAS CHARACTERIZED BY PATRIARCHAL ECONOMIC-LEGAL AUTHORITY. DURING THE PERIOD FROM ABOUT 1800 TO THE PRESENT, CERTAIN ASPECTS OF THE FAMILY IN THE UNITED STATES—SUCH AS HOUSEHOLD COMPOSITION, PERSONAL CHOICE OF A MATE, AND ROMANTIC LOVE—CHANGED BUT LITTLE, WHILE OTHERS—SUCH AS WOMEN'S STATUS, SEX CODES, AND INSTITUTIONAL EMBEDDEDNESS—UNDERWENT SUBSTANTIAL ALTERATION.

SECTION ONE

PRE-COLONIAL INFLUENCES

The attempt to investigate and understand the antecedents of the modern family in the United States confronts immediately the difficulties referred to by Freedman in his discussion of the Chinese family. The vast majority of historical sources are either descriptive of the high-status family, or else are written from a normative perspective, i.e., telling how people *should* behave instead of how they do. Thus, insights into the behavior of "average" families in pre-colonial and colonial days must be drawn from normative complaints and critiques and from a scattering of direct references, as well as from what might be called "informed conjecture." It is tempting to begin by dwelling at length upon the early antecedents such as the ancient Hebrews, the Greeks, Romans, and early Christians. Our discussion, however, will be restricted to four or five important characteristics and developments during and following the Medieval period, with detailed accounts left to other sources.[1]

During the early Middle Ages, the nuclear family and its community were highly embedded in each other personnel-wise. That is, the nuclear family had little existence apart from the kin-friend-neighbor milieu in which the individual functioned. The nuclear family was seldom perceived as a separate entity and did not arouse strong feelings of allegiance among its members. In the average family, children were viewed as burdens, or in terms of the service they could render. The flow into and out of the home of kin and friends—as well as of nuclear family members—meant that nuclear family members had virtually no privacy from each other or from other members of the social network, and that affective feelings flowed fairly freely through this broader network.[2]

In the early Medieval Church, religious ordination, but not marriage, was considered a sacrament; the family was not a holy union, but a concession to the weakness of the flesh. Thus, sex in the family was only slightly more acceptable to the religious leaders than was sex outside the family. Such negativism regarding sex in general, when coupled with the broader range of intimate relationships and lack of strong nuclear family values, means that sexual promiscuity (by later standards) was very likely quite prevalent. The nuclear family was simply embedded interactionally in its wider social network.

A second possible form of embeddedness involves the relationships between the family and/or kin group and other societal institutions. In a society such as that of the Papago, in which all economic, religious, political, and other functions are performed as aspects of kinship organization, one can speak of total institutional embeddedness in the kin group. However, in Medieval Europe this was clearly not the case. There were separate functionaries set aside in political, religious, and economic institutions. And yet there was a great amount of embeddedness of these and other social institutions in the kin-friend network. Education took place, for the masses, in the home with kin and friends. Religion has its separate location, but its reinforcement was often left to be carried out or not by the family unit. The economy had proceeded further toward nucleation, in that the majority of nuclear families were producing, property-holding units—the larger kin group having been reduced from a dominant economic position to one in which its basic role was to give economic and other assistance in time of need. Generally speaking, institutions other than economic ones were embedded more in the social network of the individual than in his nuclear family in the early Middle Ages.

The changes that had occurred by the late Middle Ages in Europe had a profound effect upon the family in the American colonies. Underlying many of the other changes was the developing concept of the privacy and sanctity of the nuclear family. Sociability, in earlier centuries, had meant that the home was open to kin and friends almost as much as to spouse and children. Rooms had not been set aside for specialized functions; family and non-family members had interacted in various circumstances. The concept of privacy was twofold. It meant the separation of the family from the outside world and the separation—if they so desired—of family members from each other. This developing separation (not completed in the Middle Ages) was accompanied by the glorification of family life and the appearance of the moral notion of marriage as a sacrament. Monogamy was already the legalized form of marriage, with important economic motives behind such legalization. Now came a distinction in the sex code, which said that, although sex within marriage is blessed by the Church, outside of marriage it is a sin. Devoutly religious people still frequently felt considerable guilt about sex, even within marriage, but the distinction was now clear between sex inside and outside the nuclear family. One important long-term effect of this new emphasis on the nuclear family unit was to reduce the personnel embeddedness of the nuclear unit in its social network; another was to alter the institutional embeddedness, in terms of functions performed, away from the network and toward the nuclear family.

Another change resulting from the increasing self-consciousness of the nuclear family and the concomitant change from institutional embeddedness in the social network to embeddedness in the nuclear family was to make more obvious the husband's dominance over his wife. In the sixteenth century, the wife's position was such that "any acts she performs without the authority of her husband or the law are null and void."[3] Some authors have argued, as does Philippe Ariès, that changes during the Middle Ages actually served to deteriorate the woman's position. This author would argue that what nucleation did was to make increasingly evident the subordinate position that women had traditionally held. This awareness, along with other factors, eventually gave rise to the women's rights movements of the nineteenth century. However, the normatively patriarchal pattern of the family's legal-authority structure was carried over into the American colonies, and will be referred to again.

A third factor arising prior to the establishment of the colonies was the concept of romantic love as distinct from other forms of love. In the upper strata of society in the early Middle Ages, parents commonly arranged the marriages of their offspring to members of appropriate kin groups. During this period, codes of etiquette and chivalry became highly developed in the courts of European nobles, as dramatized in the games at which the valiant did battle for the favor of a particular female.

Chivalry and arranged marriage were not, however, sufficient to produce the idea of romantic love as something different from the ordinary love resulting from sharing and companionship. As long as male sexual experimentation outside of marriage was relatively easy to accomplish (due to personnel embeddedness), romantic love was not distinguishable as a separate entity. However, with the strengthening of the nuclear unit and the clear normative demarcation between sex with one's spouse and with all others, the arrangement of marriages in the upper strata began to be accompanied by heightened frustration. Romantic love, ordinarily occurring after marriage and with a person other than one's own spouse, was often unrequited or frustrated, and involved idealization and strong emotion. In late Medieval Europe, among those of high status, romantic love came to be a technique of rebellion against familial control of mating. In short, the historical factors most immediately responsible for the development of romantic love as something unique or different from ordinary love included: the practice of arranging marriages, the courtly games and etiquette codes, and the increasing separation of the nuclear family—sexually and otherwise—from other societal groupings, according to the official morality. During this period, romantic love was distinguishable primarily in the upper strata and had little direct relation with either marriage or the selection of a mate.[4]

We have been speaking of the upper strata of the late Middle Ages. Among those in the upper strata, marriage was planned as a link between two important lineages (and, later, households). Mating among the masses, it should be noted, was frequently a matter of choice and had a strong emotional element. Here, then, is an instance of what Freedman refers to in discussing the Chinese family. A characteristic of the common people, seldom written about by the *literati* of the time—specifically, personal choice of a mate—came to be a goal for people at all levels of society. There were, however, a few differences between personal choice and love among the masses of Medieval Europe and the romantic love concept of the twentieth century. Affectional ties, although usually present, were not the sole basis for most marriages, nor could these ties be described by the romantic notions of "love at first sight," frustration, or idealization. Marriage was likely to be between two people who had known one another for years, and often took into account economic factors, as well as emotional attraction.

In summary, it can be said that the upper strata of the late Middle Ages were characterized by planned marriages and an increased emphasis on extra-marital romance; while, among the majority, marriage was by choice, but was based upon a complex of factors which did not yet include romantic love as a definable type. Privacy and normative sanctity; the increasing demarcation between familial and extra-familial sex; increasing institutional embeddedness in the nuclear family rather than in the social network; and patriarchy—these are some of the late Medieval influences that most affected the family in the New World.

SECTION TWO

FAMILY LIFE IN THE AMERICAN COLONIES, 1611–1800[5]

Family life in the colonies was shaped partly by the European traditions of the settlers and partly by the challenge of a continent to be explored. There were, as among Rosenfeld's Arab villagers, two sets of norms at work. Those of the official religio-political morality stressed the sanctity of the nuclear family and its position as separate from the social network, while the norms of the common people retained many elements of the personnel embeddedness in which the nuclear family was little distinguished—sexually and otherwise—from its social milieu. However, the mobility that characterized the settling of the American continent served to weaken network ties, as nuclear units moved from place to place, and thus prepared the way for the ascendancy of the nuclear family during the Victorian era of the 1800's.

Though romantic love was already a popular theme of the

literati of Europe, it was not yet directly linked to courtship and mate selection. Two factors in the early history of the colonies began to effect this connection. First, the colonists were overwhelmingly from the lower strata of European society. This meant that they brought with them a tradition of personal choice in marriage, though parents—with an eye out for an economically advantageous arrangement for their son or daughter—were ordinarily consulted regarding the choice. Yet, in general, parental influence had to be by subtle means, since choice was the rule.

The second factor that began to link romance to mate selection was the shortage of European women in the colonies, especially on the expanding frontier. To put it in economic terms: when any desirable or necessary commodity is in short supply, the desire for it becomes more compelling. The feeling is likely to be: "I've got to have that (one)!" When it is a human being of the opposite sex toward whom that feeling is projected, the internal reaction is not very different from that of the Medieval courtier to the unavailable lady. The internal pain of the courting male (or males) was in fact the emotional response that had already been labelled by the *literati* and upper strata as romance or romantic love. It ordinarily settled upon one love-object, and was a forerunner of the idea that one can love only one person at a time. Literature, both fiction and non-fiction, describing the plight of the competing males, publicized this approach to mate selection.[6] Thus, the combination of a tradition of choice, the demand for females, and the increasing emphasis upon the nuclear family apart from its milieu began to link romantic love and mate selection in the American colonies. This link was in contrast to the previous situation, in which such love was simply a sort of free-floating emotion that could strike any time, under any conditions, but most often after and outside marriage. While long-term acquaintance and economic considerations kept romantic love from becoming the sole basis for marriage in the colonies, romantic-love choice as *the* pre-condition for marriage was well on its way.

Perhaps the best-known feature of official colonial morality is its ethic of severe sexual repression. One reason for its great importance to religious and community leaders was, in all probability, the great gulf that separated the official morality from common practice. Premarital sex and pregnancy and extra-marital sex still occurred among the populace, but the official attempts to curb such practices—attempts that had become noticeable in late Medieval Europe—were continued into the colonies. Premarital sexual relations were punishable by public denouncing and extra-marital sex often meant dismissal from the Church in New England. Being thus excluded was intended to make one a social as well as a spiritual outcast, since the Church was both a social and a religious organization. Yet the fact that only a small proportion of the population belonged to the Church very likely made dismissal less than completely effective. In some cases of premarital intercourse, the couple were obliged to marry; in most cases, some sort of penance was required, at least of the female.[7]

Although the official norms are generally acknowledged to have been severe and repressive, it is extremely difficult to ascertain the way in which they affected common behavior. In fact, as historian Charles Adams points out, no one knows with certainty whether or not the harsh code, the public and sometimes severe punishment, and the penance leading to reinstatement actually acted as deterrents even among the devoutly religious. It is possible that the combination of "forbidden fruit" with the emotional satisfactions that must have accompanied the completion of penance and reinstatement resulted in increasing the behavior that the code purported to control. Be that as it may, it should be added that it has become popular to speak of the preoccupation with sex in the present-day United States. Apparently the colonists were also engrossed in the subject, though the official stress among colonial spokesmen was upon repression. We shall return to this topic in upcoming pages.

Moving now from courtship, sex codes, and sex behavior to the colonial family itself, we can see much internal similarity between this family and the common European family. The father was the actual and legal head of the family, dominating the normative decision-making processes. (A recent content analysis of colonial literature revealed about three references to overt male power over decisions to every reference to overt female power.) In addition, the authors find numerous sources noting the use of subtle power by the female, which is seen as "a reaction to or a way of dealing with male authority."[8] Such subtle influence on the part of the female is precisely what one might expect in a system that is legally and normatively patriarchal. The female gave up legal title to any resources she brought into marriage; they became resources at her husband's disposal. As the eighteenth century wore on, however, some variations in property-holding by sex began to appear, with certain colonies giving women somewhat more control over property. Nevertheless, the wife's usual lot in the colonial family was to bear and care for the couple's children and, under difficult conditions, to supervise the household. An excerpt from one written record in a family Bible from this period reads as follows:

> He had sixteen children. When the first child was a year and a half old the second child was born. The baby was but four days old when the older child died. Five times did that mother's heart bear a similar cruel loss when she had a baby in her arms; therefore when she had been married but nine years she had one living child, and five little graves bore the record of her sorrow.[9]

The mother's domestic, reproductive, and socializing (child-rearing) role was one of physical hardship, drudgery, and normative subjection to her husband; it is hardly surprising that she took great pride in those of her offspring who survived to adulthood.

The child's position in the colonial family has been characterized as one dominated by the three R's of repression, religion, and respect, although one might add that religion was often primarily used to increase the other two. A child's basic tendencies were considered to be sinful; it was his parents' task to set him straight. Legally, the child was no better off than the wife. The "father was entitled to his child's services, and he could demand that the child work for him without pay. If the child worked for an outsider, the father was entitled to his earnings."[10] Discipline, while stern, also included the first expressions of a new concept of the child. Up to this time he had been viewed as a small adult; in the colonial family, however, playfulness and mischief were sometimes dismissed with the assertion that "boys will be boys"—an expression of the belief that children are somehow different from adults and should be treated differently. But, for the most part, childishness merely served to increase parental concern about the youngster's wantonness and sinfulness. Not only was the child expected to be submissive, but he was to do his fair share in the family economy, whether with the crops, the flocks, or the housework. Adult roles were learned by the young from parents and persons like them, including older brothers and sisters. As a small adult, when the child was "off duty" he was allowed a substantial amount of freedom to roam and govern himself. In short, the child's life was dominated by his role in the family division of labor and by a repressive discipline, though he often found—or was given—time to temporarily escape into mischief and fun.

The relation of the family unit to the external world, the other institutions of the colonies, also bore a great resemblance to late Medieval European society. Partial embeddedness of the various institutions in the nuclear family, not in the kin-friend network, characterized the colonies. The economy focussed on family subsistence farms, from 70 to 90 per cent of the colonial population being in such agricultural units. The colonists built homes, made furniture and clothing, and raised food. There were trade centers where individuals could take their surpluses and exchange them for what they lacked, and where certain specialists such as the blacksmith had their shops; but, for the most part, the family was an economically self-sufficient unit. Religion, while having separate functionaries and, usually, a separate meeting place, was frequently used for socialization or disciplinary purposes in the home. In fact, families that did not use religion within the home, very often ignored the organization and its leaders as well. Recreation, when the colonists found time for it, tended to be home- or church-based, involving the entire family unit in many instances. The educational process was even more home-based than was recreation: it involved training in homemaking and motherhood for the females and the learning of farm work or an apprenticeship in some trade for the males. Formal education outside the home, even for males, was not universal, and it did not last many years for those who received it. Protection in the colonies demanded cooperation between various family units for mutual defense. The most common type of health care was the "home remedy." In short, the nuclear family was functionally central to the economy of colonial society: the male family head held property, and the family, as the unit of production, joined in a well-defined division of labor. Other institutions—religious, recreational, educational, protective, and medical—all were embedded in the nuclear family to a substantial degree. That is, the activities that characterized these institutions generally either took place within the home or involved the family unit as a whole. Only in the political sphere was there almost no direct tie between the institutional activity and the nuclear family unit.

The question of functional centrality, or institutional embeddedness, which came up in the discussions of the Papago and Chinese families, arises again in observing the United States colonial family. Two questions inferred in the various discussions of institutional embeddedness are often left unanswered. They are: 1) Is it the kin group or the nuclear family that is thought of as central to the functioning of a particular society? (2) Is this family-kin unit essentially political or economic in its centrality? In classical China, for example, Freedman speaks of the masses as nuclear family units on the land, with a balance of political power afforded by certain influential lineages. In colonial America, as in China, we find large numbers of economically important nuclear units working the land, but we don't find the politically strong kin units that were present in the Chinese upper classes. Thus, the institutional centrality of the colonial family system may be thought of as lying somewhere between the virtually total institutional embeddedness in the kin group of the small, kin-based society such as the Papago and that of the family in modern industrial society, which is the focus of the present volume. That is, institutional embeddedness in the colonial family must not be described in any total or absolute sense.

One important concomitant of the colonial type of institutional embeddedness in the nuclear family was the increasingly great concern in the colonies with keeping family units intact. The growing demarcation between the nuclear family and its social network and the importance of the family, economically and otherwise, were such that divorce laws came to be strict and narrowly delimited, with adultery (particularly on the female's part) being the single most prevalent—and often the only legal—grounds for divorce. Although an intolerable family situation could be escaped by desertion (perhaps by "heading for the frontier"), the norms and sanctions were such that this was apparently a less frequent occurrence than legalized divorce is in contemporary U.S. society.

SECTION THREE

CHANGES IN THE AMERICAN FAMILY, 1800–1970

Many discussions of changes in the family since colonial days have been plagued by one or more of the following problems. A first difficulty, which has been clarified and, to a great extent, corrected by recent writers, is the tendency of many historical accounts of the colonial family to present an idealized, or normative, conception of earlier days. The picture of a series of family units living happily in a kinship network on adjoining farms, with little or no sexual promiscuity or other internal difficulty, has been labelled by

William J. Goode the "classical extended family of Western nostalgia."[11] It is, of course, impossible to discuss changes that have occurred unless one can piece together a basically accurate picture of the past.

A second problem has been that the issue of change has been consistently posed in terms of the relation between industrialization and the family. The capitalist market economy, the political ideology of the United States, urbanization, the knowledge explosion, communication growth, agricultural productivity, and other changes that are not completely subsumed under the "industrialization" label, may all relate to the family in distinct and important ways. Nor, in fact, do all students of recent history agree that the family is necessarily the dependent variable[12] in the causal chain. It has been argued that the development of nuclear family privacy *vis-à-vis* its social network may have been a pre-condition for many of the economic-technological changes that surrounded the industrial revolution.[13] Be that as it may, the posing of the issue as one existing between the family and industrialization simply ignores a whole series of related developments—technological and ideological—which may have been associated with family change not directly connected with the industrial revolution itself.[14]

The third difficulty with much theorizing about historical changes in the family is that, in one source or another, as many as fifteen different features of the family—such as husband-wife power relations, sex codes, romantic love, courtship, women's status, and divorce—have been linked to industrialization. The results of choosing certain aspects of the family and ignoring others have been three divergent conclusions regarding the family and change: (1) industrialization caused change "X" or changes "XYZ" to occur in the family; (2) no change occurred in feature "A" or features "ABC" of the family; thus, the industrial revolution apparently had no effect; (3) characteristics "LMN" of the family's structure were the cause of certain changes that occurred in the economy. (The latter is the least frequent interpretation.) The argument over change, cause, and effect has raged, but has been persistently contaminated by either an *idealized view* of the colonial or pre-industrial family; by *ignoring other important developments* that were parallel to industrialization and which influenced the family; or by the *selective use of family features* on the part of the individual researcher or writer.

An attempt is made here to avoid such pitfalls by asking at the outset: "What changes have and have not occurred in the American

TABLE 1

Approximate Degrees of Change in the American Family Features from Colonial Days to the Present

Type of Change	Family Feature
Little or No Change	(1)* Personal choice of a mate
Slight Change	(1) Romantic love in mate selection (2) Nuclear household composition (3) Residential mobility
Moderate Change	(2) Personnel embeddedness (probably curvilinear) (2) Husband-wife power norms and behavior (2) Marital breakup (2) Socialization of children (child-rearing) (2,3) Women's status
Major Change	(1) Courtship (1) Premarital sex norms (2) Husband-wife roles and adjustments (3) Institutional embeddedness in the nuclear family (2,3) Divorce laws
Unknown	(1) Premarital sexual behavior (probably curvilinear) (2) Marital happiness

* These numbers indicate the categories into which these family features are divided in the subsequent discussion. (1) These are concerned with family formation and premarital relationships. (2) Family unit characteristics, or internal relationships. (3) Relations between family and the external world.

family since colonial days?" instead of the more difficult question of "What effect did the industrial revolution and the Western nuclear family have upon one another?" Subsequently, we shall raise the issue of whether certain changes were in fact related to the industrial revolution. Several excellent sources appearing during the 1960's discuss changes and stabilities;[15] from them and from the author's own investigation, the preliminary list shown in Table 1 was devised. The various family features listed in the table can be subsumed under three general headings: (1) *family formation,* or premarital relationships and mate selection; (2) unit characteristics, or *internal* family relationships; and (3) relations with the *external* world of social network, community, institutions, and society.

The *formation* of nuclear family units in America involves personal choice, romantic love, the mechanisms of courtship, and the issues of premarital sexual norms and behavior. As indicated earlier, personal choice of a mate was already typical of the colonists upon their arrival in the New World. Then, as now, there were extremely small numbers of high-status families attempting to keep direct control over mating, but even the arranged marriage of the small numbers of American elites has never been the prepubertal linkage that has characterized some societies. For the most part, mate selection in the U.S. has been controlled by residential patterns and value systems, with personal choice as the norm. The only change with respect to romantic love was that it was becoming more and more common as the basis for mate selection. This was, however, accompanied by significant alterations in courtship behavior. Dating (unchaperoned heterosexual activity and experience) was not even a part of nineteenth century vocabulary. Until the early 1900's, courtship had centered in the social gathering or the home, with the couple having little unchaperoned time and lacking the freedom, transportation, and places to go which eventually gave rise to dating as *the* U.S. form of courtship. Another change in courtship has seen the female begin to make direct appeal for the interest of the male, by means of more revealing clothing and self-styled makeup. The womanly "wiles," involving coyness and indirectness, which were so appropriate to chivalry and the double-standard morality, have taken a back seat to more obvious mechanisms of attention-getting.

Along with the appearance of dating as the focal point of American courtship, major changes occurred in the sexual codes governing premarital behavior. Much has been made of the colonial practice of bundling and its possible implications for premarital sexual intercourse.[16] Authors such as Charles F. Adams have noted how the officially strict norms and sanctions may have increased rather than limited premarital sex. The crucial element in premarital sex norms and behavior, however, is the rise and fall of the Victorian era during the nineteenth century, with its great stress on the nuclear family and sexual continence outside of marriage, especially for the female. The increasing strictness of the official norms from colonial days through the mid-1800's, followed by a wholesale questioning of this position during the twentieth century, may very well have had the result of decreasing slightly the incidence of premarital sex in the mid-1800's and increasing its prevalence again in this century—even beyond its incidence in colonial days. Yet we can never know for sure whether or not premarital sexual behavior followed this curvilinear pattern. What we do know is that society has moved toward an overt and often positive attitude in dealing with sexual matters. Sex education, sex research, popular literature, motion pictures: these and other media have brought about the frank and public consideration of all manner of sexual practices—a drastic departure, even from the treatment of sex in the early 1900's. An example of this change is that the pros and cons of premarital intercourse are being openly debated, not simply rejected by invoking an absolute, by many of the country's religious or moral leaders.[17] The white settlers and their colonial progeny did not ignore sexual matters. Nevertheless, the emphasis in official quarters is no longer on denouncing, control, and guilt, but has moved toward freedom, permissiveness, and openness.

Internally, the family has generally undergone moderate-to-great changes over the past two centuries. Perhaps the least change has occurred in the actual structural composition of the household. Well before the colonists came to the United States, the European household had taken on a nuclear character. The majority of nuclear families lived apart from the other members of their social network, this being an aspect of the privacy motif referred to above. The little change that did occur in household composition between the seventeenth and twentieth centuries was a decrease in the proportion of extremely large households, although the modal size category remained about the same. Another possible difference, based on the greater tendency in colonial days to incorporate an aging parent or parents into the household, has been balanced by the greater likelihood today that parents will live until their children reach maturity.

Much has been written about greater permissiveness in child-rearing and about the decline in parental authority. It seems, however, that the major changes in socialization center around the division of labor in the family and a more continuous, developmental concern on the part of the parents. The family is no longer the basic economic producing unit, a fact that frees the child from the kind of authority that could be asserted over someone in a clearly defined and inferior economic role.[18] Yet the child's role in the colonial family's division of labor, buttressed by moral training in absolutes and a tendency to perceive the child as a small adult, included a substantial permissive or self-directive element. That is, the colonial child, when "off duty," or free of responsibility, was often on his own—with internalized absolutes left to suffice. Today parents lack strong economic-labor authority and are less likely to be buttressed by absolutes, but they tend to be more consciously and continuously concerned with the child as a developing person —with achievement and other aspects of socialization. Thus, only a portion of the apparent greater permissiveness is due to reduced parental authority; the remainder is based upon a heightened parental awareness of and concern about individual personality and child-rearing *in toto*. We shall return to this in Chapters VII and VIII.

The curvilinear change in personnel embeddedness posited in Table 1 is closely related to the socialization issue just discussed. In the late Medieval period, we have noted, the nuclear family began to be distinguished from its social network. Emphasis upon the nuclear family, at the expense of the kin-friend network, continued through the colonial period and culminated in the Victorian era of the mid-1800's. Already, however, a new emphasis upon the individual was increasing; it was embodied in the conception of home architecture which made possible the privacy of family members from one another. Thus, the move from the Victorian into the Progressive era was characterized by a decrease in nuclear family values and an increase in concern with the individual and his needs for adjustment, understanding, personality development, and uniqueness. Precisely where we are today in nuclear embeddedness versus individualism cannot be determined until later in the present volume, but it is a question that the reader should keep in mind (see Figure 2).

Husband-wife power relations in the family are extremely difficult to ascertain for two primary reasons. For one thing, legal and normative authority may, as Lantz *et al.* observe, be circumvented or overridden by subtle means of influence.[19] Furthermore, there is the nagging question in the study of power anywhere, not just in the family, of whether *not* doing a task or making a decision means that the individual lacks power in that area, or whether it

FIGURE 2

Changes in Personnel Embeddedness from Colonial Days to the Present

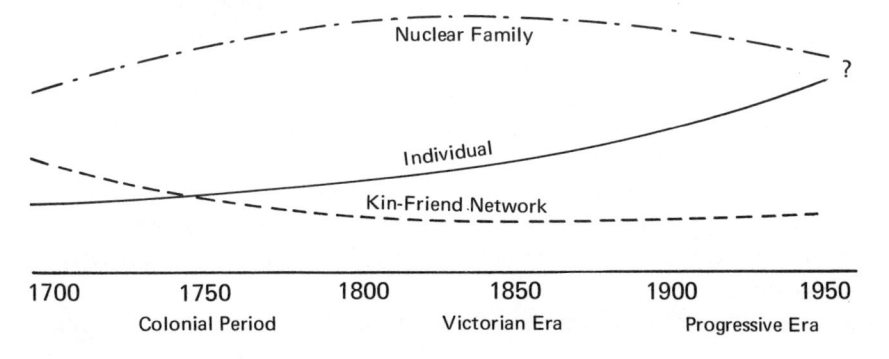

1700	1750	1800	1850	1900	1950
	Colonial Period		Victorian Era		Progressive Era

means he has delegated power or authority to the one doing the task. We do know that wives may have substantial influence in a normatively patriarchal family system. We also know that, in the modern couple that is seeking to make decisions democratically, the father may, because of his achievements or the resources he controls, find himself with veto power in many key decision-making situations. Despite these facts, it seems likely that some change has occurred in husband-wife power behavior allowing an increase in the *direct* and *acceptable* influence of the wife.

Firmer ground is reached in looking at changes in power norms or expectations rather than behavior. Patriarchy, or husband-dominance, was the general expectation in the colonial family, today this norm is competing with the norm of conscious equalitarianism and democracy in the home. The reason for speaking of moderate rather than great change in this area is that *conscious* power equality is characteristic, not of the entire U.S. family population, but of one major segment: those "white-collar" or middle-class families that are financially fairly well off.[20]

The prevalence of marital breakup is one of the more frequently used indicators of the purported "decay" of the American family. The nineteenth century witnessed a substantial increase in the number of legal grounds for divorce; this was followed in the first half of the twentieth century by a rise in the divorce rate. (A case could be made both for considering the increase in the divorce rate to be internal and for considering it to involve relations between the family and the external world.) Despite the changes in grounds and divorce rate, it is difficult to determine the extent of the increase in all forms of family breakup since colonial days. For one thing, family units in colonial days that might eventually have been disrupted by desertion were often broken by the premature death of one spouse or the other. For another thing, some of the rise in divorce rate is nothing more than an increase in the tendency to legalize marital separation. Thus, while the divorce rate has risen, the rates of family breakup by death, desertion, and separation have declined. In short, change in the legal structures has very likely been greater than the change in total rates of marital breakup. Yet the strictness of the norms and laws, and the concern of the colonists to keep families together for the sake of their economic and other functions, indicate that husband-wife relations had to be worse in colonial days than today before a couple would separate.

Another change affecting the family has to do with the position of women in society, and the concomitant alteration of husbands' and wives' roles.[21] As late as 1850 in many states, a wife had no legal control over personal property; all her belongings were legally at her husband's disposal. However, the democratic ideal, plus the growing awareness of females that they could make a living in urban, industrializing society, resulted in the women's rights movements being born. Within the past 100 years, women have gained legally and politically; ownership of property within marriage and the right to vote are two examples of these gains. They have gained educationally: in colonial days even a grade school education was thought unnecessary for a girl. A century later, the distinction was drawn at the secondary school level. High school—and, in high-status families, college—was deemed valuable for males, but impractical for females. The twentieth century ushered in the period of "coeducation," with about one-third of today's American college graduates being females. They have likewise gained substantially in the economic sphere: not only are there some 25 million U.S. women holding jobs, but they have advanced to the point that salary differentials for men and women doing the same work diverge but slightly. One must be cautious, however, not to overstate women's gains in the United States. For one thing, job-holding by women still has *supplemental* connotations economically, since a wife tends to make less money than her husband, and more income means more spent for consumer goods. In addition, job discrimination is still strongly against females, both in terms of advancement and in terms of virtual exclusion from many professional and business fields. In fact, since World War II, the glorification of wifehood and motherhood by the mass media has to some extent undone the former gains of the feminists. Thus, the female today is in a difficult position: her rise in status has been accompanied by the tendency to play down her traditional role—to speak of being "just a housewife." And yet this remains her dominant life goal due to the influence of tradition and the systematic, yet subtle, discrimination that she confronts in society.[22]

The change in the status of women in society is related to the changes in courtship practices discussed above, as well as to changes in husband and wife roles and adjustments. The basic movement has been away from predestined economic and familial roles toward an open, free-choice approach to being a husband and father or wife and mother. In colonial days, the father was expected to run the economic machinery of the family and to be a stern and able disciplinarian; the woman was expected to marry, raise children, and provide for her husband's needs. Today, the options have multiplied and traditional norms are questioned. How should the male operate as a father: as disciplinarian, provider, or buddy? How much of himself should he invest in activities that are internal to the family and how much in community and occupational affairs? Should a woman be "just a housewife" or should she balance such responsibilities with occupational employment or various forms of community service? The crucial element in all the various role decisions men and women must make is the openness, the weakness of traditional expectations, the lack of predetermination. This, of course, heightens the importance of adjustment between wife and husband; each couple must work out its own role definitions. The intricacies of these role options and the adjustments required are one of the major foci of the present volume, particularly of Chapters XI and XII.

The notion of family adjustments brings us to one of the more intriguing dimensions of the "classical extended family of Western nostalgia." It is often assumed that the family in colonial days was a happy, close-knit unit in which conflict and indecision were far overshadowed by stability and tradition. Yet, as we have indicated, the colonial family was kept together by various legal and traditional mechanisms for the sake of the economic and other functions which the nuclear unit performed. Thus, personal happiness might vary greatly from one family unit to another. It is not that unhappiness did not result in some colonial family units breaking up; it is rather that some units very likely stayed together, despite unhappiness, for the sake of their other functions. The twentieth century American family, by contrast, lacks many of the cultural or normative supports for the unit which characterized the earlier day, and finds itself held together primarily by the quality of internal relationships. Under such circumstances, happiness, satisfaction, or adjustment becomes the overt goal of the married couple. While it is impossible to discern the marital happiness of colonial families, it seems quite possible that the actual "happiness quotient," or level of happiness, is even higher today than in colonial days for two reasons. First, married couples work so hard at it today; and second, more unhappy marriages weed themselves out today than they did formerly. Whether or not this interpretation is correct, let us not make the mistake of referring nostalgically to the "happy, traditional, colonial family."

Turning to the relations between the nuclear family and the *external* world, which includes the already-discussed position of women, we find a close relation between personnel embeddedness, the dimensions of the household, and the amount of residential mobility. One of the reasons for the increasing separation of the nuclear unit from its social milieu, in terms of values and household composition, is the residential mobility of families. This mobility is not, however, so much a difference between colonial days and the present as it is a pervasive characteristic of U.S. history. The history of white colonization and colonial expansion on the American frontier is, in fact, the history of residential mobility. Granted, there was a substantially larger proportion of colonial persons who inherited farms or settled on land near their kin, but this is offset to some extent by the large numbers of working-class persons who, in the nineteenth and twentieth centuries, clustered together in the same city with their kin. There may have been an increase in the number of multiple moves by any one family unit in modern society, but this is a characteristic of a minority of the population—primarily certain professional and executive persons and their families. Furthermore, twentieth century mobility neither exists uniformly without being affected by the location of kin and friends, nor does it entail—as it often did in colonial days—virtual isolation from kin and former friends. Too much has been made of the modern family pursuing industrial and managerial work opportunities; the overall picture is more one of slightly greater freedom to choose one's residential relationship to one's kin and of somewhat greater frequency of residential movement—but not much.

The European and colonial American family systems were already basically different—in terms of institutional embeddedness—from a society such as the Papago, in which the family-kin network and social organization were almost synonymous. In the colonies, the legal and political institutions were quite separate from kinship and family ties, and other institutions, such as the economic, religious, and educational, had special functionaries as well as strong ties to the nuclear family. Nevertheless, great changes in embeddedness have occurred since colonial days. The industrial revolution, centered in the development of the factory system, directly effected one of these changes by transferring the economic productive function from the family unit and home to a separate location, to which one or more family members go to work to provide for their family's economic needs. The family as a unit is no longer producer as well as consumer, but merely consumer. Yet in the capitalist market economy, the family's role as consumer is extremely important, and the business community of today is quite cognizant of the value of having a strong nuclear family system.

Other activities that were handled by the family in an immediate and often rudimentary fashion have undergone expansion and spatial separation. Recreation, once a family endeavor at home or church and an individual pursuit around the home, has become increasingly specialized along age lines and centered in various locations other than the home. The protective function (except for a few private fall-out shelters) has ceased to be a cooperative-familial responsibility, being instead the concern of the police, firemen, and other community specialists. Health care has become the responsibility of the doctor, the drug store, and the hospital, with the family as coordinating agency. The home remedy, once the key element in medical treatment, has become nothing more than the butt of jokes.

Except for economic productivity, the educational function is perhaps the most dramatic example of expansion and parcelling out. Today the law makes it impossible, except under extreme, extenuating circumstances, for parents to keep their children at home to educate them. At five or six years of age the child is removed from the home for twenty to forty hours a week. Simultaneously, however, parents supervise and give continuing attention to their children's development.

The religious function, once of great importance to socialization and discipline, has seen its roots in the home become weakened, with its activity restricted to specific times and places apart from the home. The lessening of the carry-over between the religious institution and the home makes it possible for commentators to note a fourfold to fivefold increase in church membership since colonial days and, at the same time, to refer to the increasing secularization of society. All these developments may be referred to as institutional differentiation or the weakening of institutional embeddedness in the nuclear family; we have avoided the often-used term "loss of family functions."[23] The reason for this is that the latter term, although in common usage since the 1930's, has overtones that might cause some to think of the contemporary family as "twiddling its collective thumbs" for want of responsibilities or activities. This, however, is an incorrect representation on two counts: first, the family is still very much involved in the coordinating of physical care and of socialization. Second, while much family unit interaction occurs in the interstices of the other societal institutions (as Freedman puts it), there is an increasingly overt and central involvement of the family unit in meeting the psychological needs of its members. But more on the functions of the family today shall be reserved for Chapter V.

SECTION FOUR

SUMMARY AND CONCLUSIONS

The most striking changes in family formation or premarital conditions since colonial days have been in courtship and sex codes, with an increasing link between romantic love and mate selection. The major change—in reality, a complex of changes—in relations between the nuclear family and the larger society is in the expansion and parcelling out of certain traditional functions to other agencies and locations. By far the most numerous large-scale changes have occurred within the family itself. These have included an increase in the number of role options and definitions open to both sexes, with a concomitant multiplying of the number of necessary adjustments, and a loosening of divorce laws, making it easier to dissolve a given family unit.

Only a few of these developments can be directly related to the industrial revolution. Most important is, of course, the influence of industrialization upon institutional embeddedness—especially the economic productive function. It also seems to have had some effect upon residential mobility and upon the status of women, though the latter was also influenced by democratic ideology. Beyond these, it becomes extremely difficult to perceive direct linkages between the family and industrialization.[24]

In discussing classical China, Freedman spoke of two organizing principles: that of high-status people and that of the masses. Rosenfeld likewise found two cultural ideals at work in the Arab village: the traditional and the modern. The same issue must now be raised regarding our depiction of changes in the American family since colonial days; when we speak of "sex codes" or "husband-wife power codes," the question arises: "whose codes?" Are they everyone's codes, or are they the codes of one important group within the society? The answer, to which we shall return in detail in subsequent chapters, might be inferred from the previously-made comment that "*conscious* power equality is characteristic, not of the entire U.S. family population, but of one major segment: those 'white-collar' or middle-class families that are financially fairly well off. . . ." This equality is the norm of those who dominate American culture, i.e., the middle classes. The term "dominate" is used here in much the same sense as in the discussion of polygyny. It does not mean numerical *pre*dominance; rather, it refers to that cultural style which, due to the key position of its proponents in government, education, and the mass media, receives the widest dissemination to the populace as a whole. In a society such as the United States, there are active subcultural principles as well as the dominant ones. Chapter VI is devoted to the delineation of the various subcultural principles at work in the United States and the historic interrelations between them.

One way to view the nuclear family unit and its activities is as a unit that is becoming more specialized in a society of specialists. It is this issue, and the crucial theoretical problems concerning it, that command our attention in Chapter V.

NOTES

[1] Several excellent accounts of the antecedents of the modern family may be referred to for a fuller picture. These include Panos D. Bardis, "Family Forms and Variations Historically Considered," in Harold T. Christensen, ed., *Handbook of Marriage and the Family* (Chicago: Rand McNally, 1964), Chap. 11; Morton M. Hunt, *The Natural History of Love* (New York: Knopf, 1959); Gerald R. Leslie, *The Family in Social Context* (New York: Oxford University Press, 1967), Chaps. 6–7; and Philippe Ariès, *Centuries of Childhood* (New York: Vintage Books, 1965 ed.).

[2] Ariès' book is important for its insights and ideas; it is, however, based primarily upon interpretations of artistic works and architecture and many of the conclusions regarding the family are therefore somewhat inferential. Also, it deals with the French family and cannot be taken as a perfect representation of the English family prior to colonization of America.

[3] Ariès, *Centuries of Childhood*, p. 356.

[4] For more on this, see Hunt, *The Natural History of Love*. Literary illustrations can be found in Alfred Tennyson, *Idylls of the King* (Boston: Ticknor and Fields, 1859).

[5] We must admit that the date used to indicate the close of the colonial period—1800—is more arbitrary than most. Another possibility would have been 1776, or the date when the colonial period ended politically. Another would have been 1850, as a year by which the industrial revolution was in full swing in the United States. The year 1800 is merely a compromise, indicating the beginnings of a new country and incipient industrialization, though marking no specific break with the past.

ANTECEDENTS OF THE MODERN AMERICAN FAMILY

[6] Washington Irving, *The Legend of Sleepy Hollow* (London: Macmillan, 1920). For other literature, see the footnotes to Herman Lantz et al., "Pre-Industrial Patterns in the Colonial Family in America: A Content Analysis of Colonial Magazines," *American Sociological Review*, 33 (1968), 413–26.

[7] There are even scattered reports of capital punishment for sexual sins. See Hunt, *The Natural History of Love*, p. 230.

[8] Lantz et al., "Pre-Industrial Patterns," p. 419.

[9] Arthur W. Calhoun, *A Social History of the American Family*, Vol. I. (New York: Barnes and Noble, 1945), p. 106.

[10] Herma Kay Hill, "The Outside Substitute for the Family," in Seymour M. Farber, Piero Mustacchi, and Roger H. L. Wilson, eds., *Man and Civilization: The Family's Search for Survival* (New York: McGraw Hill, 1965), p. 6.

[11] William J. Goode, *After Divorce* (New York: Free Press, 1956), p. 3.

[12] The "dependent variable" is the factor, value, or behavior that is to be explained.

[13] H. J. Habakkuk, "Family Structure and Economic Change in Nineteenth-Century Europe," *The Journal of Economic History*, 15 (1955), 1–12.

[14] Some of the best sources discussing the issue of industrialization and the family are: Sidney M. Greenfield, "Industrialization and the Family in Sociological Theory," *American Journal of Sociology*, 67 (1961), 312–22; Frank F. Furstenberg, Jr., "Industrialization and the American Family: A Look Backward," *American Sociological Review*, 31 (1966), 326–37; William F. Ogburn and Meyer F. Nimkoff, *Technology and the Changing Family* (Boston: Houghton Mifflin, 1955).

[15] Lantz et al., "Pre-Industrial Patterns"; Furstenberg, "Industrialization and the American Family"; William J. Goode, *World Revolution and Family Patterns* (New York: Free Press, 1963).

[16] On bundling, see Henry Reed Stiles, *Bundling: Its Origin, Progress and Decline in America* (New York: Book Collectors Association, 1934).

[17] A good example is a recent article by a Protestant chaplain: Ronald M. Mazur, "Commonsense Sex," *Redbook*, July, 1969, in which the author discusses premarital sex as a viable moral option.

[18] Neil J. Smelser, "The Social Challenge to Parental Authority," in Farber et al., eds., *Man and Civilization: The Family's Search for Survival*, pp. 70–71.

[19] Lantz et al., "Pre-Industrial Patterns," p. 419.

[20] As used in this volume, the terms "middle class" and "working class," as well as the term "lower class," which is used extensively in Chapter VI, have primarily occupational and socioeconomic connotations. *Middle-class* families are those in which the household head has a professional, managerial, clerical, or sales occupation, and which are clustered in the upper portion of the prestige-income ladder. They are not, however, right at the top—those at the top are generally labelled "upper classes." The *working classes* are predominantly manual workers, including skilled craftsmen, foremen, and industrial workers who have a steady income. The *lower classes* are those who are at the bottom of the socioeconomic ladder, either due to lack of skill, handicap, or discrimination. The extent to which these occupational and socioeconomic groupings are characterized by different ways of life will be explored throughout this volume, in order to determine whether such designations are empirically useful.

[21] This should more accurately be introduced under changes in relations with the external world, but is introduced here to prepare the reader for the

"internal" issue of husband-wife roles in marriage. A role is a pattern of behavior that is associated with a particular social position, such as that of husband or wife.

[22] At least one author has argued quite persuasively, by means of occupational and other statistics, that women have actually lost status in recent years in comparison to men. See Dean D. Knudsen, "The Declining Status of Women: Popular Myths and the Failure of Functionalist Thought," *Social Forces*, 48 (1969), 183–93.

[23] On the term "loss of family functions," see William F. Ogburn, "The Family and Its Functions," *Recent Social Trends* (New York: McGraw-Hill, 1933), Chap. 13, and our discussion of Ogburn's view in Chapter V of this volume.

[24] On this, see Morris Zelditch, Jr., "Cross-Cultural Analysis of Family Structure," in Christensen, ed., *Handbook of Marriage and the Family*, pp. 492–97.

V

The Family in a Differentiated Society: Toward a Theoretical Perspective

LITERATURE ON THE FAMILY HAS ACCUMULATED ON THE SUBJECTS OF STRUCTURE, FUNCTION, AND VARIETY; IN THIS VOLUME WE SHALL DEAL WITH ALL THREE. ONE STRAND OF WRITING HAS SOUGHT TO DETERMINE WHICH TASKS THE FAMILY PERFORMS IN EVERY SOCIETY. THIS CONCERN WITH UNIVERSAL FAMILY FUNCTIONS MAY BE MORE USEFULLY EMPLOYED FOR OUR PURPOSES BY TRANSFORMING THESE FUNCTIONS INTO VARIABLES. ANOTHER STRAND, DERIVED FROM OGBURN AND OTHERS, NOTES THE FAMILY'S LOSS OF FUNCTIONS TO OTHER INSTITUTIONS AND ITS AFFECTIVE FUNCTION TODAY. USING DURKHEIM'S VIEW OF SOCIETAL INTEGRATION, THE AFFECTIVE FUNCTION IS PLACED IN SOCIETAL CONTEXT, AND GUIDING PROPOSITIONS ARE DEVELOPED. THESE PROPOSITIONS INCLUDE THE NOTIONS OF: (1) THE FAMILY'S SPECIALIZED AFFECTIVE FUNCTION; (2) ITS SPECIFIC FUNCTION AS ECONOMIC CONSUMER; (3) ITS GENERAL ROLE IN SOCIALIZATION; (4) THE COMPLEXITY AND INCONSISTENCIES IN SOCIETY AND ITS FAMILY SYSTEM; (5) THE DIVERGENT FAMILY CULTURES IN AMERICAN SOCIETY, OR THE SUBCULTURE CONCEPT. FINALLY, FIVE CONTINUA ARE DEVELOPED TO DEAL CROSS-CULTURALLY WITH FAMILY FORMATION, SOCIALIZATION, MARITAL ROLES, INSTITUTIONAL EMBEDDEDNESS, AND PERSONNEL EMBEDDEDNESS, IN ORDER THAT THE CURRENT CHARACTER OF, AND DIRECTION AND SPEED OF CHANGE WITHIN, THE AMERICAN FAMILY MAY BE BETTER UNDERSTOOD.

A review of Chapters II–IV shows that the three major foci of attention have been family structure, family functions, and family varieties. In the present chapter we propose to tie together many of the loose ends from the foregoing analysis, and to develop a quasi-theoretical framework that will be utilized throughout the remainder of the volume.[1]

The structural concerns thus far presented revolve around the degrees of institutional and personnel embeddedness in various societies, including such issues as household composition, relation between the nuclear family and kin group, and structural relations between the family system and other societal institutions. These factors will be discussed further in the present chapter, and will continue to be major emphases throughout the book.

The concept of function, as it has been employed in the sociological literature on the family, is multidimensional, having at least three distinct meanings. These three meanings may be exemplified by the following statements:

"The family is functional for society in several ways."
"The functions of the family have changed."
"The family functions in the following manner."

In the first phrase, the term "functional" has to do with the *good or benefit*, perpetuation, or integration of society. The idea of universal family functions, such as reproduction and socialization, is closely related to the issue of the family's universality referred to in Chapter III. This idea concerns the way in which the family furthers certain goals of the society in which it is operating. The second use of the idea of family functions has to do with *tasks* performed, so that when we speak of the functional centrality of the family, we are saying that the central tasks of a given society are performed within the family setting. The third statement, which changes "function" from a noun to a verb, is simply concerned with describing how the family actually *operates*. The kinship system in the United States, we might say, functions for affective ties and a certain amount of obligation. Or one can speak of certain parts of the family system functioning in an inconsistent or conflicting fashion. For example, the norm that says the American should be independent is inconsistent with the one that says he should honor his aging parents; the way in which these norms are reconciled is the way society functions at that point.

The first of the three uses of "function" is not a major concern of this volume, though we shall discuss it briefly in the next few pages. The question of changing family tasks is a basic issue in this chapter and, like the structural questions, continues to be raised in subsequent chapters. Finally, the large mass of materials describing adolescence, dating, husband-wife relations, and other aspects of the family simply depict the way in which a particular family system—that of the United States—operates.

Thus far, the concept of family varieties has been exemplified cross-culturally by the use of materials on the Nayar, Papago,

Chinese and other family systems. In turning more exclusively to the United States, the issue of variety is redefined as one of subcultures and subsocieties. Are there peoples within the United States who are sufficiently different culturally or separate socially as to be somewhat distinct from the dominant members of that society? This question will be the focus of Chapter VI, and will also arise from time to time throughout the remainder of the book.

We shall begin to synthesize the ideas of function, structure, and variety by referring briefly to the notion of universal family functions.

SECTION ONE

UNIVERSAL FAMILY FUNCTIONS

One strand of theoretical, or explanatory, writing about the family generalized the question regarding family functions in the following manner. There are certain goals that any society must accomplish in order to continue existing. It must reproduce individuals to replace the dying; it must protect its boundaries; it must motivate persons to take positions of leadership; it must solve the economic problem of physical survival; and so on.[2] Among these necessary functions are some that appear to be performed by the family in every society; these are called the "universal family functions," or functions that the family has always carried out everywhere. Kingsley Davis speaks of reproduction, maintenance, placement, and socialization (or raising the young) as universal family functions. George P. Murdock says the universal functions are reproduction, socialization, economic cooperation, and sexual relations. Ira Reiss claims there is but one universal function of the family—the "nurturant" socialization of the newborn. Other functions are often, but not always, performed by the family or kin group.[3] A particular author's *definition* of the family is, of course, closely related to the functions he sees it carrying out. Thus, a close link exists between the discussion in Chapter III of the universality of the nuclear family and the idea of universal family functions.

A distillation of a list of family functions devised by William J. Goode yields three functions, which can be viewed either from the standpoint of the family itself, or of the family-in-society. First, there is the *reproductive* function, which is dependent upon age at marriage, fertility, and other factors. From society's perspective, this might be called the replacement function. That is, for a society to survive, new members must be produced to replace those who are dying off; this occurs within families. Second, *status placement* means the determination of the individual's life chances within his society. From the standpoint of society, this is the integrative or maintenance function. It simply means that family background has historically and cross-culturally been a major determinant of one's career achievement or status in society. Third, the family, as Reiss indicates, performs the *socialization* or child-rearing function. In the family, the individual learns what to do and what not to do in order to get along in his society, in order to be consistent with its demands and expectations. Thus, from society's standpoint, this is the social control function—a result of the family's embodying and imparting the society's culture.

Goode rightly cautions the reader against assuming that the three functions he lists are universals in the sense of being constants.[4] Though the discussion of "universals" is valuable in its own right, Goode feels that such functions should be thought of as variables, with the family system of a given society meeting more or less of a specific need. For example, in some societies one's life chances are predicated almost entirely upon the family unit into which he is born. In other societies, such as the United States, the possibility of individual achievement means that the family might be better described as the base, or beginning point, defining certain limits upon status. A careful review of the literature might result in the conclusion that in the U.S. about 40 per cent of status placement is determined by family background. Or, the reader might conclude that, in one society, 90 per cent of socialization occurs within the family and kin group, while in another society the figure is less than 50 per cent. Thus, the universal functions may profitably be transformed into variable functions for the sake of comparing societies.

Bernard Farber goes even further in criticizing the notion of universal family functions. When you start by saying: "Here are the things which must be done for society to survive, and these are what the family does for its society," you are defining the goals of a society, as well as talking about tasks. In speaking of the family as doing certain things for the benefit of society, or furthering societal ends and integration, two value judgments must be made. First, we must ask whether the family is doing a good or poor job of performing its functions in a given society, thus drawing a judgment regarding its quality of performance. Also, we are likely to make the inherent judgment that equilibrium is better than change, that stability is better than alteration of society and culture. Rather, we should be reminded that, as families carry out their reproductive, status-placing, and socializing functions, they may or may not be contributing to societal integration and perpetuation. It is quite possible to conceive of high fertility, low status-placement, and socialization for change in a particular segment of a society as leading to upheaval rather than maintenance.[5] A difficulty arises, then, in the discussion of universal functions when one moves from the general notion of family functions to the specific, i.e., how the family system of a given society is doing in this regard. This obstacle is not insurmountable, for the careful student may profitably seek to discover the goals and values of a society and the relation of family functioning to these goals.[6] This is not, however, a key purpose of this book. When you read in subsequent pages about the functions of the American family, keep in mind that we are not describing how well a set of universal functions is being performed, but are merely noting the ways in which the family in the United States has historically articulated and currently articulates with this particular society and its other institutions.

SECTION TWO

THE FAMILY AND ITS CHANGING FUNCTIONS: THREE VIEWS

The attempt to discover universal family functions is left to Davis, Murdock, Reiss, and others. Rather, let us turn to three authors who have summarized the transformation of the family in Western civilization in recent times. William F. Ogburn, Ernest Burgess, and Bernard Farber have each made a contribution to understanding the modern family. Ogburn, writing in the 1930's, described the family's loss of functions. Industrialization and urbanization have resulted in the transferral of one traditional family function after another to specialized institutional settings. The economic producing function has been transferred to the factory and office; the educational function has been moved to the schoolroom; the religious function has been left almost entirely to the church or synagogue; the recreational function has gone to the theatre and stadium; the medical function has been transferred to the doctor's office and hospital. In most cases, the family members go to these places individually, not as a family unit. The result has been that the family is left to provide affection and understanding for its members, but little else.[7] In short, with the increasing differentiation and specialization of society, the family, too, has become a specialist. No longer functionally central, it now specializes in gratifying people's psychological needs.

Ernest Burgess, while more interested in describing what takes place between family members than in relating the family to the larger society, nevertheless parallels Ogburn in his conception of the family. The family, says Burgess, is moving from an institution to a companionship. Recalling our definition of an institution from Chapter I, we see truth in the statement that the institutional family would ideally be "one in which its unity would be determined by the traditional rules and regulations, specified duties and obligations, and other social pressures impinging upon the family members."[8] Its institutional characteristics include authoritarian or autocratic power, stability and permanence, perpetuation of culture, compliance with predetermined roles, and the carrying out of numerous tasks, such as economic, religious, and recreational ones, *as a unit*. The American family—or, more generally, the modern industrial family—has, over the past two centuries, moved away from an institutional character and toward a "unity which develops out of mutual affection and intimate association of husband and wife and parents and children." The characteristics of this emerging type include equalitarian decision-making, individual choice of a mate based upon affection and personality, concern in marriage with happiness and adjustment, and a great modification of the family's historic functions. "The external factors making for family stability, such as control by custom and community opinion, have been greatly weakened. The permanence of marriage more and more depends on the bonds of affection, temperamental compatibility, and mutual interests," in sum, upon companionship.[9] Although the American family has not yet arrived at the companionship type, it is currently heading in that direction.

The family, according to Bernard Farber, is moving from orderly replacement to universal, permanent availability. Orderly replacement means both persons and culture content, but the emphasis is upon the latter. It means the passing along of family culture from one generation to the next with as little change as possible. Today, however, orderly replacement is giving way to universal, permanent availability. In using this term, Farber focusses, not upon socialization, but rather upon mate selection or the formation and dissolution of family units. The individual, Farber believes, is increasingly free to choose as a mate any individual of the opposite sex with whom he comes in contact. That is, members of the opposite sex are "universally available" as potential mates. They are, furthermore, "permanently available," so that if one marital linkage proves unsatisfactory, it may be terminated and another begun.[10] Personal choice of a mate, loosening sex codes, frequent divorce—all three are consistent with the expectation of happiness and meaningful relationships in the family, and are indices of the movement toward universal, permanent availability.

Each of the three authors notes that, in a society in which the family is functionally central, or is the prime economic and socializing unit, there is apt to be great concern for keeping the individual family unit intact. Thus, in the institutional, functionally central family concerned with orderly replacement, sex is controlled (if possible), divorce is difficult to obtain, and mate selection is pretty much in the hands of the adult generation. However, when functions are expanded and parcelled out from the family unit, the result is a weakening of the cultural mechanisms for maintaining the boundaries of any given family unit. This weakening is felt to be a part of the family's recent history.

Loss of family functions, movement toward a companionship basis for marriage, and universal, permanent availability of members of the opposite sex for mating: these are some of the conceptualizations that have been developed to summarize the changes discussed in the preceding chapter. Although these conceptualizations are valuable, they are somewhat misleading and overdrawn. Thus, in Section Three, we shall—with the aid of the French sociologist, Emile Durkheim—extend and clarify the issues raised by the three authors referred to in this section.

SECTION THREE

DIVISION OF LABOR AND THE FAMILY: EXTENSIONS AND CLARIFICATIONS

Emile Durkheim, in his writing in the early twentieth century, presented a view of society and its direction of change which, while incorrect in some of its predictions, is of help in understanding family change. Durkheim's major emphasis throughout his writings is the nature of societal integration, or what it is that ties people together in society. Historically and cross-culturally, many societies (the Papago, for example) have been composed of relatively self-sufficient family-kin units, each of which carried out approximately the same activities as any other unit. These self-sufficient and similar units are not obliged, out of necessity, "either to remain united or to perish. On the contrary, since they do not need each other, as each contains within himself all that social life consists of, he can go and carry it elsewhere."[11] What, then, is it that keeps persons linked together in such societies, instead of each sub-unit wandering freely and self-sufficiently? For Durkheim, the answer lies in the strength of the behavioral norms and the interpersonal bonds—the expectations and the collective sentiments ("we" feelings) that are developed. The simple, or undifferentiated, society is held together by careful specification of the acceptable, serious punishment of the unacceptable, awareness of the ways in which "our" behavior differs from that of the people "over the hill," and by the identification of persons in a family-kin unit with their larger society. Both norms and bonds are a part of the collective conscience; the development of a strong collective conscience is necessary to societal integration in a society in which the family-kin units do not actually need each other. This, says Durkheim, is "mechanical solidarity."

Societies in the modern world are very different from undifferentiated societies. They are characterized by an ever-expanding division of labor. A single family-kin unit is no longer self-sufficient and identical to every other such unit; rather, there is an organic solidarity or integration between them. That is, they are linked together like the parts of an organism, each with a specific function to perform, but very much dependent upon the others for mutual survival. Civilized and industrialized society is held together, not so much by the feelings of the units toward each other, as by necessity.

While these ideas from Durkheim are of some interest in themselves, a certain amount of extension is necessary before they begin to illuminate the internal nature of the family. Durkheim's efforts, we have said, were directed largely toward understanding society. Seldom did he turn his attention to what goes on within the family-kin units.[12] However, a few hints can be pieced together from the following references: In the mechanically solidary or undifferentiated society, "the farmer's life does not extend outside the familial circle. Economic activity, having no consequences outside the family, is sufficiently regulated by the family, and the family itself thus serves as occupational group." But in the organically solidary society, in which the family-kin units are no longer self-sufficient, "the family, in losing the unity and indivisibility of former times, has lost with one stroke a great part of its efficacy. As it is today broken up with each generation, man passes a notable part of his existence far from all domestic influence."[13] This transformation is elsewhere described as follows. "The family, in truth, is for a long time a veritable social segment. . . . Instead of remaining an autonomous society alongside of the great society, it becomes more and more involved in the system of social organs. It even becomes one of the organs, charged with special functions. . . . It is, indeed, a law without exception that the more the social structure is by nature segmental, the more families form great, compact, undivided masses, gathered up in themselves."[14] So the family, says Durkheim, comes to be more and more of a specialist among specialists, dependent upon other such units and upon a differentiated economy for survival. Yet Durkheim has only hinted at the character of the family-kin units themselves. One key hint, for example, is found in the term "undivided masses," from the above quotation. Let us, therefore, expand upon the familial inferences found in Durkheim's writing.

In those "mechanically solidary" societies composed of self-sufficient family-kin units, what is the internal nature of those units? Cross-cultural study has led anthropologists and other social scientists to the conclusion that, no matter how simple a society is in terms of technology and division of labor, there appears to be role differentiation on at least two bases: age and sex. Morris Zelditch, for example, reports this from a survey of literature on 56 societies. Males and females, adults and children are assigned different roles, tasks, authority, and privileges in the institutionally-embedded (mechanically-solidary) society. This differentiation is centered in the various family-kin units, although each of these units is relatively similar, says Durkheim, to every other one. The care and detail with which the family-kin division of labor is spelled out is most appreciated by one familiar with anthropological literature.[15] In ideal-typical language, we are suggesting that, in a society integrated by mechanical solidarity, its sub-units—family-kin groups—will tend to be internally, or "organically," integrated by a clear division of labor. The strength of the family members' bonds to each other is not as important to its internal functioning and maintenance as are strong norms and bonds to the integration *between* families. Also, whether the nuclear family can be easily dissolved is dependent upon the extent of personnel embeddedness. If a larger kin unit, such as a patriline, is the chief unit of economic production and other functions, the marital relationship may be somewhat tenuous. If, however, the nuclear unit is the seat of many institutional functions, but is not greatly embedded in a larger kin unit (as was generally true in the American colonies), divorce may be difficult to obtain due to the nuclear family's perceived importance.

When the division of labor ceases to be primarily internal to either kin or family units, and begins to involve the relations between them, a change in the nature of the family-kin unit occurs as well. To put it categorically, as society moves from mechanical to organic solidarity, its family-kin units move from organic to mechanical solidarity. That is, the family division of labor becomes less distinct and is predicated more on choice than tradition, with relations within the family increasingly based upon strong norms and (especially) bonds. The family in the specialized society is kept together more by the development of behavioral expectations and by strong affection than by either the members' need for each other or by society's need for stable family units. Thus, if affectional bonds are weak, the unit may dissolve.

The family, then, has come to be the seat of, and based upon, primary relationships. As defined by Charles H. Cooley and refined by others, the primary relationship is one involving: (1) *Response to whole persons* rather than segments. The doctor sees modern man as a patient; the grocer sees him as a customer; the teacher sees him as a student—but who sees and knows him as he is? This is expected of the nuclear family. (2) *Communication of oneself:* with whom are pleasures shared and upon whom are troubles unloaded? Presumably this occurs within the family, with a few additional kin or friends also being confidants. (3) Personal satisfaction, or the *relationship* is seen *as an end in itself*. One's relations on the job, at school, or even socially, may be for the sake of success or some other goal. But the primary relationship is maintained for its own sake; this, likewise, is expected to occur in the family. The modern industrial family has become, if you will, a refuge from a segmented and impersonal urban life. According to the authors referred to in this section, families are ideally characterized by primariness, by companionship, and by mechanical solidarity.

The word "ideally" is used advisedly, for several qualifications must now be added to the foregoing analysis. First, you will have noticed that the unit of analysis has been left vague throughout, both structurally and temporally. The nuclear family and kin group were not distinguished by the present author; Durkheim seldom refers directly to the societal sub-units of which he speaks; Ogburn refers primarily to the nuclear family. One reason for leaving this vague is that the kind of historical discussion contained in the preceding pages is both ideal-typical (as Burgess admits) and highly condensed. One passes over much history—the strengthening of the kin group and its subsequent weakening in favor of the nuclear family, the parcelling out of functions by the nuclear family—if he refers only to the notion of an historical change from mechanical to organic solidarity in society. This exemplifies the issue of temporal or historical vagueness. Durkheim is comparing the "simple" society with the modern industrial one; Ogburn is discussing the pre-industrial and industrial families; Burgess' ideal types are the patriarchal and modern industrial family; Freedman described a classical Chinese system in which kin groups were buffers between state and family. The difficulty in synthesizing these ideal-typical summaries lies in their tendency to overestimate the changes that have occurred. Ogburn, for example, has been incorrectly interpreted by some as saying that the pre-industrial American family was a perfect example of the functionally-central family system because the institutions of the larger society were totally embedded in the family. However, the changes that have been the subject of Chapters III, IV, and V might best be defined by a series of six types, ranging from total institutional embeddedness in the family to total differentiation and specialization (see Figure 3).

In Type 1, the division of labor is encompassed by the nuclear family, with interaction including other members of the hunting-gathering band. Economic, political, and other separate functionaries are nonexistent. Type 2 also has few separate functionaries in other institutions. However, with agriculture or herding, corporate kin groups tend to develop, with personnel and institutions embedded in it; e.g., the Papago. Type 3 is found in the classical China depicted by Freedman. Here the nuclear family is somewhat less embedded in the kin group institutionally, but kin provide a balance of power *vis-à-vis* (the now-separated) political and religious functionaries. In this type, the marriage tie may be less binding than the blood tie; the same is true for Type 2. Type 4 is found in the colonial American family described in Chapter IV.

FIGURE 3

Types of Relationships Among Family, Kin Group, and Other Institutions

Type 1: Personnel and institutions embedded in nuclear family; age and sex division of labor in family (Durkheim's mechanically solidary society: e.g., hunting-gathering band)

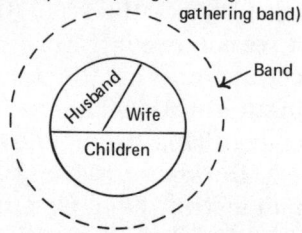

Type 2: Personnel and institutions embedded in kin group; age and sex division of labor in kin group (typical of agricultural and pastoral societies: e.g., the Papago)

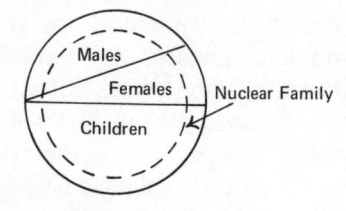

Type 3: Some institutional differentiation; kin group as buffer between state and family (e.g., high-status classical China)

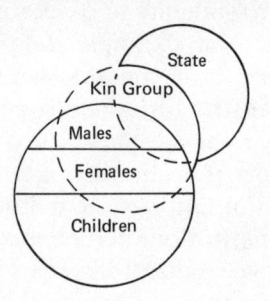

Type 4: Some institutional differentiation, including economic; personnel embedded in nuclear family (e.g., colonial America)

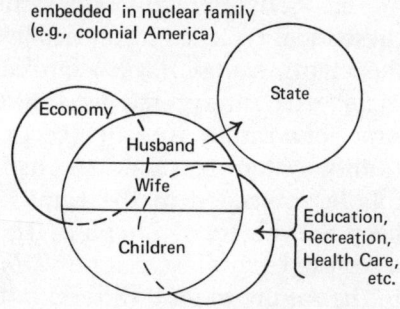

Type 5: Little institutional embeddedness; personnel embeddedness variable (modern, industrial society: e.g., contemporary U.S.)

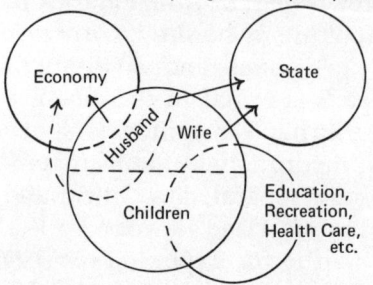

Type 6: Complete institutional differentiation; family serves the individual (Durkheim's organically solidary society)

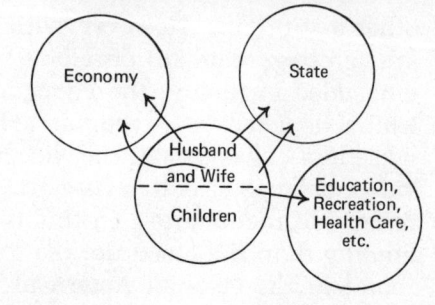

The kin group is no longer central to economic and other functions, nor does it play the role of political buffer. However, much economic, educational, and other activity still involves the nuclear family as a unit, or else takes place within the home. It is, incidentally, noteworthy that Types 1–4 are actually curvilinear in terms of institutional and personnel embeddedness. The nuclear family is basic to the simplest hunting and gathering bands and again in the early stages of industrialization, with the kin group most prominent in certain agricultural and pastoral societies.[16] Type 5 is modern, industrial society, with the family unit still playing a substantial role in education, recreation, and religion, as it tries to give general direction to the socialization process, but seldom acting *as a unit* in economic production. In addition, the wife may or may not engage in occupational employment; the stress may be variable between the family unit's importance and that of the individual in terms of personnel embeddedness. Type 6 is basically hypothetical, although certain systems, e.g., the kibbutz in Israel, have attempted to establish a differentiation closely resembling this one.[17] The historical confusion arises when an analysis such as Ogburn's is viewed as describing a change from Type 1 to Type 6, whereas in reality the change he is referring to was from Type 4 to Type 5. Thus, a necessary clarification of the ideal-typical discussions of Ogburn, Burgess, Farber, and Durkheim involves the further specification of the structural and temporal units of analysis.[18]

A second point of confusion, which we have tried to avoid (and which actually is an extension of the above concern), lies in Ogburn's term "loss of family functions" and its misinterpretations. Ogburn's point is that activities that traditionally took place within the home or involved the whole family now take place elsewhere and engage family segments. The problem with the term, however, is that it can convey the impression that the family now has little to do. The actual process has been one in which activities that were performed in a simple or rudimentary fashion within the family expand to the point where the home can no longer encompass them. This process has been referred to above by the terms "expansion" and "parcelling out" of functions. Yet, as Clark Vincent points out, even this leaves the picture one-sided. "It is interesting to speculate," says Vincent, "about what might have happened if students of the family (a) had kept in mind Ogburn's central interest in social change and (b) had emphasized that it was the *traditional content and form* of given functions, rather than functions *qua* functions, that were being performed decreasingly by the family."[19] The family may no longer be an economic producing unit, but its function as consumer has been heightened. More important, the family as a unit plays an increasingly important role in *adaptation*. By this, Vincent means that the organically structured, or specialized, society requires individuals who can adapt to residential movement, to varied demands, and to rapid changes. It is within the family that one learns—or doesn't learn—this vital aspect of modern life. While we may argue with Vincent's point regarding the economic function (since the family has always been a consuming unit for whatever the economy had to offer), his notion of the family teaching adaptability is a valuable one. The knowledge explosion and specialization have made it virtually impossible for a given family unit to encompass the demands for education of their offspring—and the laws have made it illegal for a family to try. Yet, it is within the family that direction is given to the socialization process, that a style of confronting society's expectations and opportunities is developed. The problem is not, therefore, that the term "loss of family functions" is so much incorrect as it is incomplete, leading one to view the family as inactive and of less significance than it is.[20]

The concept of the family's loss of functions necessitates a third qualification as well. Some social analysts, especially during the years when industrialization and urbanization were being decried as resulting in social disorganization, expressed the fear (or view) that the loss of traditional functions means the disintegration of the family as we know it. No longer the economic, educational, religious center of society, the family has lost its reason for being. In response to this, the suggestion has been made that, concomitant with the specialization of society, the family has become a specialist in gratifying people's psychological needs—needs for understanding, affection, and happiness.[21] But, it might be argued, what about the high rate of divorce? Does this not indicate that all is not well with the family? To say that the family, ideally, is a focus for primary relations is also to indicate where its problems will arise. The demand to gratify people's needs for love, companionship, and emotional release is a heavy burden for any social group to bear. This pressure is even greater since neolocality and decreased family size have reduced the numbers of persons sharing intense day-to-day relations. It should not, therefore, be surprising to find that those who do not achieve satisfactory relationships within the family are likely to break ties and try again. The rate of divorce, in other words, may be viewed as either a problem or a solution, depending upon one's perspective.

It should, moreover, be noted that the expectations that characterize the companionship family, i.e., happiness, adjustment, and primariness, tend to retard to some extent the movement toward what Farber calls "permanent availability." "Availability" connotes access to an individual for marriage, for sex, for intimacy. Yet, divorce and extra-marital sex tend to be limited by the specific happiness-adjustment function the family is expected to perform. A couple may, for example, have decided that they might be happier if they divorced, but may decide against it for the sake of the adjustment or happiness of their offspring. Or the individual who considers himself "intellectually free" to engage in extra-marital sex may perceive that his marital happiness would be detrimentally affected thereby, and thus forego the exercise of his freedom for the sake of greater personal adjustment, happiness, and primariness within his marriage. The point is simply that the family's "affective" function is also, at present, a crucial deterrent to rapid change.

The questions of disintegration and change must not be dismissed on the basis of the preceding generalizations. In fact, much effort in the present volume is expended toward the goal of defining the direction of change within the family system of the United States. To this end, several continua, upon which current characteristics and directions of change may be located, are posited in Section Five. But prior to presenting these continua, the historical and functional strands of Chapters IV and V will be synthesized in several propositions.

SECTION FOUR

QUASI–THEORETICAL PROPOSITIONS ABOUT THE U.S. FAMILY

Several characteristics of the contemporary family in the United States emerge quite clearly from the last two chapters, while others may be inferred therefrom. The first three pertain to the family functions that have been the subject of Chapter V. The family unit performs two specific functions in U.S. society. (1) Its *affective* function is a central basis for both the formation and the continuation of individual family units. The people of a society, like those of any group, perform tasks and establish relationships. If the family or kin unit is primarily a task group, as in the undifferentiated (institutionally-embedded) society, the development of relationships within that unit is problematic, since the bases for the persistence of the unit are tradition and functions as well as affection. When many societal tasks are performed outside the family unit, much of the family's effort is focussed on meeting people's needs for affection and understanding; the ability of the family to provide for these needs is a key determinant of whether a given unit will persist or dissolve. Furthermore, males in this society are more likely to take an active role in providing primary relations than they are in the society in which the family involves a stringent division of labor by sex. Yet, primary relations, or affectivity, is but one of the crucial functions of the contemporary U.S. family.

(2) A second specific family function is as *economic consumer*. A key reason why the larger society strives to foster nuclear family values is because this unit plays so great a role in consuming the goods of the market. As far as the capitalist market economy is concerned, in a society in which families are not units of economic production, it is permissible for individual family units to dissolve, as long as most people of marriageable age are married and raising families at any given point in time. And, it should be noted, the proportion of adult Americans who are married has increased over the past century.

In addition to the specific affective and consumer functions performed by the family, this unit plays (3) a general, though somewhat reduced, role in *socialization*. Other institutions, such as recreational and educational ones, meet many specific needs that individuals have for learning their culture. Nevertheless, the family, with its current concern for the developing individual, tends to coordinate and give direction to the influence of these other agencies. Thus, for example, one family may further the goals of the school system by encouraging achievement and cooperation, while another family may attempt to negate or neutralize the efforts of the educational institution by belittling its goals and practices. There also appears to have been some reduction in the distinction between the father role and mother role in socialization. Parents today still try to "orderly replace" their culture from one generation to the next; the major difference is in the influence of other institutions in reinforcing or altering the culture (values, beliefs, norms) received from one's family.

The themes covered in these three propositions respond to such questions as: "What functions does the family perform?" and "How does the family relate to the rest of its society?" These appear to bespeak a strongly functional perspective—a perspective that assumes a great amount of consistency and integration both among the parts of the family system and between that system and the total society. Explanation, therefore, appears to originate in function performed and consistency assumed: a characteristic is sufficiently explained by what it does and by its articulation with other characteristics. There are, however, two further propositions that act as correctives upon an overly functional stance regarding the family. (4) The family in modern society includes *inconsistent aspects and fragmentary changes;* it is not entirely coherent. The brief description of the family in recent history, found in Chapter IV, would lead us to conclude that all aspects of the American family system have not changed at the same rate of speed, nor are they necessarily consistent with each other at a given point in time, nor are they well integrated, at every juncture, into the larger society. The basis for the formation and persistence of family units, it has been argued, is love; yet the cessation of love, up to now, has not been a legal grounds for the dissolution of that unit. The individualistic value of independence and achievement and the familial value of honoring one's parents are at odds from time to time, especially when the parents reach old age. While it is not necessary to spell out all the loci of stress and inconsistency at this point, the reader should be on the lookout for such discrepancies throughout the remainder of the book.

(5) A corollary of the realities of inconsistency and stress is that there are in fact *subcultural varieties* within the contemporary United States. The author's theory of society is not based on the kind of consensual model which says that the middle-class style of life is pervasive in the sense that all social change is in that direction as people strive to be middle-class. Rather, the middle-class style is considered *dominant* in the sense that middle-class people are most able to enact their norms into law and to disseminate their views on what is right, proper, and expected behavior—whether in the family or elsewhere. This dominance is not even necessarily a numerical *pre*dominance, but is due to the key positions of the middle class in government, education, and mass communications. However, there are subcultural varieties with their own ideals and expectations; as Rosenfeld pointed out in his study of the Arab village, the influence of these ideals is not necessarily unidirectional. History and diversity must, in short, be taken seriously. A part of this seriousness involves not only the issue of inconsistencies raised above, but that of divergent princi-

ples. It is quite possible, for example, that not all portions of the U.S. population share the expectation that the father should take a major role in affectivity and in socialization. Do ethnic, racial, religious, and socioeconomic categories signify major cultural and social cleavages, or only minor differences? The concern of Chapter VI will be to outline briefly the key varieties of cultural principles found in the United States and to indicate where their problems lie and in what areas changes are taking place.

The general quasi-theoretical stance produced by these five summary propositions is based on notions of function, change, and variety. It acknowledges that much can be learned by asking about functions performed and bases for existence among a dominant segment of the population. It also admits that explanation requires an understanding of history and subculture as well; and that a society and its families will manifest disjuncture and variety as well as articulation and integration. In order to discern the mix between these elements, we shall employ Goode's suggestion that functions and characteristics should be treated as variables, or continua, rather than as constants. By developing five continua to deal with major family characteristics, we should be able to locate the contemporary American family in terms of its basic features and to define its direction and speed of change.

SECTION FIVE

FAMILY SYSTEM CHARACTERISTICS: FIVE CONTINUA

In Chapter IV the various aspects of the family in American history were grouped together under three headings: family formation, internal family relations, and the family and the external world. Internal family relations can be broken down into socialization, marital role structure, and personnel embeddedness; all of these aspects, with their logical extremes, are illustrated in the five continua of Figure 4.

Looking at the continua one at a time, it is possible to conceive of a society in which incestuous and exogamous prohibitions leave the individual only one category of persons within which to find a mate and in which arrangements are made by the parents. Or the prohibitions may be fewer, resulting in a wider range of possibili-

FIGURE 4

Five Ideal-typical Continua upon Which to Locate Family Characteristics and Changes

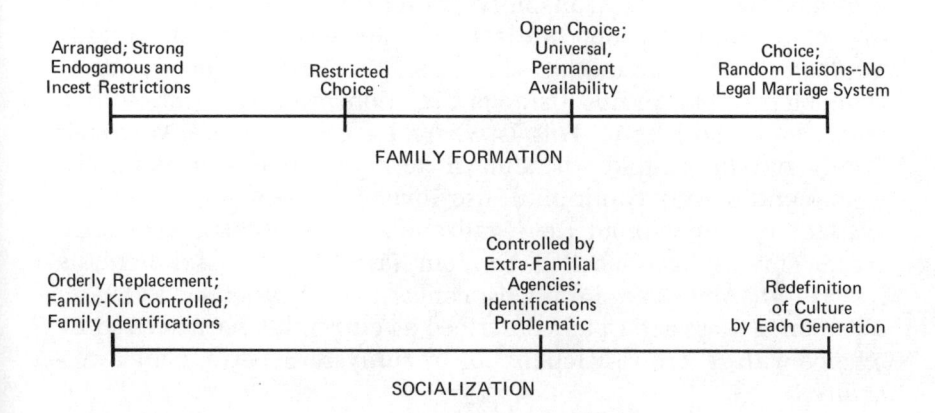

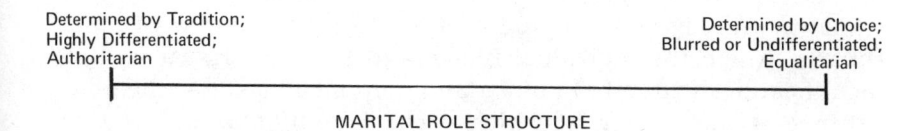

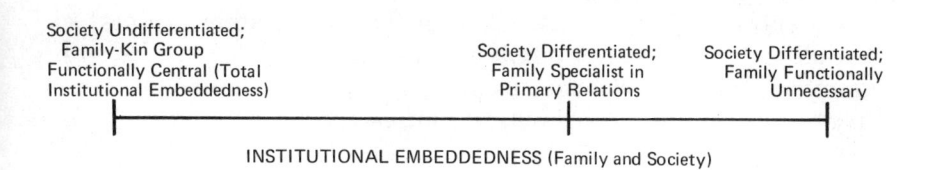

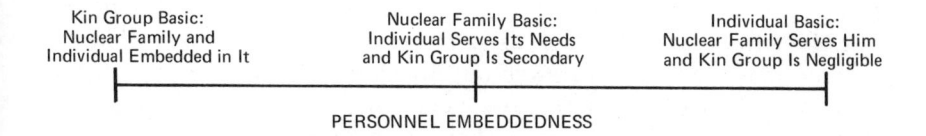

Arranged; Strong Endogamous and Incest Restrictions — Restricted Choice — Open Choice; Universal, Permanent Availability — Choice; Random Liaisons--No Legal Marriage System

FAMILY FORMATION

Orderly Replacement; Family-Kin Controlled; Family Identifications — Controlled by Extra-Familial Agencies; Identifications Problematic — Redefinition of Culture by Each Generation

SOCIALIZATION

Determined by Tradition; Highly Differentiated; Authoritarian — Determined by Choice; Blurred or Undifferentiated; Equalitarian

MARITAL ROLE STRUCTURE

Society Undifferentiated; Family-Kin Group Functionally Central (Total Institutional Embeddedness) — Society Differentiated; Family Specialist in Primary Relations — Society Differentiated; Family Functionally Unnecessary

INSTITUTIONAL EMBEDDEDNESS (Family and Society)

Kin Group Basic: Nuclear Family and Individual Embedded in It — Nuclear Family Basic: Individual Serves Its Needs and Kin Group Is Secondary — Individual Basic: Nuclear Family Serves Him and Kin Group Is Negligible

PERSONNEL EMBEDDEDNESS

ties, but the parents may still work out the pairings. Restricted choice, as in colonial America, is characterized by the individual's choosing his own mate, but with residential immobility, religious and racial status, or other restrictions severely limiting the range within which the choice operates. The notion of open choice, or universal, permanent availability (as indicated earlier), is that all the members of the opposite sex in one's society are potentially available to him for mating. They are, furthermore, permanently available, so that an unsatisfactory relationship can be terminated and a new one begun. This is where Farber feels the American family system is rapidly heading in terms of mate selection. The logical end of this continuum also involves universal, permanent availability, but without the legalization of either marriage or divorce. This we have labelled "random liaisons." The issue here, as far as the American family is concerned, is whether its mate selection is most accurately described as currently characterized by "choice with severe restrictions" or by "universal, permanent availability."

The socialization continuum has, at one extreme, the society in which culture is redefined by each succeeding generation only enough to be consistent with small technological advances, in which the family and kin group control the learning process, and, thus, in which the individual is likely to find his crucial positive identifications with other family-kin group members.[22] At the other extreme is the society in which each generation completely rethinks and reworks its culture, i.e., in which socialization, or the passing along of culture, does not take place. Somewhere in the middle would be the society characterized by some redefinition, in which extra-familial agencies control the socialization process, so that identification with a family member is as problematic as with a football coach, movie star, teacher, or any other significant member of one's society. How closely, we might ask, does the extra-familial socialization model fit the contemporary United States?

Family roles may be traditionally determined, so that the society includes only one definition of what it means to be a father, mother, or son or daughter of a certain age. In this case, there are no role definition options open to the individual. Such a society, as noted earlier, tends to have as part of its traditional definition of family roles a carefully worked out division of labor and an authoritarian control of resources and decisions. Opposed to this is the society in which definition of the father or mother role is determined by choice. The choices are such that the members of the unit are likely to share equally in decision-making and control of resources; they may divide economic, socialization, and affective roles in any way they see fit—since tradition dictates no predetermined family division of labor. The question concerning family roles which will engage us throughout this work is the extent to which there is freedom of choice in the contemporary U.S. family.

The fourth continuum is really a reduction of certain aspects of Figure 3. The extremes include the undifferentiated society, with all functions totally embedded in the family or kin group, and the totally differentiated society, whose family system is therefore functionally unnecessary. In between are Ogburn's family, specializing in primary relations, and Burgess' companionship unit. To what extent, we might ask, do major functions now take place outside the home and involve subsegments of the family? Has the family stabilized at the companionship level, or is its present character merely a stage on the way to eventual disintegration?

The final continuum is related in many ways to the preceding four. Yet the multidimensional nature of the "personnel embeddedness" concept demands that we spend a bit more time with it. There are two stages, or types, of personnel embeddedness, each with an interactional and a value element. *Kin group embeddedness* means that the kin group is the primary milieu for social interaction and is valued more highly than either the nuclear family or the individual. The nuclear family in this situation has no existence apart from, or privacy within, its kin group; and kin solidarity takes precedence over that between nuclear family members. To put it briefly, both the individual and his nuclear family operate within and serve the needs of the larger group. A second form of personnel embeddedness is found if the kin group and its community are weak, but the individual is still expected to operate primarily within, and serve the needs of, the *nuclear family*. "He is the black sheep of the family"; "he has disgraced us": these are phrases that indicate that "the family" is actually considered more important than the individual and his needs. However, if the family is viewed as basically serving the needs of the individual, and concerned with his unique welfare; and if both family and kin interaction are less important than extra-familial activity, one cannot speak of personnel embeddedness, but of *individualism* and independence. "Where did we fail him?" "What makes for achievement?" These questions bespeak an individualistic orientation within the society. It is generally acknowledged that the culture of the contemporary U.S. is not characterized by kin group dominance, with the nuclear family and individual highly embedded in the kin group. The difficult question, however (and one which will occupy us throughout this volume) is whether the correct representation of mid-twentieth century America depicts the individual as operating within and serving the needs of the nuclear family, or depicts the family as serving the individual's needs and helping him to operate as a unique individual. Looking at the continuum as a logical system, and recalling the ideal types of Figure 3, it should be noted that the simplest band is characterized by nuclear family embeddedness, with the more complex agricultural and pastoral societies closer to the left-hand end of the continuum than either the band or modern industrial society.

Many of the issues raised by these five continua will arise time and again in the chapters on socialization, mate selection, husband-wife interaction, kinship, aging, crisis, and family dissolution. However, we must first expand upon the theme of definable subcultural types within the contemporary United States.

NOTES

[1] By "quasi-theoretical," we mean that the framework has a certain amount of explanatory usefulness, but also provides a basis for organizing the descriptive materials.

[2] D. F. Aberle et al., "The Functional Prerequisites of a Society," *Ethics*, 60 (1950), 100–11.

[3] Ira Reiss, "The Universality of the Family: A Conceptual Analysis," *Journal of Marriage and the Family*, 27 (1965), 443–53.

[4] William J. Goode. "The Sociology of the Family," in Robert K. Merton, Leonard Broom, and Leonard S. Cottrell, eds., *Sociology Today* (New York: Basic Books, 1959), Chap. 7.

[5] Bernard Farber, *Family: Organization and Interaction* (San Francisco: Chandler, 1964), pp. 23–28.

[6] Harold Christensen, "The Intrusion of Values," in Christensen, ed., *Handbook of Marriage and the Family* (Chicago: Rand McNally, 1964), pp. 974–75, points out that the scholar "can use some goal or desired end (value) as the criterion against which to measure its phenomenon—but of course without making any judgment as to whether the end itself is good or bad."

[7] William F. Ogburn, "The Family and Its Functions," in *Recent Social Trends* (New York: McGraw-Hill, 1933), Chap. 13.

[8] Ernest W. Burgess, Harvey J. Locke, and Mary Margaret Thomes, *The Family*, 3rd ed. (New York: Litton Educational Publishing, copyright © 1963), p. 3, by permission of Van Nostrand Reinhold Company.

[9] *Ibid.*, p. 4.

[10] Farber, *Family: Organization and Interaction*, pp. 106–9.

[11] Emile Durkheim, *The Division of Labor in Society*, trans. George Simpson (New York: Free Press, 1964 ed.), p. 151.

[12] For some of his lesser-known references to the family, see Herbert Bynder, "Emile Durkheim and the Sociology of the Family," *Journal of Marriage and the Family*, 31 (1969), 527–33.

[13] Durkheim, *The Division of Labor in Society*, p. 17.

[14] *Ibid.*, pp. 210, 292.

[15] Some of this literature is summarized and excerpted in William N. Stephens, *The Family in Cross-Cultural Perspective* (New York: Holt, Rinehart and Winston, 1963), Chap. 6.

[16] Two sources in which the curvilinear pattern of nuclear family in the band, corporate kin groups in agricultural and pastoral societies, and nuclear family dominance again in the industrial state is postulated are M. F. Nimkoff and Russell Middleton, "Types of Family and Types of Economy," *American Journal of Sociology*, 66 (1960), 225; and Robert F. Winch and Rae Lesser Blumberg, "Societal Complexity and Familial Organization," in Robert F. Winch and Louis Wolf Goodman, eds., *Selected Studies in Marriage and the Family* (New York: Holt, Rinehart and Winston, 1968 ed.), p. 92.

[17] For a discussion of the kibbutz family, and some additional references, see Yonina Talmon, "The Family in a Revolutionary Movement—The Case of the Kibbutz in Israel," in Meyer F. Nimkoff, ed., *Comparative Family Systems* (Boston: Houghton Mifflin, 1965), Chap. 13.

[18] Note that these six types, as depicted in Figure 3, should not be considered as a unilineal continuum through which all societies must pass in the process of change. Furthermore, they describe society in terms of the family perspective. The same individual plays multiple roles; the issue here is whether he plays them as a member of the family and within the family setting, or whether many of his roles have been differentiated off to separate locations and specific times. The interwoven fabric of the society is not captured in Figure 3.

[19] Clark E. Vincent, "Mental Health and the Family," *Journal of Marriage and the Family*, 29 (1967), 26; see also Clark E. Vincent, "Familia Spongia: The Adaptive Function," *Journal of Marriage and the Family*, 28 (1966), 29–36.

[20] For a further critique of the "loss of family functions" conception, see John N. Edwards, "The Future of the Family Revisited," *Journal of Marriage and the Family*, 29 (1967), 505–11.

[21] Frank Musgrove, *The Family, Education, and Society* (London: Routledge and Kegan Paul, 1966), pp. 31, 35–40, 99, discusses this phenomenon.

[22] By "positive identification" is meant the attempt to model one's behavior after that of another person. The process of identification is both complex and important, and will be referred to in greater detail in Chapters VII and VIII.

VI

Family Subcultures and Subsocieties in the United States

IN THIS CHAPTER WE DESCRIBE MIDDLE-CLASS AND LOWER-CLASS MODELS OF FAMILY BEHAVIOR. SUBSEQUENTLY, RELIGIOUS, ETHNIC, AND RACIAL SUB-DIVISIONS ARE INTRODUCED, AND THE KEY PROBLEMS FACING THEM ARE NOTED. FOR THE RELIGIOUS SUBSOCIETY, THE PROBLEM HAS BEEN TO STAY SEPARATE IN A SOCIETY THAT TENDS TO ASSIMILATE ITS PARTS. FOR THE EUROPEAN ETHNIC GROUPS, THE PROBLEM HAS BEEN TO KEEP THEIR CULTURAL HERITAGE ALIVE AND MEANINGFUL IN THE FACE OF THEIR DESIRE FOR, AND ABILITY TO GAIN, ASSIMILATION. FOR BLACKS AND OTHER RACIAL MINORITIES, THE PROBLEM HAS BEEN THEIR INABILITY TO ACHIEVE ASSIMILATION INTO THE DOMINANT SOCIETY AFTER HAVING INCORPORATED MANY ELEMENTS OF THE DOMINANT CULTURE. THE ISSUES CONCERNING BLACK FAMILIES IN AMERICA ARE STATED IN TERMS OF TWO OPPOSING MODELS, ONE BASED ON THE CONCEPT OF FAMILY DISORGANIZATION AND THE OTHER ON THE NOTION OF RESILIENCE AND STRENGTH.

The United States is a society characterized by a Western, urban, and industrial form of culture. Within that society there are familial attitudes and practices that are so common as to be considered virtually cultural universals.[1] Among these cultural forms are monogamy, legal marriage, legal dissolution of marriage prior to remarriage, joint residence of spouses and their dependent children, and responsibility of the parents for the care and rearing of their children. Both legal and social sanctions of various sorts tend to restrict deviation from these universals.

There is, however, an order of deviation that, as Ruth Cavan puts it, "is subordinate to the basic culture and gives a quasi-organization to aggregates of people who accept the basic culture but are distinctive in ways in which they implement it, or in less fundamental phases of culture."[2] Thus, within the basic culture, there may be great variation in acceptance or rejection of birth control, husband-wife role relationships, socialization of children, importance of kin, and other aspects of the family. These variations tend to divide the society into subcategories of persons whose intensity of interaction with each other is greater than it is with those whose culture differs substantially. Nevertheless, the congruence between subcultures (particular configurations of attitudes and behaviors) and subsocieties (networks of interacting persons) is not perfect. "The subcultural system of the United States," says Cavan, "is a composite of social classes and of ethnic-religious and racial groups. They are combined into a vertical hierarchy according to general principles of relative status and along a horizontal spacing according to the degree of mutual acceptability. When groups are unacceptable to each other, they tend to form parallel social-class systems."[3] This "horizontal spacing" is, in fact, the division of society into subsocieties, whose cultures may in some instances be virtually identical. On the other hand, persons in a subsociety may be characterized by great internal cultural diversity.

The approach of the present chapter is to begin by outlining two subcultural models that are found in American society. Subsequently, the notions of religious, ethnic, and racial subsocieties will be introduced, with the hope that several key questions regarding such categorizations may be resolved, and the problems confronting these groups made plain.

SECTION ONE

MIDDLE-CLASS AND LOWER-CLASS FAMILY MODELS

Much has been said already about the middle-class family in the United States. The changes between colonial days and the present, listed in Chapter IV, are for the most part comparisons of the colonial family with the modern, middle-class type. While this approach is valid, due to the dominance of middle-class forms today, it is historically only partially correct. This is because both the modern urban middle-class and urban lower-class family systems can be traced back to colonial days, with certain similarities and certain divergencies. Thus, beginning with the middle-class model, we shall attempt to clarify the historical processes and connections.

During colonial days, the vast majority of Anglo-American families lived at or near the subsistence level. They were agricultural, following the cultural patterns described in Chapter IV. With the industrial revolution began a whole complex of developments that eventuated in both the urban middle and urban lower class, the former becoming dominant. The move from agriculture to industry and the cities was spearheaded by a small number of creative Anglo-American Protestants, who embodied the individualism-work-success motif idealized by the colonists. Along with the industrialists large numbers of people came to the city to work in the factories. However, the nineteenth and twentieth centuries did not belong simply to the wealthy industrialists and their workers; rather, this was the period of the emergence of the middle classes. From a small number of independent businessmen, the middle class grew with the differentiation and expansion of government, education, legal and medical services, and with the vast increase in commercial and office personnel in the industrial complex. These persons—professionals, managers, salesmen, and clerks—are occupationally typical of that category known as the middle classes. Economically, these are the persons who, along with their families, have risen above the subsistence level, enabling them to turn their attention to self-respect, experience and personality needs, and child development. It was the women within this group of predominantly white Anglo-American Protestant urbanites who found the time and the rationale for the women's rights movements. This push for sexual equality had substantial impact upon relationships within the family as well as outside.

What, then, are the basic aspects of the *middle-class family style* as it developed during the nineteenth and early twentieth centuries? (1) Economic and work values are central, including, if need be, residential mobility in pursuit of opportunity. This is somewhat more typical of professional and managerial families (often referred to as upper-middle-class) than it is of sales and clerical ones, but it is often used to characterize the entire middle-class category. (2) Husband-wife relations are predicated on happiness, communication, and mutual gratification. Even in the sexual sphere, in which formerly it was only the husband who sought pleasure, the stress on equality and mutual needs has resulted in a concern for mutual satisfaction. Love is expected to be fundamental, not only to the selection of one's mate, but to the household as well. (3) Socialization of children emphasizes sheltering during their younger days. The world of childhood is to be insulated to some extent from the woes and cares of adults. In addition, the child is taught that he must get along with other people, and that he should learn to do things for himself. He is expected to internalize the value of deferred gratification, or putting off immediate goals and pleasures for the sake of greater goals in the future, e.g., postponing marriage for the sake of a college education. Getting along, independence, deferred gratification—these are, after all, the values that middle-class parents believe have gotten them where they are.

This middle-class configuration is oriented toward success and respectability as defined by the official societal values. Children learn to identify with their parents more as general symbols of success than in terms of the specific occupational or other roles they play. The intensity of emotional ties between family members is great; punishment is likely to center here. This family differs at many points from the typical colonial farm family; two keys to its divergence are the fact that the husband's economic role is played outside the home and that the family's focus of attention is no longer subsistence or survival.

This latter point leads directly to the *lower-class model*. Economically, this model is a function of the continuing struggle for survival among persons who find themselves surrounded by affluence and who may perceive the cards stacked against them. These are the individuals and families who never really made it in the industrial world, though they live in an urban, rather than rural, environment. Typical of this group is the unskilled laborer, who, lacking skills, education, and sometimes opportunity, lives out his life at or below the subsistence level. The first-generation non-Protestants from Europe and, the post-slavery Afro-Americans were incorporated into American society primarily at this level.

The lower-class family model is the most direct descendent of the colonial type at several points, but the change from rural to urban has caused some substantial alterations. (1) The segregation of roles between husbands and wives is quite similar in the modern lower-class and colonial families. Sex is the husband's pleasure and the wife's duty. The husband expects to take little hand in household tasks and child-rearing, since these are "women's work." (2) A second point of similarity between the colonial family and the modern, urban lower-class is in socialization. The primary concern of the parents is to teach order, obedience, and limits to their children; within this framework, the child is given considerable freedom. This freedom is not the kind of independence training that characterizes the attempt of middle-class parents to get their offspring to "do things for themselves," but is a freedom from adult supervision for periods of time.

Several changes or differences between colonial and modern lower-class families are related to the rural agricultural and urban industrial settings in which they exist(ed) and function(ed). (3) The husband, in both cases, perceives himself as patriarch, or as dominant, having delegated household and child responsibilities to the wife. However, when his economic role is both insecure and performed outside the home, the husband finds himself less able to assert consistent and *acceptable* authority within the home. That is, his actual status in the home is likely to be lower in the urban lower-class family than in the colonial farm family. (4) The economic insecurity of the lower-class family is related to greater familial instability as well. On the other hand, in the colonial agrarian family, social sanctions, the legal system, and functions performed were more likely to hold economically marginal families together—though some, of course, did separate. Perhaps of greater note today is the number of economically disadvantaged families that *do* stay together despite weak cultural supports for the unit. (5) Much unskilled urban work does not provide the individual with a sense of inherent worth; however, the meaning that the farmer finds in his productive labors in the soil has probably been overdrawn. It seems that the shorter work week today makes it possible for the urban lower classes to pursue the leisure activities that are at the heart of their value systems. Kin and friend contacts, and the activities that can be provided by the paycheck give meaning to the life of the economically disadvantaged urbanite. Deferred gratification and success striving are much more likely to be found in the middle-class than in the lower-class family, which is convinced that such striving is either undesirable or useless.

Here, then, are two models of family life today.[4] Each has some roots in the colonial family and other roots in the industrial-urban revolution. One stresses equality, personality, respectability, and success; the other stresses role segregation, order and freedom, leisure gratifications, and survival. But how are such cultural themes or configurations related to specific societal categories within the United States population? We have already indicated the relationship of the middle-class style to the white Anglo-American Protestant population. But what of the other religious, ethnic, and racial divisions of society? They are the foci of attention in the sections that follow.

SECTION TWO

THE RELIGIOUS SUBCULTURE AND SUBSOCIETY

"Certain subcultural groups achieve almost complete and relatively permanent isolation, for example, the Amish, Doukhobors, and Hutterites, and, in the past, the Shakers and the Oneida Community."[5] Cavan is here referring to groups of religious immigrants who have kept themselves both culturally and socially apart from the peoples around them. The Amish and Hutterites are perhaps the best-known examples of religious subsocieties in America. We shall briefly describe the latter.

The Hutterites "are not only an ethnic group," says one of them, "but also one of the world's important religious minorities which have in recent years come under the close observation of sociologists and others."[6] Hutterite colonies are located in the Dakotas, Montana, and in Alberta, Manitoba, and Saskatchewan, Canada.[7] They are one of three surviving Anabaptist groups, and are able to trace their history back to early sixteenth century Europe. Beginning in Moravia and the Tyrol of Austria, their pacifism, civil disobedience, and communal economy—all viewed by them as New Testament Christian principles—caused them to be persecuted and driven to the Ukraine and then, in the 1870's, to the United States. They have a social organization that can be adapted to the grazing and crop areas of any nation. The Hutterites are large-scale farmers who are generally quite economically successful in raising draft horses, cattle, pigs, sheep, geese, ducks, turkeys, chickens, bees, and crops such as wheat and oats. They have not hesitated to sell surpluses to those in the "outside world," nor have they rejected the technological advances that make their economic endeavors more profitable. About their economic success and social forms, a Jehovah's Witnesses missionary commented: "Them Hutterites are a case where religion is just something to keep the economics going." John Bennett notes that, while such a view is mistaken, it does illustrate the point that "the colony's religious activity is sometimes less conspicuous than its economic and decision-making apparatus."[8] To this, Paul Gross, himself a Hutterite, responds:

> most of our critics are unable to look beyond the sphere of dollars and cents. To them we appear to be economic competitors who deliberately plan our way of life so as to compete more efficiently with our neighbors.
> But serious students of our way of life have discovered that the basis of our communal existence is not economic but religious. Take away our colonies within which we are insulated from the crime and disease of the world, and our young people would soon be forced to give up their faith and join the mad world in its headlong plunge into perdition.[9]

Are the Hutterites to be numbered among the Protestants? While the historical and temporal answer would seem to be "yes," they themselves deny any such identification. In addition to their strict adherence to the communal form of organization, there are at least three other points at which they differ from most reformed groups: they refuse to bear arms, they refuse to take legal oaths, and they refuse to assume civil authority to uphold what they feel are unjust and barbarous laws.[10]

The decision-making apparatus, to which Bennett refers, centers around the council of five to seven men. The council always includes the ministers, householder, and field manager, and usually one or two heads of economic departments as well. Council members sit in order of rank and "make practical day-to-day decisions, grant permission for travel, judge minor disagreements, and help the colony to run efficiently by making many semiroutine decisions."[11] The colony consists of an elaborate set of functionally differentiated roles; status distinctions are commensurate to these roles. Paradoxically, however, the colony is at the same time an extended set of kin, involving male relatives and their wives and children in a brotherly and egalitarian network. While the bureaucratic and kinship principles often seem at variance with each other, the group identifications with which colony members have been embued since birth tend to keep strains and conflicts to a minimum.[12] The way in which group identification and decision-making actually work is well illustrated by Hostetler's description of the yearly meeting:

> The various enterprises are carefully considered by the colony at the yearly meeting. Whether to expand, mechanize or diminish one enterprise, such as hog or turkey

raising, will be important for the welfare of the whole colony. Important factors entering into decision making for the productive enterprises are: the cleavage between the old and young men, since the younger are more prone to support mechanization; the ability of the person in charge of a given enterprise; and the ability of the group to arrive at an amicable consensus. Since consensus is more important for "the good of the colony," than sheer efficiency, the Hutterites have refrained generally from speculative production.[13]

The three groups of Hutterites—who call themselves Schmieden Leut, Lehrer Leut, and Darius Leut—are endogamous, not only with respect to the outside world, but with respect to each other. Though there have been a few exceptions (a member of one Leut marrying one from another Leut), the slight but important differences in styles of dress and technology stand in the way of Leut intermarriage. Within a Leut, the rule is colony exogamy, i.e., a male from one colony will ordinarily marry a female from another. One reason why kin ties seldom conflict with the system of social ranking is that kinship, as in the urban-industrial world, is primarily to provide primary relationships. While these relationships may be somewhat more intense among the Hutterites, they nevertheless are not the basis for the colony's division of labor. Seldom, for example, does an offspring inherit his father's role in the colony.

Perhaps the best way to understand the Hutterite in his family and colony life is to follow him from birth until death—in summary fashion. The socialization process prepares the individual for two key events: baptism and death. Baptism, at about age twenty, is more than an expression of religious faith; it is the act by which the Hutterite identifies with the colony and its way of life. The success of socialization for incorporation "is evidenced not only by the stability of the colonies as social systems, but also by the extremely low rate of defection."[14] Arthur P. Mange notes that during the 50-year period from 1900 to 1949, only 98 males and 7 females—mostly late teenagers—left the Schmieden Leut colonies. This was a period during which the population increased from 500 to nearly 4,000.[15]

Until the age of three, children stay at home as "house children." They learn early that the colony comes before the individual. Punishment or discipline is usually physical and occurs frequently; however, the child also learns through petting and fond attention that he is very much wanted. A "good" baby, says Hostetler, "has two major attributes. He sleeps a lot, at least during colony work periods, and he will go to anyone. In other words, he does not disrupt the colony time schedule and he accepts all colony members."[16]

From ages three to five the child attends kindergarten or nursery school. Here: (1) he begins to be weaned from his family; (2) he becomes acquainted with those in the peer group, with whom he will spend his life; (3) he learns to respect authority; (4) he learns to tolerate a restricted environment; and (5) he is rewarded for cooperativeness and passivity. Self control and obedience are inculcated as basic principles; the child is now expected to be quiet around adults. "The child can easily interpret these changes as rejection. He has fallen to the lowest status group within the colony, but he has also started the steady, rewarding climb up the steps that lead to full, responsible membership in the colony."[17]

For the ten years following kindergarten, the young Hutterite attends both the German and English school within the colony. Many of the functions of the kindergarten are merely continued and intensified during this period, cooperativeness and respect for authority being especially crucial. Children are expected to make mistakes and misbehave during this period, for that is their nature. They must be willing to accept their place in the social structure, caring for those younger than they and reacting obediently to those older.

At age 15 the young person assumes adult work responsibilities, but does not reach full adult status until baptism. Between age 15 and baptism there is some experimentation with the "ways of the world." Comic books, radios, nail polish, jewelry, even cigarettes may be obtained surreptitiously and stored, particularly by girls, in special places. The young person is left free by the adults to compare these objects with the communal life he sees around him; in most cases he eventually chooses the latter. The expectation of both personal and economic security

> is undoubtedly one of the main causes of the relatively high stability of Hutterian life, and the low rate of defection. As one outspoken young Hutterite put it: "Well, it's a pretty good life, you know. You go away from it once in a while, but you always come back. Where else can you get a good deal like this for a lifetime?"[18]

The main reason that experimentation is allowed during youth is, of course, that the adults are quite sure that Hutterite culture has been reinforced sufficiently during the early years and that the young person has already internalized or accepted the Hutterite norms and values and will return to them.

Dating begins sometime after age 15 and is likely to last for two to six years. The freedom surrounding Hutterian courtship is seen in the great variation both in parental control or permissiveness and in the openness or secretiveness of premarital relationships. Dating is facilitated by the interchange of labor between colonies, during which time eligible young men and women may find free time to be together. Much of this period of courtship, experimentation, and responsibility can be viewed as providing the young person with an opportunity to evaluate himself with respect to the peer group, the opposite sex, and the colony. His interest in the outside world aids him in understanding what it means to be a Hutterite.

Prior to marriage, the young person makes the decision to be baptized, thus becoming a full member of the colony. "The goal of child rearing among the Hutterites is the individual's voluntary decision to submit himself to the *Gemein*. All the child's life has been, in effect, a preparation for this major rite of passage."[19] While each stage since kindergarten has brought the growing Hutterite closer to his parents, baptism results in their treating him as both an offspring and a colony member. He has now chosen the colony's way of life, has rejected the world, and is thus almost removed from the young people's circle. The last step is, of course, marriage.

Mate selection is, in fact, quite similar to that in the urban-industrial United States. It is based upon individual choice and love, with parents and kin exerting pressure in the same way as they do in the outside world; i.e., by verbal encouragement or discouragement, by arranging meetings, but without force and with few sanctions. The key difference is in the range of interactional possibilities; at this point the comparison breaks down. "In contrast to the long, rigorous preparation for baptism, the preparation for marriage is incidental."[20] While the wedding is a joyous occasion— even more so if several occur simultaneously—post-wedding adjustment for the groom is negligible. His brothers may simply move out and his bride move in. For the bride, the adjustment involves the drastic step of leaving her colony to live among a few other former members of her colony of orientation and a large number of strangers.

The separation of the sexes in adulthood is one of status and also of function. This distinction has been summarized thus: "Hutterian men are colony citizens first, executives and managers second, and laborers third; Hutterian women are housewives and mothers first, light laborers second, and citizens third."[21] Males are believed to be superior both physically and mentally to females. Thus, the women do not participate formally in colony decision-making, nor do they produce economically for trading in the outside world. Their economic responsibilities, perhaps for the raising of geese or chickens, involve only goods being raised for colony consumption. Yet, as pointed out by Lantz *et al.* in discussing the colonial family, such women have much indirect influence upon decision-making, and their patently inferior status gives them a certain amount of freedom.

Men of the colony are very likely to be known and referred to according to their functional roles: John may be the turkey man and Paul the hog man. Minute status gradations accompany these economic tasks and help the individual to understand his place in the colony. Several observers have noted the effect that these distinctions and the stress on consensus have on primary relationships. In the lifelong struggle to avoid conflict and to develop consensus, a certain amount of spontaneity is lost. Even in the relation between brothers, since openness of expression and communication may lead to dissension, the only safe practice is to hold fast the reign of self-expression.

When the person can no longer contribute a full day's labor to the colony, he is retired. Although the aged lose that status which accrues to a specific functional role, the traditionalism of the Hutterites causes them to be greatly respected by the younger members of the colony. Death is seen, not as the end, but as the beginning of a new day; pre-death anxieties regarding property and inheritance disposal are minimized by the Hutterian way.

What is the crucial problem that the Hutterites, and similar separatist subsocieties, face in the modern United States? It is the problem of *staying separate in a society that tends to reach out and assimilate its parts, culturally and socially*. But as long as succeeding generations continue to become convinced that their way is right and best, the Hutterites are likely to survive as a definable subsociety.

SECTION THREE

THE ETHNIC SUBCULTURE AND SUBSOCIETY

Throughout the previous discussion, the terms "subculture" and "subsociety" have been employed, and the terms "ethnic group" and "minority" have been avoided. Yet, because the latter terms are frequently used in describing American society, some understanding of them is essential. The most useful definitions can be found in Shibutani and Kwan's book, *Ethnic Stratification*, in which minority groups are described as the "underprivileged in a system of ethnic stratification," and as "people of low standing—people who receive unequal treatment and who therefore come to regard themselves as objects of discrimination."[22] An ethnic group, say the authors "consists of those who conceive of themselves as being alike by virtue of their common ancestry, real or fictitious, and who are so regarded by others."[23] Thus, a minority may or may not be an ethnic group, depending upon whether or not there is a sense of corporate identity, and an ethnic group may or may not be a minority, depending upon whether it is discriminated against in society.

Historically, the groups in America that have been most often defined as ethnic are the non-Protestant European immigrants—including Irish, Polish, and Italian Catholics and the Jewish people—though the latter are hard to distinguish analytically from a religious subculture. According to most observers, the history of such groups in America is of a movement from ethnic minority status to ethnic group to quasi-ethnic group. Speaking of their patriarchal family system, for example, Ruth Cavan asserts that "this type of family organization has faded under the strain of urban-industrial life and the acculturation of immigrants and their children into the prevailing patterns of Anglo-American culture."[24]

Just how complete is the fading or abolishing of the ethnic culture patterns? Paul J. Campisi feels that, within a period of 20 to 25 years after arrival, the Italian immigrant family was almost completely assimilated by the dominant society and its culture. This assimilation occurs as the younger generation grows up and as their aging parents begin to realize that success is predicated upon becoming increasingly like the "old Americans."[25] Features of the family, from patriarchal control to rejection of birth control, are altered radically under the influence of the Anglo-American style.

Will Herberg, in his book *Protestant-Catholic-Jew*, describes a more complex and less complete process of assimilation through which the Catholic and Jewish immigrant groups have passed. The first generation, arriving in the late 1800's, attempted to hold on to the ways of their fathers and became an enclave within their new society. Language, family forms, and belief systems were retained, and awareness of differences was intensified by the tendency of these families to cluster together residentially, especially in the growing urban centers along the East Coast. The result was considerable persecution of and discrimination against these groups by the Anglo-American Protestants among whom they settled.

As the members of the second generation moved out into the school system and peer culture, the conflict of old and new was no longer only intergroup, but became intergenerational and intrafamilial as well. "Frequently, though not always, the man of the second generation attempted to resolve his dilemma by forsaking the ethnic group in which he found himself."[26] The struggle to be incorporated into the American social, economic, and political system was long and hard, but was successful because of the second generation's ability to assume the dominant cultural forms and their willingness to aid each other educationally and otherwise. Mutual aid and a mutual rejection of many key aspects of the old culture occurred simultaneously.

It is at this point that Campisi's discussion of the assimilative process ends. Herberg, however, notes a further change after 1920. At this point, the stream of immigrants ceased, and the third generation appeared. This generation "became American in a sense that had been, by and large, impossible for the immigrants and their children. That problem, at least, was solved; but its solution paradoxically rendered more acute the perennial problem of 'belonging' and self-identification." Herberg then goes on to describe how this problem was resolved:

> They wished to belong to a group. But what group could they belong to? The old-line ethnic group, with its foreign language and culture, was not for them; they were Americans. But the old family religion, the old ethnic religion, could serve where language and culture could not.

With modifications, this religion could be made to serve the American value system and still be used for identification, confirming "the tie that bound them to their forebears, whom they now no longer had any reason to reject, whom indeed, for the sake of a 'heritage,' they now wanted to 'remember.' "[27]

As far as the family is concerned, the problem for the third and subsequent generations has been twofold. On the one hand, many of the ritual practices by which the ethnic-religious ties had been reaffirmed have already been emptied of their former significance and lack a meaningful content. On the other hand, the dominant value system continues to beat away at the remaining features of the old system, e.g., rejection of birth control among Catholics. There are, in fact, but few points at which the family culture of these ethnic groups does not resemble that of either the middle-class or lower-class model described above. What, then, is the central problem for these groups at the present time? First, it must be stated that, unlike the Hutterites, Amish, and other separatists, they have desired assimilation—and have found it possible. *Their key problem has been to keep alive any subcultural characteristics in a society in which they have achieved assimilation.*

SECTION FOUR

RACIAL GROUPS: THE BLACK AMERICAN FAMILY

The everyday division between racial categories—into black, yellow, red, and white peoples—fits quite well into the scholarly discussions of race in America, in which Negroes, Orientals, and Indians have typically been distinguished from White Americans.[28] While much that has been said about religious and ethnic groups applies to these so-called racial categories as well, there are also some points of divergence both in history and in current problems. Because of their numerical and structural importance in American society, this section will focus upon blacks, or Afro-Americans— those labelled "Negroes," until recently, in most investigations.

Seldom has there been a subject within social science literature about which more value judgments have been allowed to creep in. From the turn of this century until the present, writers (both black and white) have had extreme difficulty in discussing the Afro-American without bias and prejudice, conscious and unconscious. The literature, therefore, must be handled with great caution; it seems to the present writer that the most valuable approach might be to isolate the various areas of misconception and disagreement and to try to make sense out of them. Thus, we shall divide our discussion into historical issues and current issues regarding black families and culture.

History of the Afro-American

African history involves great kingships and a multitude of small societies. Yet the history of the *Afro-American* begins primarily in exploitation and cruelty. It begins in West Africa with the killing and capture of large numbers of men and women, the transporting of the captured to the New World, and their enslavement—usually as agricultural laborers—in a strange land. Their African heritage faded during the period of indentured servanthood, especially under the influence of legalized and non-terminable slavery. Eventually slavery was superseded by their "emancipation" and by the weakening of the plantation system crucial to the existence of slavery.

The preceding paragraph is clearly not a full coverage of the 200-250 years it summarizes. However, we are concerned here with the effect of the occurrences of these years. What happened to the Afro-American during this period? We must answer this by spelling out two versions of the story. One version is well exemplified in the concentration camp analogy so many commentators have adopted.[29] During the Second World War, some of the inmates of Nazi concentration camps in Germany became, over time, childishly silly. Their relations with each other became unstable; they became pathological liars and dishonest in all their dealings. In effect, they regressed to childhood. Eventually, they identified with and imitated their captors, coming to view each other through Gestapo eyes and sometimes outdoing the Gestapo in cruelty to fellow prisoners.

What caused this type of behavior? The Gestapo used terror and torture, intimidation, isolation, and secrecy. Prisoners were rewarded for compliance with the Gestapo, and, above all, there was a "complete break with the outside world."[30] In a similar manner, says Stanley Elkins, the role of child was forced on the slaves. The master was the "father," who disciplined, taught respect, and held complete control over the life of the slave, the master was also the only person with whom identification might occur. Under these conditions, personal relations among the slaves; including those within the family, were extremely tenuous. But didn't the culture brought from Africa act as a stabilizing influence upon relationships? The negative answer to this question is arrived at by two different logical paths, depending upon the writer. Melville Herskovitz' response is that the characteristics of the slave family—female dominance, common-law marriage, illegitimacy, and weak ties—can be traced back to the polygynous family of West Africa. In other words, the culture the blacks brought with them increased, rather than diminished, the instability of relationships during slavery. A more prevalent argument is that posed by E. Franklin Frazier: The culture brought from Africa had no stabilizing influence upon relationships because that culture was virtually obliterated by experience in the New World. The "rare and isolated instances of survivals associated with the Negro family only indicate how completely the African social organization was wiped out by slavery."[31] The enslaved people were moved randomly from place to place, without any concern for tribal or national groupings. This, plus the conditions described by Elkins, served (over several generations) to destroy most vestiges of African culture.

Because internal stability had been provided (so the argument goes) by the white system and not by their own relationships, and because slaves had previously had little or no freedom to govern their own destinies, the result of emancipation could only be disastrous.

> When the invading armies disrupted the plantation organization, thousands of Negroes were set adrift and began to wander footloose about the country. Not only were the sentimental and habitual ties between spouses severed but even Negro women often abandoned their children. Among the demoralized elements in the newly emancipated Negroes promiscuous sexual relationships and frequent changing of spouses became the rule.[32]

Such a description, without an offsetting account of the non-demoralized elements, leaves the reader to infer that this pattern was typical. And Frazier's picture of post-war anarchy is echoed by Jessie Bernard, who writes that "in 1865, desertions were innumerable. . . . When the Negroes were moving around to test their freedom, many of them seized the opportunity to desert their wives and children. . . . The young and strong deserted the aged, the feeble, the children, leaving them to shift for themselves."[33] This is a view of the historical process: cultural obliteration, suppression and order under slavery, and anarchy upon emancipation.

There is, however, a second possible perspective on the same era—one that may be pieced together with the help of a different analogy, the insights of Andrew Billingsley, and a few alternative inferences. Helmut Schelsky writes at length, not about the concentration camp, but about the family in post-World War II Germany. He begins by tearing down a stereotype:

> In general, such times of disorder and distress are considered to be a cause for the disruption and weakening of the family; it is astonishing, therefore, that we must designate the effect of the difficult social experiences which I have mentioned as a *heightening of the stability of the German family*. With the collapse of political and economic order and in the face of the immediate peril to which almost everyone was subjected, marriage and the family were considered to be the natural point of stability and protection. . . . The family was often knitted together in the struggle for mere existence, where it was a matter of thriving or perishing, to such a degree that the personal tensions, the bored indifference of the usual marital "co-existence" gave way to a conscious and heightened sense of belonging together.[34]

The family was felt by the German people to be the last element of stability in a disintegrating world. "Therefore," Schelsky asserts, "the displaced farmer or the 'declassed' official . . . lives with clear consciousness and decisiveness 'only for the family,' an expression which I heard often enough in the families I investigated."[35] Solidarity between husbands and wives and between old and young is evidenced in the minimization of tensions and in the astonishingly slight amount of child neglect. When the rest of the society crumbled, the German people retreated into the family and lived for it. In addition, the balance of power and importance swung toward the female, causing the largest percentage of German families to take on an equalitarian character.

Before pursuing the possible use of Schelsky's account as an analogue to the post-slavery family among Afro-Americans, let us back up a bit to the family in Africa. Did the social systems of West Africa, from whence blacks were brought to America, act as a foundation for common-law marriages, weak relationships, and illegitimacy in the New World, as Herskovitz claimed? African history was one of family and lineage stability, but this stability, as well as African culture, was completely disrupted by the movement of Africans to America as slaves. What was not disrupted was the basic humanity and mutual concern which were functions of the African heritage. Then with emancipation and the destruction of the southern way of life, large numbers of Afro-Americans retreated into their family units and attempted to find economic and social stability within them. Migrations, first urbanward and then northward, ordinarily involved family units—not footloose individuals. Whole kin groups often moved, one family at a time, to the same location where economic opportunity was reported to be greater.

Which picture of Afro-American history is correct? Was it the "concentration camp influence," with its dehumanization, weakening of peer relationships, and with the opportunity it gave the "emancipated" to sever all ties and renounce all responsibility? Or was it a post-defeat world, with the Afro-American drawing upon a basic fund of humanity and upon mutual support—often within the family—in the struggle for stability and survival in a crumbling social system? An obvious possibility is that both analogies are partially correct: after emancipation, weak ties became weaker and strong ties became stronger. This, however, evades the issue of which pattern was dominant in the late 1800's. It seems to this writer that the weakness of family ties under slavery has been overdrawn, and that the dominant pattern following emancipation was family and kin solidarity as the blacks sought equilibrium and opportunity. If the post-war Germany analogy is, in fact, the more accurate, how can one account for the predominance, in the historical literature, of descriptions of weak ties among the slaves? At least a part of the answer lies in the attempts of white scholars (and black scholars educated in a white society) to ease the guilt for the white race's inhumanity. That is, if slavery dehumanized the blacks and weakened their ties to one another, then the selling of slaves—the breaking up of units—does not seem quite so inhumane. But if, in fact, the traffic in human chattel destroyed family ties that were meaningful and supportive to the individual, the crime becomes more appalling. In other words, because some white scholars wished to believe that black ties were weak, they wrote as if that had, in fact, been the case.

Of course, the particular conclusion the reader draws regarding the slavery and post-slavery family among Afro-Americans is bound to be consistent with his conclusions concerning black families today. Keeping this in mind, let us seek to unravel the tangled strands of contemporary debate.

The Black American Family Today

There are two tendencies in the study of the American family: one is to ignore black families altogether; the other is to treat them as social problems. The classic statement of this latter approach is found in Frazier's work on the family. "The mass migration of Negroes to the cities of the North resulted in considerable family disorganization." Life for the urban Negroes, he feels, is casual, precarious, and fragmentary.

> It lacks continuity and its roots do not go deeper than the contingencies of daily living. . . . Without the direction provided by family traditions and the discipline of parents, large numbers of Negro children grow up without aims and ambitions.[36]

Frazier's characterization of the Negro family gained wide attention when it was repeated and programmed by Daniel P. Moynihan:

> The evidence—not final, but powerfully persuasive—is that the Negro family in the urban ghettoes is crumbling. . . . In a word, a national effort towards the problem of Negro Americans must be directed towards the question of family structure. The object should be to strengthen the Negro family so as to enable it to raise and support its members as do other families.[37]

Proponents of this view say that the black family is disintegrating, that it is disorganized, traditionless, free-floating, and matricentric. To them, the "free-floating" nature of rural southern and urban lower-class families means that sex relations are promiscuous, illegitimate births are prevalent, and marriage is not a part of the mores. As for the matricentric, or matriarchal, nature of the family, Moynihan claims that the Negro community has been forced into such a pattern "which, because it is so out of line with the rest of the American society, seriously retards the progress of the group as a whole, and imposes a crushing burden on the Negro male and, in consequence, on a great many Negro women as well."[38] The household headed by a mother or grandmother is defined as a problem, since there is no male present, and as problem-producing, since the absence of a male makes achievement by the younger generation even more problematic. As Moynihan puts it: "White children without fathers at least perceive all about them the pattern of men working. Negro children without fathers flounder—

and fail."[39] One characterization thus becomes complete: Afro-Americans developed weak family ties during slavery; even these were loosened by emancipation. They then began the long process of trying to internalize the ways of the dominant society (including the concept of stable marriage), but the clustering together in urban ghettoes and rural areas arrested the process. As a matter of fact, at present, acculturation appears to have become reversed, so that instability and weakness of relationships are once again becoming more prevalent.

What of the other picture—the vast numbers of family units struggling together after slavery to make it in a white world? Billingsley picks up this theme. How can a people survive under oppression? One way is "to adapt the most basic of its institutions, the family, to meet the often conflicting demands placed on it."[40] Disagreeing directly with Moynihan and others, Billingsley states: "We do not view the Negro family as a causal nexus in a 'tangle of pathology' which feeds on itself. Rather, we view the Negro family in theoretical perspective as a subsystem of the larger society. It is, in our view, an absorbing, adaptive, and amazingly resilient mechanism for the socialization of its children and the civilization of its society."[41] Is it disorganized and unstable? Frazier admitted that, while there is considerable family disorganization among the lower classes, "there is a core of stable families even in this class."[42] To this, Billingsley adds that the large numbers of stable black working-class families never make the news and seldom the pages of social science reports. The majority of "poor Negroes live in nuclear families headed by men who work hard every day, and are still unable to earn enough to pull their families out of poverty."[43] It certainly cannot be surprising, says Bernard, to learn that lower-class black husbands "were rated least satisfactory in the role of provider. What is unexpected, in fact, is that relatively so few were. Only 10 per cent of the wives felt that they were really missing out so far as level of living was concerned."[44] This fact, however, is surprising only if instability is expected or assumed.

Is the Afro-American family free-floating? Does it have weak ties and loose (by middle-class white standards) morality? Frazier admits that adequate information to answer these questions is lacking and that sexual promiscuity and weak marriage appear— from the data available—to be confined largely to the lower classes. Billingsley, referring to illegitimacy, adds that white middle-class adoption processes are such that "both women are protected from condemnation, for they both have 'done the right thing.' This contrasts sharply with the general efforts to expose to ridicule the Negro woman who has an illegitimate child and chooses to keep her own child, or must do so because of the policies of adoption agencies."[45]

Finally, are black families matricentric? Frazier himself, from whom Moynihan drew heavily in preparing his report, finds in the 1940 census that only 21.7 per cent of black families are headed by females.[46] One-fourth to one-third of Negro families in cities, says Frazier, are without a male head. Yet, when it comes to defining a "Negro problem," Frazier and his successors subtly allow this proportion to take on the character of typicality. There is a form of matrifocality that may be used to describe the black lower-class family, but it is hardly racially based and must be distinguished from male absence. Lee Rainwater depicts this form of matrifocality as follows:

> Because of the high degree of conjugal role segregation, both white and Negro lower-class families tend to be matrifocal in comparison to middle-class families. They are matrifocal in the sense that the wife makes most of the decisions that keep the family going and has the greatest sense of responsibility to the family. In white as well as Negro lower-class families women tend to look to their female relatives for support and counsel, and to treat their husbands as essentially uninterested in the day-to-day problems of family living.[47]

Schelsky notes the conditions of social and economic disintegration which give rise to such a family style.

> The shifting of social functions and social balance in the family in favor of the wife is a phenomenon which is peculiar to industrial society in and of itself; the process, however, was vastly accelerated in Germany by the war and postwar events and, not only because women on their own part took over many more tasks and much more authority in the family and in public life, but also largely because the events themselves effected a lessening of the social self-consciousness of the husband.[48]

Thus, what Rainwater and Frazier have been saying about black families (which is reinforced, to some extent, by Schelsky's account of Germany) is that they are primarily stable units, struggling together to survive in a white-dominated society. They are not typically weak or promiscuous in their relationships, but the way in which deviant behavior, such as illegitimacy, is treated accounts for some of the supposed differences between blacks and whites.

Finally, they are characteristically matrifocal only in the sense of the lower-class model itself.

One of the problems with the two characterizations is, of course, a semantic one. The use of terms such as "the majority," "a large number," "vast numbers," and "a large portion," can be misleading when interpreted to mean "typically," or "in general." Furthermore, not all black families follow the same pattern, nor are black families simply a reflection of the white middle-class and lower-class models in all their particulars. Wherein lie the differences among blacks, and what is the significance of these differences?

For Jessie Bernard, the resolution of the debate regarding the nature of Afro-American society is to be found in distinguishing members of two black cultures: the *acculturated* and the *externally adapted*. The former have internalized the moral norms of Western society; the latter are pleasure-loving and consumption-oriented. "The great chasm between the two Negro worlds is so great as to be, for all intents and purposes, all but unbridgeable, at least until now. Fear and hostility—even hatred and resentment—characterize the relations, or lack of relations, between them."[49] This great chasm of mutual rejection, drawn to some extent from Frazier's account in *Black Bourgeoisie,* can be used to explain the simultaneous increase in education and in illegitimacy, in achievement and in family instability. One set of phenomena are occurring among the acculturated and the other among the externally adapted, and there is little overlap.

This split has strong social class overtones: the acculturated are predominantly well off economically and socially, while the externally adapted are for the most part disadvantaged. There are, however, a few exceptions, such as the Black Muslims, who are economically disadvantaged, but who have adopted the family values and moral codes of the middle-class model.[50]

The key to Bernard's conception is mutual rejection and separation—even combat between these two cultural and social categories. Yet, within her own treatise, Bernard refers to research that calls into question this complete separation. Zena Smith Blau, for example, found that "fully 90 per cent of the middle-class Negro women came from working-class backgrounds, in contrast to 35 per cent in the white middle-class."[51] If there were mutual rejection between the two ways of life, how did these 90 per cent become motivated to adopt the middle-class morality and success values? Billingsley claims that, not only is there not mutual rejection; but that, at present, there is an increasing sense of identity and peoplehood in the black communities of America. Those who have achieved middle-class positions are not severing their connections with the disadvantaged Negro population, but are identifying with their problems. Here once again there appears to be a great disagreement between writers: rejection, separation, and hatred of one another on the one hand; identification and a sense of peoplehood on the other.

In this case, it may not be necessary, as in the case of the historical models, to simply accept the one that seems most "reasonable." Rather, it is at least possible that both are correct and that they describe an historical process. Perhaps when Frazier was describing the bourgeoisie, they were, in fact, trying very hard to be middle-class and not "Negro"; while today these same professionals and white-collar workers are admitting their common Afro-American heritage with other blacks in this country. In other words, the 1960's may be seen as the decade when the "Negroes" became "Afro-Americans"; when a minority began the process of becoming an *ethnic* minority. Billingsley himself notes this change within his lifetime. In the 1940's, he says, we were still ambivalent about our heritage. African students were treated with disdain, white students with adulation. Even since World War II, large numbers of blacks still feel a twinge of inferiority regarding their African heritage. "Yet the image is changing radically and rapidly."[52] Billingsley's discussion of the ability of the strong individual in a black family to "pull others up," as long as they are responsive to his efforts on their behalf, is well known in the writings on the ethnic minorities in American society.

To summarize, there are obvious cultural differences among blacks as one looks at different sectors of the socioeconomic ladder. However, it is doubtful if this bespeaks two black subsocieties characterized by mutual rejection, hatred, and combat. There may have been a time when the desire for assimilation caused the black middle classes to try to reject their racial ties; on the other hand, Billingsley's programmatic concern may have led him to overplay the ethnic identification of today's middle-class blacks with their race. However, the current direction of change appears to be toward an increased racial, or—if you will—ethnic identity among blacks.

When we turn from the internal similarities or differences among blacks to the issue of white and black cultural similarity or difference, we find that the preceding conclusion could lead us in either of two directions. On the one hand, saying that there are not two black subsocieties—but rather variations as one moves up and down the socioeconomic ladder—could be interpreted to mean that blacks merely reflect white culture, the only difference being that there are a larger proportion of blacks toward the lower end of the continuum. On the other hand, the perception of an increase in ethnic identification among blacks could be interpreted to mean that they are developing a more and more distinctive cultural style *vis-à-vis* whites. It is in the resolution of this dilemma that Afro-Americans resemble most closely the other ethnic groups. Various authors and researchers agree that, while simple black-white comparisons have often ignored socioeconomic level, even the employing of social class, or socioeconomic level, does not obliterate the differences between whites and blacks. After all, says Billingsley, social class "was not invented to account for the racial factor."[53] But what is this *racial factor*? Education, income, and occupation controls do not completely close the gap in marital stability that exists between the races. Bernard suggests that "the presence of these externally adapted men accounts for the relatively lower proportion of Negroes in stable marriages."[54] Yet how do you explain the prevalence of such men? Bernard mentions several possible explanations for racial differences—great striving (perhaps to compensate for discrimination), inconsistency between different measures of one's status—but these are not directed toward explaining why there are so many "externally adapted" men. Several authors, in commenting upon Bernard's article, make an attempt to explain the racial factor. Catherine S. Chilman, for example, states it thus:

> Cultural differences between Negroes and Caucasians in the United States undoubtedly do play a part in the higher rates of Negro family instability. However, other probable factors must be mentioned: the greater stress that Negro families are likely to suffer from the manifold pressures of prejudice as they operate in reference to housing, recreation, social acceptance, ghettoization, employment discrimination, intimidation, and so on.[55]

Such discrimination, especially in the occupational structure, is felt by Billingsley to be one important reason why racial comparisons that "control for social class" are not comparing comparable experiences.[56] Rainwater speaks of the effect of ghettoization, which is even more obvious than that of discrimination. A negative picture of oneself may develop in a white lower-class family; but, for the Negro, there is the "reality of blackness

> . . . one of the effects of ghettoization is to mask the ultimate enemy so that the understanding of the fact of victimization by a caste system comes as a late acquisition laid over conceptions of self and of other Negroes derived from intimate, and to the child often traumatic, experience within the ghetto community.[57]

That conditions of life for the blacks in the ghetto appear to be getting worse is one point of agreement between Billingsley, Moynihan, and other contemporary observers. A slightly higher rate of illegitimacy and a lower proportion of stable family units are the symptoms or signs. Nevertheless, there are other effects of ghettoization, of course, besides those defined negatively by the middle classes. One is the black cultural style that has gradually emerged during the years of urban separation. This style includes music, humor, art, and literature, the foundation for which can be traced back to remnants of African culture and to the slavery and post-slavery treatment of blacks in this country. This style is an essential ingredient of the present increase in ethnic identity. Also, the residential power base has fostered the emergence of a black political leadership, which has also—in the form of black power—begun to be a rallying point for a new sense of positive identity within the black community. In short, there is a racial factor, a modicum of cultural difference between blacks and whites—a divergence that may be increasing.

The portion of this increasing divergence which most writers define as undesirable is that pertaining to family stability. Once again, however, these writers disagree regarding both the problem and its solution. Many readers of the Moynihan report have interpreted it as saying that the Afro-American family of today is self-perpetuating in the production of individuals with negative identities, little ambition, and tendencies toward weak relationships. If the family were straightened out (a process that would include the addition of a strong father figure), the other problems of the black in American society would take care of themselves (see Figure 5). This, says Rainwater, is an incomplete interpretation of Moynihan. Instead, Moynihan was saying that "the socioeconomic system constrains the family in ways that lead to disorganization and that family disorganization then feeds back into the system to sustain and perpetuate social and economic disadvantage."[58] The critics of the Moynihan report feel that it is simply saying: "Get a father into

FIGURE 5

Views of the Place of Black Families in the Scheme of Discrimination and Disadvantage in American Society

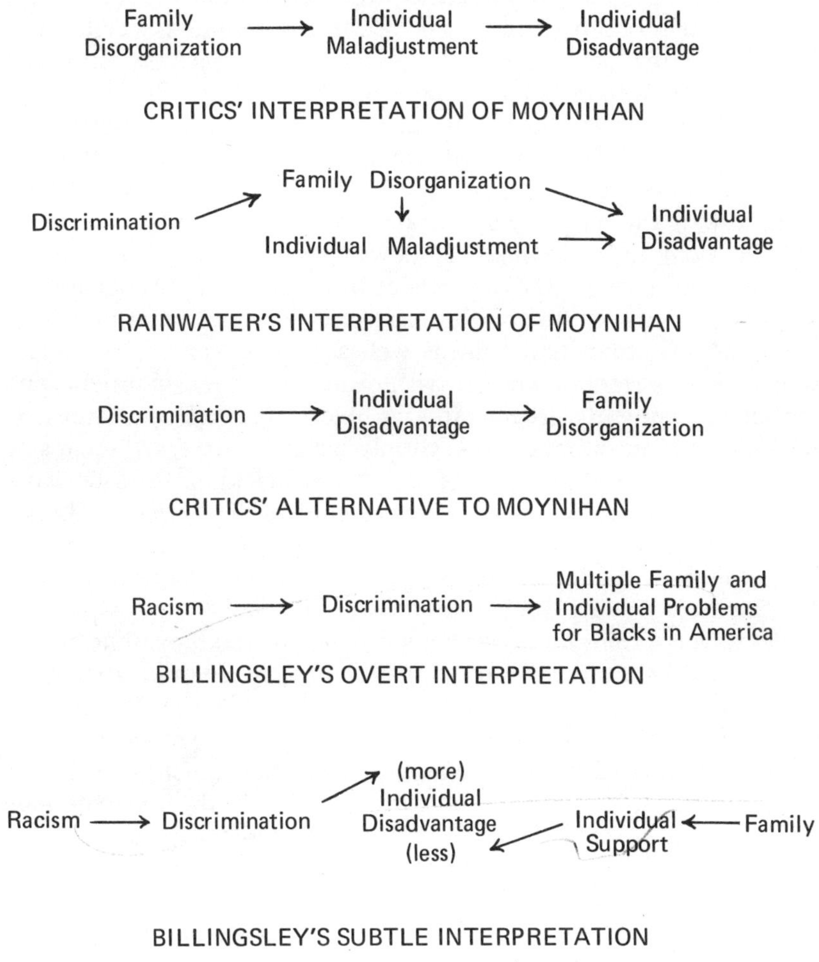

Family Disorganization ⟶ Individual Maladjustment ⟶ Individual Disadvantage

CRITICS' INTERPRETATION OF MOYNIHAN

Discrimination ⟶ Family Disorganization ↓ Individual Maladjustment ⟶ Individual Disadvantage

RAINWATER'S INTERPRETATION OF MOYNIHAN

Discrimination ⟶ Individual Disadvantage ⟶ Family Disorganization

CRITICS' ALTERNATIVE TO MOYNIHAN

Racism ⟶ Discrimination ⟶ Multiple Family and Individual Problems for Blacks in America

BILLINGSLEY'S OVERT INTERPRETATION

Racism ⟶ Discrimination ⟶ (more) Individual Disadvantage (less) ⟵ Individual Support ⟵ Family

BILLINGSLEY'S SUBTLE INTERPRETATION

the home and over time the disadvantage of the black male in society will be abolished." Their response is to reverse the order: "Stop discrimination against blacks, especially males, and the family will eventually stabilize." The problem, they say, is not with the family but with the economic and social system.[59] Or, more plainly, it is time to stop talking about the "black problem" and begin to work on the "white problem."

There are at least two interpretations of the contemporary

black family which can be found in Billingsley's book. One is that the specter of racism "limits the viability of Negro families in hundreds of ways."[60] Racist attitudes and the resultant discrimination cause problems for the family unit, for the individual, and for the general position of blacks in a white-dominated society. Yet, throughout his book, another interpretation appears—one that notes the strength of black families and the way in which they act as a buffer against the debilitating effects of white racism and discrimination. It is the strength of the black family and its social network which makes possible upward mobility and stable relationships among the majority of blacks in a society calculated at every turn to hold these individuals down and weaken relationships. Warmth and love are the heritage of most maturing blacks and, in contrast to many white middle-class families, this love often comes from persons other than (but as well as) members of the nuclear family. Furthermore, concern with order, neatness, manners, and morals is frequently greater among blacks than among whites on the same socioeconomic level, simply because these are means to respectability—and, because of prejudice, blacks have to be *more* "respectable" than whites to be considered so. Thus, says Billingsley, the issue is not why there are so many unstable black families, but rather how the family and social network have made it possible for blacks to develop such a high level of stability and aspiration under adverse conditions. Perhaps the part of the Moynihan report which was most offensive to its critics was the solution that grew logically out of the definition of the problem. The solution is to strengthen the family, to see to it that there is a male in every household. Such a program, claimed the critics, must begin in the economic area, not within the family itself. If the income issue were solved, so that the male could contribute regularly to the family's maintenance, the family structure situation would take care of itself. It is noteworthy that both of these solutions must be effected by the white society. To these proposed solutions, black leaders have responded that the problem to be solved by the white community is its own racism and prejudice. White leaders could do well to turn their attention and concern to the study, understanding, and resolving of prejudice and race hatred—emotions accompanied by debilitating and insidious effects upon the prejudiced themselves.

By the same token, several solutions have been proposed by black leaders to their own problems. The three most prevalent might be labelled assimilation, separation, and power. The assimilative or incorporative approach is epitomized by the non-violent civil rights movement and the writings of men such as Martin Luther King. Its goal is for the black man to be a part of the society and to share equally in its abundance; the means is to eliminate the racism and hatred of the whites through love and patient understanding. The desire for assimilation was not, of course, originated recently, but has been an expectation of many black Americans for decades.

Some blacks, seeing the hope of assimilation go unrealized, have swung to the opposite pole. "Since they (the whites) reject us, we reject them." Here, in essence, you have the separatist movement so well illustrated by the Black Muslims. The group, no longer a "back to Africa" movement, has placed much of its emphasis upon having a separate area of the country (or several areas) in which the blacks may relocate themselves and run their own affairs.[61]

To many blacks today, both the assimilative and the separatist approaches sound too idealistic. The whites, they feel, are not really going to incorporate us, nor are they going to give us an area in which we can practice self-government. Therefore, for some, the solution is revolution. For others, it is black power, which takes several forms and has several goals. One of these goals is quasi-assimilative; a second is quasi-separatist. Both goals are well-expressed in a programmatic statement by Billingsley. The Negro family is not going to be strengthened by direct government intervention, nor by income measures alone. The solution lies in more control by blacks over their own life conditions.

> We have been arguing that the best way to insure the viability of the Negro family life is to insure that the major institutions of the wider society are open and responsive to the Negro experience, and at the same time to insure that there are strong and viable institutions within the Negro community itself, controlled and managed by Negro people.[62]

Assimilation of people and cultural style into the larger society and, at the same time, greater control over their own communities: these are two goals of black power. The means to such goals are frequently debated. Can these goals be achieved by political participation and power, or must there be a more substantial revolution in the economic and political system?[63] Disagreements among black spokesmen, as well as slowness of change in the white community, keep this important issue unresolved.

How can we summarize what has been said regarding the place of the black family within American society? For substantial numbers within the ghetto community, family instability is perpetuating itself, even intensifying. For even larger numbers, however, the Afro-American family appears to have been a buffer between the individual and the more debilitating aspects of racism. The majority of black households are nuclear family units, with the husband holding a steady job. In addition, there are numerous nuclear units that have been augmented (Billingsley's term) by the presence of one or more additional kin—a grandmother, uncle, or cousin. These augmented families are reminiscent of those of the European immigrants, who frequently lived together for the sake of mutual support and the sharing of resources during the period of discrimination.

The problem for blacks in America has differed greatly from that of the Hutterites and that of the European ethnic groups. The problem for blacks has been that, *after incorporating much of the dominant culture, they have not been allowed into the dominant society*. The solution hardly seems, to this writer, to be some program directed primarily at black families. Rather, the crucial issues revolve around white attitudes and behavior, as well as around various black efforts which must assume that there will be little *voluntary* change in the white community. Precisely how the black family fits into this total scheme—as problem and resource —the reader must ultimately decide for himself. Help on that decision must come from more and better research on the Afro-American family, based neither on biases nor on "preferred" types, but on empirical reality.

We have now completed a review of cross-cultural variations, the historical antecedents of the American family, the basic family types within the contemporary United States, and the theoretical and conceptual tools that are of value in understanding the family. At this point, the focus shifts to the family life cycle, beginning with socialization and continuing through mate selection to old age and family response to challenges. Throughout the subsequent chapters, the middle-class model, as "dominant" in the U.S., will be the prime object of analysis; although lower-class and other differing models will be brought in for comparison, when they are significant.

NOTES

[1] The terms "cultural universal" and "cultural alternative," which will be used extensively in the discussion of premarital sex in Chapter IX, are defined by Ralph Linton as follows: "There are those ideas, habits, and conditioned emotional responses which are common to all sane, adult members of the society." These are *cultural universals*. "There are in every culture a considerable number of traits which are shared by certain individuals but which are not common to all the members of the society or even to all the members of any one of the socially recognized categories." These are *cultural alternatives*. Ralph Linton, *The Study of Man* (New York: Appleton-Century, 1936), pp. 272-73.

[2] Ruth Shonle Cavan, "Subcultural Variations and Mobility," in Harold T. Christensen, ed., *Handbook of Marriage and the Family* (Chicago: Rand McNally, 1964), p. 536.

[3] Cavan, "Subcultural Variations and Mobility," p. 541.

[4] For more on the middle-class model, see Gerald Leslie, *The Family in Social Context* (New York: Oxford University Press, 1967), Chap. 9. On the lower-class model, see Arthur Besner, "Economic Deprivation and Family Patterns," in Lola M. Irelan, ed., *Low-Income Life Styles*, Department of Health, Education, and Welfare, Welfare Administration Publication No. 14 (1966), pp. 15-29. On working-class families, which are between the middle-class and lower-class on the socioeconomic ladder, see Mirra Komarovsky, *Blue-Collar Marriage* (New York: Random House, 1964). For a brief introduction to upper-class family patterns, see Leslie, *The Family in Social Context*, pp. 304-7.

[5] Cavan, "Subcultural Variations and Mobility," p. 536.

[6] Paul S. Gross, *The Hutterite Way* (Saskatoon, Canada: Freeman, 1965), p. 1.

[7] Besides Gross, *The Hutterite Way*, see John W. Bennett, *Hutterian Brethren* (Stanford, Calif.: Stanford University Press, 1967); John A. Hostetler and Gertrude Enders Huntington, *The Hutterites in North America* (New York: Holt, Rinehart and Winston, 1967); S. C. Lee and Audrey Brattrud, "Marriage Under a Monastic Mode of Life: A Preliminary Report on the Hutterite Family in South Dakota," *Journal of Marriage and the Family*, 29 (1967), 512-20.

[8] Bennett, *Hutterian Brethren*, p. 108.

[9] Gross, *The Hutterite Way*, p. 3.

[10] *Ibid.*, p. 6.

[11] Hostetler and Huntington, *The Hutterites in North America*, p. 29.

[12] See Bennett, *Hutterian Brethren*, p. 109, on these two principles.

[13] Hostetler and Huntington, *The Hutterites in North America*, p. 40.

[14] Bennett, *Hutterian Brethren*, p. 110.

[15] Arthur Mange, *The Population Structure of a Human Isolate* (Ph.D. Diss. University of Wisconsin, 1963).

[16] Hostetler and Huntington, *The Hutterites in North America*, p. 60.

[17] *Ibid.*, p. 67.

[18] Bennett, *Hutterian Brethren*, p. 129.

[19] Hostetler and Huntington, *The Hutterites in North America*, p. 81.

[20] *Ibid.*, p. 84.

[21] Bennett, *Hutterian Brethren*, p. 114.

[22] Tamotsu Shibutani and Kian M. Kwan, *Ethnic Stratification* (New York: Macmillan, 1965), p. 35.

[23] *Ibid.*, p. 47.

[24] Cavan, "Subcultural Variations and Mobility," p. 549.

[25] Paul J. Campisi, "Ethnic Family Patterns: The Italian Family in the United States," *American Journal of Sociology*, 53 (1948), 448.
[26] Will Herberg, *Protestant-Catholic-Jew* (Garden City, N.Y.: Doubleday, 1960), p. 28.
[27] *Ibid.*, pp. 30–31.
[28] Though they are sometimes treated as a racial minority, Mexican Americans would be better dealt with as an ethnic group.
[29] Stanley M. Elkins, *Slavery: A Problem in American Institutional and Intellectual Life* (New York: Grosset and Dunlap, 1963), was the first to present this.
[30] Elkins, *Slavery*, p. 104.
[31] For these two interpretations see Melville J. Herskovitz, *The Myth of the Negro Past* (New York: Harper and Brothers, 1941); E. Franklin Frazier, *The Negro in the United States* (New York: Macmillan, 1957 ed.), pp. 11, 12.
[32] Frazier, *The Negro in the United States*, p. 313.
[33] Jessie Bernard, *Marriage and Family Among Negroes* (Englewood Cliffs, N.J.: Prentice-Hall, 1966), p. 110.
[34] Helmut Schelsky, "The Family in Germany," *Marriage and Family Living*, 16 (1954), 331–32.
[35] *Ibid.*, p. 332.
[36] Frazier, *The Negro in the United States*, p. 636.
[37] Daniel P. Moynihan, *The Negro Family: The Case for National Action*, Department of Labor (1965), abstract and p. 47.
[38] *Ibid.*, p. 29.
[39] *Ibid.*, p. 35.
[40] Andrew Billingsley, *Black Families in White America* (Englewood Cliffs, N.J.: Prentice-Hall, 1968), p. 21.
[41] *Ibid.*, p. 33.
[42] Frazier, *The Negro in the United States*, p. 324.
[43] Billingsley, *Black Families in White America*, pp. 137, 139.
[44] Bernard, *Marriage and Family Among Negroes*, p. 97.
[45] Frazier, *The Negro in the United States*, pp. 635, 319; Billingsley, *Black Families in White America*, pp. 162–63.
[46] Frazier, *The Negro in the United States*, p. 317.
[47] Lee Rainwater, "Crucible of Identity: The Negro Lower-Class Family," *Daedalus* (Winter, 1966), p. 190.
[48] Schelsky, "The Family in Germany," p. 335.
[49] Bernard, *Marriage and Family Among Negroes*, pp. 33, 58.
[50] *Ibid.*, p. 46. On the family values of the Muslims, see Harry Edwards, "Black Muslim and Negro Christian Family Relationships," *Journal of Marriage and the Family*, 30 (1968), 604–11.
[51] Zena Smith Blau, "Exposure to Child-Rearing Experts: A Structural Interpretation of Class-Color Difference," *American Journal of Sociology*, 69 (1964), 605–7, quoted in Bernard, *Marriage and Family Among Negroes*, p. 45.
[52] Billingsley, *Black Families in White America*, p. 39.
[53] *Ibid.*, p. 200.
[54] Jessie Bernard, "Marital Stability and Patterns of Status Variables," *Journal of Marriage and the Family*, 28 (1966), 438.
[55] Catherine S. Chilman, "Marital Stability and Patterns of Status Variables: A Comment," *Journal of Marriage and the Family*, 28 (1966), 447.
[56] Billingsley, *Black Families in White America*, p. 88.
[57] Rainwater, "Crucible of Identity," pp. 204–5.
[58] Lee Rainwater and William L. Yancey, *The Moynihan Report and*

the Politics of Controversy (Cambridge, Mass.: M.I.T. Press), 1967, p. 309.
[59] Billingsley, *Black Families in White America*, p. 199, expresses this view.
[60] *Ibid.*, p. 155.
[61] *The Autobiography of Malcolm X* (New York: Grove Press, 1966 ed.).
[62] Billingsley, *Black Families in White America*, pp. 190–91.
[63] Stokely Carmichael and Charles V. Hamilton, *Black Power* (New York: Random House, 1967).

VII

The Socialization Process

SOCIALIZATION IS THE PROCESS BY WHICH THE INDIVIDUAL INCORPORATES THE ATTITUDES AND BEHAVIORS CONSIDERED APPROPRIATE BY ANY GROUP OR SOCIETY. IT INVOLVES SELF-CONCEPT (IDENTITY FORMATION), WHICH INCLUDES CONSCIENCE DEVELOPMENT AND THE TWIN PROBLEMS OF IDENTIFICATION AND EGO STRUGGLE—ALL OF WHICH ARE RELATED TO INTRAPERSONAL AND INTERPERSONAL ADJUSTMENT. THERE ARE DIFFERENCES IN SOCIALIZATION, NOT ONLY BETWEEN SOCIETIES, BUT AMONG THE SUBCULTURAL GROUPS OF A GIVEN SOCIETY. THE SOCIALIZATION PROCESS IS THE MEANS WHEREBY DIFFERENCES ARE PERPETUATED. RAPID SOCIAL CHANGE AND EMPHASIS UPON PEER EXPERTISE HAVE RESULTED IN THE CURRENT PHENOMENON OF "REARING BY THE BOOK."

Every individual comes into the world with certain physical, emotional, and intellectual characteristics—a certain heredity. However, the infant has, at birth, the capacity to become a Chinese Communist, a Bushman, or an American—and what he does become depends greatly upon his socialization. This view, held by many social psychologists and anthropologists today, is well expressed by Margaret Mead:

> We are forced to conclude that human nature is almost unbelievably malleable, responding accurately and contrastingly to contrasting cultural conditions. The differences between individuals who are members of different cultures, like the differences between individuals within a culture, are almost entirely to be laid to differences in conditioning, especially during early childhood, and the form of this conditioning is culturally determined.[1]

Socialization (Mead's "conditioning") may be defined as *the process of learning or of teaching one how to behave in any group or society*. It is learning the culture, or ways, of a group; the process encompasses both the teachers and the learners, the socializing agents and the socialized. While the early years of childhood are stressed in much of the literature on socialization, the process actually continues throughout life, as a person changes roles and confronts new expectations.[2] During childhood, however, much of the individual's culture becomes fixed or internalized—as anyone who has moved from one society to another after childhood can attest.

Our biological inheritance *permits* and *requires* socialization, but also *limits* it.[3] No culture can demand that the individual run faster, lift more, or solve harder problems, than is humanly possible. But, within the bounds of these limitations, the potentialities are almost limitless. We tend to be unaware of much of our own socialization process, simply taking it for granted that our beliefs are "good," and that we know "the way" things should be done. Yet there are extreme differences between ours and other cultures, involving even aspects of our attitudes and behavior that we may consider to be inherently "human." Economic competitiveness is not universal. Aggressive behavior may be rewarded in one cultural setting, passivity and amiability in another. Mead's summary of the differences between the Arapesh and Mungdugumor of New Guinea illustrates the variability in cultural styles:

> We found the Arapesh—both men and women—displaying a personality that, out of our historically limited preoccupations, we would call maternal in its parental aspects, and feminine in its sexual aspects. We found men, as well as women, trained to be cooperative, unaggressive, responsive to the needs and demands of others. We found no idea that sex was a powerful driving force either for men or for women. In marked contrast to these attitudes, we found among the Mungdugumor that both men and women developed as ruthless, aggressive, positively sexed individuals, with the maternal cherishing aspects of personality at a minimum. Both men and women approximated to a personality type that we in our culture would find only in an undisciplined and very violent male.[4]

The setting for such cultural differences may be diagrammed as shown in Figure 6. Within the limits set by human endowment, each culture tends to reinforce certain attributes, while rejecting or punishing others. The result is that a particular type of personality comes to be dominant. Societies do differ, however, in the amount of variability (the size of the wedge-shaped section of Figure 6) they allow. Some, like the Mungdugumor, reward and value a very narrow range of personality types, so that only a small number of individuals diverge from the very specific cultural ideal. Such a

FIGURE 6

Cultural Possibilities and Limitations

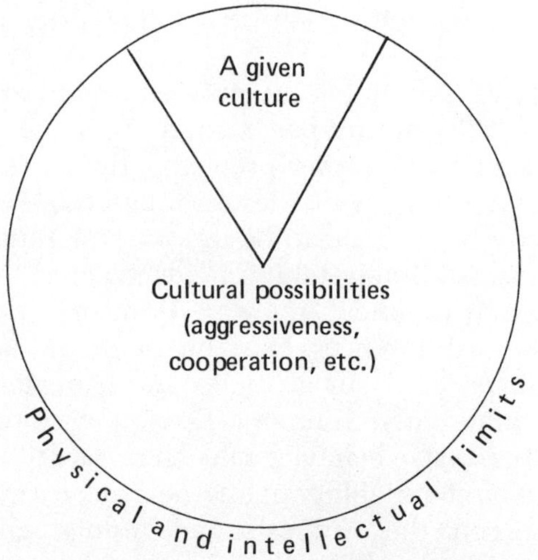

A given culture

Cultural possibilities (aggressiveness, cooperation, etc.)

Physical and intellectual limits

society is called *homogeneous* with respect to its culture. Other societies—the United States, for example—not only include several subcultural styles, but also reward a wider range of cultural possibilities, making these societies more *heterogeneous* in this respect. In addition, a given member of a heterogeneous society may be more strongly affected than a member of a homogeneous society by the pressures of conflicting cultural principles, such as expectations of cooperativeness and competitiveness, honesty and success.[5] There are, then, differences between societies, both in the range of acceptable socialization patterns and in the range of alternatives offered the individual.

A particular pattern of socialization and culture also determines who will be the deviant in a society. Though it is impossible to know with certainty, Mead assumes—and other writers concur—that the range of hereditary types, or innate dispositions, is virtually the same from one society to another. Yet each culture tends to cultivate and value a specific portion of the range of possibilities. Thus, there may be a fundamental discrepancy between an individual's innate disposition and the kind of personality rewarded by the society into which he is born. Under these conditions, the socialization process may never bring that person to the point of conforming to society's expectations. Thus, in the past, the

Cheyenne Indian boy who, by nature, was shy, fearful, and non-aggressive, and who never overcame these tendencies, may never have reached the cultural ideal of courage and bravery. If he failed to "measure up" during puberty, when he was required to demonstrate his ability to be a brave, he may have been forced to become a transvestite, taking on both the appearance and social role of the Cheyenne woman.[6] The same boy might have been incorporated with relative ease into Arapesh culture. One reason for cultural deviance is, of course, that socialization is an imperfect process in two ways. First, as indicated by the Cheyenne example, it does not result in molding every individual to the cultural ideal; second, the individual is not *completely* socialized and, consequently, acts upon his society as well as being acted upon by its socializing agents.[7]

Without dwelling further upon the great diversities of socialization and cultural patterns in different societies, we shall now consider some general principles of socialization, after which we shall examine socialization in the United States.

SECTION ONE

SOME PRINCIPLES OF SOCIALIZATION

Socialization is the process by which the individual learns to control his biological drives, is taught what behavior is acceptable and what is unacceptable, and develops an identity or self-concept. At least three relatively comprehensive theories have been developed to explain various aspects of this process. These are psychoanalytic theory, learning theory, and role-symbolic interaction theory. Though the theories are sometimes viewed as contradictory, they are better seen as emphasizing different components of the human experience. Psychoanalytic theory stresses the importance of biological endowment and drives, as well as unconscious processes. Learning theory stresses responses to stimuli and mental or psychological processes. Role theory and symbolic interaction theory stress sociological processes or the importance of the socializing agents.[8] In this text we shall focus on role theory and symbolic interaction theory, though each of the three types will contribute to the discussion at certain points.

Socialization, we have said, involves self-concept or identity clarification.[9] Identity means a sense of the categories or groups to which one belongs and some conception of the kind of person he is. The child learns very early to relate himself to his environment. First, he cries or gurgles in response to a specific physical state. Soon he cries or yells to bring his mother, that "object" that has appeared in the past when he needed help. He learns what behavior is rewarded and what is not; by the repetition of rewarded behavior he begins to fix that action as part of his personality. (Of course, rewarded behavior must be defined by the goals of the individual. If the goal sought is simply the attention of the socializing agents, misbehavior may serve as well as acceptable behavior.)

The child also begins to do more than repeat rewarded and avoid unrewarded behavior. He makes the transition from the question "Am I a good boy?" to the internal feeling "I am a good boy." By noticing his parents' and others' general reaction to him, he begins to evaluate himself as a good boy, bad boy, smart boy, or nuisance. This is what Charles H. Cooley calls the *looking-glass self:* I see myself in the looking-glass or reflected by other people.[10] Many and repeated "reflections" begin to cohere and to become part of the self-concept, which is formed by extremely early experiences and reactions. It is relatively easy, for example, to see how a second (or later) child might develop a concept of himself as humorous or funny. As he makes his first, halting attempts to walk, to talk, or to eat, the older child may laugh. If this continues, and if the parents join in good-naturedly, the younger child may begin to view himself as a comic; this aspect of his self-concept may last for years—or a lifetime. In short, one portion of self-concept formation is described by the looking-glass self notion.

Conscience and Guilt

Part of one's self-concept is his *conscience*, involving the sense of right and wrong. As Freud and his followers noted, the individual learns to control his biological impulses, and to feel guilty when he fails to control them. At first, we have said, the child will ordinarily do "right" to avoid punishment; that is, he tries to do what he knows his parents will not punish. Later, he may feel good or bad, accordingly, when he does something that these significant other people would consider good or bad if they knew about it. He is thus reacting to what George Herbert Mead has called a *generalized other*, the internalized demands of the significant people in one's milieu.[11] Guilt is, therefore, the self-punishment that you administer when you do what might have been punished by others if they had seen you do it. By means of socialization, different consciences are taught to respond with guilt feelings to different behaviors. It is at this point that certain types of criminal behavior become understandable. The pickpocket who is the son of a professional pockpocket and part of a criminal subculture may feel little guilt about his behavior, only a concern not to be caught by the "bad guys," i.e., the authorities. When one's socialization has not taught him that something is wrong, he may not feel guilty, even though he is punished for it. On the other hand, when one has been taught that something is wrong, and is later told by others that it is not, he may agree rationally that it is right, but still find his emotions reacting with a sense of guilt to his newly acquired behavior. For example, the young person who has been raised in a conservative religious tradition that defines smoking, drinking, and dancing as sinful, may, when he arrives at college, be told that "everybody does it," and yet have great difficulty convincing himself that this type of behavior is acceptable. The individual with an underdeveloped conscience, who behaves according to the accepted patterns of his group and society only when others are around, is called a psychopath.[12] Cultural and socialization differences play a big part in accounting for differences in conscience and guilt about specific acts, whether they be masturbating, head-hunting, or walking on the grave of one's ancestors.

This brings us to a general proposition regarding the relationship between cultural homogeneity or heterogeneity and conscience development: In the homogeneous society, the process of socialization may so uniformly reinforce the accepted definitions of right and wrong as to overdevelop the conscience of the members of that society. The result is that a serious breach of conduct may be followed by punishment or, if the individual is not caught, by such remorse and guilt as to lead, in the extreme instance, to suicide.[13] By contrast, the heterogeneous society may present the individual with so many conflicting conceptions of right and wrong as to either weaken his conscience and sense of guilt or to cause him to adopt the standards of whatever milieu he happens to be in —a sort of "conscience relativity."

Ego Struggle

Conceptions of right and wrong, and their internalization, are but one portion of self-concept development. Two other important aspects of the process may be introduced as ego struggle and ego identification. *Ego struggle* is the attempt of the growing individual to discover and assert his uniqueness. Early in his life the infant does not distinguish between self and non-self. Yet he soon discovers his own boundaries and a sense of himself as separate from those about him. While the socializing agents impinge upon him in many ways during his early years, the child finds himself increasingly aware of and concerned about "I-ness" and "they-ness." Ambivalence toward and aggression against the socializing agents are likely by-products of this struggle; these attitudes tend to intensify as one moves from childhood into the teenage years. One reason for such ambivalence and struggle may be that one's innate disposition is somewhat at variance with his society's demands. Another is simply that he begins to evaluate these demands by means of his rational faculties. Thus, one of the most difficult parental tasks is to give the child a "proper" amount of freedom so that his sense of identity can develop in a manner consistent with his capacities.

The fact that ego struggle is at least partially successful for many persons helps to account for the fact that cultural change does occur. Each new generation accepts, but also rethinks and alters, the behavioral norms and attitudes of the previous generation. This leads us to a second propositional distinction between the homogeneous and heterogeneous society. The struggle, ambivalence, and rethinking are likely to be greater in the latter than in the former, since the individual in the heterogeneous society is exposed to divergent principles, to which he can compare those of his most immediate socializers. That is, ego struggle is more widespread and more intense in the heterogeneous than in the homogeneous society.

Identification

Opposite to ego struggle, but of equal importance in socialization, is the process of *identification*. How does the growing boy learn how he is supposed to behave as a male, a job-holder, a father, and a husband? He learns from significant other people, whom he sees playing these roles. Identification, according to Winch, pertains to "the more or less lasting influence one person exerts on the behavior of another."[14] Identification is not a single variable in the type of relationship described; it involves either personal or positional influence, or both. A "role model" is someone in a particular position, such as that of father or husband, from whom one learns how to behave when he assumes that same position. When I use my own father in this fashion, I can be said to have identified with him, or to have modelled my behavior as a father after him. But identification is broader than the concept of role model; it also may mean trying to be the kind of person we conceive someone else to be or striving toward some abstract characteristic he embodies. Thus, I may "identify" with my father's character or his success, while either rejecting or not even knowing the specifics of his role behavior. Identification, then, may be positional or personal.

Furthermore, identification may mean either trying to emulate, complement, or to negate the behavior of another. The child may try to be like his father, or he may try to be whatever he conceives his father not to be. In common parlance, however, the term "identification," when unmodified, signifies positive identification, or trying to be like some other person. The complex of processes and meanings subsumed under the term "identification" is not unrelated to the concept of conscience development. Identification actually personalizes the question of where one gets his standards of right and wrong, although it also questions the origin of other attitudes and aspects of behavior.

As a process, identification involves three steps: (1) *awareness* of someone's *modus operandi*. The individual cannot identify with someone he knows nothing about. He may read about the way in which a certain contemporary, historical, or fictional person acts or performs his roles. More often, however, actually seeing the person in operation makes one aware of his characteristics. Furthermore, intensity and continuity of observation increase the likelihood of identification, making members of the same nuclear family a prime target for the process. After one becomes aware of the behavior of the role or character model, the next step in identification is (2) *evaluation*. It is at this point that the process may become either positive or negative. Though often unconscious, the reaction is: "This is the way (or not the way) to behave in the role of father," or "This is the way (or not the way) to react to the situation." Identification very often involves evaluations of a whole complex of behaviors by the same person; this is what is meant by "intensity."

The process is not complete until the step of (3) *incorporation* is made. Incorporation often means "filing away for future reference," rather than immediate implementation. That is, the role of father may be modelled after one's own father, although it is not assumed for many years. Thus, the completed process might be illustrated as follows:

(a) "I see how he plays the role of father."
(b) "That is the proper way to play the role of father."
(c) "When I become a father I shall play the role the way he does."

Who are likely objects of identification? Immediate possibilities, as indicated above, are one's parents and siblings. Works by Robert Winch, David Lynn, and Orville Brim have analyzed the intricate way in which the same-sex parent or an older sibling may influence the growing individual.[15] A proposition, modified slightly from one by Winch, is that, the more central the nuclear family is to the functioning of the society, the more likely it is that the individual will establish his major identifications within that unit. Conversely, the less central the nuclear family is to the functioning of the society, the more likely it is that the individual will establish his major identifications outside that unit.[16] Precisely how this proposition fits the historical facts regarding the family in the United States will be considered in Section Two.

Personality Integration

One further way to conceptualize the process of self-concept formation is in terms of the problem of personality integration. Each individual achieves two forms of integration, or adjustment, to a greater or lesser degree. The first is *intrapersonal*, or psychological, adjustment, which involves the reconciling of your preferred self-concept, or how you wish you were, with your actual self-concept, or the way you perceive yourself to be. You may see yourself as a great lover and athlete, but you may be afraid of girls and unable to catch a ball. In such a case you must find some way of reconciling these, perhaps by lowering your goals, or by excelling as a musician or scientist. Without such a reconciliation, you may be headed for mental difficulties. Unfortunately, the individual cannot simply go to a blackboard and list his preferred and actual concepts and then proceed to make them agree. Neither may be immediately available to the individual for manipulation. A great part of psychotherapy is predicated upon the hypothesis that behavior is modified when one brings his preferred self-concept into line with the way he actually knows himself to be; this achievement requires that he uncover or become aware of both.

A second form of adjustment with regard to the self-concept is *interpersonal*, or social, adjustment. Each person must attempt to behave at least somewhat consistently with the expectations of others. That is, he must reconcile how he acts with how others think he ought to act. For example, a man may see himself as non-aggressive and friendly, and may live in accordance with his preferred self-concept, but his wife may chide him for lack of aggressiveness and for not getting ahead. Or, if he tries to keep peace in the family by aggressive behavior on the job, the result may be intrapersonal difficulties, e.g., ulcers, due to the divergence of his preferred and actual self-concepts. When one's preferred self-concept and other people's expectations are inconsistent, the conflict may be resolved by placing greater importance upon one or the other. You may have developed no clear or strong preferred self-concept, or part of this self-concept may be a concern to act in a way which is pleasing to others; in either case the demands of others will dominate. Or you may live according to your internalized principles and preferences, often based on strong ancestral role models, while ignoring the expectations of peers. Fortunate, it would seem, is the man or woman for whom what he thinks he ought to be, what he perceives himself to be, and what others expect him to be all coincide.

The discussion of personality integration has necessarily taken us beyond the period of childhood in order to gain a broader perspective on the socialization process. With these tools and concepts in mind, let us turn now to the specific historico-cultural context with which we are most concerned: socialization in the United States.

SECTION TWO

SOCIALIZATION IN THE UNITED STATES

The Principles Applied

The nuclear family in colonial America had achieved a substantial degree of privacy with respect to its social network. Interrelations were fairly intense (in the sense in which that term was used above). That is, the child saw his parents at work, at play, at worship, under conditions of discipline, fun, and relaxation. The family was the hub of many societal functions; where this is so, we have postulated that positive identification within that unit is extremely likely. Not only did the child see his parents carrying out the various aspects of their roles, but there were few alternative role models for the child to emulate. Thus, even when the child had rankled under his own socialization, such as at the hands of a stern disciplinarian, he was likely to follow a similar pattern with his children later in life. Though he might have thought as he was being punished: "If I live through this I'll never treat my kids this way," when he became a father he did, in fact, behave as his father did, because that is "the way fathers are." Furthermore, the other models available to him, perhaps an uncle or an older sibling, were more likely to reinforce than to negate the model presented by the father.

What about a social setting in which non-familial socialization and divergent subcultural patterns vie with the family for influence in socialization, and in which the father plays his basic economic role outside the family? The proposition presented in the preceding section states that, the less central the nuclear family is to the functioning of the society, the more likely it is that the individual will establish his major identifications outside that unit. The pattern in the contemporary U.S. is not quite as simple as this proposition might indicate. The growing individual is most certainly confronted with multiple role model possibilities. He is unlikely to know precisely what his father does when he is away from home, but he may think he knows what the football coach or the movie actor does. That is, the son is aware of his father's home behavior, but not his economic or extra-home role. On the other hand, daughters appear almost as likely to identify with their mothers today as in the colonial family. The intensity of their interaction—frequently greater than in the colonial family, due to smaller families today—virtually offsets the influence of competing agents of socialization outside the home. Therefore, one major change from the colonial family to today's family is the weaker identification of sons with their father's role behaviors.

Even this difference must be qualified, however. The foregoing discussion had focussed upon positional identification, making the point that the range of possible role identifications between son and father is much more limited today, since many facets of the father's role are played elsewhere. Forms of personal identification between a son and his father, however, are quite prevalent today. There may be identification with a general characteristic of one's father, such as his success, or an aspect of his character, such as his honesty. Yet, on the whole, the proposition still holds: The modelling of day-to-day behavior after members of the nuclear family is somewhat less likely today than in the colonial family. In fact, precisely where the individual will find his role models, and whether or not they will reinforce one another, is problematic.[17]

This leads to an interesting point of speculation: If finding adequate sources of identification is currently more difficult than it was in the colonial family, can we conclude that ego struggle is, therefore, easier? Once again, the conclusion is not quite that simple. The colonial child, we have said, was given time free from supervision; in this way he resembled the Hutterite teenager with his cigarettes, movie magazines, and radio. Yet, in both of these instances, the intensity of the role models was such that the socializing agents were confident that the growing individual would internalize his group's standards and eventually cease to dabble in alternatives. In other words, the child might perceive himself as having substantial freedom, not realizing that the lack of clear-cut alternatives and the intensity of relations with significant others prevent ego struggle from ever really becoming an issue.

Ego struggle *is* an issue in the modern industrial world; but it is not necessarily an easy one. Parents are often quite successful in altering the child's unique development. They may, in some instances, dominate a child for the satisfaction of having someone to dominate. You may have seen cartoons in which the father has taken a beating from his superiors at work, and upon arriving home, finds occasion to spank or scold his son. Or a parent may demand excessive achievement on the child's part in order to compensate for his own mediocre accomplishments, thus helping to solve his own (the parent's) identity problems. Ambitions that were thwarted in the father's youth, in athletics for example, may be achieved through his offspring. Or—and this is a criticism often levelled at the middle-class mother—the parent may be so devoted to the child and attentive to his every need as to overprotect and, thus, thwart the child's unique development of his potentialities. To conclude by saying that ego struggle was the greater problem in the colonial family, and that today it is identification, would be an oversimplification. Due to a lack of awareness of adequate alternatives, ego struggle was not recognized as a problem in the colonial family. Neither is it the case that parents today limit themselves to simply presenting alternatives and teaching their children how to think critically in order to make their own behavioral decisions. On the contrary, parents are still quite concerned to "orderly replace" their culture in their offspring, but the impinging of alternatives limits their ability to do so. The result is that identification is more problematic today than it was in the colonial family; ego struggle is more possible today, but is kept problematic by the conscious awareness of alternatives weighed against the indoctrinating efforts of parents and other socializing agents. Intrapersonal and interpersonal adjustment, when placed in an historical context, are quite closely related to the questions of identification and ego struggle just discussed. Both philosophical and empirical analyses have referred to a change in socialization emphasis over time toward more concern with interpersonal adjustment.[18] In colonial days, the behavioral standards of one's parents and other ancestral models were generally internalized and reinforced by one's experiences. When the individual did encounter divergent expectations, it was assumed that he would behave according to his internalized standards, i.e., his preferred self-concept based on strong identifications. In contemporary society, however, parents have learned by their own experiences that, in order to be a successful member of society, one must be adaptable and flexible. In addition, most of the old behavioral absolutes have been called into question on what are assumed to be rational bases. Therefore, Miller and Swanson feel that today's "bureaucratic-type" parents have as their major socializing principle teaching their child how to get along. The child

> must learn to produce a relationship that uses the symbols of genuine friendship as its currency without the actual commitment of the real thing. He must learn to be a "nice guy"—affable, unthreatening, responsible, competent, adaptive. It is this kind of skill in which the parents must train him.[19]

When it comes to a choice between following one's internalized standards and the demands of others, today's child is taught to follow the latter. This does not mean, as Melvin Kohn cautions, that socialization today undermines self-direction.[20] Rather, the interpretation must be phrased to indicate that the preferred self-concept itself includes as a major element getting along with people, fitting in, and cooperating. The individual in American society has changed, says David Riesman, from being inner-directed, with behavior based upon a preferred self-concept drawn from ancestral models, to being other-directed, with behavior based on conforming to the expectations of one's peers.[21] Riesman does not mean, as some have interpreted him, that today people worry about what others think while formerly they did not. Instead, the issue is who the others are whose opinions and expectations influence us. In an earlier day it was the family and those of the ascending generation (often persons no longer alive) who tended to dominate; today it is presumably whatever group the individual is a part of at the moment.

Riesman's ideas are intuitively appealing but have been somewhat difficult to test empirically. Thus, our conclusions, while consistent with much historical information on American socialization, should be thought of as tentative. The data are too sparse and are drawn together from too many sources to be considered final. One further qualification on the foregoing generalizations concerns the subcultural differences in socialization that can be found in United States society. These require some specification.

Middle-class and Lower-class Styles of Socialization Compared

We have already noted the substantial differences in life style between the affluent masses of American society—the middle classes—and the lower classes, who must strive to maintain an economic subsistence level. Only brief mention was made of the working classes, that large aggregate of manual workers who enjoy stable employment and a standard of living that includes many of the luxuries that characterize the affluent. Once again, in this section we shall begin by comparing the middle and lower classes, but we shall subsequently bring in the working classes.

Available evidence from studies conducted over a 35- to 40-year period indicates that the following are some of the more important differences between middle-class and lower-class socialization. (See Table 2.) Middle-class parents have consistently been found to be more emotionally warm and expressive toward their child, showing pleasure in him and generally bolstering his sense of self-esteem. This difference is particularly acute in the case of fathers; Kohn has described the role of the middle-class father thus:

> Middle-class mothers want their husbands to be supportive of the children (especially of sons), with their responsibility for imposing restraints being of decidedly secondary importance. . . . Most middle-class fathers agree with their wives and play a role close to what their wives would have them play.[22]

TABLE 2
Some Differences between Middle-class and Lower-class Socialization

Aspects of Socialization	Middle Class	Lower Class
Parental warmth and demonstration of affection	High	Low
Role of father	Supportive of child	Little role in socialization
Style of verbal communication	Reasoning and discussion	Much use of commands
Basis for discipline	Behavioral intent	Behavioral consequences
Use of physical punishment	Moderately low	High
Tolerance of children's impulses	High	Moderately low
Demand for responsible independence	High	Moderately low

SOURCES: These are brought together from numerous sources; among them are: Urie Bronfenbrenner, "Socialization and Social Class Through Time and Space," in Eleanor E. Maccoby, Theodore M. Newcomb, and Eugene L. Hartley, eds., *Readings in Social Psychology* (New York: Henry Holt, 1958), pp. 400–25; Kohn, "Social Class and Parent-Child Relationships: An Interpretation," *American Journal of Sociology*, 68 (1963), 471–80; Grace F. Brody, "Socioeconomic Differences in Stated Maternal Child-Rearing Practices and in Observed Maternal Behavior," *Journal of Marriage and the Family*, 30 (1968), 656–60; Arthur Besner, "Economic Deprivation and Family Patterns," in Lola M. Irelan, ed., *Low-Income Life Styles,* Department of Health, Education, and Welfare, Welfare Administration Publication No. 14 (1966), pp. 15–29; Urie Bronfenbrenner, "The Changing American Child—A Speculative Analysis," *Journal of Social Issues,* 17 (1961), 6–18; E. E. Maccoby and P. K. Gibbs, "Methods of Child-Rearing in Two Social Classes," in W. E. Martin and C. E. Stendler, eds., *Readings in Child Development* (New York: Harcourt Brace, 1954), pp. 380–96; Melvin L. Kohn and Eleanor E. Carroll, "Social Class and the Allocation of Parental Responsibilities," *Sociometry,* 23 (1960), 372–92; Catherine S. Chilman, "Child-Rearing and Family Relationships of the Very Poor," *Welfare in Review* (1965), pp. 9–19. Additional references can be found in Chilman's article and in Bronfenbrenner's paper in *Readings in Social Psychology.*

The lower-class husband, on the other hand, ordinarily plays a minor role in child-rearing and, as Rainwater points out, "often his wife prefers it that way."[23] The support the middle-class father offers takes many forms: discussing events and goals, helping with homework, teaching skills, as well as complimenting and encouraging his child. There is, however, an apparent middle-class bias present in the conclusions regarding warmth in the family. If, as some feel, the lower-class nuclear family is more embedded personnel-wise in its social network than is the middle-class family, then emotional warmth for the lower-class child may not be less; it may simply be more dispersed, coming from a grandmother or other extra-familial member of the social network.

In middle-class families, a great deal of emphasis is placed upon the development and use of verbal skills. Lower-class parents are less likely to live and work in the realm of ideas, or to give substantial attention to explanation, reasoning, and understanding of motives. This holds for interaction with children as well as between husband and wife. It takes not only inclination but *time* to reason and discuss; the middle-class tendency is reinforced by the likelihood of there being a smaller number of children, giving parents more time to spend with each one, and by the greater likelihood that the middle-class mother will be a full-time housewife. In the lower-class family, lack of both verbal skills and time combine to increase the use of commands and physical response.

A key area in which the foregoing difference appears is child discipline. In the first place, the basis for discipline tends to hinge on the question of behavioral intent in the middle class, while in the lower class it is predicated upon behavioral consequences. The middle-class parent is concerned with the motives of the child rather than strictly with the negatively-defined outcomes of specific behavior. By way of illustration, let us suppose that a six-year-old child turns over his glass of milk. An immediate attempt is made by the middle-class parent to assess his intent. Did he spill the milk because he was trying to cut up his own meat? If so, encourage him. Did he turn it over because he was angry at having beans for supper? Then he must be scolded or punished. The decision regarding behavioral intent must be made almost spontaneously, therefore, it is possible that the parent may make a mistaken assessment. The lower-class parent, when faced with the same situation, defines this behavior by the six year old as punishable, since it is disruptive of routine and damaging to furniture, as well as indicating lack of control. A second difference in discipline concerns the use of physical punishment. Middle-class parents usually employ reasoning, shame, and sometimes a threat of love withdrawal, while lower-class parents are more likely to respond in a more physical manner. The last two class differences in socialization to be discussed are middle-class parents' greater tolerance of children's impulses and spontaneous outbursts and their greater demand for responsible independence. Lower-class parents are likely to punish impulsive behavior when it occurs, but their style of socialization and discipline is not an effective deterrent and, in fact, may foster the behavior it aims to control. An important distinction is captured by the term "responsible independence." By this is meant self-reliance, learning how to do things for yourself —but always within the bounds of the middle-class value system. The middle-class parent is excited when his child learns to tie his shoes at age four, to make his bed and put his clothes away, to set up a stand and sell lemonade. All these are signs of responsible or, to use Farber's term, "sponsored" independence. For the lower-class parent, a crucial element in socialization might be called freedom or "unsponsored independence."[24] Robert Sears *et al.* argued that earlier findings "of greater freedom of movement for the lower-class child were more properly interpreted not as 'permissiveness' but as 'a reflection of rejection, a pushing of the child out of the way.' "[25] To overstate it, the child is simply turned out with the expectation that he will return home when he is hungry, sleepy or injured. This approach on the part of lower-class parents, incidentally, is one of the historical connections between the modern subsistence-level urban family and the American subsistence farm of the past. In both instances, as noted in Chapter VI, when the child was not carrying out his family responsibilities, he was generally unsupervised. The major difference is in the proportion of free time available. Agrarian family economic endeavor and division of labor ordinarily left the growing individual with only a fraction of his time to himself. Urban lower-class life leaves the child with far less family responsibility and, thus, with much more time to spend in unsponsored independence, or staying out of the way.

How does the pattern of socialization in the working class (here defined as those families in which the husband is a stably employed manual worker with some skill) differ from the middle-class and lower-class models sketched above? At the outset, one must be aware of the inherent difficulties with the literature on working- and lower-class families. Some studies have used the terms almost interchangeably, while others have used "working class" to designate both working and lower classes. Nevertheless, the evidence, to the extent that it can be differentiated, points to the following distinctions. If middle-class socialization is best characterized by independence, interchange, and affection, and lower-class socialization by freedom and discipline, working-class socialization is oriented toward *respectability*—a concern with limits, neatness, and control. Consistently, Bronfenbrenner asserts, the working-class parent has "emphasized what are usually regarded as the traditional middle-class virtues of cleanliness, conformity, and control. . . ."[26] In addition, the mother, rather than desiring her working-class husband to stay out of the way or to be merely supportive, wishes him to help her with the directive function. This, however, he is generally unwilling to do. Kohn explains it thus:

> It is not that they (working-class fathers) see the constraining role as less important than do their wives, but that many of them see no reason why they should have to shoulder the responsibility. From their point of view, the important thing is that the child be taught what limits he must not transgress. It does not matter much who does the teaching, and since mother has primary responsibility for child care, the job should be hers.[27]

Although the differences between middle-class, lower-class, and working-class socialization appear to have remained over the 30- to 40-year period during which the studies have been carried out, the gap between middle- and working-class styles appears to be narrowing. To some extent, this may be a function of the rise in standard of living among the stable working classes. Bronfenbrenner, however, feels that the narrowing is due to the fact that the working-class parent is making more use of middle-class techniques and sources of information, thus reducing the cultural difference between them:[28] These sources include child-care manuals such as *Infant Care* and Benjamin Spock's *Baby and Child Care*, to which we shall refer below. Some have even coined the term "middle mass" to incorporate the skilled and stable working classes and the less affluent segments of the middle class, e.g., salesmen and clerks.[29] Yet Brody's and other studies in the late 1960's continue to produce sufficient differences to justify—at least temporarily—the continued use of middle-class, working-class, and lower-class models.

A study by Arnold Green is an excellent point of departure for linking middle- and lower-class differences in socialization with the earlier discussions of identification and personality integration.[30] Middle-class parents ordinarily have more socioeconomic rewards to offer and grant more affectional rewards to their children than do lower-class parents. Since reward is related to identification, it follows that identification with parents is more likely in the middle-class family. There are, however, some peculiar problems of personality integration presented by the middle-class family setting. Remember that independence is demanded of the middle-class child, especially the male; that the child is in an affectionate family setting; and that punishment is characterized by shame and by the threat of love withdrawal. According to Green, if all of these elements are strong, this approach to socialization may confront the individual with the possibility of neurosis. Though he never defines it, the neurosis of which Green speaks is nothing more than an undercurrent of anxiety and nervous upset, resulting from a combination of a somewhat confused self-concept and the internalized threat of love withdrawal. In most cases of such neurosis, the individual continues to function in society, but is unduly worried about himself, his responsibilities and role, about others, or about the world in abstraction. How does this neurosis develop?

The child is taught and expected by his mother to be loving and responsive, and is thus bound to her by a close emotional tie. Yet punishment often centers in that very love relationship, so that the child in his early years is made to feel that being loved is dependent upon acting in a certain way—upon good or almost perfect behavior. Furthermore, in the case of the male child, both parents, but particularly the father, expect him to be aggressive and competitive outside the home, while his home environment stresses giving, consideration, and affection. Thus, the gelling of his self-concept, of what he is and wants to be, is made difficult. This is not to say that more than a small fraction of middle-class families produce neurotic offspring. The point is, however, that when middle-class socialization *does* cause a problem, intrapersonal maladjustment is the direction it is likely to take.

Included in Green's study was a brief comparison of middle-class socialization with socialization in the homes of recent Polish immigrants in the coal mining areas of Pennsylvania. Punishment in these homes was found by Green to be haphazard, overt, and spontaneous. Unsponsored freedom for the child is maximized and neurosis, or conflict within the self, is averted. Though Green does not pursue the comparison, it would seem to follow that, in a situation of spontaneous and often antagonistic human relations, personality adjustment problems are more likely to be interpersonal than intrapersonal.

At least one study has verified the conclusion that problems in middle-class personality development tend to take the form of intrapersonal neuroses, while the more usual forms personality disorders take in the lower class are interpersonal neuroses and character disorders.[31] Elsewhere, however, both inter- and intrapersonal adjustment difficulties have been found to be more prevalent in the lower-class family. Yet, apart from consideration of differences between the middle class and lower class, it does seem that when middle-class socialization causes the individual problems, they tend to be of an intrapersonal nature. The reader is left to pursue, on his own, considerations of schizophrenia, violence, and other forms of maladjustment suggested by the foregoing discussion.

Rearing by the Book

The orderly replacement of family culture from one generation to the next is most easily accomplished in a society that looks to ancestral models for authority, wisdom, and guidance. In the United States of the 1960's, however, Dr. Spock and *Parents' Magazine* have been extremely successful in "displacing grandmother as the authority on child development."[32] The result of looking to our peers or contemporaries for guidance, as Martha Wolfenstein so beautifully demonstrates, is that, instead of receiving accumulated and relatively unchanging advice, the American parent tends to get advice that fluctuates with the latest fad. She shows how, in 1890, the dominant viewpoint was to indulge the child; by 1920, scheduling and a certain aloofness predominated; and, by 1945, indulgent mothering was once again recommended.[33]

This swing of the pendulum is actually between two viewpoints regarding the nature and development of the child. These viewpoints are labelled the "traditional" and "developmental" by Evelyn Duvall.[34] The traditional view, which has some of its roots in Puritan ideology, reached its greatest strength during the Victorian era in Great Britain; this view sees the necessity of curbing the child's impulses. He is less wise than his parents, so the reasonable form of socialization should stress nuclear family values and obedience and reserve on the child's part. A typical reaction to the offspring who deviates from his family's expectations would be: "He is the black sheep *of the family*." The developmental view, expounded by Freud, John B. Watson, John Dewey and others, presents the idea that the child should be allowed to develop his own potentialities at his own speed and in his own way, thus maximizing creativity and uniqueness. This latter approach, of course, fits well this society's emphasis upon newness, creativity, change, and individualism. A typical reaction to an offspring's deviance is: "Where did we go wrong?" or "Where did we fail *him?*" In fact, the traditional and developmental emphases in socialization are closely related to personnel embeddedness in the nuclear family and individualism, respectively. It is not surprising that the over-all long-range trend has been—although there have been fluctuations—toward the developmental, or individualistic, position.[35] It cannot, however, be concluded that individualism now predominates in U.S. society, but rather that the two views are currently vying for ascendency.

In the next chapter, we move to a consideration of the period of adolescence; our summary of socialization will appear at the close of that discussion.

NOTES

[1] Margaret Mead, *Sex and Temperament* (New York: New American Library, Mentor Books, 1950 ed.), p. 191.

[2] For a good discussion of socialization after childhood, see Orville G. Brim, Jr., and Stanton Wheeler, *Socialization After Childhood: Two Essays* (New York: Wiley & Sons, 1966).

[3] On the first two, see Frederick Elkin, *The Child and Society* (New York: Random House, 1960), pp. 10–11.

[4] Mead, *Sex and Temperament*, p. 190.

[5] For a discussion of the range of cultural values in American society, and conflicts between these values, see Robin M. Williams, Jr., *American Society: A Sociological Interpretation* (New York: Knopf, 1960 ed.), Chaps. 10–14.

[6] On the Cheyenne, an excellent source is G .B. Grinnell, *The Cheyenne Indians: Their History and Ways of Life*, 2 vols. (New Haven, Conn.: Yale University Press, 1923).

[7] The latter point is well made in Dennis H. Wrong, "The Oversocialized Conception of Man in Modern Sociology," *American Sociological Review*, 26 (1961), 183–93.

[8] For a brief discussion of the three theories, see Elkin, *The Child and Society*, pp. 18–44. For a lengthier discussion, see Morton Deutsch and Robert M. Krauss, *Theories in Social Psychology* (New York: Basic Books, 1965), Chaps. 4–6.

[9] An approach to personality or self-concept formation that diverges from ours, but which is nevertheless interesting, is Bingham Dai, "A Socio-Psychiatric Approach to Personality Organization," *American Sociological Review*, 17 (1952), 44–49.

[10] Charles H. Cooley, *Human Nature and the Social Order* (New York: Scribner's, 1902), p. 184.

[11] George H. Mead, *Mind, Self and Society* (Chicago: University of Chicago Press, 1934), pp. 154f.

[12] John Bowlby, *Child Care and the Growth of Love* (London: Penguin, 1953); Theodore R. Sarbin, and Donal S. Jones, "Intrapersonal Factors in Delinquency: A Preliminary Report," *Nervous Child*, 11 (1955), 23–27.

[13] Durkheim's brief discussion of fatalistic suicide might be interpreted to include such an instance of oppressive demands and a strong sense of guilt. See Emile Durkheim, *Suicide* (New York: Free Press, 1951), p. 276.

[14] Robert F. Winch, *Identification and Its Familial Determinants* (Indianapolis: Bobbs-Merrill, 1962), p. 142.
[15] Winch, *Identification and Its Familial Determinants;* David B. Lynn, "The Process of Learning Parental and Sex-Role Identification," *Journal of Marriage and the Family,* 28 (1966), esp. 446–70; Orville G. Brim, Jr., "Family Structure and Sex-Role Learning by Children," *Sociometry,* 21 (1958), 1–16.
[16] Robert F. Winch, *The Modern Family* (New York: Holt, Rinehart and Winston, 1963 ed.), p. 480.
[17] Portions of the preceding discussion are adapted from Winch's ideas in *Identification and Its Familial Determinants.* On measuring parental identification, see S. W. Gray and R. Klaus, "The Measurement of Parental Identification," *Genetic Psychology Monographs,* 54 (1956), 87–114.
[18] See, for example, Daniel Miller and Guy Swanson, *The Changing American Parent* (New York: Wiley & Sons, 1958); Frank Musgrove, *The Family, Education, and Society* (London: Routledge and Kegan Paul, 1966); David Riesman, Nathan Glazer, and Reuel Denney, *The Lonely Crowd* (New Haven, Conn.: Yale University Press, 1950).
[19] Miller and Swanson, *The Changing American Parent,* p. 203.
[20] Melvin L. Kohn, "Social Class and Parent-Child Relationships: An Interpretation," *American Journal of Sociology,* 68 (1963), 476.
[21] Riesman et al., *The Lonely Crowd.*
[22] Kohn, "Social Class and Parent-Child Relationships: An Intepretation," p. 479.
[23] Lee Rainwater, *Family Design: Marital Sexuality, Family Size, and Contraception* (Chicago: Aldine, 1965), p. 60.
[24] Bernard Farber, *Family: Organization and Interaction* (San Francisco: Chandler, 1964), pp. 367–78.
[25] Referred to in Bronfenbrenner, "Socialization and Social Class Through Time and Space," p. 401.
[26] *Ibid.,* p. 423.
[27] Kohn, "Social Class and Parent-Child Relationships: An Interpretation," p. 479.
[28] Bronfenbrenner, "Socialization and Social Class Through Time and Space," p. 420.
[29] On the middle-mass concept, see Bennett M. Berger, *Working-Class Suburb* (Berkeley and Los Angeles: University of California Press, 1960), p. 96; Richard F. Curtis, "Differential Association and the Stratification of the Urban Community," *Social Forces,* 42 (1963), 72; Bert N. Adams and James E. Butler, "Occupational Status and Husband-Wife Social Participation," *Social Forces,* 45 (1967), 503, 506–7.
[30] Arnold W. Green, "The Middle-Class Male Child and Neurosis," *American Sociological Review,* 11 (1946), 31–41.
[31] August B. Hollingshead, "Factors Associated with Prevalence of Mental Illness," in Eleanor E. Maccoby, Theodore M. Newcombe, and Eugene L. Hartley, eds., *Readings in Social Psychology* (New York: Henry Holt, 1958), 425–36. See also August B. Hollingshead and F. C. Redlich, *Social Class and Mental Illness* (New York: Wiley & Sons, 1958), for a fuller account.
[32] Robert F. Winch, *The Modern Family* (New York: Holt, Rinehart and Winston, 1963 ed.), p. 448.
[33] Martha Wolfenstein, "Trends in Infant Care," *American Journal of Orthopsychiatry,* 23 (1953), 120–30.
[34] Evelyn M. Duvall, "Conceptions of Parenthood," *American Journal of Sociology,* 52 (1946), 193–203.

[35] There is some question regarding the period since 1950. Wolfstein and Winch feel that there has been some movement away from indulgence and permissiveness toward order and control. Michael Gordon, however, finds no such change in *Infant Care* or in Dr. Spock's manual, though he admits that it may have occurred in popular periodicals. Michael Gordon, "*Infant Care* Revisited," *Journal of Marriage and the Family*, 30 (1968), 578–83.

VIII

Adolescence

ADOLESCENCE IS A CULTURE-BOUND AND RECENT PHENOMENON UPON WHICH OPINION IS DIVIDED REGARDING BOTH ITS SIGNIFICANCE AND ITS AGE-BOUNDARIES. SOME OF THE IDEAL-TYPICAL VIEWS OF THE ADOLESCENT EMPHASIZE HIS IDEALISM, HIS HONESTY, HIS REBELLION, HIS SEARCH FOR RECOGNITION, OR HIS IRRESPONSIBILITY. CURRENT ATTEMPTS TO ASCERTAIN THE FACTS ABOUT ADOLESCENCE IN THE UNITED STATES FOCUS ON SUCH ASPECTS AS THE EMANCIPATION PROCESS, THE NOTION OF A "YOUTH CULTURE," AND THE GENERATION GAP. THE COLLEGE ADOLESCENT, DUE TO HIS LENGTHY POSTPONEMENT OF ADULT STATUS, IS OF PARTICULAR INTEREST. THE CHAPTER CLOSES WITH THE AUTHOR'S RECONCILIATION OF THE CONFLICTING DEFINITIONS OF ADOLESCENCE AND A GENERAL SUMMARY OF SOCIALIZATION IN THE UNITED STATES.

An adolescent is an individual defined by his society as too old to be a child and too young to be an adult. The answer to the question "What is adolescence?" has been stated in physiological, emotional, intellectual, and cultural terms. To some, it is fundamentally the period of *incipient physiological maturity*. Rapid growth, glandular activity, and surface bodily changes give the adolescent his unique character. For others, adolescence is primarily *emotional*. It is the period of emotional intensity, internal stress, and ambivalence during which former interpersonal commitments are tested. Still others see it as basically *intellectual*, involving idealism and the questioning of the value systems and behavior of the older generation. Finally, there are some who define it *culturally*, as a period of fads and cultural limbo following physical maturity and preceding adult status. How do these four definitions fit the data on adolescence? The answer to this question must await the completion of our discussion.

Adolescence as a period of physical maturation has, of course, always existed; adolescence as defined in terms of emotions, intellect, and culture is felt by F. Musgrove and others to be a phenomenon of recent centuries. "The adolescent as a distinct species,"

Musgrove asserts, "is the creation of modern social attitudes and institutions."[1] As recently as the time of Alexis de Tocqueville, i.e., the early 1800's, the young, vigorous, expanding United States could give its young social tasks and roles.[2] Now, however, the adolescent is produced by being "excluded from responsible participation in affairs, rewarded for dependency, penalized for inconvenient displays of initiative, and so rendered sufficiently irresponsible to confirm the prevailing teenager-stereotype."[3] He is made into an ineffectual outsider.

Not only is the adolescent (according to the authors quoted above), a product of recent history, but (according to others, such as Margaret Mead) he is also culture-bound. The Samoan girl, says Mead, painlessly, quietly "slips from childhood into womanhood, loitering by the way, doing her share of the family work, but guarding herself against a reputation for too great proficiency which might lead to early marriage."[4] Instead of being the most stressful period in the Samoan girl's life, it is perhaps the most pleasant time she will ever know. The patterns observed in both Samoa and Dobu suggest that "adolescence is not necessarily a period of stress and strain, that these familiar and unlovely symptoms flow from cultural anxieties."[5] That is, the problems by which we tend to define the period are aspects of American civilization, not of youth in general—and physiological changes alone cannot account for this variation.

But what of the adolescent period in the United States; what are its boundaries? Neither sociological nor physiological criteria are entirely unambiguous or satisfactory in defining its scope. The beginning of adolescence may, without great distortion, be considered synonymous with the onset of puberty. Yet one must decide which physiological changes to treat as most basic. While the appearance of pubic hair, or the growth of the female's breasts might be used, a frequently employed index of the onset of puberty is first ejaculation by the male and first menses for the female. Even such an unambiguous criterion as the latter, coming ordinarily about the twelfth year of life, has been found by Alfred Kinsey *et al.* to range from age nine to age twenty-five.[6]

Determination of the end of adolescence is even more difficult. For certain high-status families in American society it might be the debut, coming anywhere between 17 and 22 years of age. For the masses, however, possible criteria might include graduation from high school, graduation from college, entering military service, beginning one's first full-time job, moving out of the parental home, and marriage. All these factors cannot coincide, and there is no ceremony marking the assumption of adult status. Therefore, the passage from adolescence into adulthood is more a gradual occurrence than an abrupt or clearly demarcated transition. If two or three factors, such as college graduation, marriage, and the first full-time job, do coincide, the end of adolescence may be fairly clear-cut. Yet adolescence continues to be something of a vague concept in its empirical referent; perhaps the very ambiguity of its duration and nature increase the difficulty of the period.

SECTION ONE

THE ADOLESCENT AS AN IDEAL-TYPE

The young person in American society has not yet assumed adult responsibilities; many adult observers believe that this fact makes it possible for him to do several things. First, as an outsider, the young person is typically perceived as playing the role of social critic. He desires honesty and, yet, finds many aspects of his complex society which are dishonest; as an idealist, he sees many inconsistencies in his society. The combination of idealism and honesty in the adolescent gives rise to a general despising of sham and pretense. In addition, he begins to move out from under the direct control of parents, teachers, and other authorities, but is not yet considered or allowed to be a responsible member of society. The need to rebel but to be supported, when coupled with irresponsibility, results in his being depressed by conformity, both in himself and in others. Finally, he seeks identity and recognition, to be somebody among his peers. According to the adult world, the typical adolescent is thus bothered by sham and pretense, by conformity, and by lack of recognition.

The little novel by J. D. Salinger, *Catcher in the Rye*, is a portrait of an adolescent who gets fed up with school and spends 36 hours at Christmastime wandering through the streets of New York City in search of something, namely himself.[7] Many adolescents can identify quite readily with the strivings of Holden Caulfield, the late-teenage star of the story, for it is possible to see exemplified in some of his experiences the ideal-typical problems believed to beset the adolescent. First, Holden Caulfield liberally dispenses the term "phonies" to describe those given to sham or pretense. Most pointed in this regard is his depiction of Christmas at Radio City:

> All these angels start coming out of the boxes and everywhere, guys carrying crucifixes and stuff all over the place, and the whole bunch of them—thousands of them—singing "Come All Ye Faithful" like mad. Big deal. I can't see anything religious or pretty about a bunch of actors carrying crucifixes all over the stage. When they were finished and started going out the boxes again, you could tell they could hardly wait to get a cigarette or something.[8]

Sally Hayes kept saying how beautiful it all was, and

> I said old Jesus probably would have puked if he could see it—all those fancy costumes and all. Sally said I was a sacrilegious atheist. I probably am. But the thing Jesus would've really liked would be the guy that plays the kettle drums in the orchestra.[9]

And Holden proceeds to describe the kettle drummer's sincerity and intensity.

Holden is depressed by authority and conformity, and often expresses this depression in the phrase "I could have puked." He tells of an old guy about 50 who came into his dormitory on Veteran's Day and wanted to see if his initials were still in the bathroom door.

> He kept talking to us the whole time, telling how the days he spent here were the happiest of his life, and giving us a lot of advice for the future and all. Boy, did he depress me! I don't mean he was a bad guy—he wasn't. But you don't have to be a bad guy to depress somebody—you can be a *good* guy and do it. All you have to do to depress somebody is give them a lot of phony advice while you're looking for your initials in some can door—that's all you have to do.[10]

In attempting to get out of the rut, Holden proposes to Sally Hayes that they get a car and go up to Massachusetts or Vermont and get a cabin and chop wood and live there. Sally replies: "You just can't *do* something like that."[11] With this he becomes depressed with Sally and soon leaves her behind.

Our "typical" adolescent appreciates sincerity, wants to escape from conformity and authority, and wants to be recognized. When his brother died, Holden smashed all the garage windows with his fist and could not attend the funeral because he was in the hospital himself. Once in a while Salinger allows his hero a moment of pleasure; it is almost always related to recognition and a certain amount of freedom from restraint. For example, he describes a "swell kid" in New York City as follows:

> He was walking in the street instead of on the sidewalk, but right next to the curb. He was singing and humming, and walking a straight line. He was just singing for the hell of it, you could tell. The cars zoomed by, brakes screeched all over the place, his parents paid no attention to him, and he kept on walking next to the curb and singing. . . . It made me feel better.[12]

How close is the ideal-typical picture of the American adolescent—with his honesty, idealism, rebellion, and irresponsibility—to reality? What is known of the adolescent's relations with parents and peers which might help us to discern the accuracy of the popular stereotypes? These questions are the subjects of Section Two.

SECTION TWO

ADOLESCENTS, PARENTS, AND PEERS

Adolescence as a process can be thought of as the movement from dependence upon and control by parents and other adults through a period of intensive peer group activity and influence and, finally, to the assumption of adult roles. Emancipation, youth culture, and the presumed generation gap are aspects of this process upon which much attention has been focussed.

Emancipation

Douvan and Adelson's description of the emancipation process is an excellent introduction to our discussion.

> The direction of adolescent growth is clearly toward emancipation from the family. The period begins with the child almost entirely dependent on the family, needing its say-so for what he can and cannot do, still tied to his parents emotionally, still clinging to their ideas and ideals. It ends with the child reaching adulthood, freer to make up his mind about what he will and will not do, holding (if he so wishes) his own beliefs and values, and if need be looking elsewhere than the family for love and support.[13]

TABLE 3

Levels of Independence in Relation to Different Aspects of Autonomy

Level of Independence	Rank in Various Aspects of Autonomy		
	Behavioral	Emotional	Value
Passive	Variable	Low	Low
Sponsored	High	High	Low
Unsponsored	High	High	High

The end result is the autonomous or independent individual; a careful reading of the above quotation yields three types of autonomy. First, there is *emotional* autonomy, as the individual gives up ties to his family and looks elsewhere for love, support, confidence, and so on. Second, as the individual achieves freedom to decide what he will and will not do he gains *behavioral* autonomy. Finally, the move from his parents' ideas and ideals toward his own beliefs and attitudes can be called *value* autonomy.[14]

Of course, not every individual moves through the emancipation process at the same speed nor with the same degree of completeness in all three areas of autonomy. Bernard Farber draws a distinction between sponsored and unsponsored independence. The former characterizes the individual whose emotional and behavioral independence develop within the bounds of the parental value system; the latter characterizes the individual who, in the course of achieving independence, rejects many parental values and performs acts that meet with parental disapproval. In addition, there is the adolescent who, while making certain behavioral decisions for himself, never really accomplishes either emotional or value autonomy. Thus, Farber's ideas and those of Douvan and Adelson might be related as in Table 3.[15]

Differences in level of independence are not distributed randomly within the American population, but are related to such factors as socioeconomic class and the individual's sex. Middle-class socialization, with its emphasis on warmth and affection and its supportive tendencies, yields primarily adolescents characterized by sponsored independence—as indicated in Table 2. Lower-class socialization, however, is less warm and more concerned with control and direction, the result being that in order to achieve independence, the lower-class adolescent is more likely to have to resort to unsponsored acts.[16]

Sex differences are equally noticeable in the literature on socialization. "In the sphere of emotional independence from the family, boys by and large outdistance girls."[17] College women, says Mirra Komarovsky, "are somewhat more attached to parents, less likely to make decisions contrary to the wishes of the parents, more frequently experience homesickness than is the case with the male undergraduates."[18] What these and other such references indicate is that, while the middle-class male is best characterized by sponsored independence, the middle-class female might be somewhat more inclined to remain passive, particularly in the area of emotional autonomy.

Another aspect of the emancipation process concerns confidence. Douvan and Adelson note that the adolescent boy who continues to rely on his parents for behavioral advice appears to be less confident than other boys. In a recent and as yet unpublished study of high school seniors, the author was able to trace the emancipation process from confident dependence upon one's parents to confidence in one's own ability to cope with various situations. Some of these seniors seemed perfectly calm about the prospect of graduating and either going to college or to work; but, upon further questioning, it became apparent that their confidence was actually in their parents' ability to handle things and to cushion all shocks. At the other extreme were a substantial minority of seniors who indicated a basic *self*-confidence and a respect for their parents on a virtually adult-to-adult basis. By far the largest number were, however, in midstream, expressing some desire for parental guidance and some lack of confidence both in themselves and in their parents' ability to handle new situations for them. Thus, assurance, or confidence, appears to be curvilinear during the emancipation process, moving from that invested in parents, through a period of uncertainty, and to mature confidence in oneself and appreciation of parents (see Figure 7). It is also noteworthy that more females were still at stage one and more males at stage three in this high school sample, a finding that is consistent with the sex differences reported above.

Youth Culture

Another important aspect of emancipation, or the movement toward autonomy, involves the peer group, the adolescent's age companions. Much debate has centered around the question: Is there a distinctive youth culture or not? For years the developing child thinks that everyone is pretty much like his parents. Then, in the pre-teen years, he becomes aware of differences, but is likely to

FIGURE 7

The Confidence of the Adolescent at Various Stages of the Emancipation Process

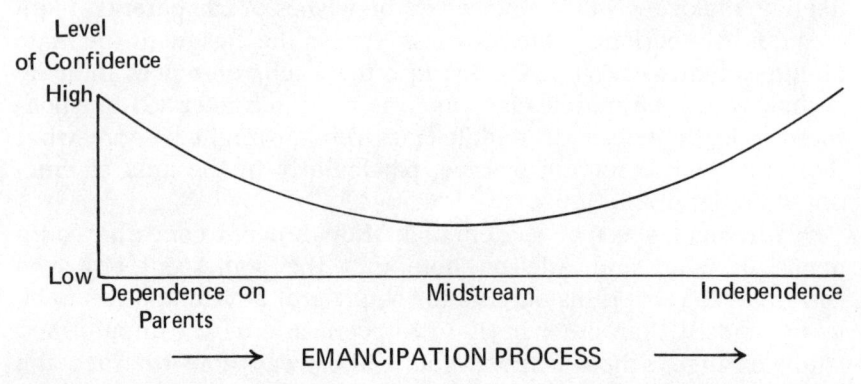

[Graph: U-shaped curve showing Level of Confidence (Low to High) on vertical axis and Emancipation Process (Dependence on Parents → Midstream → Independence) on horizontal axis]

be convinced by his parents that their ways are best. Now, in the adolescent years he discovers that rational criteria for saying that his parents' ways are best do not always hold up. The peer group defines its own standards, apart from the values of any single set of parents. These standards include concern with cars, sports, social activities, and popularity, and are often at odds with those values parents and school officials state they would like to see in young people. James Coleman, David Gottlieb and Charles Ramsey, and Gary Schwartz and Don Merten have written at length about these phenomena, which they call "youth culture."[19]

On the other side of the debate are those who argue that youth culture is a myth. Bennett Berger states that "there is absolutely no good body of data on adolescents, Coleman's included, which indicates the existence of a really deviant system of norms which govern adolescent life. . . ."[20] Those taking this side of the debate believe that youth culture is basically a sort of organized or patterned rebellion, the only genuine manifestations of which are fads that dabble in irrelevancies, while basic parental patterns and values remain intact.

As is the case in so many sociological debates, several authors have made great efforts to resolve the issue on some middle ground. Schwartz and Merten feel that the reality of a youth culture does not rest upon the repudiation or undermining of basic adult values. Rather, it is sufficient that youth experiment with and elaborate on "some of the partially unrealized or alternative possibilities in the adult moral order."[21] Gottlieb and Ramsey go even further in stating that the existence of a youth culture should not be predicated on its being in conflict with adult values.

> For us, differences may be sufficient but they are not necessary in investigating adolescent behavior. In the case of the adolescent the question is not deviation from some universal norm but rather how involvement in and commitment to the peer group influence the behavior and beliefs of the participant. Once we can pinpoint areas of influence and how they operate we will be better able to evaluate the meaning of adolescent cultures.[22]

Berger, they are saying, overstates the cruciality of differences; it is sufficient that adolescents find their own common denominators apart from the values and norms of any given set of parents or adults. David Friesen takes a slightly different approach to reconciling the debate. He finds that when students are asked about future-oriented and enduring values as distinct from the value needs of the high school system a different pattern emerges. The same students who affirm the importance of athletics and popularity within the social system of the high school assert that academic success is most important to their futures.[23] Coleman's results, Friesen finds, were not predicated either on the actual behavior of the high schoolers, nor upon what they felt would be important in the long run. It is possible, therefore, that the emphasis upon athletics and popularity may, in fact, be based upon the desire for new worlds to conquer among those already doing well scholastically. Or it may even be based to some extent on the "grass being greener" in some pasture other than that in which they now find themselves.

Although the present author would rather, for the sake of consistency, restrict use of the term "culture" for distinct differences in attitudes and values, let us for the moment accept Gottlieb and Ramsey's claim that the key is the extent to which the peer group defines its own standards. There are two reasons why the adolescent peer group must do this. First, society—meaning the adult world—does a poor job of defining roles for youth. The adolescent begins to drive at one age, drink at another, and vote at another. He is not yet wanted as an economic contributor, but his sex powers are developed and active. It is in the peer group that he must hammer out the relation between these factors. Thus, despite the fact that many parents and other adults are open to and desirous of intergenerational conversation, the young person is likely to feel that the adult world is responsible for his role dilemmas and, therefore, is unable to accept adult counseling in the solution of these dilemmas.

The second reason why the peer group must define its own standards is the social segregation of youth. Notice, in the following quotations, the use of terms that are virtually synonymous with the idea of segregation. "Youth," say Gottlieb and Ramsey, "are set apart. Only vaguely defined courses of action are recommended to them...."[24] Musgrove says his data are consistent with those

> American investigations which have shown adolescents belittled by their elders, regarded as a separate, inferior, and even threatening population, exposed to contradictory expectations and demands from the general body of adults, and consigned, as Hollingshead has said, to "an ill-defined no-man's land that lies between the protected dependency of childhood, where the parent is dominant, and the independent world of the adult, where the person is relatively free from parental controls."[25]

Historically, as in the case of the child, the treatment of the adolescent, not as an incipient adult, but as a distinct kind of person is a fairly recent phenomenon. In industrial society the growing individual is no longer of much value in the family's division of labor, nor is he needed in economic production. He is, therefore, age-segregated in the school system and community and left to define his activity and value patterns within the peer group. These patterns, however, ordinarily reflect what youth perceive to be the most basic, if unverbalized, values of the adult world. Popularity and material goods, such as cars, may be central to adolescent society, but perhaps the reason for this is that they are seen by young people to be of great importance in the adult world.

Adolescents, we have said, are segregated and allowed to define their own cultural forms within the peer group. As long as these activities take the form of recreation and study, and of inoffensive fads, they are condoned or at least permitted by the adult society. But when a few display an unwanted criticism of adult values, or when the fads are interpreted as symbolizing the questioning or rejection of society's dominant values, the result is suppression and the "belittling" of which Musgrove speaks.

What, then, are the significant conclusions to be drawn regarding youth culture and society, and what are their implications? Adolescents in general reflect adult values, with an overlay of supposedly distinctive youthful interests. Irresponsibility is forced upon them by adults; as long as they stay out of the way and continue preparing for "legitimate" adult roles, they are tolerated.

In other words, adolescents generally accept the dominant values and culture, but are not allowed into the dominant society in a responsible way. This, you may recall, is precisely the problem that has historically plagued racial minorities in the United States; the analogy between young people and blacks in the U.S. is most informative. The major difference is that adolescents are constantly being incorporated into the adult world and new ones are constantly entering the age group, while the racial minority is kept socially separate throughout the lifetime of the individual. Adolescents are, in short, currently more accurately described as a distinct society than as a distinct culture.

Conflict with Parents and the Generation Gap

Until now, we have referred to the prevalence of value similarity between adolescents and their parents, asserting that the crucial factor giving adolescence its character is the segregation of youth from adult society and concerns. There is a substantial body of literature on adolescence which stresses conflict between young people and their parents in the United States. Kingsley Davis begins by describing societal conditions under which parents and youth would not be in conflict. Stable rural society, with emancipation from parental authority marked by gradual and institutionalized steps, and with no great postponement of marriage and adulthood following puberty, is likely to be characterized by little parent-youth conflict. But American urban society, with its weak or unclear parental role models, much extra-familial socialization, rapid change, postponed adulthood, and individual choice of adult roles, is productive of intergenerational conflicts.[26]

One of these factors, rapid social and cultural change, means that within a generation, i.e., 20–25 years, there is historically significant change. Clifford Kirkpatrick, in his text, speaks of the breakdown of *one-way empathy* that results from the rapidity of change. By one-way empathy is meant the ability of one party to put itself in the other one's shoes, but not vice versa. The parent has already been an adolescent, but the adolescent has not yet been a parent. Yet, if the parent says, "I was once your age," the adolescent may respond or think to himself that things were different then. Youth may feel that a parent who danced the Charleston or Fox Trot in his or her youth simply could not understand the problems and struggles of Beatle-era youth. Thus, one-way empathy breaks down in the response of the young person that his parents' experiences and ideas are outdated, that "things were different then."

Another portion of parent-youth difficulties, Kirkpatrick claims, can be explained by the *clash of inferiority complexes.* Adolescents feel inferior because they lack experience and poise and because they know that they do. Overcompensation toward parents may mean that what is lacked in these respects is made up in defiance, aggressiveness, and pseudo-sophistication. On the other hand, parents often feel inferior because of an underlying impression that they really don't understand, because of a declining attractiveness and sex power in the face of youthful virility and attractiveness, and because of an awareness that in many cases they have achieved less than they had hoped to. Age, then, even without true wisdom, may be glorified because age is what the parent has. The combination of enforced authority without wisdom and defiance without poise may result in a circular and escalating conflict between the generations.[27]

Conflict there is, but what is its focus? Is it the ideologies and values of the older generation? Schwartz and Merten say "No." Open intergenerational conflict revolves, not so much around the values of the adult world, but around "the question of how much control adults rightfully can exercise over adolescents."[28] Since tolerance of adolescent deviance is limited at best, autonomy must be sought—as we said earlier—in minor acts of defiance toward adult authority.

The generation gap, according to these authors, is nothing more than the result of youthful rebellion against adult control. Yet it seems more complex than that. In the first place, there is no doubt that parents are attempting as much as ever before to implant their culture in their offspring. As Douvan and Adelson put it:

> . . . the American parent does not separate himself enough from the child; instead he will want to live in the child, excessively, trying to re-realize, in the child's freshness, in the opportunity to make a new life, his own lost autonomies.[29]

Ironically, however, the frantic attempt to control the thinking and behavior of the young is accompanied by the parents' perception that they are actually losing control, that there is a major cultural as well as social gap separating them from their children. Part of this perception is based upon the parents' own doubts about society's goals and values, which, however, they are unable to express actively because of their role commitments and life patterns of work, economic indebtedness, family, and leisure. Instead, such doubts are projected onto the uncommitted, the young, so that the adolescent fads are infused—from the adults standpoint—with sinister and symbolic implications for society's values. In short, a portion of the generation gap is based upon adult perception, doubt, and projection. That certain adults are aware of this is well illustrated in the following excerpt from a conference on the family held in the mid-1960's:

> Dr. Krech: "How much of the competition between the generations is in the mind of the perceiver?"
> Dr. Lee: "I would say this is its chief existence. . . ."
> Dr. Kirkendall: "I think that the extent to which this competition does exist may be a product in part of the extent to which parents and other adults feel it does."[30]

Projection and perception often result in what has been called the self-fulfilling prophecy. That is, if you talk and act as if something is true, the long-term result is likely to be the strengthening of those very conditions. The majority of youth do not desire an open break with their parents and other adults, but the combination of adult pressures for conformity, plus social segregation, plus pervasive adult concern about the value gap, tends to increase the very phenomena it seeks to control.

Besides adult perceptions and projections, there are aspects of adolescence in the contemporary United States which widen the gap. First, the mass media have made young people more aware than ever before of what is happening in the adult world from which they are systematically excluded. Second, events of the 1960's resulted in a vocal minority of adolescents taking direct issue with the perceived inconsistencies in the society. Furthermore, the repressive response of adult "authorities" to such criticism and protest has served only to enlist the support—both tacit and open—of formerly uninvolved youth.

At present, the vast majority of young people are still following the prescribed paths to societal position as defined by the dominant values of their society. The parent-youth conflict of which we speak is basically forced upon the adolescent if he is to gain behavioral autonomy instead of remaining passive. However, what was once almost entirely an adult-imposed *social* gap appears to be changing gradually to include cultural elements as well.

Much of the generation gap, in Douvan and Adelson's terms, can be traced to adult unwillingness to yield behavioral autonomy to adolescents because they are afraid it may include value autonomy (unsponsored independence) as well; that fear is gradually being realized. One way, perhaps, to summarize the current state of adolescence in the United States is to look briefly at the last stages of the emancipation process among those who postpone the traditional responsibilities of adulthood the longest: college students.

SECTION THREE

THE COLLEGE ADOLESCENT

One of the basic factors in adolescence, to which we referred at the beginning of this chapter, is the postponement of adulthood. An aspect of postponement that is descriptive of the college student is deferred gratification. This means putting off desires, such as going to work and perhaps getting married, for the sake of greater fulfillment later on.[31] The college student defers adulthood and gets a college education, it is often said, with the hope that it will "pay off" or increase his life chances in the long run.

Clearly, the dominant value orientation of the college population according to adult middle-class society is expected to be a form of sponsored independence. This is the orientation that sees education as utilitarian, with its major purpose being the obtaining of one's passport to society's affluence and goals. Social life, reasonably good grades, some influence on campus, kicks when they come: all these are means to the end of a law career, a corporation slot, or the finding of a good husband. Why should you stay in school, or why should you support the college of your choice? Because, says the TV ad, the college graduate will make $150,000 more in his lifetime than the non-college graduate. This is the educational motivation fostered by the mass educational system and the adult world: the student is there, very simply, to get a degree.

The same perspective on college students, which is based primarily on surface manifestations, concludes that there are two campus variations from the theme of sponsored independence: the activist and the retreatist. The former sees flaws and inconsistencies in the dominant culture and society and is seeking by various means to change them. The latter has truly "opted out" and is seeking fulfillment neither by a middle-class position nor by social reform, but by personal release and self-expression.

The sponsored, the activist, and the retreatist: such classification of college students is highly oversimplified despite its apparent usefulness to middle-class adults. It misses entirely the college students whom Kenneth Keniston calls the "apparently unalienated." These are the young people who go through college living by the rules—passing courses, buying new clothes, cheering at football games—but who, according to Keniston, "show a lack of deep commitment to adult values and roles. . . . Rather, they view the adult world they expect to enter with a subtle distrust, a lack of high expectations, hopes, or dreams, and an often unstated feeling that they will have to 'settle' for less than they would hope for if they let themselves hope."[32] On the surface they are living by middle-class society's goals and expectations; inside they are not really "sold" or committed. Nor does the threefold classification clarify the situation of those who, according to Berger and others, look like deviants because they are caught up in the "fads which dabble in irrelevancies," but are inwardly committed to the middle-class goals of success, material possessions, and a respectable life pattern. These "outward deviants," who are not really seriously questioning or rejecting adult culture, but merely biding their time until they are allowed in, are the basis for Edgar Friedenberg's claim that adolescents are vanishing in the U.S. They make it possible for many adults to "console" themselves with the observation concerning youthful activists that "in another ten years they will be using the same energy in selling encyclopedias." In other words, there are at least four definable types of college-age young people: (1) those internally and externally committed to middle-class values and norms; (2) Keniston's externally committed but internally questioning and uncommitted; (3) Berger and Friedenberg's externally uncommitted but internally committed; and (4) those who are both internally and externally questioning the middle-class system. It is quite possible that the second category predominates numerically, but the empirical classification of young people according to these types is of little consequence compared to the importance of understanding the significance of the categories themselves.[33]

SECTION FOUR

SOCIALIZATION AND ADOLESCENTS: SUMMARY AND CONCLUSIONS

We close the discussion of adolescence by returning to the question raised at the outset. How can the adolescent period in the U.S. best be characterized? Is it primarily the period of incipient physiological maturity, of emotional intensity and upheaval, of intellectual questioning, or of postponement-segregation-cultural limbo?

Since the first is a uniform human occurrence—while adolescence appears to be variable—physiological changes do not seem useful in defining the peculiar character of adolescence in United States society. In order to come to grips with the other three parts of the question, we must now recall the discussion of ego struggle and identification. It may be true that in colonial days identification was easy and ego struggle difficult; however, it must not be inferred from that statement that the opposite is the case today. Friedenberg, in *The Vanishing Adolescent* and other books, states his belief that the young person may be freer from parental domination than he was formerly, but that the school system has taken over the chore of squelching deviance—and, with it, creativity. The creative person, says Friedenberg, often gets in trouble, while the person who cooperates, works hard, and plays the role of the good school "organization man" is rewarded.[34] Musgrove, while agreeing that the adolescent has trouble with ego struggle, sees the school as basically an extension of parental demands.[35] Thus, the young person may be freer from actual parental domination, but he is not freer from the extension of parental domination into the school system. Regardless of their differences concerning the relation between family and school, both authors suggest that the contemporary child is not presented with clear and intense role models; neither does he receive support, in his ego struggle, from the key socializing agents. He is thus prepared for life as a chameleon, an other-directed man, who can adapt to many social and organizational settings, but who has not gained a clear picture of the kind of person he is.

This is, of course, a somewhat overdrawn characterization of the pitfalls in American socialization. It does, however, suggest that the process can cause the individual trouble with both identification and ego struggle. It is, simply, difficult for the individual to develop into a mature adult, with a clear self-concept.[36] A tentative answer to the definitional problem regarding adolescence would therefore be as follows. If we consider adolescence to be a period of intellectual questioning and idealism, then, in our society there are likely to be only a few adolescents—only a few who ever overtly question, even if they are not really committed to the dominant pattern. (We might, however, disagree on two counts with Friedenberg's assumption that they are "vanishing." First, there may never have been many young people who overtly questioned the dominant values during any earlier historical period. Second, if our preceding discussion is correct, the 1960's may have seen a substantial increase in their numbers.) Thus, the postponement of adult status following physiological maturity, when accompanied by social segregation and ill-defined cultural roles, is enough to cause the kind of emotional stress usually thought to characterize adolescence.[37]

How do the conclusions of Chapters VII and VIII relate to the socialization continuum presented in Chapter V? Orderly replacement of culture from parents to children is somewhat problematic, but not to the extent that socialization has been taken over by extra-familial agencies. Rather, many of these agencies should be viewed as extensions of parental influence and others as in competition with parents. In either case, because parents are concerned about the possibility of losing control of their children's development, they try very hard to control their behavior and influence their values. Though socialization is an extremely complex and multifaceted process, we might summarize by reproducing the continuum and indicating approximately where the author feels socialization in the contemporary U.S. should be located (see Figure 8). The reader should, of course, feel free to relocate this complex of factors wherever he believes the facts would warrant.

FIGURE 8

The Approximate Location of Socialization in the Contemporary U.S. on the Socialization Continuum

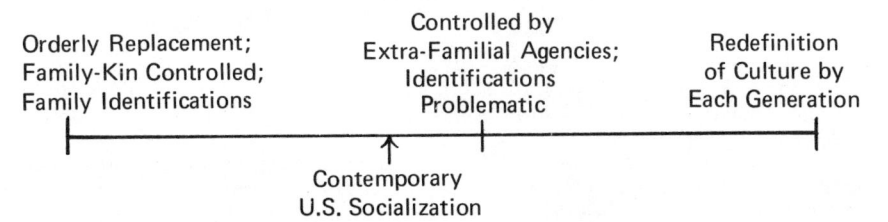

Orderly Replacement; Family-Kin Controlled; Family Identifications	Controlled by Extra-Familial Agencies; Identifications Problematic	Redefinition of Culture by Each Generation

↑
Contemporary
U.S. Socialization

One further aspect of the young person's emancipation, or movement from his family of orientation to his own family of procreation, involves heterosexual relations with peers. Therefore, in Chapters IX and X we turn our attention to dating, love, and mate selection in the U.S.

NOTES

[1] F. Musgrove, *Youth and the Social Order* (London: Routledge and Kegan Paul, 1964), p. 13.
[2] Elizabeth Douvan and Joseph Adelson, *The Adolescent Experience* (New York: Wiley & Sons, 1966), p. 127.
[3] Musgrove, *Youth and the Social Order*, p. 16.
[4] Margaret Mead, "Adolescence in Primitive and in Modern Society," in Eleanor E. Maccoby, Theodore M. Newcombe, and Eugene L. Hartley, eds., *Readings in Social Psychology* (New York: Henry Holt, 1958), p. 343.
[5] *Ibid.*, p. 347.
[6] Alfred C. Kinsey, et al. *Sexual Behavior in the Human Female* (Philadelphia: Saunders, 1953), p. 123.
[7] J. D. Salinger, *The Catcher in the Rye* (Boston: Little, Brown, 1945).
[8] *Ibid.*, p. 178.
[9] *Ibid.*
[10] *Ibid.*, p. 219.
[11] *Ibid.*, p. 171.
[12] *Ibid.*, p. 150.
[13] Douvan and Adelson, *The Adolescent Experience*, p. 125.
[14] *Ibid.*, p. 130.
[15] Farber's description of four independence levels, based upon combinations of sponsored and unsponsored independence, differs from Table 3. For his divisions, see Bernard Farber, *Family: Organization and Interaction* (San Francisco: Chandler, 1964), pp. 376–77.
[16] See Farber, *Family: Organization and Interaction*, pp. 369–70.
[17] Douvan and Adelson, *The Adolescent Experience*, p. 149.
[18] Mirra Komarovsky, "Functional Analysis of Sex Roles," *American Sociological Review*, 15 (1950), 513.
[19] See James S. Coleman, *The Adolescent Society* (New York: Free Press, 1961), p. 329; David Gottlieb and Charles Ramsey, *The American Adolescent* (Homewood, Ill.: Dorsey Press, 1964), p. 43; David Friesen, "Academic-Athletic-Popularity Syndrome in the Canadian High School Society (1967)," *Adolescence*, 3 (1968), 50; Kenneth Keniston, *The Uncommitted* (New York: Dell, 1960).
[20] Bennett Berger, "Adolescence and Beyond," *Social Problems*, 10 (1963), 395. See also Frederick Elkin and William A. Westley, "The Myth of the Adolescent Peer Culture," *American Sociological Review*, 20 (1955), 680–84.
[21] Gary Schwartz and Don Merten, "The Language of Adolescence: An Anthropological Approach to the Youth Culture," *American Journal of Sociology*, 72 (1967), 460.

[22] Gottlieb and Ramsey, *The American Adolescent*, p. 33.
[23] Friesen, "Academic-Athletic-Popularity," p. 40.
[24] Gottlieb and Ramsey, *The American Adolescent*, p. 249.
[25] Musgrove, *Youth and the Social Order*, p. 105.
[26] Kingsley Davis, "The Sociology of Parent-Youth Conflict," *American Sociological Review*, 5 (1940), 523–34.
[27] Clifford Kirkpatrick, *The Family: As Process and Institution* (New York: Ronald Press, 1963 ed.), pp. 266–67.
[28] Schwartz and Merten, "The Language of Adolescence," p. 459.
[29] Douvan and Adelson, *The Adolescent Experience*, p. 129.
[30] Seymour M. Farber, Piero Mustacchi, and Roger H. L. Wilson, eds., *Man and Civilization: The Family's Search for Survival* (New York: McGraw-Hill, 1965), p. 158.
[31] For a good discussion of deferred gratification and achievement, see Murray A. Straus, "Deferred Gratification, Social Class, and the Achievement Syndrome," *American Sociological Review*, 27 (1962), 326–35.
[32] Keniston, *The Uncommitted*, p. 396.
[33] Another classification of college students, developed by Martin Trow and Burton Clark in their essay, "Determinants of College Student Sub-Culture," divides them into vocational, non-conformist, academic, and collegiate. For a summary, see Gottlieb and Ramsey, *The American Adolescent*, p. 191.
[34] Edgar Friedenberg, *The Vanishing Adolescent* (New York: Dell, 1959).
[35] Frank Musgrove, *The Family, Education, and Society* (London: Routledge and Kegan Paul, 1966), p. 131.
[36] Of course, a portion of the reason for the self-concept problem or "identity crisis" that is so much discussed today is simply an increased emphasis in twentieth century America upon introspection and self-awareness. That is, the crisis is at least partially a result of the continual posing of the question: "Who am I?"
[37] For more on adolescence, see Glen Elder, "Adolescent Socialization and Development," in Edgar Borgatta and William W. Lambert, eds., *Handbook of Personality Theory and Research* (Chicago: Rand McNally, 1968), pp. 239–364, and the papers on youth in transition, in the proceedings of the American Orthopsychiatric Association, reported in the *American Journal of Orthopsychiatry*, 39 (1969), 181–227, 306–19.

IX

Premarital Relationships in the United States

DATING, A TWENTIETH CENTURY PHENOMENON ON THE AMERICAN SCENE, HAS BECOME SO PERVASIVE AS TO VIRTUALLY EMBODY THE CURRENT MATE SELECTION PROCESSES OF THE UNITED STATES. BESIDES RECREATION AND MATE SELECTION, DATING FUNCTIONS FOR SOCIALIZATION, EGO NEEDS, AND STATUS ACHIEVEMENT. SOME OF ITS MORE PROBLEMATIC ASPECTS INCLUDE PARENTAL INTRUSION, HETEROGENEOUS DATING, EMPHASIS ON PHYSICAL ATTRACTIVENESS, SOCIAL AWKWARDNESS, AND INSINCERITY. DUE TO BEHAVIORAL AND SUBSEQUENT ATTITUDE CHANGES, THE PROHIBITION OF PREMARITAL SEX HAS BEEN TRANSFORMED INTO A CULTURAL ALTERNATIVE IN MIDDLE-CLASS AMERICA, AND IS INCREASINGLY BECOMING A MATTER OF NON-MORAL INDIVIDUAL CHOICE.

One of the crucial tasks of the emancipation process during adolescence is the selecting of a mate and the establishing of one's family of procreation. Historically, three clearly definable approaches to mate selection and the heterosexual contacts that precede it can be discerned; each of these approaches is closely linked to one of the types of personnel embeddedness. The first, *arranged marriage*, is found most frequently in those societies or subsocieties in which the individual and nuclear family are embedded in the larger kinship group. Such marriages are arranged primarily for the purpose of fostering or strengthening the appropriate kin linkages and have definite economic overtones. Concern with domestic or individual happiness is strictly secondary.

The second and third approaches to mate selection are both based on individual choice, and are thus different in degree rather than in kind. Nevertheless, it is in this quantitative difference that dating as a basis for heterosexual relationships appears. *Restricted choice* occurs when the domestic unit is considered all-important, and when it is felt that the preferences of the individuals involved form the most adequate basis for establishing a sound unit. However, this choice has historically been restricted by several influences. One of these is the overt and expected intervention of parents in numerous ways, including the chaperoning of the heterosexual activity of teenagers. A second restrictive influence is the relative residential stability of the population, so that choice is made among persons with whom the individual has been acquainted most or all of his or her life. The third restriction is the length of time during which premarital relationships occur. The courtship period itself is quite brief, so that when a young person begins to bestow courtship attention upon a member of the opposite sex, it is assumed that he has "serious intentions." Thus, the choice takes place under the considerable influence of significant others, often within the bounds of lengthy acquaintance, and usually within the scope of a few months or years.

Open choice, of which there is no pure example in the world at present, would best characterize a situation of complete family subservience to individual needs and desires. This is exemplified in Farber's ideal-typical model of universal and permanent availability. According to this idea, all members of the opposite sex are potentially available to me for mating, with no "artificial" restrictions. Furthermore, they are permanently available, so that if my first attempt to find a satisfying relationship fails I am free to sever these ties and try again, for my individual needs and happiness are all-important.

The closest approximation to the open choice basis for mate selection is a result of historical developments within the United States. Prior to the twentieth century, the majority of courtships resembled fairly closely the "restricted choice" alternative. Most young people lived at home until an early marriage. Though mate choice was individual, adult expectations were that heterosexual contacts would occur under the watchful eye of parents; it often required ruses or subtle means to escape surveillance. Yet the seeds of change were present in the nineteenth century. Industrialization and mobility were increasing and higher education was expanding, a development that postponed adulthood. Particularly with the spread of co-education during the first 20 years of this century, increasing numbers of young people spent several unmarried years living away from home and parental supervision. While co-educational colleges were expected to assume a position *in loco parentis,* college adolescents had much less difficulty than those living at home in arranging rendezvous apart from adult supervision.

Concurrent with the spread of co-education in the United

States, the growth of cities and an advancing technology increased the number and types of places for urban entertainment, as well as improving the means for getting to them. Motion pictures, night clubs, theaters, sporting events; these and other places became ever more available to the unchaperoned young couple. Engagement in such activities came to be known as "dating," and was thought of as a form of recreation with little relation to courtship. The same opportunities were available to high school age people, but their young age plus the fact that they lived at home meant that it would be several more years before dating would be prevalent and acceptable at the high school level. Yet from this recent beginning under the influence of postponed adulthood, individual mobility, and urban entertainment, dating has come to be an ubiquitous and multipurpose aspect of premarital relationships in the United States. Let us, then, begin by examining its nature and functions.

SECTION ONE

THE NATURE AND FUNCTIONS OF DATING

The Dating Continuum

Geoffrey Gorer, an English anthropologist, describes American dating practices as a competitive game in which each side makes points; he concludes that "the ideal date is one in which both partners are so popular, so skilled, and so self-assured that the result is a draw."[1] One of the first sociological descriptions of dating produced in the United States, that of Willard Waller, is consistent both with Gorer's comments and with the early history of dating as a recreational pursuit. Waller described the "Rating and Dating Complex," based on research done at Pennsylvania State College in the early 1930's.[2] Dating, says Waller, is a "dalliance" relationship, a recreational activity; the qualities rated highly in a date—campus leadership, money, a car, and good clothes—are not the same as the personality- and character-based qualities desired in a mate.

Since Waller's article appeared in 1937, his distinction between courtship and dating (the former serious and the latter not) has apparently become increasingly inappropriate. Instead, it seems justifiable to replace it with the concept of a *dating contin-*

uum with various identifiable stages (casual dating, going steady, engagement) and with multiple purposes.

There are at least three reasons for this change in conceptualization. A first reason why the term "courtship," as distinct from dating, is less appropriate is that young people themselves don't use it. The teenage male seldom announces to his roommate or parents: "I'm going courting tonight," but rather "I have a date," or "I'm going out tonight." Courtship, when used in everyday speech, seems to have connotations of a bygone day.

Another reason why the word "dating" has incorporated the significance of the term "courtship" is its intensiveness and extensiveness within the teenage population. Not only is it no longer restricted to college students; dating has spread back into the pre-high-school years. Samuel Lowrie, in 1950–1951 studies involving over 2,800 midwestern high school and university students, found that dating experience had begun for the majority at ages 14 or 15.[3] Lowrie's students were predominantly of middle-class origins; during the 1950's and 1960's others reported the age at first date to be closer to 13 for the majority of middle-class youngsters, and about two years later in the working and lower classes. In a study of several hundred University of Wisconsin undergraduates carried out during 1966, the present author found that *regular* dating, as distinct from initial date, had begun at age 14 for the majority of the girls and at 15 for most of the boys. It seems likely, therefore, that Lowrie's 1950 research detected one point in the spread of dating, over four or five decades, from the college population back to the early teenage years. Dating, then, has become a primary activity for virtually all young people in the United States, covering for many of them a period of as many as ten years.

The third and perhaps most compelling reason for abandoning Waller's distinction between recreational dating and serious courtship in favor of a dating continuum involves direct attempts to replicate Waller's research.[4] Robert Blood, for example, finds no sharp break between the characteristics desired in a casual date and those valued in a more serious relationship by University of Michigan students. As he puts it:

> The BMOC-fraternity-car-clothes-money complex has already been scrapped by Michigan girls in their casual dating preferences so that thinking of marriage requires no further significant changes in their orientation. Conversely, the personality-type items . . . , which were frequently chosen both as campus norms and as personal

preferences in casual dating, continue to receive extensive support as qualifications for a potential marriage partner.[5]

In a more recent study, Ira Reiss has noted at a co-educational college in Virginia that the competitive-materialistic values Waller described are present as a subdominant value-set—mainly within the Greek organizations. However, among the Greeks these same values appear to be related both to casual dating and to mate selection.[6]

In summary, then, the disuse of the term "courtship," the ubiquity of dating, and the fact that dating appears to be motivated by serious as well as recreational purposes, make it reasonable to think of the dating continuum as comprising the heart of the courtship system of the contemporary United States.

General Functions of Dating

Dating is more than a recreational outlet and the vehicle of mate selection in the United States. By drawing upon discussions by William Kephart, Robert Winch, and James Skipper and Gilbert Nass, it is possible to formulate a list of five complex functions that this system of heterosexual contacts performs for the individual in society.[7] (1) Dating is a form of *recreation*. "It provides entertainment for the individuals involved and is a source of immediate enjoyment."[8] (2) It is a form of *socialization*. It gives the individual an opportunity to learn about members of the opposite sex at close range, to develop techniques of interaction, to play roles, and to increasingly define his self-concept as he observes others' reactions to him as a person. (3) It serves for the meeting of *ego needs*. The young person—like all people—needs understanding, serious conversation, and to be considered important. A satisfactory dating experience may help the individual over the rocky period of independence struggle and postponement of adulthood which is called adolescence. (4) Dating functions for the society as a means of *status placement*. This is a function performed strictly by the family or kin unit in many societies, so that the unit into which an individual is born determines the category of persons into which he will marry as well as his adult status in the society. In the United States, where personal choice is basic to mate selection, the dating system makes it possible for certain persons to be rated highly desirable and thus to raise their status within the peer group. Thus, the dating system helps to control the operation of free choice by parcelling out prospective mates according to their status value. (5) Finally, of course, dating functions for the *selection of a marriage partner*. This is, after all, the end result of at least one dating relationship for the individual. Most young people do not begin each date by asking "Would I want to marry this person?" Yet somewhere in the course of one's dating experience this latent question is answered in the affirmative. Mate selection is, therefore, both the cause and the final effect of the dating continuum.

Stages and Specific Functions of the Dating Continuum

The dating continuum may be thought of as consisting of a series of gradual changes in seriousness, including such identifiable stages as random or casual dating, going steady, engagement, and marriage. In addition, some groups of young people recognize certain intermediate stages as "going steadily," a relationship not quite as exclusive as going steady, and "pinning," a serious step prior to engagement among some organized school groups.

The five general dating functions listed above are not *all* performed at *all* stages of *all* dating relationships. Recreation, and to a lesser extent socialization and status achievement, are the sole functions of many casual dating experiences. However, the meeting of ego needs and, increasing seriousness may be concurrent aspects of a relationship as it becomes more intense and lasting. And, of course, the mate selection function can be considered synonymous with the final stage of the dating continuum.

Besides the more general functions performed by dating, there are several functions, or purposes, that are more specific to a particular stage on the continuum. Of special interest in this regard is going steady, that stage which ordinarily embodies the transition from a recreational to a serious relationship. Research at the University of Wisconsin by Robert Herman and, later, by the present author has revealed several important motives for going steady.[9] Herman, who asked his students about their high school experience, found that a frequent reason given for going steady was that "Everyone's doing it"; i.e., it is a high school fad. Many students, however, expressed other reasons as well. Going steady makes it possible to guarantee being able to go to activities; it is good "date security." It also helps the young person to avoid the anxieties of competition for desirable dates. And, even on the high school level, to some it is a pledge of serious interest and intent— although the consummation in marriage may be understood by both couple members to be many years in the future, and may never come to pass.

Looking at reasons for going steady among college students, the author found several of Herman's motives still present, but of lesser importance. Date security was still a secondary reason expressed by girls for going steady, and freedom from competition was sometimes expressed by boys, but seriousness and ego needs had become dominant. College students of both sexes expressed as the most basic reasons either love for their partner or the need to feel wanted and important. A minority (some 10 per cent) of the male students also indicated that a reason for going steady is to guarantee a sexual outlet, a subject to which we shall return later in the chapter. In short, even a specific stage of the dating continuum, such as going steady, can have differing significance to different persons as well as to the same person at different ages.

Thus far we have reviewed the general functions of dating, the stages of the dating continuum, and the functions of and reasons for going steady. Clyde McDaniel has attempted to synthesize several previous analyses of the dating process, giving particular emphasis to the changing role played by the female. Drawing upon Winch's work, McDaniel claims that the possible roles played by females during dating are assertive, or receptive, or some combination of the two. Assertive daters are achievement-oriented and competitive, autonomous, dominant, and hostile. Receptive daters are deferential, succorous (desirous of help), prone to vicariousness (gaining pleasure from others' achievements), and anxious.

> Girls, in the early stage of courtship, are inexperienced and unsophisticated with regard to appropriate role behavior. They are assertive initially because they view their right to act as aggressors in social interaction as identical with boys' right to act as aggressors. In heterosexual interaction on dates, however, they are made aware of their inappropriate role behavior through negative reinforcement from boys. In this way, they learn that receptivity is more frequently approved than assertiveness.[10]

Waller's and Gorer's descriptions of dating as a competitive recreational activity seem to McDaniel to fit the early stage of dating, with mutual assertiveness on the part of the couple members, quite well. However, socialization into appropriate roles occurs, and the later or more serious stages of dating are characterized by the female playing a more acceptable receptive role in the relationship.

McDaniel's interesting analysis does an injustice to previous research, especially Lowrie's and Waller's, when it tries to fit the differing views onto a single, non-historical continuum. However, it does raise certain intriguing questions. In closing, he reiterates the "cycle wherein girls learn through trial and error to become receptive." It may not be overstating the case, McDaniel feels, to assert that "if they do not become receptive, they never get married."[11] One cannot help but wonder if McDaniel's closing assertion might have been more correct in an earlier period of American history than it is today. In the colonial and Victorian eras of role separation and normative patriarchy, the female who could not learn to be receptive may have had great difficulty in finding a mate. Today, however, substantial change in the status of women and a blurring or loosening of role specifications makes one question the extent to which female receptivity is a *necessary* condition for marriage.

A second question raised by McDaniel's closing assertion concerns the relation between role playing and personality. To the extent that McDaniel is correct, it is quite possible that a female with an assertive personality will play a receptive role in dating in order to obtain a mate. What is the likely effect on the marriage when the wife's assertiveness is subsequently manifested? Will serious conflict occur? These are issues for further research, not idle speculation.

The process of love and breakup is investigated by Clifford Kirkpatrick and Theodore Caplow in a well-executed study involving 399 students at the University of Minnesota. They find that the early stages of a dating relationship tend to be controlled by the male, due to his role as initiator. At the more serious stages, however, it is generally the female who exercises greater control over the continuation or termination of the relationship. The period of heartache and adjustment following most breakups is extremely brief. Dating is described by the authors as a selective process through which the less stable and less compatible relationships are weeded out.[12] It is a total courtship continuum, but many relationships terminate at an early stage due to loss of interest, an alternative attraction, or some other reason. In the next chapter we shall examine at length the key factors in this weeding or filtering out process which leads to mate selection.

Two further comments regarding dating as a courtship continuum seem to be in order. First, personal choice of a mate is thought by many to be an extremely problematic basis for a stable marriage.[13] Yet it should be added that extended dating, or a lengthy dating experience, is conducive to the making of an adequate choice at a time when institutional or traditional controls are weak. Alan Bayer states it this way: "It is the *length* of the dating experience prior to marriage which may have a crucial impact on the subsequent outcome."[14] Presumably, the more extensive one's contact with members of the opposite sex, the greater are his chances of making an intelligent choice of a mate. Second, discussion with students and academicians from Taiwan, India, and certain African nations has led this author to the conclusion that dating is considered by many persons in these countries to be one index of modernization. One reason is that it represents freedom from adult control over mating and kinship, therefore symbolizing among the young leadership of these countries the rejection of traditional ways and entrance into the modern world. Dating is thus not unique to and functional for the family system of the United States alone, but has a symbolic value in certain other nations as well.

SECTION TWO

PROBLEMATIC ASPECTS OF DATING

It is quite possible that the reader may have surmised by this time that dating, according to the present author, is the courtship system *par excellence*. This is not, however, an accurate conclusion to derive from the foregoing discussion of the nature and functions of the dating system of the United States. It cannot be overemphasized that dating is a recent phenomenon. Five or six decades has been sufficient time to establish dating as the basis of the courtship process in the United States, but the specific norms governing the process continue to be in flux. With the fluidity of the cultural content of the adolescent period, each new generation redefines the dating codes or norms of the previous generation (and an adolescent generation is, of course, less than ten years long). The expectations and practices undergo constant re-evaluation, and the following problems arise within the dating system.[15]

Parental Influence

Parents naturally take an interest in the dating behavior of their sons and daughters. Alan Bates found in interviews with young people several years ago that a high proportion of their parents had tried to influence their dating (see Table 4). In a later study, Marvin Sussman reported that parents in 81 per cent of his middle-class New Haven sample "admitted they either persuaded or threatened their children with withdrawal of support during periods when they were courting persons of whom they disapproved."[16] While most parents feel compelled to speak out on the subject, the reaction of young people to the intrusion varies from acceptance to resentment and conflict. This, then, is one aspect of current practices in which the choice falls short of being "open," but is still a cross between restricted and open, between externally (adult) influenced and youth or participant-run.[17]

TABLE 4

Per Cent of Parents Attempting to Influence the Dating Behavior of Their Sons and Daughters

	Fathers' Influence	Mothers' Influence
Sons	49.1	79.4
Daughters	68.7	97.1

SOURCE: Alan Bates, "Parental Roles in Courtship," *Social Forces*, 20 (1942), 483–86.

It may be argued that since parental approval of the mate selected seems to be related to success in marriage for the offspring, such intrusion is therefore vindicated. Yet great parental insight is but one possible interpretation. Another plausible explanation for the relation between parental approval and marital success might be that when parents disapprove they tend to cause trouble for the young couple after marriage, increasing the likelihood of dissolution of the marriage. Whichever interpretation one accepts, it must be concluded that, with a participant-run dating system and weak cultural supports for parental intrusion, parental approval will remain a problematic aspect of courtship in the United States.

Intergroup or Heterogeneous Dating

Dating someone of a different background from your own is a problem primarily in relation to the issue of parental intrusion, as well as that of kin and friends. If the young person were entirely free from group constraints, difficulties posed by interclass, interreligious, and interracial dating would very likely be minimal. Either he would avoid such relationships because he had internalized the importance of the differences represented, or else he would engage in heterogeneous dating with no thought of problems involved. (Note we are speaking here of heterogeneous dating, not marriage). Parents or other significant persons, in arguing against heterogeneous dating, may be motivated by a sincere belief that such relations are problem-producing if they culminate in marriage. Yet in this last phrase lies a part of the problem: while these "others" are focussing on the possibility of marriage, the young people involved may be seeking enjoyment and experience, with little or no thought of marriage. Thus, the fact that the dating continuum serves for both socialization and mate selection may become the basis for misunderstanding. A second issue in intergroup dating may be a basic value disagreement between the generations, or between persons in the same social network. The older generation may consider group values to be very important, but these persons may be considered by the younger generation to be snobbish and bigoted. Such differences, the young people may feel, "simply don't matter any more." The key point regarding group heterogeneity is what it signifies, i.e., divergent values and norms; any trouble in intergroup dating is likely to be caused by disagreements concerning the importance of these divergences. This issue must be raised again when we discuss mate selection in Chapter X.

Physical Attractiveness

One of the most problematic factors in dating concerns physical attractiveness. Elaine Walster *et al.* (who investigated a computer dance among University of Minnesota freshmen) and Glen Elder agree that sheer attractiveness is an overriding determinant of liking, and is particularly crucial in boys' reactions to girls.[18] This is the negative side of the status-placement function discussed above. While girls may be penalized more than boys, neither sex avoids the difficulties besetting the generally unattractive young person in a participant-run dating system. It is ironic that, at a time in life when, perhaps more than any other, emotional security is needed, the dating system is as likely to frustrate these needs as to meet them. For every individual who achieves status in the peer group there is one who loses status because he lacks those qualities valued by the peer group—and one such quality is physical attractiveness. Under a system of arranged marriage, face and body are not quite so important, and equality of opportunity is at least theoretically easier to effect. Even in American society, the reader may have noticed from time to time the homely debutante on the "society" page of the newspaper. In such a case, lineage and economic value increase the individual's chances, and help to balance the competition based upon looks. In general, however, physical attractiveness is one of the more variable and crucial elements in the American courtship system.

Social Awkwardness

Social awkwardness and conversational inferiority are on the opposite side of the coin of socialization through dating. One learns by means of the dating experience, we said, how to interact with members of the opposite sex and how to play various roles. But if the participants run the system, as they do in the United States, a premium is put on social and conversational abilities at the outset; those who are deficient in these departments may have difficulty both in obtaining a date and in handling themselves once they have obtained it. Ideally, dating should afford the opportunity for socialization, for developing social skills; it may, however, thwart development as the individual flounders in the attempt to make a good impression. This is a theme played upon in the mass media; glamour magazines and teen magazines are good examples. These publications demonstrate quite well how the dating system falls short of providing for the socialization function: one must practice elsewhere, the reader is told, in order to be a good conversationalist on the date.[19] Dating may simply serve in many cases to exaggerate tendencies already present for the smooth to become more so, and for the awkward likewise to become increasingly less adept at handling social situations.

Insincerity

Insincerity is a problem that grows out of the fact that dating serves both for enjoyment and for mate selection. An obvious possibility is that one party is serious while the other is seeking enjoyment; in such a case, the meeting of ego needs becomes highly problematic. This is where "the line" appears, as the less emotionally involved member of a couple tries to convince the more serious party that he cares more than he actually does. Skipper and Nass remind us that, in a dating situation characterized by differential interest, "the individual with the greater emotional commitment . . . will have the least control over the relationship."[20] The fluid and multipurpose nature of the dating continuum means that differences of motive and commitment are likely to be frequent in dating, thereby thwarting the individual's attempts to gain understanding and security.

Most of what has been said thus far regarding the nature, functions, and problems of the American dating system holds for young people at all levels of the socioeconomic ladder. Lower-class and middle-class courtship do, however, diverge at a few points. According to a national sample study analyzed by Alan Bayer, young people in lower-class families start dating later than those in the middle class.[21] The dating activity of the former is governed by lesser financial resources, and is oriented toward sex and marriage more immediately and directly than that in the middle class. One reason for this is that only a small proportion of lower-class young people postpone marriage in order to attend college. Thus, the continuum of dating experience in the lower class is foreshortened both by a late start and by a generally earlier age at marriage than in the middle class. In the chapter on marital dissolution we shall return to the issue of early marriage and its relation to marital permanence.

Dating serves as the courtship continuum of the contemporary United States. Yet the system is characterized by the convergence of familial and individualistic pressures: it is a participant-run system, but parents continue to influence the choice; mate selection is open, but is likely to be made within the bounds of certain social categories. The recency of dating, its multipurpose nature, and the fluid and sometimes contradictory character of its expectations makes it a problem-producing experience for many young people. One issue in premarital relations, sexual intercourse, is treated as a problem by many commentators. We shall turn to this issue in Section Three.

SECTION THREE

PREMARITAL SEXUAL RELATIONS

The subject of human sexual relations has within the past generation come to be considered a suitable topic for conversation and research in American society. The forerunner of current discussions of sex in the modern industrial world is found in the ethnographic reports of anthropologists studying a wide variety of pre-industrial societies.[22] All societies, it seems, control in some manner the possible sexual behaviors; the two most universal forms of control appear to be the incest taboo and marriage. In addition, accounts of such practices as premarital sex, extra-marital sex, masturbation, and homosexuality indicate that these activities may be encouraged, permitted, ignored, condemned, or suppressed, depending upon the society and its norms. Furthermore, there may be variations in correspondence between verbalized norms and typical behavior.

Among the sex practices mentioned above, the one that has received most widespread cross-cultural acceptance is premarital intercourse. After analyzing a large sample of societies, George Peter Murdock stated that "premarital license prevails in seventy per cent of our cases. In the rest, the taboo falls primarily upon females and appears to be largely a precaution against child-bearing out of wedlock rather than a moral requirement."[23] The arrangements in the majority of societies that permit premarital sex include safeguards against exploitation of the female and equal and legitimate status for children born out of wedlock. In other words, where the practice is accepted as a part of the society's culture, there are few stressful and guilt-producing features attached to it. The greater problems occur in those societies that officially prohibit premarital sex, since it is extremely difficult to enforce the prohibition, nor is it considered by many societal leaders important enough to enforce.

Sex outside of marriage, unlike sex before marriage, is *not* permitted by a majority of societies. Many factors concerning the stability and integration of societies and their family systems are related to the control of extra-marital sex. We therefore introduce our discussion of premarital sex with the statement that sex practices are usually consistent with other characteristics of a culture. If a culture is changing rapidly, as that of the United States seems to be, a rethinking of previously accepted sexual norms occurs, making it likely that there will be inconsistencies between various aspects of the culture.

Extent and Significance of Premarital Sex in the United States

The massive research on sex in the United States carried out by Alfred Kinsey and his associates burst upon the public following World War II.[24] Because it noted the prevalence of many types of sexual practices and the discrepancy between the expressed and behavioral morality of the middle classes, the research was perceived as a threat by many persons. Researchers attacked the methodology, editorialists rejected the conclusions, and moral leaders accused the authors of undermining the moral fibre of the nation.[25] While many of the same criticisms would apply to other sociological research, the significant fact is that the Kinsey studies were felt to deserve extensive critical attention. They were correctly viewed as heralding a new day of openness and frankness regarding sexual matters; the result has been a flood of studies examining sex, which continues unabated to the present.[26]

One focus of the Kinsey research—as well as of notable studies by Louis Terman, Winston Ehrmann, and Ira Reiss—is premarital sex relations. By drawing upon the findings of these and other authors and by tracing changes over time, it is possible to derive a fairly accurate estimate of the current prevalence of premarital sexual intercourse in the United States. Approximately 70 per cent of the single male population engage in intercourse prior to marriage, while for females the figure is closer to 50 per cent.

Granted, the male may have a more active biological drive for "sex where he finds it," and may feel freer due to the absence of pregnancy fears, but there is more to the sex difference than this. There is, first of all, lingering evidence of a double standard that considers premarital intercourse more morally reprehensible in a female than in a male. Reiss, for example, speaks of the millions of males who are engaged in reducing the number of virgins, while at the same time holding a deep desire for a virgin mate. Secondly, a basic middle-class distinction between males and females appears to be that, according to Ehrmann, females base their indulgence in premarital intercourse upon romanticism and males upon eroticism. To elaborate, many a female indicates that her premarital intercourse has been only with the man who later became her husband. Her sex expression, as a respectable girl, is seldom of the sort defined by the official morality as promiscuous or random; it is, rather, profoundly related to love and to a single partner. Sex is best viewed premaritally (when it occurs) as an expression of love on the part of the middle-class female, and as an erotic release on the part of the male, who nevertheless desires a virgin bride. This serves to clarify Ehrmann's conclusion that, in the middle class, degree of physical intimacy varies inversely among males and directly among females with intensity of affection.[27] Some question is now being raised regarding the current validity of Ehrmann's conclusion concerning males. Erwin Smigel and Rita Seiden, writing the "Decline and Fall of the Double Standard," claim that "young men today are probably less promiscuous and more monogamous, and their relationships tend to be more stable. Both sexes are approaching a single standard based on sex with affection."[28] In other words, during the 1960's the inverse relation between affection and intercourse which Ehrmann found for middle-class males may have been changing toward a direct relationship, so that, as seriousness of intent on the part of both males and females increases, so does the probability of a couple engaging in premarital intercourse.

Throughout the preceding paragraph the phrase "middle-class males and females" has been used several times. This is because the percentage approximations—70 and 50—are over-all figures. For the lower classes the per cents are some 15 to 20 points higher for each sex; for the middle classes they are correspondingly lower (see Table 5 for our estimates by sex and social class).

TABLE 5

Per Cent of Males and Females (by Social Class) Engaging in Premarital Intercourse

Sex and Social Class	Per Cent Engaging in Premarital Intercourse
Middle-class males	50
Middle-class females	30
Lower-class males	85
Lower-class females	65

The figures on premarital sex reported in the array of studies summarized by Gerald Leslie may also be misleading in another way. Many of these studies are based on an unmarried population at a given point in time, and are usually called cross-sectional studies. The question: "Have you ever engaged in sexual intercourse?" when asked of unmarried persons, must be interpreted: "Have you ever engaged in sexual intercourse up to now?" However, what the researcher ordinarily wants to know is how many persons engage in intercourse at any time prior to marriage. Thus, the most accurate studies of premarital sex must involve married persons describing the entire period of their dating or courtship experience.

The foregoing criticism is particularly applicable to research on college populations. A study of college norms and behaviors, carried out by David Heise at the University of Wisconsin during 1966, involved approximately 800 undergraduates. Table 6 shows the per cent of males and females stating that they had engaged in premarital intercourse, according to their year in college.[29] A simple statistical mistake, in summarizing the data of Table 6, would

TABLE 6

Engagement in Premarital Intercourse by 800 University of Wisconsin Students, by Sex and Year in College

Sex and Year in College	Per Cent Engaging in Premarital Intercourse
Males	
Freshmen	25
Sophomores	30
Juniors	60
Seniors	70
Females	
Freshmen	15
Sophomores	20
Juniors	30
Seniors	35

be to sum the totals for males and females and thus conclude that about 45 per cent of the males and 24 per cent of the females in this sample indulge in sex prior to marriage. This would, of course, be a serious underestimate, since such data must be handled cumulatively instead of by computing an average. The fact is that the correct figure for males in this sample is very likely 75–80 per cent, while for females it is 40–45, for we may safely assume that even some of the seniors will engage in intercourse in the future, but before their marriage. Despite Smigel and Seiden's claim of a single standard, it seems that this critical discussion is especially applicable to middle-class or college females, who are still quite likely to restrict their sexual involvements until the immediate premarital period.

Having looked at the extent and significance of premarital intercourse by sex and social class, let us discuss briefly the current trends. Available data indicate, as asserted in Chapter IV, that the greatest increase in the incidence of premarital sex in this country occurred in the early years of the twentieth century, particularly in the 1920's. There has been only a slight change in behavior since then. What seems to have been happening is that attitudes and verbalized norms have been slowly changing so as to congrue more closely with the individual-choice–based practices. It is as yet too early to assess the effect of the birth control pill upon behavior. There are some, however, who feel it will have little or no effect whatsoever on the prevalence of premarital sex. Listen to Smigel and Seiden:

> But we doubt that the pill has added materially to the increase in the numbers of young adults or adolescents who have had premarital sex. Effective techniques of birth control existed, and were used, before the pill. True, the pill makes birth control easier to manage (except for the memory requirement), but romantic love is still important; it makes taking the pill, when no definite partner is available, undesirable. What the pill does is to give sexual freedom to those who are having steady sexual relationships, for then the use of the pill adds to romantic love by making elaborate preparations unnecessary.[30]

Those who would use the pill to prevent a premarital pregnancy would have indulged in intercourse even without it. What would have to happen to change behavior drastically would be, not just freedom from pregnancy fears, but a separation of sex from affection or "romantic love," as Smigel and Seiden put it. The female's reason, it is suggested, is either: "I am in love with him," in which case she is about as likely to engage in intercourse even without the pill, or else it is: "I was swept away by emotion and affection," an argument for spontaneity which is difficult to make convincing if one has been taking the pill for a week, or a month.

Value Positions on Premarital Sex

Smigel and Seiden believe that "sex with affection" is now coming to be the single standard of premarital sexual behavior. The figures quoted throughout the preceding discussion would tend to belie any notion of a single standard. Some engage in premarital sex, others do not; both indulgence and abstinence may be based upon a multiplicity of reasons. Disagreements rage in the adult population of the United States regarding the acceptability of premarital sex; the various current value positions are neatly summarized by Isadore Rubin, editor of a little magazine entitled *Sexology*. Rubin feels there are six major competing value systems at present.[31] (1) *Traditional repressive asceticism* is a value still embodied in the official codes and laws of many states. Seven states have fines for premarital intercourse ranging from $10 to $100; Oregon has a maximum penalty of $500 or five years in prison. Other states have sentences ranging from three months to three years. Though such laws are seldom enforced, the logic behind them is still asserted by many religious or other moral leaders in the United States. Sex is linked to procreation and is to be avoided outside of marriage; even within marriage, some spokesmen for this view feel sex should be utilized only with procreation in view. Sex behavior is handled in terms of absolutes—"thou shalt" or "thou shalt not." Both the study and the discussion of sex tend to be considerably restricted by this approach, since the rightness or wrongness of specific practices is not subject to debate.

(2) *Enlightened asceticism* is best exemplified in the views of David Mace. Mace sees asceticism or control in the sexual and in other spheres of life as a necessary safeguard in American culture against the softness and weakness that result from overindulgence. He sees self-mastery as necessary to avoid individual weakness and national collapse. On these grounds he opposes the slackening of the sex codes. However, he takes neither a dogmatic nor a negative attitude toward sex and is an ardent exponent of the open forum for studying and discussing the issue. In fact, his discussions of premarital sex with Walter Stokes and Albert Ellis are among the more valuable expositions on this issue—an issue that he feels requires debate in order to be understood, due to the contradictory nature of the present norms.[32]

(3) *Humanistic liberalism* is best exemplified in the ideas and works of Lester Kirkendall of Oregon State. He, too, opposes inflexible absolutes, but is above all concerned with interpersonal relations. Morality does not concern the omission or commission of certain acts, but, rather, the consequences of those acts for relations between the actors. Kirkendall searches for a value system that will supply internalized controls for the individual at a time when the older, institutional controls, such as religion (he feels), are breaking down. The "sex with affection" or "permissiveness with affection" position that Smigel and Seiden claim is dominant today is fairly close to the philosophy embodied in humanistic liberalism.[33]

(4) *Humanistic radicalism* likewise starts with concern for the human being, but states the need for major societal changes.

Walter Stokes, a spokesman for this position, accepts Kirkendall's humanism, but proposes that society should make sexual freedom possible for young people. In order to do this, the official morality will have to remove the cultural baggage that makes for guilt. Thus, Stokes envisions a cultural engineering project that may take generations. This project involves forgetting the Puritan heritage and approaching premarital sex as a natural act, rather than as a moral issue.

(5) *The fun morality* has as its most consistent theoretical or academic spokesman Albert Ellis, and as one of its practical advocates Hugh Hefner of *Playboy Magazine*. Without compromise, Ellis upholds the view that sex is pleasurable and that the more such fun a human being has, the better and more psychologically sound a person he is likely to be. He believes that premarital intercourse should be encouraged for well-informed and adjusted persons. (Of course, Stokes might respond that, unfortunately, there are not very many such people in American society at present.)

(6) The sixth position, that of *sexual anarchy*, had as a philosopher the late French jurist René Guyon. Guyon attacked chastity, virginity, and monogamy, and called for the complete removal of all sex taboos and controls; in effect, he called for complete or universal availability for sex. The only restriction would be against doing violence to or injuring one's fellow.

It is unfortunate that Rubin or someone else has not attempted to determine the distribution of these six value positions within the population. This author's estimate, based upon available evidence, is that humanistic liberalism is the most prevalent empirically, followed by traditional asceticism, the fun morality, enlightened asceticism, with sexual anarchy having a few advocates, and with humanistic radicalism being more of an action program than an empirically discernible type. The reader may, however, review the available literature and draw his own conclusions regarding the empirical distribution of these value positions.

Premarital Sex As a Cultural Alternative

A cultural universal, as described in Chapter VI, is a belief, practice, or prohibition that is agreed upon (at least verbally) by virtually all of the members of a given culture. In American society, two universals are monogamy and the prohibition of infanticide. Thus, you are not likely to find forums being held on infanticide as desirable or undesirable. Instead, we speak absolutely about it and expect almost universal agreement. A cultural alternative, on the other hand, is a belief, practice, or prohibition upon which opinion is divided in the various segments of society. Open give-and-take is expected when such an issue is broached. Within the official morality of American middle-class society, the past century has seen the prohibition of premarital sex move from being almost a cultural universal to being an alternative. Whereas at one time the inveighing of the religious leader against the practice was enough to arouse virtually unanimous verbal agreement, such a stand today would be met with open agreement by some, doubt by others, and laughter by others. In fact, those who hold to the formerly quasi-universal position of premarital chastity often find themselves on the defensive in the face of the vociferous spokesmen for sexual liberalism. In any case, the "proper" view is no longer clear-cut, no longer prescribed in the dominant middle-class norms.

The changes that have increased the prevalence of premarital sex and that have made it attitudinally a "legitimate" alternative are defined by many writers as directionless and problem-producing. Without clear guidelines, the possibilities of exploitation, insecurity, or guilt are great. Peter Blau, for example, notes the female's sexual dilemma: she increases a man's love by granting favors, but if she dispenses them too readily she depreciates their value and their power to arouse an enduring attachment.[34] The problem of insincerity, referred to in the discussion of dating, is especially acute in the area of premarital sex. How can the female know *for sure* that the male is serious in intent? The answer is simple: she can't. She can only take, or avoid taking, a calculated risk—without knowing whether either her indulgence or her abstinence will increase or decrease his interest. The pressure on the young person's sexual decisions is also heightened in situations in which peer-group and parental standards diverge, as they still tend to do.[35] Parental values may cause the young person to feel guilty if he does engage in premarital sex, while a certain peer group may cause him to feel guilty if he doesn't.

The changes that are defined as problematic for the individual are seen by some writers, we have said, as anarchic and directionless within society. Vance Packard indicates this confusion or lack of direction in the title of his book, *The Sexual Wilderness*. The changes, he feels, are currently "too chaotic and varied to describe yet as a revolution. A revolution implies a clear movement in an understood and generally supported direction."[36] While one could stop to argue with his conception of revolution, the important fact is that Packard finds no direction or trend in the changes in sex practices and attitudes—only chaos.

There is, however, another way to interpret the changes that have made premarital intercourse a legitimate alternative to continence. The past century has seen a movement *away from two double standards*. One of these demanded, during the Victorian era, a higher level of morality for females than for males. The other double standard involved a substantial discrepancy between verbal norms and behavior. It is easy to see the problems caused by the competing value systems today, but one can only imagine and infer from the literature of that era the individual difficulties caused by the two double standards. Restrictions, guilt, and lack of pleasure in sex for the female, resort to prostitutes for the male, and the results of hypocritical verbal norms may have made family and individual adjustment even more difficult than they are today. Though the process of change is still in midstream, its direction seems to be toward a reduction of the former confusions.

The last phrase is questionable if one assumes that the competing value systems are the end of the process. But they are not. They are, rather, a stage on the way *toward an individual-choice approach* to premarital sex. Indications supporting this conclusion can be traced historically as follows. The post-World War II era of the Kinsey reports saw the emergence of a new openness regarding sexual matters. This was followed in the 1950's with a period of titillation and obsession with sex. Some deplored it, some embraced it, and many wanted advice—which their peers and societal experts were only too ready to give. During the early 1960's, one found in the United States the competing value systems described by Rubin; this is where the majority of middle-class adults still appear to be at the beginning of the 1970's. That is, they are still debating the moral implications of premarital intercourse. Among young people, however, the beginnings of a further development can be discerned. There are signs during the last half of the 1960's that evangelism in support of some value stance and the seeking of advice have both begun to give way to a more *laissez faire* attitude. Each should define his own morality or "do his own thing" in this area: whether he wants to indulge or abstain until marriage is his business. There seems to be an increasing "patient indifference" on the part of young people in response to the expert's presentation of the latest facts on premarital sex replacing the old fascination and commitment regarding sexual matters. This conclusion is, however, not based upon research but upon the author's contact with young people during the 1960's; the reader may want to debate the question of just how far the adolescent peer group has progressed toward this sort of naturalism or individualistic morality in the area of premarital sex.

Though some would brand these developments as anarchy, it is unquestionable that individualism is more advanced in this area than in many others relating to our family system, in which domestic and individualist values are competing at present. The reason for this advanced individual freedom in premarital sex becomes apparent when we compare it with extra-marital sex. Extra-marital sex is seen as a threat to marital adjustment and thus to the nuclear family; the conflict of the value of domestic adjustment with the individual value of sexual freedom is decided at present in favor of the former. By contrast, with pregnancy fears at a minimum, adults find it increasingly difficult to argue against premarital intercourse on the grounds that it is detrimental to the stability of the family system.[37] Furthermore, that premarital sex is becoming an individual matter within the adolescent peer group is consistent with the combination of a participant-run dating system and emphasis upon individual adjustment in the family. Individual adjustment, a basic criterion of family success, has become central to premarital relationships as well. Thus, one's sexual adjustment prior to marriage competes with adherence to the traditional notion of sexual continence for the sake of a virgin bride and legitimate offspring.[38] Young people increasingly predicate their indulgence in or abstinence from premarital sex upon whether or not it is perceived as making for good personal adjustment—a sense of wellbeing.

In the lower class, many of the changes we have been discussing have simply not occurred. Premarital intercourse has been widespread for centuries, and is still more so than in the middle-class. An important difference, however, is that premarital intercourse in the lower classes is still primarily a matter of exploitation for the male and defenselessness and/or ignorance on the part of the female. The distinction between this approach and that of the middle class, with its adjustment basis and its concern for female as well as male enjoyment, is embodied in Reiss' description of "respectable" permissiveness in the middle class. This new type of permissiveness places a high value on intellectual autonomy and, while it may be defined as deviant behavior by parents, it is not viewed as such by the young people themselves.[39]

In summary, neither intercourse nor sexual continence can be considered normative in adolescent society.[40] Rather, the norm shows signs of becoming simply individual choice, without either the Freudian fascination or the moral overtones that still preoccupy the adult generation. Individualism in this area is likely to be defined as anarchy rather than as freedom by that large number of persons who prefer well-defined guidelines (traditions) to the necessity of making an individual evaluation and choice. But, whether the changes in premarital sexual attitudes and behavior are defined as anarchic, directionless, and problem-producing—or as freeing, confusion-reducing, and adjustment-based—continues to be primarily a matter of the value position of the observer.

SECTION FOUR

CONCLUSIONS

Dating is the focus of the participant-run courtship system of the United States, having become the basis of a continuum that ranges from casual heterosexual relationships to mate selection. Of recent origin, dating includes aspects in which individual and nuclear family values reinforce each other, e.g., the view that personal choice is the most adequate basis for a happy or adjusted marriage. It also includes aspects in which individual and nuclear family values are in conflict, examples being parental intrusion and the strictures against heterogeneous dating. Dating has become institutionalized as the courtship system, but the norms governing behavior within the system are fluid and often problem-producing for the individual.

Premarital sex is an element of heterosexual activity which is more widespread in the lower class than in the middle class. In the middle class there are currently several competing value approaches to premarital sex, with humanistic liberalism, or "sex with affection," apparently predominating empirically. However, there are signs that premarital intercourse is becoming increasingly a matter of individual choice among middle-class young people, without either commanding the undue attention or possessing the moral overtones that it still does among middle-class adults. One reason for this is that this phenomenon poses so little threat to the family system. As William O'Neill indicates: "Conservatives continue to be unhappy about the rise of promiscuity and, of course, they resist it when they can. But it proved to be something they could live with."[41] Whether these developments are viewed positively or negatively is as likely to be based upon the biases of the writer as upon empirical evidence that such individualism is either good or bad for the individual himself.

The result of the dating continuum is still marriage for most persons, and much research has been done to determine which factors govern the choice of a mate. In Chapter X we examine these factors.

NOTES

[1] Geoffrey Gorer, *The American People: A Study in National Character* (New York: Norton, 1964 ed.), p. 114.

[2] Willard Waller, "The Rating and Dating Complex," *American Sociological Review,* 2 (1937), 727–34.

[3] Samuel H. Lowrie, "Factors Involved in the Frequency of Dating," *Marriage and Family Living,* 18 (1956), 46–51.

[4] For a list of the studies replicating Waller's work, see Ira L. Reiss, "Social Class and Campus Dating," *Social Problems,* 13 (1965), 193–205.

[5] Robert O. Blood, "A Retest of Waller's Rating Complex," *Marriage and Family Living,* 17 (1955), 41–47.

[6] Reiss, "Social Class and Campus Dating," pp. 194, 204.

[7] William M. Kephart, *The Family, Society, and the Individual* (Boston: Houghton Mifflin, 1961 ed.); Robert F. Winch, "The Functions of Dating in Middle-Class America," in Robert F. Winch and Louis Wolf Goodman, eds., *Selected Studies in Marriage and the Family,* 3rd ed. (New York: Holt, Rinehart and Winston, 1968), pp. 505–7; James K. Skipper and Gilbert Nass, "Dating Behavior: A Framework for Analysis and an Illustration," *Journal of Marriage and the Family,* 28 (1966), 412–20.

[8] Skipper and Nass, "Dating Behavior: A Framework for Analysis and an Illustration," p. 412.

[9] Robert D. Herman, "The 'Going-Steady' Complex: A Re-examination," *Marriage and Family Living,* 17 (1955), 36–40.

[10] Clyde O. McDaniel, "Dating Roles and Reasons for Dating," *Journal of Marriage and the Family,* 31 (1969), 100.

[11] *Ibid.,* p. 106.

[12] Clifford Kirkpatrick and Theodore Caplow, "Courtship in a Group of Minnesota Students," *American Journal of Sociology,* 51 (1945), 114–25; Kirkpatrick and Caplow, "Emotional Trends in the Courtship Experience of College Students as Expressed by Graphs, with Some Observations on Methodological Implications," *American Sociological Review,* 10 (1945), 619–26.

[13] This statement itself is dependent upon the definition of the word "stable." If stable simply means permanent, then the mode of choice is far less important than the strictness of the laws governing dissolution of the unit. If stable means satisfying or happy, individual choice is probably a better basis for stability than is arranged marriage, despite the fact that a loosening of the laws may allow more of the unsatisfactory units to dissolve.

[14] Alan E. Bayer, "Early Dating and Early Marriage," *Journal of Marriage and the Family*, 30 (1968), 632.

[15] Much of the following discussion of problems in dating is adapted from Kephart, *The Family, Society, and the Individual*, pp. 293–300.

[16] Marvin B. Sussman, "Parental Participation in Mate Selection and Its Effect Upon Family Continuity," *Social Forces*, 32 (1953), 76–81.

[17] On the significance of the term "participant-run," see Ira L. Reiss, *The Social Context of Premarital Sexual Permissiveness* (New York: Holt, Rinehart and Winston, 1967), pp. 165, 176, *et passim*.

[18] Elaine Walster, Vera Aronson, Darcy Abrahams, and Leon Rottman, "Importance of Physical Attractiveness in Dating Behavior," *Journal of Personality and Social Psychology*, 4 (1966), 508–16, and Glen H. Elder, Jr., "Appearance and Education in Marriage Mobility," *American Sociological Review*, 34 (1969), 519–33.

[19] Of interest in this regard is a syndicated newspaper editorial by Jenkin Lloyd Jones, in which he criticizes the teen magazines' approach to conversational problems. See Jenkin Lloyd Jones, "Late-Teen Smoothness: Con in Conversation," *Wisconsin State Journal*, September 12, 1965.

[20] Skipper and Nass, "Dating Behavior," p. 413. Many years earlier this was labelled by Willard Waller as "the principle of least interest." See Waller, "The Rating and Dating Complex," p. 733.

[21] Bayer, "Early Dating and Early Marriage," pp. 628–32.

[22] The works of men like Bronislaw Malinowski were often read by the "civilized" but culture-bound public more to titillate than to inform. Good examples of anthropological works dealing with sex are Malinowski's, *Sex and Repression in Savage Society* (London: Routledge and Kegan Paul, 1927), and Malinowski, *The Sexual Life of Savages in Northwestern Melanesia* (New York: Liveright, 1929).

[23] George Peter Murdock, *Social Structure* (New York: Macmillan, 1949), p. 265.

[24] Alfred C. Kinsey *et al.*, *Sexual Behavior in the Human Male* (Philadelphia: Saunders, 1948), and Kinsey *et al.*, *Sexual Behavior in the Human Female* (Philadelphia: Saunders, 1953).

[25] See especially Jerome Himelhoch and Sylvia F. Fava, eds., *Sexual Behavior in American Society* (New York: Norton, 1955).

[26] For a review of studies before 1960, see Winston Ehrmann, *Premarital Dating Behavior* (New York: Holt, Rinehart and Winston, 1959), pp. 33–34. For later studies, see Reiss, *Social Context of Premarital Sexual Permissiveness*.

[27] Ehrmann, *Premarital Dating Behavior*, p. 338.

[28] Erwin O. Smigel and Rita Seiden, "The Decline and Fall of the Double Standard," *The Annals*, 376 (1968), 17. For an important normative interpretation, see Hallowell Pope and Dean D. Knudsen, "Premarital Sexual Norms, the Family, and Social Change," *Journal of Marriage and the Family*, 27 (1965), 314–23.

[29] The figures in this study are not to be interpreted as typical of *any* population, even undergraduates at the University of Wisconsin. They are presented to illustrate the difficulty in investigating cumulative phenomena by cross-sectional methods.

[30] Smigel and Seiden, "The Decline and Fall of the Double Standard," p. 17.

[31] Isadore Rubin, "Transition in Sex Values—Implications for the Education of Adolescents," *Journal of Marriage and the Family*, 27 (1965), 185–89. On many of these value positions, see "Premarital Sexual Behavior: A Symposium," *Marriage and Family Living*, 24 (1962), 254–78, which includes the views of Lester Kirkendall, Thomas Poffenberger, Richard Klemer,

Ira Reiss, Walter Stokes, and Blaine Porter. The symposium is reprinted in Edwin Schur, *The Family and the Sexual Revolution* (Bloomington: Indiana University Press, 1965).

[32] Tapes of these debates are available from the National Council on Family Relations, Minneapolis, Minnesota.

[33] The excellent research of Ira Reiss also concludes that sex with affection is probably the "most popular youth standard." See Reiss, *Social Context of Premarital Sexual Permissiveness*, p. 174.

[34] Peter M. Blau, *Exchange and Power in Social Life* (New York: Wiley & Sons, 1964), p. 80.

[35] On parental and peer influence, see Reiss, *Social Context of Premarital Sexual Permissiveness*, pp. 162–75, and Alfred M. Mirande, "Reference Group Theory and Adolescent Sexual Behavior," *Journal of Marriage and the Family*, 30 (1968), 572–77.

[36] Vance Packard, *The Sexual Wilderness* (New York: McKay, 1968), p. 17.

[37] In their 1965 article, Pope and Knudsen argue that premarital sexual norms are "connected with maintenance of family lines and position," and will continue to be so unless "social arrangements that allow separation of premarital coitus from unwed parenthood are also adopted." See Pope and Knudsen, "Premarital Sexual Norms," p. 322. This author would argue that much of that separation has, in fact, been accomplished.

[38] One illustration of concern with sexual adjustment, which has become prevalent enough among college student couples to receive attention from the press, is "the arrangement." This is a situation in which an unmarried young man and woman live together as if they were married, in order to discover, if possible, whether or not they are suited for each other sexually and otherwise, without the responsibilities and legal entanglements of marriage. This differs from the historical radical and bohemian rejection of marriage and the nuclear family in that the majority of the participants indicate their expectation of marriage and a home in the not-too-distant future.

[39] Reiss, *Social Context of Premarital Sexual Permissiveness*, p. 178.

[40] Jeffrey Hadden and Marie Borgatta show how it is possible to overstate the changes that have occurred, making it appear that premarital intercourse is now "normative." They state it thus: ". . . in a college newspaper an editorial may assert that sex on the campus is so commonplace as to be a part of the mores. This kind of statement does not take into account the distinction between permissive patterns and normative patterns at another level. Persons are not prepared to ask the corollary question" concerning premarital sex as a new moral norm: "Is it immoral *not* to be involved in premarital sexual affairs?" (Italics added.) The fact that our answer to such a question is likely to be: "Of course not," indicates that premarital intercourse cannot be considered the "new norm." See Jeffrey K. Hadden and Marie L. Borgatta, eds., *Marriage and the Family* (Itasca, Ill.: Peacock, 1969), p. 219.

[41] Wiliam L. O'Neill, *Divorce in the Progressive Era* (New Haven, Conn.: Yale University Press, 1967), p. 141.

X

Love and Mate Selection in the United States

ROMANTIC LOVE IN THE WESTERN WORLD DIFFERS FROM THAT IN MANY OTHER SOCIETIES IN HAVING BEEN INSTITUTIONALIZED AS THE BASIS FOR MATE SELECTION. LOVE DOES NOT, HOWEVER, OCCUR IN VACUO. SOME OF THE CONDITIONS THAT MAY SERVE TO LIMIT LOVE AND MATE SELECTION INCLUDE THE INCEST TABOO, PROPINQUITY, AND VARIOUS SUBSOCIETAL CATEGORIES SUCH AS RACE AND RELIGION. FACTORS THAT HAVE BEEN TREATED BY DIFFERENT AUTHORS AS ENHANCING LOVE AND INCREASING THE LIKELIHOOD OF MARRIAGE ARE: COMMON INTERESTS, SHARED VALUES, COMPLEMENTARY NEEDS, EMPATHY, AND PARENTAL IMAGE. YET MATE SELECTION IS TOO COMPLEX TO BE REDUCED TO A SET OF SINGLE FACTORS; UNDERSTANDING IS IMPROVED WHEN SELECTION IS TREATED AS A PROCESS. AN IMPORTANT EXAMPLE OF NON-UNIVERSAL AVAILABILITY IN AMERICAN MATE SELECTION IS RACIAL INTERMARRIAGE; A CONSIDERATION OF THIS ISSUE CLOSES THE CHAPTER.

Love, Kin Group, and Mate Selection

Love is an innate disposition, a complex emotion, which—like humor, anger, hate, fear, and jealousy—is a universal potentiality in human beings.[1] As universal potentialities, emotions that manifest themselves behaviorally may pose a threat to the structures and solidarities of societies. The behavioral manifestation of anger is injury or murder, and, while societies permit anger, drastic measures are taken against injury and murder in an attempt to control the disruptive aspects of the emotion. Fear—when expressed in either immobility or flight—can dissolve social solidarity. Therefore, a society must devise means to control fear; for example, magic may be used to allay anxiety and increase courage. The emotional attraction of one person for another, which we call love, has as its behavioral manifestation sex relations. However, sexual relations have been defined in most societies as integrally related to procreation and mating. Thus it is that three strong controls have been placed upon love in order to avoid or channel its behavioral manifestation. The most universal of these controls involves the *incest taboo,* which is based, as we said in Chapter II, upon the great potentiality for the development of love among immediate kin and upon the equally great desire in human societies for mating to occur exogamously with respect to this category of kin. The second control, which is imposed most stringently when sexual relations are defined as strictly a matter of procreation, concerns the *prohibition of homosexuality,* since the sexual expression of emotional attachment between two members of the same sex cannot result in procreation.[2] Of primary interest in the present chapter is the third control, that over *choice of a marriage partner.* This is not as widespread as the first two; it is also different from incest and homosexuality prohibitions in the extent to which it controls not only the sexual manifestation of love, but the development of the emotion as well.

Why should a society attempt to control the non-incestuous development of love between members of the opposite sex? The most obvious answer, if the above argument is correct, must be that the members of that society are convinced that if love were given free reign it would be detrimental to structures and solidarities. By the expression "giving free reign" to love, we mean allowing heterosexual love to be the basis for mating and procreation. Thus, a further question arises: What kinds of social structures and solidarities would be threatened if love were permitted to operate as the sole basis for mate selection? It would be detrimental in a society whose basic functions are performed and controlled by kin groups. If economic productivity, political authority, inheritance, residential location, and religious symbols are controlled by the lineage or kin group, it is imperative that the marriage linkages of its offspring be arranged, or at least limited. Individuals and nuclear families are embedded in the kin group, which controls mate choice in order to guarantee the appropriate continuation of solidarities and functions. The "free reign" of romantic love is minimized by such mechanisms as child marriage, stringent definition of eligibles, and isolation from potential mates.[3]

Romantic love is not unique to the Western world. It can "break out" in any society if given the opportunity. Variation from one society to another in the prevalence and desirability of love is thus not a matter of emotional capabilities, but of definition and control. Love is an inadequate basis for mating and sex relations in the kin-centered society, and is therefore defined negatively and controlled by the kin group. A love relationship may develop between mates, but this is not the basis for, nor even a necessary concomitant of, their marriage. "Kinfolk or immediate family," says Goode

> can disregard the question of who marries whom, only if a marriage is not seen as a link between kin lines, only if no property, power, lineage honor, totemic relationships, and the like are believed to flow from the kin lines through the spouses to their offspring. Universally, howver, these are believed to follow kin lines.[4]

The logical alternative to kin control of mating would be found in a system in which kin lines are totally unimportant and solidarities and functions are individual-based, with the domestic unit—if it existed—serving individual needs. In such a society, which can be observed nowhere in the empirical world, entirely free choice could be permitted; this choice would very likely be based strictly upon emotional attraction. Such a scheme is related to Farber's "universal availability" conceptualization.

Between the two polar alternatives described above, i.e., complete kin control and completely free choice, can be found several degrees of restriction upon love and mating. In the colonial American family, for example—in which the nuclear family dominated many functions and vied with the kin group for solidarity—choice was individual, but was greatly restricted by nuclear family and kin influences. In the contemporary U.S. family, in which individual values and functions compete with both nuclear family and kin solidarity, mate selection is by choice, based on love; but family and kin still use various methods, often successful, to influence the process.

Love is, therefore, an emotional potential that is controlled to varying degrees by the different societies of the world. The amount of control varies directly with the degree to which institutional functions and personnel are embedded within the kin group. In modern American society, love has been institutionalized as the basis for personal choice of a mate, but even in this society diverse means are employed by family and kin to restrict the opportunity for love to develop.

Normatively, then, an American will cite love as the reason for his marriage. Love may cause marriage, but (1) what is love? (2) what causes it? and (3) how is it controlled in American society? The first question has seldom been answered directly. A novelist may view love viscerally and sexually, giving descriptions of the attraction one human being holds for another. A poet may ennoble love through the use of adjectives and hyperbole, as he "counts the ways" in which he is drawn to his beloved. The sociologist Robert Winch reduces love to a two-fold definition, more casual than descriptive, which sees love as resulting from the person (1) having certain attributes highly prized by me, and (2) meeting specific personal or psychological needs which I have.[5] Goode is perhaps most realistic when, after attempting a definition of his own, he admits that verbal definitions of the emotion called love "are notoriously open to attack."[6] It is better to refer to the experience without attempting an inclusive and conclusive definition, such as one might give for fear or anger, and to assume that most readers are sufficiently familiar with the phenomenon to provide their own intuitive perception of its significance. Thus, we shall move on to a consideration of controls upon and causes of love in the United States, an approach that will very likely lead us closer to an understanding of love than if we expended further effort trying to define it.

SECTION ONE

NEGATIVE FACTORS IN MATE SELECTION

The negative or limiting factors in mate selection are those concerned with the question: Who *won't* you marry? These factors include not only kin and family controls or restrictions, but any other conditions that limit the field of eligible persons. Though the direction of change in American society may be toward an increase in universal availability, the contemporary family system is still far from embodying that principal. There is considerable personal choice in the selection of a mate, but there are also factors that operate to limit that choice. In this section we shall discuss three of the more important of these factors.

Incest Taboos

The prohibition against marrying close kin has already been discussed at length, therefore, it will only be referred to here. In the United States, as in the great majority of societies, this taboo involves parents and siblings, as well as other close kin of the ascending generation such as aunts, uncles, and grandparents. First cousins are also ordinarily excluded from marriage, though examples of cousin marriage are reported from time to time. No distinction is made between parallel and cross cousins in terms of eligibility for marriage.

Propinquity

One seldom marries someone whom he has not seen, met, and interacted with; he is more likely to interact with someone located nearby than with someone located at a distance. This statement of self-evident fact introduces a second limiting condition upon mate selection—propinquity, or proximity. This obvious factor in mate selection was first described in detail by James H. S. Bossard in 1932. After investigating 5,000 marriages in Philadelphia, Bossard discovered that one-third of the couples applying for marriage licenses lived within five city blocks of each other, and more than half lived twenty or fewer blocks apart.[7]

Subsequently, other researchers reported the same results: the closer to one another two persons live, the more likely they are to get married. Many writers interpreted the findings as another manifestation of homogamy. That is, people of the same social and cultural group tend to live close together. Thus, they interact more frequently and, therefore, marry each other. In 1958, Alvin Katz and Reuben Hill reviewed and summarized the research on propinquity by means of three propositions.[8] (1) *Marriage is normative,* or follows subcultural lines. This, of course, embodies the homogamy interpretation of many previous writers. (2) Within the normative field of eligibles, *the probability of marriage varies directly with the probability of interaction.* Many of us have heard stories about the couple who correspond by letter for years and marry at their first actual meeting. This is the exception which proves the rule that the possibility of frequent interaction is the logical precondition for dating and marriage. (3) The authors note that *the probability of interaction is lessened by intervening opportunities for interaction.* This might be called the density factor; it becomes apparent when we consider the likelihood of two persons on adjoining farms one-half mile apart interacting and becoming well-acquainted, in comparison to the likelihood of two residents of dormitories or apartment buildings one-half mile apart becoming acquainted.

The locational character of any given individual's life is not stable. He may move from place to place, thus complicating the operation of propinquity. Thus, for example, we can say that a student at the University of Pennsylvania is more likely to marry a co-ed at the University of Pennsylvania than a co-ed at the University of Florida, unless he resided near the Florida co-ed at an earlier stage of their lives. This does not void the propinquity factor, but merely complicates it.

Homogamy in Mate Selection

The third and final negative, or limiting, factor in American mate selection is in reality a complex of social structural categories. When availability allows, the person chosen as a mate is ordinarily from the same general social background as oneself. If, for example, one is a WASP (white, Anglo-Saxon, Protestant), the chances are pretty good that he will marry another WASP. Four categories within U.S. society have received substantial research attention with respect to their limitation upon mate selection. These are race, religion, ethnic or nationality group, and social class.

Studies of *racial* homogamy, or marriage within the same racial group, have generally divided the population into white and black and—if included in the sample—American Indian, Mexican, and Oriental.[9] The norms restricting racial intermarriage are extremely stringent; this issue will be dealt with at length in the last section of this chapter. Many of the investigations of *religious* intermarriage have been based on the threefold division into Protestants, Catholics, and Jews; although a few have further subdivided Protestants into the largest denominational groupings, such as Presbyterians, Methodists, Baptists, Lutherans, and Episcopalians, and Jews into Orthodox, Conservative, and Reformed. *Ethnic* or nationality categories are difficult to distinguish definitively from both racial and religious. Mexicans, for example, are actually an ethnic group, but are often treated as a racial category. Also, the members of many nationality groups are almost all of the same religion; e.g., the vast majority of Italians are Roman Catholics, while Scandinavians are largely Lutheran. The United States is comprised of numerous ethnic groups, including Irish, Spanish, Italian, Japanese, Chinese, Filipino, Hungarian, Norwegian, German, Polish, and English. In some studies of ethnic homogamy, these numerous national aggregates have been combined into more inclusive groupings such as southeastern European, northwest European, and so on. It is apparent that the possibilities of confusion, both within the ethnic category and between ethnic category and race or religion, are substantial; studies of ethnic homogamy must, therefore, be interpreted cautiously. *Social class,* or status grouping, is the only one of the four structural designations that the individual himself is unlikely to make. The individual may say: "I am a white Irish Catholic," but is unlikely to add to this: "I am upper middle class," or "I am working class." Thus, while an observer will recognize that there are actual differences in education, income, and occupation within U.S. society, and that these differences have behavioral manifestations, it may be argued that social class designations are actually artifacts of the investigator. Some studies of social class homogamy have divided the population into but two categories, middle class and working class, or—according to occupation—white collar and blue collar. Others have dichotomized each of these into upper and lower, while still other researchers have used as many as six or seven class divisions. Of course, the rate of intermarriage reported is bound to fluctuate as a result of the number of categories employed. Since social class divisions are made by observers using various indicators, and not by the population itself,[10] it might be well to indicate the possible interpretations of social class endogamy which seem viable. According to Bruce Eckland, class endogamy may be explained by: (1) similar values, which reflect within-class cultural similarity; (2) residential segregation along class lines (noted in the discussion of propinquity); (3) the close relation between class and ethnicity-race; (4) family pressure to marry one's "own kind"; (5) educational advantages or disadvantages that cause class differences to persist. These five interpretations show once again the interrelations between the four categories used in homogamy studies. Therefore, keeping in mind these cautions concerning interrelationships between categories and the arbitrary nature of the number of subdivisions within each of the four, let us turn to the research on homogamy rates.

The general tendency in American society is for homogeneity between mates (according to the four categories) to persist. Bruce Eckland summarizes the rates of homogamy (drawn from numerous studies) as follows: "Most studies in the United States report a very high rate, over 99 percent, for racial endogamy, an overall rate perhaps as high as 90 percent for religious homogamy, and moderately high rates, 50 percent to 80 percent for class homogamy. . . ."[11] The 90 per cent rate of religious homogamy is based primarily upon studies that divide the population into only three religious categories—Protestant, Catholic, and Jewish.[12] When a further breakdown of Protestant and Jewish groups is employed, the rate is only slightly above the lower limit for social class reported by Eckland. Also, Eckland's 80 per cent figure for class endogamy is based upon those studies that dichotomize the population into middle and working class, while his 50 per cent limit is drawn from studies employing six or seven divisions. Finally, Eckland does not deal with ethnic homogamy, but if six to ten of the most populous nationality groupings are considered, the homogamy rate is fairly close to that for religion when the same number of categories is used. Thus, racial homogamy is most nearly complete at present; the rates for the other three social categories are fairly similar and dependent to a large extent on how many subdivisions are made.

When we turn from the consideration of comparative rates to that of trends in rates, we find that racial and social class intermarriage rates are changing hardly at all, while those for religion and ethnic group are increasing.[13] A key reason for the increase in religious intermarriage is the decreasing salience of the religious subdivisions in American life; as the importance of such differences diminishes, emphasis upon homogamy according to religion also diminishes. This trend is much more noticeable when the three general religious categories—Protestants, Catholics, and Jews—are subdivided than it is when only intermarriages among the three are considered. The increase in religious intermarriage is a gradual, but perceptible, process in the twentieth century United States. A key cause of the decrease in ethnic group solidarity was the cessation of large-scale immigration during the 1920's, resulting in the "Americanization" of the immigrants and their offspring.[14] It is quite likely, therefore, that in the foreseeable future rates of homogamy will be highest within racial categories, next for social class and the three general religious categories, and lowest for the religious and ethnic subdivisions.[15]

The influence of social categories upon mate selection in the United States can be recapitulated by reviewing the significance of four terms: consciousness, availability, visibility, and salience. The question, "What social categories do you belong to?" is not always, and perhaps *not* even usually, verbalized or *consciously applied* to one's dating partners. Yet limitation does occur, if not as a conscious process, then as a result of feeling more "at home" with a partner of similar background or as a result of the residential segregation imposed by parents' choice of location. The mention of residential segregation leads to the second issue in homogamy, that of *availability*. August Hollingshead's and John Thomas' articles on homogamy illustrate the importance of this factor. Hollingshead found in New Haven that only 6.2 per cent of the Catholic marriages were with non-Catholics, while Thomas reported that, for the state of Connecticut as a whole, 40.2 per cent of Catholics who married, married persons of other religious faiths.[16] This divergence, Thomas feels, is to be explained principally by availability. That is, the Catholic who grows up in a predominantly Protestant community is much more likely to marry a Protestant than is the Catholic who grows up in a ghetto-like Catholic neighborhood in a city such as New Haven. Thus, the non-availability of persons of one's own background is a key factor in various sorts of intermarriage (and is related to the propinquity factor discussed earlier).

A third influence upon the operation of background categories in limiting mate selection is *visibility*. Due to the visibility factor, it is not difficult to see why religious intermarriage is more frequent than racial intermarriage. However, even more important is the fourth and final influence upon homogamy—*salience*. Two persons of different races who say: "Sure we are of different races, but what difference does it make?" may very well get married. But an interracial couple who says: "We are strongly attracted, but, conditions being what they are, our racial difference would be bound to cause our children and us lots of heartaches," is demonstrating that their racial difference is salient to them. The salience or non-salience of each of the four social categories could be illustrated in a similar way by asking: "Does their background heterogeneity matter to the couple, or doesn't it?" If it matters, it may not stand in the way of dating for enjoyment or experience, but it may very well stop them from marrying. Farber makes a very good point when he says that "intermarriage is occurring not only because of a breakdown in parental control over mate selection, but also because the traditional social categories for inmarriage are themselves becoming vague and diffuse."[17] This decrease in salience is particularly noticeable in college populations, but does not hold for racial barriers as it does for the other three social categories.[18] The question of salience or non-salience is really one of values, of what matters to the individual. An individual who highly values a particular aspect of his background or group to which he belongs is unlikely to compromise it for the sake of marriage. The notion of values, however, when viewed in a broader perspective, introduces us to the positive, or selective, factors in mate selection. Thus, at this point let us examine those factors that determine the answer to the question: "Among the eligibles, which one will you pick?"

SECTION TWO

POSITIVE FACTORS IN MATE SELECTION

Values in Mate Selection

After incest taboo, propinquity, and the pressure of social group ties have narrowed the field of eligibles, the young person finds other factors affecting his dating and mate selection. A question that is likely to arise as one becomes more seriously inclined toward a dating partner might be expressed thus: "Do we see eye to eye on the things that matter to me?" Salience and similarity, or mutual non-salience (a matter's being considered as unimportant by both members of the couple), is important not only regarding religious, racial, ethnic and status distinctions, but also regarding values of a more personal nature, such as desired marital roles, number of children desired, and so on. However, it must be admitted that there is marked disagreement concerning the importance of values as possible selective factors. Robert H. Coombs, in an article entitled "A Value Theory of Mate Selection," suggests that most other theories can be incorporated into and explained by a value theory that includes background factors, propinquity, and personal values.[19] Eckland reviews the mate selection theories and qualifies the influence of values on mate selection. "Apparently," he says, "our *perception* that other persons share with us the same or similar value orientations and beliefs facilitates considerably our attraction to them." (Italics added.) This idea that perception of consensus is more crucial than actual consensus is consistent with many social psychological studies of friendship attraction.[20] However, Eloise Snyder's study of 561 students, who were primarily of rural background, beclouds the issue by asserting that similarity of attitudes among marital pairs appears to be "the result of the adjustive interaction shared by the couple and not necessarily an affinity present at the outset of the relationship."[21] In other words, attraction may be the basis for increased perception of value consensus or even for an actual increase in consensus, or consensus may produce attraction.

Thus, values may have some influence upon mate selection which is separate from that based upon salient social categories, but the extent of this positive influence is impossible to ascertain from the available studies.

Common Interests

Occasionally news comes of two musicians who are marrying in order to make beautiful music together forever. George Bernard Shaw portrays his acquaintances, the Webbs, thus: "two typewriters beating as one." One or a few common interests may be the major motivating force behind a marriage, but such a case is exceptional enough to be newsworthy. Unquestionably, common interests, or activities enjoyed together, form one foundation for a durable dating relationship; this relationship, in turn, is the typical prelude to marriage in U.S. society. Yet, a direct link between such interests and the ultimate choice of a mate is doubtful in most cases. Related research by Purnell Benson has shown that certain kinds of common interests may be detrimental to a satisfactory engagement or marriage, and that there is little or no relation between the *number* of common interests and adjustment in either engagement or marriage. Common familistic interests, such as home, children, and religion, are characteristic of well-adjusted engaged persons, while individualistic and pleasure-seeking interests, such as success, drinking, money, travel, commercial entertainments, and companionship as a means to avoid loneliness, are more prevalent among poorly-adjusted engaged couples.[22]

If Benson's findings are slightly reinterpreted, the interests related to good adjustment can be seen to be values of the sort discussed in the previous section, while the pleasure-seeking interests are the enjoyments and activities that are the major focus of the term "common interests." Does this, then, mean that common activity-interests, though important in the early stages of a relationship, come to be detrimental as the relationship becomes more serious? Is the long-term result of activity-interests either an unhappy engagement or an unhappy marriage? It seems that a better interpretation of Benson's results would be as follows: Common activity-interests may be an excellent beginning point for a premarital relationship. However, if that relation reaches the engagement stage with the couple members still having nothing more in common than the activities and personal pleasures that originally brought them together, then the engagement is precarious. Common activities, without the presence of a deeper and more serious value consensus, form a superficial and inadequate basis for a stable engagement and marriage—unless an activity has been transformed into a basic value or goal, as in the case of the Webbs and the musicians. The "superficial" activity-based engagement or marriage may illustrate Charles Bolton's concept of escalated commitment, in which a couple has been impelled toward marriage by various "pushes," including pressure from significant others.[23]

Benson's research, the reader may have noticed, does *not* say that persons do not marry on the basis of pleasure-seeking interests, but rather than this is an inadequate basis for a *satisfactory* marriage. To the present author it seems that any increased societal tendency to define marriage as a *voidable* relationship might be accompanied by an increased tendency to marry for reasons of enjoyment, without any deeper value commitments. Farber speaks of the movement in American society toward *permanent* availability, so that if a marriage does not work out, the couple members are free to break ties and try again. If this movement has progressed since Benson wrote in the early 1950's, common-activity interests may actually be more prevalent as a basis for mate selection at the present time. Couple members may feel that common interests and enjoyment are sufficient to justify marriage, regardless of whether or not they are an adequate basis for its permanence. This, however, is an interpretation that can be held only tentatively, pending further research on activity-interests and mate selection.

Complementary Needs

"Birds of a feather flock together." "Opposites attract." For centuries these two aphorisms have existed side by side in the chronicles of human thought. Both have likewise made their way into the scholarship pertaining to mate selection in American society. The former concept is inherent in the previously-discussed tendency toward categorical homogamy, while the latter is embodied in Robert Winch's recent argument that love, and therefore mate selection, is attributable to the need for complementarity. Winch, the reader will recall, included as part of his definition of love, attraction to another who shows promise of meeting one's psychological needs. He explicates this throughout his book on *Mate-Selection*, indicating that the way needs are gratified is by finding a partner whose personality characteristics are the opposite of, but complementary to, one's own.[24] If you are basically a submissive person, you will seek as a mate someone who will dominate you. If you are "nurturant" (need to have things done for you), your choice of a mate will be a succorant, or receptive, person (that is, someone who is gratified by doing things for others). Winch's intensive study of 25 married student couples at Northwestern University revealed the presence of these and other complementary need patterns, which Winch assumed to have been a key factor in their selection of each other as mates. What is attractive about this theory is its fascinating simplicity and intuitive rationality. The problem with it is the inconclusive nature of the subsequent evidence. Winch and his students, Thomas and Virginia Ktsanes, have been among the few who have been able to compile any evidence that complementary psychological undercurrents are operative in the mate selection process.[25] On the other hand, research by Schellenberg and Bee, by Bowerman and Day, and by others, has found a random relation between complementarity and mate selection.[26] That is, for every couple characterized by a particular form of complementarity, there can be found another couple whose members share the same general personality traits. In a study of 47 married and 50 engaged couples, J. Richard Udry noted a tendency to project one's own traits onto the partner. Furthermore, he found no evidence of general complementarity in mate selection, though some asymmetrical specific complementarity was discovered.[27] Winch's traits are too broad and inclusive, Udry feels, to be useful as predictors of mate choice. Winch and his critics have questioned each others' methods and interpretations; the evidence, according to both Eckland and Winch himself, is still inconclusive.[28]

Winch, it should be noted, does not say, either in his book or in his later articles on complementarity, that this is the only factor in mate selection in the U.S. Rather, he feels, it operates to weed out the bad bets after homogeneity considerations have already greatly limited the field of eligibles. In his latest article, he adds that perhaps complementarity should be supplemented by the concept of role compatibility.[29] Thus, despite our attempts to isolate and examine individually the factors in mate selection, the interrelations between them once again become apparent. These interrelations will be the topic of a later section of this chapter, after several additional positive factors have been introduced.

Other Psychological Factors in Mate Selection

Various researchers have proposed several other psychological factors to account for mate selection, but the evidence for their influence is meager. Ernest Burgess and Paul Wallin, and Anselm

Strauss, writing prior to the appearance of Winch's complementary needs theory and using data on a well-educated sample of 373 engaged or recently married persons, find that *personality needs* influence mate choice. Burgess and Wallin claim that "a high proportion of persons fail to find the satisfaction of their chief personality needs in their relation with their mates. Yet the fulfillment of personality needs appears to be of primary importance in mate selection."[30] In other words, the individual has needs and he finds a mate whom he feels will come closest to meeting them. However, the mate is unlikely to be able to meet all of one's needs, nor, for that matter, may he or she be able to satisfy any of them completely. What sorts of needs are Burgess and Wallin talking about? Strauss gives some hints in the following observations:

> The person had as a child emotional experiences which have developed in her the need for recognition, approval, gentle consideration, emotional support, and the like. These psychological necessities, whether consciously or unwittingly sought, quite understandably enter into the girl's anticipations of married life and more or less determine her ideal. . . .[31]

Little evidence has been compiled since the Burgess-Wallin-Strauss research that would indicate more precisely the manner in which these needs operate in mate selection. Perhaps they operate as Winch claims: the person searches out as a mate someone who is perceived as able to meet one's own needs because that person's needs and personality are opposite and complementary. Strauss does hint that this notion is also related to some sort of ideal mate that the individual seeks. His own needs help to structure the ideal, and that ideal may in turn influence his mate choice. The majority of persons, or so the argument goes, develop some conception of the kind of person they want in a mate and carry it with them throughout their dating experience. This *ideal mate concept* may consist of physical characteristics, personality characteristics, cultural traits, or some combination of all three. However, the problem with the ideal mate concept as a positive factor in mate selection is very similar to that raised by Snyder concerning values. Udry writes:

> What is the significance of ideal mate conceptions for mate selection? From this study, it appears that the ideal mate is not an actual basis of mate selection. . . . mates are selected on some other basis without regard to pre-existing ideal mate images. Furthermore, the ideal mate images are not attributed to selected persons, but probably change in response to new relationships into which

the person enters. Ideal mate images can therefore be seen as resultants—reflecting need structures, changing in response to changing interpersonal relationships, responding to experiences with particular people—rather than determinants of heterosexual selections.[32]

As we noted above, Strauss believed that the ideal mate image had influenced the mate choice of at least some of his sample; he also thought that this image might have served to exclude certain categories of persons from consideration. In other words, he feels that the ideal acts as a limiting factor for many persons, and as a selective factor for some. Yet we are again confronted with overlapping concepts: Strauss finds that for many persons the ideal includes the qualities that we discussed earlier under the heading of "homogamy." The concept of the ideal mate, like one's value system, can be interpreted broadly enough to incorporate most of the other factors. However, if homogamy is omitted from the ideal mate concept, we are forced to agree with Udry's assessment of the inutility of the ideal mate image as a selective factor in mate selection—at least until further evidence is provided.

A third psychological or personality factor in mate selection, which has been linked by Strauss and others with the ideal mate image, is *parental image*. A narrow application of this factor is indicated in the words of the song: "I want a girl just like the girl that married dear old Dad." However, Burgess and Wallin find several patterns of attraction besides that based upon the similarity of one's chosen mate to the opposite-sex parent. Other patterns include attraction to a person who: is similar to the same-sex parent, is the opposite of one or the other parent, combines characteristics of both parents, even has the traits of a surrogate parent.[33] In light of this multiplicity of possibilities and the ordinarily *post hoc* nature of the linkages, Eckland's conclusion should not be too surprising. He maintains that though it "would seem reasonable to expect parent images to either encourage or discourage a person marrying someone like his parent, no clear evidence has been produced to support the hypothesis."[34]

Several years ago Clifford Kirkpatrick and Charles Hobart studied 306 couples at the University of Indiana.[35] These couples included 62 who were "favorite dates," 66 who were going steady, 75 who were engaged, and 103 who were married. The authors' major concerns were to trace disagreements and *empathic ability* (or the ability to predict the action, thoughts, and feelings of one's partner accurately, i.e., to put yourself in your partner's shoes). The researchers found that empathic ability was much greater between those going steady than it was between those in the favorite date category. Similarly, the ability was greater in married couples than in engaged couples. Yet, since this was not a longitudinal study, following the same couples through all four stages, these differences had to be interpreted cautiously. Is it length of association that increases empathic ability, or is it a matter of selectivity, with the non-empathic couples weeding themselves out at certain points? According to the authors, the latter explanation is more satisfactory than the former, since *within* each of the four categories there was no correlation between length of dating and empathy score. Kirkpatrick and Hobart conclude that when a couple defines its relationship as "steady" or "married," this is a sign that it is time to find out more about one's partner, thereby increasing empathic ability. Of course, with increased empathy, one may either like or dislike what he knows about his partner, so that empathy may act either to perpetuate or to terminate the relationship. Can this factor, therefore, be considered a positive factor in mate selection? Only if it is combined with values and interests to comprise an "understanding-agreement" factor—another interrelation between factors!

What conclusion can be drawn regarding personality needs, ideal mate image, parent image, and empathy as factors in mate selection? With the present state of research, empathy appears to be the most closely correlated with mate selection. However, part of the difficulty with the others may simply be the need for better measuring instruments and more data. Another part of the difficulty appears to lie in the attempt to treat these and the other positive and negative factors as if they were static, rather than as in process. A third difficulty lies in the actual complex relationships between the various factors that we have isolated analytically and discussed individually. Let us, therefore, spend some time discussing these last two difficulties.

SECTION THREE

MATE SELECTION AS PROCESS

Winch never claimed, we have said, that complementary needs comprise the only factor in mate selection, but rather that they act as a final filter, weeding out the bad bets and aiding the individual in his choice. The notion of a filtering process leads us to the consideration of an extremely provocative article by Alan Kerckhoff and Keith Davis. Stated summarily, the authors' claim is that it is not a matter of either homogamy or heterogamy, i.e., of marrying likes in background or unlikes in needs. Instead, all these factors —background group memberships, values and interests, and complementary needs—may in fact operate at various stages of a single courtship, from its inception to marriage.[36] Thus, if these factors are salient, the individual will limit his dating experience at the outset to those persons who are of roughly the same social background as himself. When he begins dating, race, religion, and social class have already limited his choices, though this limitation may be unconscious or determined by residential location and other parental influences.

Once the original filtering process based upon background factors has taken place, the early stages of dating involve doing enjoyable things together. Many relationships never survive this period of enjoyment, since the enjoyment simply wears off. But those relationships that do survive the idealized and companionship stage find a third factor entering the picture. This is the complementarity with which Winch was most concerned. There develops, over time, a much more realistic appraisal of the good and bad points in the dating partner (increased empathic ability) and, according to Kerckhoff and Davis, there appears a much more personality-based bond between partners. When this complementary psychological bond develops, there is a much greater likelihood of mating occurring. In short, you have a filtering process that begins with homogeneous limitation, moves through enjoyment, idealization, and a searching for commonness, and ends with a complementary bond that leads to marriage. Of course, many relationships weed themselves out along the way.

Though this is a somewhat oversimplified and pat summary of Kerckhoff and Davis' filtering process, it does cover the essential elements. One problem in the empirical process, which Kerckhoff and Davis point out, is that the history of a particular dating relationship may find the first two factors reversed. An individual may be dating serveral persons he enjoys, and may not narrow the field of eligibles on the basis of race or social class until he finds himself becoming increasingly serious about one of the partners. And, as hinted above, if a couple marries because they enjoy one another, they may later discover basic value and category incompatibilities—too late to weed out the relationship without a divorce.

Kerckhoff and Davis, then, have provided us with an ordering of several factors in mate selection, operating at different stages of the dating process. The main problem, besides that of the actual order, concerns the evidence for complementary needs as a key part of the process; the evidence for it is not convincing.

A second attempt to deal with mate selection processually, or operationally, rather than statically is found in an article by Charles Bolton. Based upon intensive research with 20 married couples, Bolton's study departs radically from the numerous attempts to isolate and determine specific factors in mate selection. Mate selection, he feels, has unfortunately been treated as a decision or a single operation, instead of as a developmental process. He feels that perhaps mate selection should be viewed as "a process in which the *transactions between individuals* in certain societal contexts are determinants of turning points and commitments out of which marriage emerges."[37] Marriage is problematic in the sense that both homogamy and heterogamy are inadequate explanations for mate selection; the interactions and change in commitments during a developing relationship must be taken seriously. Information is thus needed on what transpires—not only on what initially composed the situation and characteristics of the couple members.

Marriages are not merely functions of the needs, values, and backgrounds that the members of a couple bring to the relationship. The process of increasing commitment develops an existence of its own, and is carried forward by a series of *escalators*, factors that "push" the couple toward marriage. Among these escalators are: (1) *value-activity* involvement, which is based upon both a patterning of time spent together and an increasing congruence of values and goals, as Snyder pointed out. A second escalator is (2) *commitment*, due to the formal and public redefinition that occurs as a couple moves through the stages of seriousness toward marriage. A good example of a commitment escalator is the engagement announcement, following which couples are propelled on into marriage by that very commitment. Closely related to this is the (3) *"habitualized"* escalator, which causes the individual to avoid the grief reaction and psychological upheaval that would accompany the dissolution of an intensifying relationship. A fourth escalator is based upon (4) *identity* needs, as the individual defines himself as "Jane's fiancé," or "Tom's steady." The dating and mate selection process is related to the young person's search for identity and recognition, and the dating partner offers one means of asserting one's identity. Relinquishing this identity can be a painful process. (5) The *image* of the partner serves to perpetuate the relationship, as the romanticized conception of the partner and self-esteem, based upon one's ability to "pick 'em," combine to intensify involvement.

Bolton himself indicates other escalators and other ways in which escalators operate to carry a relationship toward marriage. His major point, however, is that the transactions that take place within a relationship itself are generally overlooked in favor of the traditional factors used to account for mate selection. It is, to be sure, as difficult to argue with Bolton's assertions as it is disconcerting to have to admit the inadequacy of attempts to understand mate selection in the United States by simply isolating and specifying individual factors.

SECTION FOUR

CRITIQUE AND TENTATIVE CONCLUSIONS

Throughout the discussion of some ten factors in mate selection, the issues of convolution and combination have arisen time and again. One author will define values broadly enough to include the effect of propinquity, background categories, and common interests. Another's definition of value will encompass personality needs, homogamy desires, and parental image within the "ideal mate" conception. Winch, while stressing complementary needs, acknowledges the fact that notions of homogamy and role compatibility must be added to the explanation of mate selection.[38] Kirkpatrick and Hobart find that empathy and agreement, when taken together, yield substantial insight into mate selection. Kerckhoff and Davis suggest that homogamy, values and interests, and complementary needs may indeed work processually to filter out the bad bets. Finally, Charles Bolton cautions us that homogamy and heterogamy considerations are not enough; they must be augmented by the consideration of process itself. A relationship, as it progresses, takes on an existence that may serve to perpetuate it despite discoveries by the couple members of value divergences, of the imperfect meeting of each other's needs, and so on.

All these observations make it impossible to accept one explanation based upon a single factor, and reject the others. Rather, some sort of intuitive interpretation, supported by a knowledge of history, is about as far as the current state of research will carry us. Farber has tried such an historical weighting of factors while commenting upon Kerckhoff and Davis' filtering process. The idea of the companionship family, says Farber, is that individuals seek personal happiness, adjustment, and freedom within the family setting. This is the type of family toward which the U.S. is moving. Now, Farber adds, in a society in which the trend is also toward permanent availability (so that if things don't work out the couple may divorce and try again), one mate selection factor-complex stands out. Mutual enjoyment and general goal similarity take precedence over both background homogamy and complementarity in the selection process. If, he says, the most salient aspect of marriage were its permanence, we would be much more careful than we are to filter out background factors and to determine deeper psychological compatibility. Complementarity may be necessary and desired under institutionalized conditions, or under conditions of permanent mating; however, under conditions of availability, interests and congeniality of goals appear to override both complementarity and categorical distinctions in the U.S. selection process. Permanent availability, therefore, implies that the basic interests of the individual may change, as may his goals, in the course of his lifetime; since these interests and goals were the prime bases for the marriage, it may be voided by such changes. Farber feels that what may happen is that a marriage already consummated on the basis of interests and certain shared goals may be severely tested if social categories and needs are found to be incompatible.

This, then, is one attempt to compare the importance of several mate selection factors. The present author cannot, however, accept Farber's interpretation in its entirety. For one thing, while the movement toward universal and permanent availability is apparent, it does not seem to have progressed quite as far as Farber assumes it has. Within the racial categories, the three general religious divisions, and the major social classes, homogamy is still the rule. Furthermore, propinquity acts both to reinforce homogamy and to further limit the field of eligibles, though the mobility of the individual complicates the operation of propinquity. It is unquestionable that the incest taboo, homogamy considerations (when they are salient), and propinquity act to greatly limit the number of possible mates available to the individual. But *limitation* is only part of the mate selection process: there are "pulls" or *selective* factors and, as Bolton reminds us, "pushes," or *intensification* and processual factors. Among the selective factors, the most fruitful seem to be common interests and perceived value consensus (which includes the idea of goals referred to by Farber), and empathy. The couple in the United States who find that they can predict one another's behavior and responses, who enjoy one another's company, and who at least assume that they agree on certain important goals and attitudes, are very likely to get married.

It would be most convenient if limitations plus interests, empathy, and values accounted for all the variability in mate choices, but this is simply not so. Many youthful marriages may occur to escape an unhappy home, or because of a premarital pregnancy; in such cases the importance of background homogamy, value consensus, and empathy may be minimal. Also, in American society, people expect to be married by a certain age. If the "right one" has not come along by the time the individual reaches his mid-20's, he may stop waiting for the right one and choose someone who shows an interest. In addition, any given relationship may, over time, develop pressures for continuation and intensification, as Bolton noted. These pushes toward marriage cannot be accounted for by what the two individuals bring into the dating process with them; they are processual elements of the relationship as it develops. Finally, love—which is, after all, what we are trying to explain—is not uniformly intense from one marriage to the next. Kephart, in a study of more than 1,000 college students, found that some females were open to the possibility of marrying someone who had qualities they desired in a mate, but with whom they were not in love.[39]

To say that the task of understanding mate selection is incomplete would be an understatement. A beginning has been made, but three major problems remain. First, the need for *further research* is obvious. Perhaps, with sufficient research, certain psychological needs, along with the limiting conditions and the empathy-agreement variables that are already somewhat substantiated, will be found to be clear predictors of mate selection. Second, *specification* may be valuable. More sophisticated research may lead us to agree with Kephart that sex-specific theories are needed, rather than an overarching framework. That is, we may find that the determinants of mate choice for males and females are not exactly the same. Or it may be that different explanations are needed for mate selection among (with respect to age) early marriers, "normal"

FIGURE 9

The Author's View of Mate Selection or Family Formation in the Contemporary United States in Relation to the Family Formation Continuum

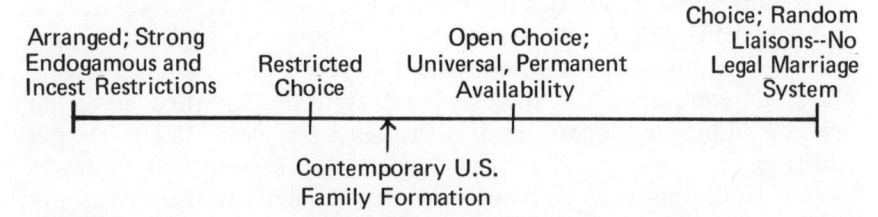

```
Arranged; Strong                        Open Choice;          Choice; Random
Endogamous and      Restricted       Universal, Permanent     Liaisons--No
Incest Restrictions   Choice            Availability          Legal Marriage
                                                              System
|------------------------|-----------------|-------------------|
                                 ↑
                         Contemporary U.S.
                         Family Formation
```

marriers, and late marriers. Perhaps the "pushes" into marriage are greater among both early and late marriers, while homogamy, empathy, and value-interest agreement can apply fairly well to those who marry between ages 20 and 25 in the U.S. The third problem may not be solved by research alone. How can the *pushes* toward marriage be incorporated into the explanation? Bolton has convinced us of the necessity of doing so, but has not generated the required methodological tools. Even if and when such tools are developed, it may still be necessary to admit the presence of other fortuitous, or *chance*, factors that cannot be rationally handled. These problems will not, of course, keep writers from trying to explain rationally "who marries whom and why" in the United States. This author's reading of the data places mate selection in the contemporary U.S. as shown in Figure 9, in which we utilize the Family Formation Continuum proposed in Chapter V. As always, the interpretation is tentative and subject to the reader's reinterpretation and relocation.

One aspect of mate selection upon which the evidence is clear is the tendency for marriage to occur between persons of a generally similar social background. Prime among homogamous considerations is race; a discussion of black-white intermarriage closes this chapter.

SECTION FIVE

RACIAL HOMOGAMY: A CASE IN NON–UNIVERSAL AVAILABILITY[40]

For most white persons in the United States, the field of eligibles simply does not include members of the black race; conversely, the field of eligibles for most black persons does not include whites. While the issue of racial homogamy includes Orientals and others, the following discussion concentrates on the norms, laws, and motives (and their respective behavioral manifestations) governing intermarriage between whites and blacks in the U.S.

Norms Governing Black-White Intermarriage

The question of norms, or expectations, regarding marriage by race has historically focussed in the anti-amalgamation doctrine, which says that the various races were meant to be separate. Gunnar Myrdal's classic study in the mid-1940's, published as *An American Dilemma,* makes it clear what Americans, both white and black, believe regarding racial intermarriage.[41] For many years white Americans argued more strongly and publicly against black-white intermarriage than did blacks. They based these feelings upon notions of the inherent inferiority of black people, frequently bolstered by religious pronouncements concerning the curse of Canaan (translated by the ministers as a curse on black people). The lower one's social class position, the greater his *expressed* opposition to intermarriage was likely to be. Educated whites also demonstrated substantial prejudice, but were better able to hide it. In some cases, because these whites felt less of a threat of intermarriage, they were more able to talk a liberal line.

Whites have justified the position they assign to blacks with the feeling: "They are doing the best they can." If a black person or family escapes from the bottom he can be treated as an exception to the basic inferiority. Some white people refer to the inferior position that black people have been assigned in this society as a rationalization for their strong feelings against marriage with blacks. That is, to many whites, blacks have been considered inferior and thus not suitable as mates.

Since the time of Myrdal's writings, there has been a needed increase in racial pride among blacks (especially black leaders). Along with this development has come an argument against marriage with whites. This argument is based on the grounds of the need for blacks to recognize their own identity and heritage as a race; and, in some cases, on the basis of the inherent degeneracy of whites.[42] The result is that today there are conspicuous pressures within *both* races for endogamy, as well as opposing pressures toward intermarriage from liberal elements of the population trying to manifest their lack of concern for the racial barrier. Which pressure is greater? Perhaps by the close of this discussion we can decide.

A second major question regarding the norms is: Where will

change occur in interracial matters? This, says Myrdal, depends on the "rank order of discrimination" (see Figure 10).[43] Items at the top of the list are, according to Myrdal, those areas in which whites are most desirous of remaining separate from blacks, while those at the bottom of the list are most important to blacks to change. Though it is possible to argue that there has been some rearranging of priorities in the years since Myrdal wrote, the important point is that the likely direction of change is approximately from bottom to top, with intermarriage being one of the last areas of desegregation and equality accepted into the norms of both races.

Intermarriage Laws

Recent changes in anti-miscegenation, or intermarriage, laws in the United States have been tremendous. As recently as 1960, 29 states, mostly southern and western, still had such laws. In 1964 it was 19 states; in 1966 it was 17; and in 1967 it was 16. In 1967, such laws were declared unconstitutional by the Supreme Court. Will this decision have any direct effect upon rates of intermarriage? Though it is too early to tell, the answer seems to be probably not in and of itself—at least as long as the norms against intermarriage remain strong.

Black-White Intermarriage: How Many and Who?

A New York attorney recently claimed that there are 1,000,000 racially intermarried persons in the United States, of which 810,000 are either passing or don't even know that they are intermarried. The idea that they "don't even know" signifies that the person may have a black ancestor in his past somewhere, bringing up the question of whether or not a marriage is a racial

FIGURE 10

Myrdal's Rank Order of Discrimination of Whites Against Blacks

RANK ORDER OF DISCRIMINATION	Black Desire for Change	White Desire for Perpetuation
Intermarriage and sex with white women	↑	
Close interpersonal relations and behavioral cues		
Use of public facilities		
Political involvement: voting, office holding, etc.		
Law, police, and court treatment		
Economics: credit, jobs, etc.		↓

intermarriage if none of the phenotypic manifestations are discernible. The notion that someone has one-fourth or one-sixteenth colored blood, and therefore his marriage is interracial if he marries a white person, is simply not scientifically defensible. It is much more appropriate to discuss rates of intermarriage in terms of their overt numbers, rather than being concerned with those who are passing or "don't know."

We do not know the national frequency of racial intermarriage. Figures are available for New York State and Boston for the early years of this century, and for California, Hawaii, Michigan, and Nebraska during the 1950's and 1960's. "For the period 1916 through 1937, Negro-white marriages in New York State exclusive of New York City varied from 1.7 to 4.8 per cent of all marriages involving Negroes. . . ."[44] The equivalent percentages for whites would, of course, be even lower. In Boston, the highest period of racial intermarriage appears to have been 1850–1900. In the 1900–1904 period and the 1914–1918 period, the racial intermarriage rate declined from 14 to 5 per 100 marriages involving blacks.[45] Since that time, the rate of intermarriage in Boston has averaged 3.9 per 100 black marriages and 0.12 per 100 white marriages, with a slight, but perceptible decline up until the Second World War.[46] The decline in intermarriages in Boston after the turn of the century was almost entirely due to a decline in marriages involving black grooms and white brides.

Figures for Boston and New York State stop at about 1938, forcing us to look elsewhere for more recent trends. David Heer, studying 1950–1960 data for four states, concludes that at least for California, Michigan, Hawaii, and Nebraska there are current indications of an upward trend in interracial marriage.[47] Thus, by piecing together the earlier and later data, though they are from different locations, we may tentatively conclude that the rate of black-white intermarriage has been curvilinear, declining from the late 1800's to about 1940, and rising gradually since that time. However, even in Hawaii, the state with the highest present intermarriage rate, the average rate for whites between 1956 and 1964 was only 24 in 10,000, or .24 per cent.[48] To say that the rate is rising is *not*, therefore, to assert that large numbers of blacks and whites are now intermarrying in the United States.

The second aspect of black and white behavior with respect to intermarriage concerns not *how many*, but *who*. Who are the intermarriers? Among whites, racial intermarriage seems most typically to have involved widowed or divorced persons more than those never married; older more often than younger persons (perhaps a function of their reduced field or eligibles); urban rather than rural people; native-born white women and foreign-born white men more than their opposites; and low-social-class white women. As for blacks who intermarry, Drake and Cayton listed the following as the types of Chicago blacks who intermarry with whites: intellectuals and bohemians, who are not responsive to social restrictions; members of cults that include disregard of racial differences as part of their social philosophy; and lower-class blacks, without pride of race.[49] Kingsley Davis had stated a few years earlier that intermarriage more often than not includes a high-status black man and a low-status white woman—though this assertion has since been questioned, as we shall see below.

Intermarriage by sex includes but two possibilities: a white female and a black male, or a black female and a white male. The rank order of discrimination, including as it does the high value placed by whites upon "protecting our women," might lead the reader to expect that racial intermarriage would more often involve a white man and a black woman. This is incorrect, however: black men and white women are by far the more frequent marital partners, some 80 per cent of interracial marriages being of this type. In view of Myrdal's "rank order," how can this be explained? According to Kingsley Davis, there may be two possible explanations. First is the *attractiveness-accessibility* hypothesis. Since sexual relations have traditionally been relatively open between white males and black females in the United States, marriage has not been necessary between them in order for the male to legitimate such an interest. If, however, a black male is attracted to a white female, the stringency of the norms is such that he has been forced to legitimate that interest by marriage. That is, the very weakness of the controls governing white male exploitation of black females has made it less necessary for them to marry in order to pursue that interest.

A second hypothesis, based on the notion that the marriage of high-status black males and low-status white females is more frequent than any other combination, is the *economic penalty* hypothesis. Given the current discriminatory and prejudicial aspects of U.S. society (this thesis goes), the economic-occupational penalty is great for the white male with a black wife. Yet the black male with a white wife is penalized hardly at all, and may even be helped by his wife's race. The difficulty with this second explanation is that recent data have not shown any great discrepancy between the social status background of the white and black partners to an intermarriage. Todd Pavela's exploratory study in Indiana includes this conclusion: "It would appear that such intermarriage now occurs between persons who are, by and large, economically, educationally, and culturally equal and who have a strong emotional attachment, be it rationalization or real."[50] Bernard likewise notes that, in general, "racial intermarriages as of 1960 tended to be as homogamous educationally as marriages between Negro men and women. The wives of Negro men—whether white or Negro—tended to average more schooling than their husbands, reflecting the generally lower level of schooling of Negro men."[51] Thus, Davis' accessibility hypothesis seems to be more useful today than that based upon economic penalties, though, of course, the latter may have been more applicable when first propounded.

Motives for Racial Intermarriage in the United States

What motives are behind racial intermarriage in the United States, when the norms of both races are so strongly against it? Though the seeking of motives can sometimes be a fruitless exercise in intuition, several explanations that have been proposed recently might be of interest to the reader. A first motive is *repudiation*. Cavan sums up this viewpoint well when she asserts that an interracial marriage "indicates either that the person has not been thoroughly integrated into his social group or has withdrawn from it for some reason. His needs are not met there; he seeks elsewhere for contacts, friendship, and marriage."[52] He may feel like a misfit, he may have been rejected, and he is manifesting a mutual rejection by overstepping the bounds of one of his group's strongest norms.

A second motive that is akin to and perhaps a part of the first is *identity* reinforcement. Earlier in the chapter we noted how the individual may establish his identity through his mate choice. If a part of this identity is a liberal life approach and a concern to deal with people on a personal rather than a categorical basis, he may seek to demonstrate this identity by means of an interracial marriage. It would seem to the present author, nevertheless, that this motive would very likely be coupled with one of the others, rather than being the sole factor in an interracial marriage.

Psychoanalytically-oriented writers have voiced a third motive for racial intermarriage, based upon *Oedipal fear*. Racial intermarriage, or marriage across any major social barrier, is a result of the person's being strongly attracted to his opposite-sex parent; his heterogamy or intermarriage reinforces the incest taboo, subtly convincing him that he is not in reality trying to marry his own parent. This idea is as difficult to test as it is intriguing.

The fourth motive for racial intermarriage, alluded to earlier in the chapter, is that racial categories are simply *not salient*, or don't matter, to the individual.[53] It seems doubtful to the present author, however, that non-salience is currently the basis for many black-white intermarriages in the United States. Race is simply made salient by societal structures and attitudes in too many ways. An increase in this motive would signify a real move toward universal availability in this area of mate selection. Whether or not the Supreme Court decision and a liberalization of attitudes will have this effect in the near future is conjectural, though it is possible that the small increase in racial intermarriage rates since World War II is accounted for by such so-called "non-salient" unions. Yet a lot of societal restructuring appears to be necessary before racial intermarriage can become prevalent, and before such marriages can be a matter of non-salience, instead of a reaction to something in the individual's life history. At present, the pressures toward racial endogamy still seem to outweigh the opposing pressures toward non-salience and universal availability.

NOTES

[1] William J. Goode draws this conclusion in his article, "The Theoretical Importance of Love," *American Sociological Review*, 24 (1959), 38–47.

[2] One side-effect of birth control, with the resultant increase in the separation of sexual relations from procreation, has been to raise the question of the legitimacy of homosexuality. Though not likely to be accepted as part of the mores, there is more debate on the practice in American society than there has been in the past and more than currently exists in many other societies.

[3] Goode, "The Theoretical Importance of Love," pp. 43–44.

[4] *Ibid.*, p. 43.

[5] Robert F. Winch, *Mate-Selection: A Study of Complementary Needs* (New York: Harper and Brothers, 1958).

[6] Goode, "The Theoretical Importance of Love," p. 41.

[7] James H. S. Bossard, "Residential Propinquity as a Factor in Mate Selection," *American Journal of Sociology*, 38 (1932), 219–24.

[8] Alvin M. Katz and Reuben Hill, "Residential Propinquity and Marital Selection: A Review of Theory, Method, and Fact," *Marriage and Family Living*, 20 (1958), 27–35.

[9] Homogamy and heterogamy—the marriage of people who are alike and the marriage of people who are different—are simply opposite sides of the same coin. The same holds for endogamy and intermarriage—marriage within one's group and marriage outside one's group. These terms are used almost interchangeably in the literature; their relationship can be seen in the fact that if the rate of religious endogamy is 90 per cent, then the rate of religious intermarriage can be seen to be 10 per cent.

[10] Many studies since World War II show that people do have a general notion of the meaning of the terms "upper class," "middle class," "working class," and "lower class." This is partially a function of the constant use of these terms by sociologists since the early 1930's.

[11] Bruce K. Eckland, "Theories of Mate Selection," *Eugenics Quarterly*, 15 (1968), 79.

[12] August B. Hollingshead, "Cultural Factors in the Selection of Marriage Mates," *American Sociological Review*, 15 (1950), 622. This article is a good example of a study based upon the trichotomization of religious bodies into Protestant, Catholic, and Jewish.

[13] See Bernard Farber, *Family: Organization and Interaction* (San Francisco: Chandler, 1964), 151.

[14] This is reported in Will Herberg, *Protestant, Catholic, Jew* (Garden City, N.Y.: Doubleday, 1955).

[15] The reader may want to reexamine the author's interpretation by reviewing the following studies of homogamy and heterogamy: T. C. Hunt, "Occupational Status and Marriage Selection," *American Sociological Review*, 5 (1940), 495–504; Ernest W. Burgess and Paul Wallin, "Homogamy in Social Characteristics," *American Journal of Sociology*, 49 (1943), 117–24; Richard Centers, "Marital Selection and Occupational Strata," *American Journal of Sociology*, 54 (1949), 530–35; Simon Dinitz, Franklin Banks, and Benjamin Pasamanick, "Mate Selection and Social Class: Changes During the Past Quarter Century," *Marriage and Family Living*, 22 (1960), 348–51; Harvey J. Locke, Georges Sabagh, and Mary Margaret Thomes, "Inter-faith Marriages," *Social Problems*, 4 (1957), 329–33; David M. Heer, "The Trend of Interfaith Marriages in Canada: 1922–1957," *American Sociological Review*, 27 (1962), 245–50; Lee G. Burchinal and Loren E. Chancellor, "Ages at Marriage, Occupations of Grooms, and Interreligious Marriage Rates," *Social Forces*, 40 (1962), 348–54; Burchinal and Chancellor, "Survival Rates Among Religiously Homogamous and Interreligious Marriages," *Social Forces*, 41 (1963), 353–62; Glenn M. Vernon, "Bias in Professional Publications Concerning Interfaith Marriages," *Religious Education*, 55 (1960), 261–64. Several studies on racial intermarriage are listed in note 45f.

[16] Hollingshead, "Cultural Factors," p. 622, and John L. Thomas, "The Factor of Religion in the Selection of Marriage Mates," *American Sociological Review*, 16 (1951), 487–92.

[17] Farber, *Family: Organization and Interaction*, p. 152.

[18] On this, see Gerald R. Leslie and Arthur H. Richardson, "Family versus Campus Influences in Relation to Mate Selection," *Social Problems*, 4 (1956), 117–21, and Albert I. Gordon, *Intermarriage: Interfaith, Interracial, Interethnic* (Boston: Beacon, 1964), p. 38. The strictness of racial endogamy norms in U.S. society will be considered at length in Section Five of this chapter.

[19] Robert H. Coombs, "A Value Theory of Mate Selection," *The Family Life Coordinator*, 10 (1961), 51–54.

[20] Eckland, "Theories of Mate Selection," p. 80. On perceived similarity, see Anthony J. Smith, "Similarity of Values and Its Relation to Acceptance and the Projection of Similarity," *Journal of Psychology*, 43 (1957), 251–60; Joseph A. Precker, "Values as a Factor in the Selection of Associates," *Disser-*

tation Abstracts, 12 (1952), 107; Carl W. Backman and Paul F. Secord, "Liking, Selective Interaction, and Misperception in Congruent Interpersonal Relations," *Sociometry,* 25 (1962), 321–35.

[21] Eloise C. Snyder, "Attitudes: A Study of Homogamy and Marital Selectivity," *Journal of Marriage and the Family,* 26 (1964), 336.

[22] Purnell Benson, "The Interests of Happily Married Couples," *Marriage and Family Living,* 14 (1952), 276–80; Benson, "The Common Interest Myth in Marriage," *Social Problems,* 3 (1955), 27–34.

[23] Charles D. Bolton, "Mate Selection as the Development of a Relationship," *Marriage and Family Living,* 23 (1961), 234–40.

[24] Winch, *Mate-Selection.*

[25] Robert Winch, "The Theory of Complementary Needs in Mate Selection: Final Results on the Test of the General Hypothesis," *American Sociological Review,* 20 (1955), 552–55; Robert Winch and Thomas and Virginia Ktsanes, "Empirical Elaboration of the Theory of Complementary Needs in Mate-Selection," *Journal of Abnormal and Social Psychology,* 51 (1955), 508–14; Winch, Ktsanes and Ktsanes, "The Theory of Complementary Needs in Mate-Selection: An Analytic and Descriptive Study," *American Sociological Review,* 19 (1954), 241–49; Thomas Ktsanes, "Mate Selection on the Basis of Personality Type: A Study Utilizing an Empirical Typology of Personality," *American Sociological Review,* 20 (1955), 547–51; Horace Gray, "Psychological Types in Married People," *Journal of Social Psychology,* 29 (1949), 189–200.

[26] Charles E. Bowerman and Barbara R. Day, "A Test of the Theory of Complementary Needs As Applied to Couples During Courtship," *American Sociological Review,* 21 (1956), 602–5, and James A. Schellenberg and Lawrence S. Bee, "A Re-examination of the Theory of Complementary Needs in Mate Selection," *Marriage and Family Living,* 22 (1960), 227–32.

[27] J. Richard Udry, "Complementarity in Mate Selection: A Perceptual Approach," *Marriage and Family Living,* 25 (1963), 281–89.

[28] Eckland, "Theories of Mate Selection," p. 78; Winch, "Another Look at the Theory of Complementary Needs in Mate-Selection," *Journal of Marriage and the Family,* 29 (1967), 756–62.

[29] Winch, "Another Look."

[30] Ernest W. Burgess and Paul Wallin, *Engagement and Marriage* (Philadelphia: Lippincott, 1953), p. 202.

[31] Anselm Strauss, "The Ideal and the Chosen Mate," *American Journal of Sociology,* 52 (1946), 207.

[32] J. Richard Udry, "The Influence of the Ideal Mate Image on Mate Selection and Mate Perception," *Journal of Marriage and the Family,* 27 (1965), 477–82.

[33] Burgess and Wallin, *Engagement and Marriage,* p. 197.

[34] Eckland, "Theories of Mate Selection." As in the case of common interests, there are data that show that if the spouse resembles one's ideal and one's opposite-sex parent, their marital adjustment is better. This, however, cannot be used as evidence for mate choice, only for later satisfaction. On this, see Eleanor Braun Luckey, "Perceptual Congruence of Self and Family Concepts as Related to Marital Interaction," *Sociometry,* 24 (1961), 234–50.

[35] Clifford Kirkpatrick and Charles Hobart, "Disagreement, Disagreement Estimate, and Non-Empathic Imputations for Intimacy Groups Varying from Favorite Date to Married," *American Sociological Review,* 19 (1954), 10–19.

[36] Alan Kerckhoff and Keith E. Davis, "Value Consensus and Need Complementarity in Mate Selection," *American Sociological Review,* 27 (1962), 295–303.

[37] Bolton, "Mate Selection" p. 235.
[38] On the notion of role compatibility as a factor in mate selection, see Bernard I. Murstein, "Empirical Tests of Role, Complementary Needs, and Homogamy Theories of Marital Choice," *Journal of Marriage and the Family*, 29 (1967), 689–96.
[39] William Kephart, "Some Correlates of Romantic Love," *Journal of Marriage and the Family*, 29 (1967), 470–74.
[40] The author is indebted to H. Kent Geiger for several of the ideas found in the following section.
[41] Gunnar Myrdal, *An American Dilemma* (New York: Harper and Brothers, 1944).
[42] Andrew Billingsley notes this increase in racial pride and solidarity, in *Black Families in White America* (Englewood Cliffs, N.J.: Prentice-Hall, 1968), pp. 11, 39.
[43] Myrdal, *An American Dilemma*, pp. 60–61.
[44] Ruth Shonle Cavan, *The American Family* (New York: Crowell, 1969 ed.), pp. 204–5.
[45] David M. Heer, "Negro-White Marriage in the United States," *Journal of Marriage and the Family*, 28 (1966), 267.
[46] Cavan, *The American Family*, 204–5.
[47] Heer, "Negro-White Marriage," p. 266.
[48] *Ibid.*, p. 264.
[49] St. Clair Drake and Horace Cayton, *Black Metropolis* (New York: Harcourt, Brace, 1945), pp. 137–39.
[50] Todd Pavela, "An Exploratory Study of Negro-White Intermarriage in Indiana," *Journal of Marriage and the Family*, 26 (1964), 211.
[51] Jessie Bernard, "Note on Educational Homogamy in Negro-White and White-Negro Marriages, 1960," *Journal of Marriage and the Family*, 28 (1966), 274–76.
[52] Cavan, *The American Family*, p. 206.
[53] On this, see Frank Musgrove, *The Family, Education, and Society* (London: Routledge and Kegan Paul, 1966), pp. 67–68.

XI

Marriage: Processes and Roles

MARRIAGE IS A MIXTURE OF CHANGE AND PATTERN. THE HABIT PATTERNS OF COUPLE MEMBERS MESH AND THEIR ROLE CHOICES BECOME FIXED ROUTINES IN THE EARLY YEARS OF MARRIAGE. HOWEVER, THESE ROUTINES ARE NOT COMPLETELY FIXED BECAUSE ABRUPT AND GRADUAL TRANSITIONS CONSTANTLY RESULT IN THE NECESSITY FOR NEW ADJUSTMENTS AND ROLES. CHILDBIRTH, TASK ACCOMPLISHMENT, DEPARTURE OF OFFSPRING, RETIREMENT, AND DEATH ARE EXAMPLES OF ABRUPT TRANSITIONS; WHILE GRADUAL TRANSITIONS ARE EXEMPLIFIED IN THE FAMILY BY DEFERRED GRATIFICATION, GOAL FAILURE, THE EFFECTS OF DETERIORATION, AND BEHAVIORAL INTENSIFICATION. THE PROCESSUAL PERSPECTIVE, WHILE LITTLE-USED IN EMPIRICAL STUDIES OF THE FAMILY, SEEMS TO PROVIDE INSIGHT INTO THE MARRIAGE RELATIONSHIP. A SECOND VALUABLE PERSPECTIVE IS THAT WHICH VIEWS MARRIAGE AS CONSISTING OF ROLE CHOICES, PATTERNS, AND CONFLICTS. IN THE COURSE OF U.S. HISTORY, THE ROLE PATTERNS OF MALES AND FEMALES HAVE BECOME INCREASINGLY A MATTER OF CHOICE RATHER THAN TRADITION OR PRESCRIPTION; THE ISSUES INVOLVED IN HUSBAND-FATHER AND WIFE-MOTHER ROLE CHOICES AND BEHAVIOR COMPRISE THE CLOSING SECTIONS OF CHAPTER XI.

SECTION ONE

MARRIAGE AS A PROCESS

A young man and woman have dated, have narrowed the field of potential mates through various conscious and unconscious means, and have finally ceremonialized their relationship in marriage. The early months of marriage are likely to be characterized by a sense of euphoria, or general emotional well-being, and also by experimentation and pattern development. Eventually, however, the euphoric solidarity peculiar to the newly-married begins to recede, and the husband and wife find themselves faced with daily adjustment to each other. The two couple members, in view of the separate habit systems they brought into the marriage, must begin to adjust to the fact that they are now a dyad—a marriage—and experimentation and routinization become predominant. "The social form created by marriage must find its way," remarks Willard Waller, "by a rather tentative process, making many false starts but attaining at last a tolerable living pattern. . . . Some patterns will be highly successful; these will tend to stabilize in the form of powerful habits."[1] Involved in the formation of collective habits is, among other things, the interchange of tastes and of likes and dislikes.

Not all patterns are successful; conflict also emerges. It may appear due to a basic, but heretofore undiscovered, value disagreement—perhaps over politics, or over leisure activity, or over whether the wife should work or not. Oftentimes, however, the conflict revolves about some seemingly inconsequential aspect of everyday behavior, brought by a couple member into the marriage. It may be a disagreement over the preparation of foods or the time for meals; it might concern bedtime routine; or even something as simple as toothbrushing. Whatever their bases, such conflicts as occur may produce a blockage of communication or may produce a new form of solidarity as accommodations and adjustments are made. Strictly speaking, then, "engagement or no engagement, every new marriage is an undefined situation, just as every new status involves undefined elements for the neophyte."[2] Yet, during the early months, routines *do* develop, and the marriage itself becomes a problem; or it becomes a mutual meeting of internal situations and a joint facing of the external world; or it becomes some combination of problem and solution.

Routines and patterns develop, but never become completely fixed. This is because transitions, some abrupt and some gradual, are constantly occurring to alter former patterns. The *abrupt transitions*, which have received considerable research attention, include not only the marriage ceremony, but parenthood, occupational change, task accomplishment, the departure of children, residential movement, retirement, and death. These are transitions both for the individual, affecting his personality integration and energy management either positively or negatively, and for the nuclear family unit, demanding new roles and adjustments. Preparation for such transitions can never be complete. The pregnancy period, for example, may give a couple time to discuss parental roles and the readjustment of household routines, but it can never truly prepare the husband and wife for the transition to parenthood. In fact, becoming a mother appears to require an even greater role transition—from wife to wife and mother—than that from single to married.[3] The key question to ask about response to abrupt transitions concerns task accomplishment, or how capable the couple members are of accomplishing the necessary changes. "The lack of prior models is stressful," the Rapoports state, "but it also provides new opportunities for creativity." The "new patterns are crystallized within a few weeks after the critical transition period of intensive involvements."[4] Whether or not the couple members can accomplish the tasks required by the transition is a matter of coping ability, or the ability to adjust, as well as a matter of the clarity of role models. If the young female, for example, upon becoming a mother, has a clear picture of the way in which new mothers operate, and if that picture is applicable to her and not to some earlier and different era, this model can help her to accomplish the required tasks. If, however, she either lacks a clear model, or if that model is no longer applicable, then coping ability is put at a premium. It seems likely, therefore, that coping ability is more important today than it would have been in a traditional family setting, since even those young mothers who have a distinct picture of how their mothers behaved are apt to feel that cultural change has largely nullified the applicability of the model.

Fully as important to understanding the family are the *gradual transitions*, those changes that cannot be fixed at a given point in time, but which nevertheless influence both the personality of the individual and his family life. Few writers have attempted to deal with such changes; Bernice Neugarten's research is probably the most insightful and useful, though it takes an individual rather than a family perspective.[5] Neugarten notes at the outset that, except for Erik Erikson's eight stages of ego development, dynamic theories of personality have generally assumed "that the personality is stabilized, if not fixed, by the time early adulthood is reached."[6] Personality is, to Neugarten and her associates, a moving complexity of intrapsychic and socioadaptive elements. In their volume *Personality in Middle and Late Life,* they summarize the results of several exploratory studies of personality processes. The studies were carried out as part of the Kansas City Studies of Adult Life, based upon probability samples of Kansas City residents between the ages of 40 and 90, the total pool consisting of 701 men and women.

The intrapsychic aspects of personality include perceptions, impulses, and mental abilities, and their operation is related to the aging process in terms of continuity, simplification, and deterioration. According to Neugarten, "personalities maintain their characteristic patterns of organization as individuals move from middle into old age."[7] Responses to various stimuli in old age can, therefore, be traced to earlier tendencies within the personality, and continuity observed. The sources of change are twofold: simplification and deterioration. Energy supply becomes less, cognitive or thinking processes become impaired, and impulse control becomes somewhat erratic; all these forms of deterioration increase the tendencies on the part of the individual to become inwardly oriented or preoccupied with self. Along with the increased interiority that accompanies the various forms of deterioration, Neugarten asserts:

> there seems to go a certain reduction in the complexity of the personality. With the shrinkage in psychological life space and with decreased ego energy, an increasing dedication to a central core of values and to a set of habit patterns and a sloughing off of earlier cathexes which lose saliency for the individual seem to occur. It is probably this quality which has led to frequent observations, on the one hand, that behavior in a normal old person is more consistent and more predictable than in a younger one—that, as individuals age, they become increasingly like themselves—and, on the other hand, that the personality structure stands more clearly revealed in an older than in a younger person.[8]

Simplification of personality, we might add, is a lifelong process. The adolescent seeks for identity by experimentation with various types of behavior and attitudes, as he struggles to make sense of his impulses and of the conflicting norms being presented to him by others. When the adolescent becomes a young adult, these behaviors and attitudes do not automatically become fixed—either by marriage, occupational experience, or parenthood. Rather, experimentation continues. Specific responses do, however, begin to be rank ordered in their salience to him; simplification involves the reinforcing of those responses that are most rewarding and an increasing ignoring of alternative possibilities.

The socioadaptive aspects of personality consist of the individual's ways of relating to the external environment. Though they are affected by simplification and deterioration processes, they are influenced even more by work status, health, financial resources, and marital status than simply by chronological age. Continuity in this area of personality may mean that the individual continues to demonstrate socioadaptive abilities in social interaction and role performance for years after intrapsychic deterioration has begun. Or socioadaptive adjustment may be altered by what Neugarten calls "accumulation." As a result, says Neugarten

> of the life history with its accumulating record of adaptations to both biological and social events, there is a continually changing basis within the individual for perceiving and responding to new events in the outer world.[9]

The aging individual may, as we have said, continue to adapt to social demands after intrapsychic deterioration is well under way. Or, on the other hand, various setbacks in the external world may impair one's socioadaptation even before the deterioration based on age has become noticeable. The intrapsychic and socioadaptive aspects of the personality are related, but they also operate separately, with the former being much more closely and directly related to chronological age than is the latter.

Neugarten and her research associates are concerned primarily with individual personality processes during adult life, not with family experience. Nevertheless, their ideas are extremely useful in understanding the gradual transitions that influence the relations between husbands and wives. The following illustrations show how these insights may be applied to marriage.

The young couple may start their life together looking forward to success and achievement on the part of the husband. As experience accumulates and success continues to recede, there may come the realization that their goals have not been, and may never be, reached. Perhaps at age 40, but more often gradually, the husband admits to himself that he has not accomplished what he set out to do. This realization may be accompanied by the husband's awareness of his diminishing energy. A realistic husband may be able to lower his sights without severe ego difficulties. More often, however, his response will be discouragement and/or anticipatory disengagement. The discouragement of the husband in middle age may demand succor on the part of the wife, but the accumulation of marital experience may not have prepared her to provide it. By anticipatory disengagement we mean that the husband gradually begins to look forward to the time when he can stop striving and can leave his occupational role. (For some working-class persons who find little inherent meaning in their jobs, anticipatory disengagement may be an aspect of their entire working life, so that there is no attitudinal discontinuity at retirement.) Admission of failure to achieve one's goals may therefore be accompanied by changes in socioadaptive personality, and may demand a personality reorientation on the wife's part which she is unable to accomplish.

Our second illustration is actually a problem in deterioration that has ramifications for husband-wife relations. One form of deterioration not discussed directly by Neugarten involves appearance. In a society in which a crucial element in marriage is the physical attraction of the male to the female, the gradual lessening of the wife's beauty, due both to child-bearing and to the direct influence of time, may have serious implications for her personality as well as for her marriage. Unquestionably, the husband and wife whose accumulated experiences and habit patterns have provided alternative bases of solidarity are best prepared to maintain both intra- and interpersonal continuity as physical decline progresses. In some instances, however, the wife becomes oriented to the past or to a fantasy regarding her current beauty, while the husband begins to look elsewhere for new attractions. Changing orientations that result from deterioration may, therefore, affect both personality adjustment and marriage.

A final illustration of a gradual transition involves two possibilities: intensification or simplification. The husband and wife who in the early years of marriage show slightly divergent tendencies—in the handling of money, for example—may over time either intensify or simplify their interaction patterns in this area. He wants to lay it away in case of an emergency, a "rainy day," while she has been brought up to believe that money is to be spent. In an area of disagreement such as this, simplification may occur if the husband and wife decide not to discuss the issue, but to allow the wife a certain amount of money for household expenses, to allow her to handle the family budgeting, or to arrange some other method of avoiding conflict. A possibility other than blocking off the area and simplifying the pattern is intensification of the situation. Intensification is a result of the interplay between accumulation of experiences and simplification which happens as follows. At first, both husband and wife are characterized by subordinate as well as dominant tendencies. Thus, there are times when he desires to spend and she wants to save for the future. However, frequent conflicts over their dominant tendencies drive them toward opposite poles. These accumulated conflicts result in the simplification of orientations toward this specific issue: he increasingly responds with criticism and anger to her expenditure patterns, while she becomes increasingly bitter about his inability to relax and enjoy money. A tendency that had resulted in periodic disagreement has become, over time, a constant and painful antagonism. The same sort of intensification may occur with respect to similarities, as well as opposing tendencies, with the result that married persons become more and more alike as they move through life together.

Marriage as a process consists of abrupt and gradual transitions and the effect of these transitions on the course of personality development, interpersonal accommodations, and role alterations. It is in the varying abilities of couples to readjust, and in such processes as task accomplishment, accumulation, deterioration, and simplification, that we are apt to find much of the explanation for marriage outcomes. Unfortunately, little research on marriage has as yet been published employing a processual perspective.[10] However, as we look at roles, interactions, and adjustments statically, it is good to keep in mind that marriage is always in flux, always changing. Transitions and personality alterations require constant redefinition of a marriage; in the redefinition process is found the basis for both the excitement and the difficulties inherent in modern marriage.

SECTION TWO

MARRIAGE AS CHANGING ROLES

A couple get married and immediately set about discovering their own and each other's views on how they should behave as husband and wife. The patterns that develop—out of the interplay between expectations, experimentation, and personality—become their particular definitions of husband and wife *roles*. A role consists, therefore, of the ways in which one characteristically behaves in a particular position, such as that of husband, clerk, father, or citizen. This section deals with the question of how the roles of husband-father and wife-mother have changed during the history of the United States family, the three foci being role differentiation, role blurring, and role choice and conflict—in that order.

Role Differentiation

An important change in the family, introduced in Chapter V, is the increasing functional differentiation of modern industrial society, so that economic, political, religious, educational, and other institutional functions are less and less embedded within either the nuclear family or the kin group. Talcott Parsons describes the process of differentiation thus:

> Differentiation refers to the process by which simple structures are divided into functionally differing components, these components becoming relatively independent of one another, and then recombined into more complex structures in which the functions of the differentiated units are complementary. A key example in the development of industrial society everywhere is the differentiation . . . of the unit of economic production from the kinship household. . . .[11]

The key word in Parsons' definition is "independent." His example concerns the way in which the economic productive role has been removed from the family setting and is performed outside the home in the modern industrial community.

Parsons' conception of differentiation as it pertains to the family was influenced greatly by his collaboration with Robert Bales, a social psychologist interested in small groups. Bales, in earlier research, had noted that in any small, task-oriented group there tends to evolve a task or *instrumental* leader, whose job it is to lead the way in solving the problem at hand, and a social-emotional or *expressive* leader, who acts to maintain morale and control conflict. By reducing strain, the expressive leader makes a positive contribution to the group's perpetuation and thus to its ability to accomplish its task. The same person in a group, the "great man," may play both the task and social-emotional leadership roles, but more often the roles are played by two different persons.

Utilizing this perspective drawn from small group research, Parsons' co-worker, Morris Zelditch, discovered in cross-cultural research that the same differentiation of leadership roles occurs within the nuclear family. In the majority of societies, the husband plays the role of instrumental leader, governing the family's economic division of labor, while the wife is the expressive leader.[12]

From this starting point, Parsons feels he can answer those who would complain that the husband has lost power in the family to the wife. What has happened is that the removal of the economic producing function from the home to an outside setting, plus the increase in the importance of happiness and emotional satisfactions to family solidarity, has resulted in the husband's playing his major role in the outside world, while the wife's role of social-emotional leadership has become central to the family unit *per se.* Thus, it is not that the husband's role has lost importance, but that it is now being performed in an extra-familial milieu. The male has not so much simply lost authority; rather the kind of authority he formerly held within the family cannot now be appropriately exercised because the family no longer engages as a unit in the kind of economic activities over which men exercise authority. He formerly ran the economic machinery of the family; now the wife runs the social-emotional machinery of the family (see Figure 11 for a diagrammatic representation).[13]

Role Blurring

The concept of increasing role differentiation, resulting in the husband's dominant life role being actually removed from the family setting, is employed by Parsons, Zelditch, Smelser, and others to account for many characteristics of the industrial family. There is, however, another strand of literature—some of it popular and some based upon research—that stresses, not differentiation, but the *blurring* of men's and women's roles and behaviors. Charles Winick expresses the conviction in several writings that "the most significant and visible aspect of the contemporary American sexual scene is the tremendous decline, since World War II, in sexual dimorphism. Sex roles have become substantially neutered and environmental differences increasingly blurred."[14] Writing not as a social observer but as a small group researcher, Robert Leik finds that male instrumentality and female emotionality, which are ap-

FIGURE 11

Diagram of Parsons' View of the Differentiation of Economic Production from the Family Unit as a Result of the Industrial Revolution

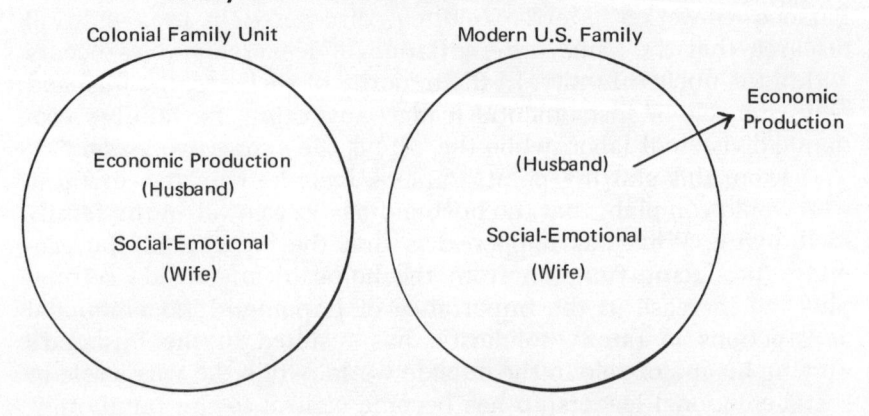

Colonial Family Unit

Economic Production (Husband)

Social-Emotional (Wife)

Modern U.S. Family

(Husband)

Social-Emotional (Wife)

Economic Production

parent in random groupings, "tend to disappear when subjects interact with their own families. Particularly is this true for instrumentality, because of a dual role for mothers."[15] Alice Rossi adds, in speaking of parental roles, that it would not surprise many investigators of the family

> if women scored higher than men on the expressive dimension and men scored higher on the instrumental dimension of the parental role. Yet quite the opposite might actually result. Men spend relatively little time with their children, and it is time of a particular kind: evenings, weekdays, and vacations, when the activities and mood of the family are heavily on the expressive side. Women carry the major burden of the instrumental dimension of parenting.[16]

Zelditch himself points out that "the American middle-class family approaches most clearly to equal allocation (or 'no allocation') of instrumental and expressive activities."[17]

One way in which the historical process of role blurring is described is by the terms "conventional" and "companionate" roles, also called traditional and equalitarian roles.[18] Conventional, or traditional, roles find the husband dominant and the wife subordinate, with the roles of males and females within the home predetermined by tradition. Companionate, or equalitarian, roles involve similarity, choice, and equality—all of which, when compared with the traditional-conventional roles of the colonial and Victorian past, can be considered to exemplify role blurring.

Are the notions of role differentiation and role blurring in conflict, or do they describe divergent aspects of reality? This question can best be answered by beginning with two varying orientations to the study of the family—those of Talcott Parsons and Ernest Burgess. Parsons, when writing about the family, is concerned about the relation of part to whole, of the family to the larger society and its institutions. When he describes role differentiation and specialization, it is a society-wide process that includes as one of its features the removal of the husband's economic productive role from the home. Burgess, on the other hand, is chiefly interested in what goes on within the family unit itself, in the "unity of interacting personalities" which we call "family." From this perspective it is possible to agree with Parsons that differentiation is important and still to focus on the question: "But how do husbands and wives act *when they are at home*?" Though this is a somewhat oversimplified reconciliation of the "differentiation" and "blurring" viewpoints, it does demonstrate that there are two perfectly valid, though interrelated, questions to ask about the modern family: (1) What effect does increased societal differentiation and the removal of the economic productive function from the home have upon the family? (2) How do husbands and wives act in relation to each other and their children?

Role Choice and Conflict

One reason why the second question is valid is because role definitions for spouses and parents are not entirely determined by tradition. Because they are given such alternatives as whether or not the wife will work, or how the man will play the father role, it is incumbent upon couple members not only to think out and make choices regarding their own roles, but to discover their spouse's role definitions as well.

Several studies have shown the intricacies involved in role choice and agreement, and the problems caused by disagreement. Annabelle Bender Motz's study of 337 married couples at Indiana University, carried out in the early 1950's, has significance beyond the setting in which it was done. Using the conceptions of conventional and companionate roles, her chief problem for investigation was: "How do conceptions of husband-wife roles, and the playing of those roles in later life, vary according to the present situation of the actor?"[19] The overall results indicated that families tended to favor the companionate role for the husband and the conventional role for the wife. This, of course, is not consistent—since it would seem impossible for one spouse to be either companionate or conventional without the other being the same—but it does point up the internal variations by sex and by current economic role within the family. The most important set of findings is related to the employment status of these students' wives. Women working full-time desired *conventional* roles for both themselves and their husbands, while those working part-time or not at all tended to desire *companionate* roles for both. Incidentally, companionate roles from the female's perspective meant that she would have a choice of whether to work or not, rather than being restricted automatically to the role of housewife. Also, wives whose husbands were unemployed, i.e., full-time students, tended to desire conventional roles, while those whose husbands were working and going to school tended to choose companionate roles for later life.

The husbands were more willing to conceive of their wives as playing companionate roles if the wives were not presently working full-time. What is the conclusion? When desires are compared with current conditions, they appear to be rationalizations of, or even reactions against, the actual role situation. In fact, the notion of the "grass being greener on the other side of the fence" is very close to being applicable to these married student couples in which many of the husbands receive economic support from wives, parents, or both.

A second study that adds to that by Motz in telling us something of role expectations and behavior is one that was published the same year by Robert Ort.[20] He looks at roles and role conflicts in relation to marital happiness. First, he finds a low probability that a spouse who rates himself or herself as happily married will have a marriage partner who rates himself or herself as equally happy. There is, then, great variation and only a low correlation between husbands' and wives' perceived happiness. Secondly, says Ort, happiness appears to be a function of how well one plays the role or roles that he expects or desires for himself, and how well the spouse plays the role or roles desired for him by the other spouse. The question that arises from these two findings (the study includes many other interesting findings) is whether or not the low correlation between husbands' and wives' happiness is because it is difficult for *both* marriage partners to play out their desired roles at the same time. We shall return to this issue.

Role desires, for oneself and one's spouse, thus appear to be one of the crucial aspects of marriage which demands adjustment and communication on the part of the couple members. Robert Stuckert adds that it is particularly important that the wife perceive her husband's role expectations for himself correctly, since she must do more of the adjusting in marriage than he.[21] Yet, accurate perception is not enough; it may, in fact, result in conflict if husband and wife expectations for themselves and each other differ too greatly. Role choice, therefore, makes disagreement and conflict a possibility; conflict may, in turn, disrupt the marriage itself. Yet, while role consensus is important to happiness, conflict or disagreement does not inevitably lead to marital dissolution. Inaccurate perception of role expectations and disagreement based upon accurate perception do not necessarily result in dissatisfaction with the marriage if these problems are accepted as typical of marriages in general.[22] "Sure we have our disagreements," this view says, "but so does everyone else we know." Burgess and Locke present a second caution regarding the direct influence of role conflict upon a marriage: "Even if a mate does not live up to the expectations of the other or up to his conception of his role in marriage, the marriage may survive because of the expectations of one or both of the permanent nature of marriage."[23]

It must be concluded that role choice is at least a problematic aspect of modern marriage, since choice may lead to communication, adjustment, and primariness, or to conflict and dissolution. Let us at this point, then, review the kinds of role choices confronting males and females in the U.S. family.

SECTION THREE

HUSBAND–FATHER ROLE CHOICES

The constant outpouring of words about the American woman in recent years, says Myron Brenton in his book *The American Male*, "has made it seem as though the male either had no problems or didn't count enough to have them aired."[24] The American male does, however, confront several issues that demand resolution. First, he must reconcile his sedentary role with the traditional image of the male as subduer of nature. Second, he must determine —with the removal of his economic role from the home—how much of his time and energy he will invest in the extra-familial world and how much he will reserve for his family. Finally, he must reconcile the democratic ideology of the present with the lingering image of the male as patriarch, as the authority over his wife and children. Let us look briefly at each of these issues.

The "Feminization" of Occupations

The shift of the husband's economic role out of the home, and the increasing importance to the family of the feminine social-emotional role, are not felt by Robert Winch to be a sufficient explanation for the blurring of sex-role distinctions in U.S. society. Winch observes that, cross-culturally, the family systems in which the husband is most apt to be the dominant figure are those in which the importance of human strength and endurance, in which males ordinarily excel, are central to the economic institution.[25] That is, family economic maintenance based upon the physical strength of the male tends to result in his having the key role in the family as well.

In modern industrial society the introduction of steam, electricity, and petroleum have reduced the importance of human strength to societal maintenance to a fraction of what it has been cross-culturally and historically. Viewed in these terms, technology has resulted, in a sense, in the "feminization" of the occupational structure—not just in its removal from the home. This statement should not be construed to mean that the market no longer favors the male. It does, however, mean that sex distinctions in hiring and salary are much less likely than they were formerly to be based upon the notion of male superiority in handling a particular job. Perception on the part of the male of his occupational "replaceability" by the opposite sex, while it may never actually occur within his lifetime, may be a severe jolt to his self-concept. This particular problem for the male would seem to be most acute at the lower-middle-class level, where sales and clerical personnel may be more painfully aware of their replaceability than either professionals or manual workers.

Home versus Community

In a day of institutional non-embeddedness, the male is confronted with a completely new decision: "How much of myself shall I invest in my occupation and community, and how much shall I invest in my family?" Not only are there few guidelines for him to follow in making the choice, but there is great disagreement among wives in their expectations for their husbands in this area. One of the popular newspaper columnists, after publishing a letter from a wife who complained bitterly that her husband spent all of his energy at work and had nothing left, sexually or emotionally, to give to her or the children, opened the issue to a public forum. The results were most instructive. A large number of wives agreed entirely with this woman's complaint, and expressed the wish that their husbands would spend a little less time and energy trying to "get ahead," and a little more in meeting their wives' and children's needs. Yet an equally large number of wives argued vehemently that they would rather have a husband who is a success and who provides well for his wife and children than to be married to a family man with little ambition.

Since the guidelines are virtually nonexistent, it remains for husbands to work out in terms of personality traits and in interaction with their wives precisely how they shall divide their time and energy resources. Most men can keep busy with their occupations and community affairs as much of the time as they are willing to give. Thus, those who *want* to escape the home are likely to employ the ready-made excuse of extra-familial demands.[26]

Husband and Father

Not unrelated to the foregoing issue is the question of how the male will perform as husband and father. Does he try to be patriarch, making the key decisions himself and restricting his wife to housewifery and motherhood? Does he reject "woman's work" around the house; does he do it grudgingly or willingly? As Brenton notes, it is not doing what was formerly women's work that causes him trouble, it is worrying about it because of the vestiges of patriarchal values.[27] It is not so much the decline in paternal and male authority that is a problem in itself; the problem arises when the couple disagree or when the husband is unduly concerned about the position he has presumably lost.

Perhaps the most open issue confronting the male in the home is the definition of the father role. As head of the family's economic division of labor in an agrarian society, the father's responsibilities were clear. But in the modern industrial world what should a father be? Should he be the *grand inquisitor*—the final authority and high court of appeals? This approach is caricatured in the description of the mother who has taken all the misbehavior that she can stand from her children. Finally, at about 3:30 in the afternoon she announces, "Just wait 'til your father gets home." Father is thus expected to walk in the door and spank or scold the child for actions he did not even witness. Such a role is acceptable to some fathers because it convinces them that they have not yielded their position as patriarch, despite the fact that they are not at home much of the time.

Should the father be the *everyday Santa Claus,* who wouldn't dare come home from a business trip without "something for the kids"? This pattern is caricatured in the father returning home to be greeted, not by, "We're glad you're home, Dad," but rather, "What did you bring us, Dad?" This is a viable approach for many fathers who invest neither time nor energy in their offspring, but who do have money.

Finally, should the father try to be the *buddy and pal,* who can't really appreciate his children until they are big enough to catch a ball, or to enjoy camping? This is caricatured in the cartoon that depicts the teenage son's response when his aging and paunchy father enters the room clad in his baseball uniform: "Gee,

Dad, I want a Father, not a pal!" There are advice-givers and critics to match each of these role choices; Brenton depicts the dilemma as follows:

> If he concentrates on being a pal to his son, he's evading his role as authority figure. If he has a nurturant bent, some of the psychiatrists call him a motherly father. If he doesn't do any nurturing to speak of, he's accused of distancing himself from his children. If he's the sole disciplinarian, he takes on, in his youngsters' eyes, the image of an ogre. If he doesn't discipline them sufficiently, he's a weak father. If he's well off and gives his children all the material advantages he didn't have, he's spoiling them, leaving them unprepared for life's hard knocks. If he's well off but doesn't spoil them the way other fathers in the community do their boys and girls, he gains the reputation of a latter-day Scrooge. . . . And, repeatedly, the accusing voices tell him that he has given up his rightful place as head of the family, as guide and mentor to his children.[28]

Obviously, for most fathers, the performance of the father role includes some sort of combination of possibilities, often with one simply tending to be dominant. Sociological research has done little to determine the empirical distribution of "fathering" styles, though it is hypothetically reasonable to assume that the "Inquisitor" or authority approach might be more of a working- or lower-class orientation, with the "Santa Claus" orientation being primarily middle-class. Nor, for that matter, has sociological research indicated much concerning the effect of different approaches to the father and husband roles upon marital adjustment and child development.[29] The crucial issue at this point is that the norms and guidelines are sufficiently ill-defined as to leave the man to determine his role specifications in accordance with his personality and the expectations of his wife.

SECTION FOUR

WIFE–MOTHER ROLE CHOICES

About the year 1950 a movie was made which strikingly illustrated the "woman's dilemma." The heroine of *The Red Shoes*, unable to choose between her love for her husband and her career as a ballerina, resolves her problem by suicide. Most women, in real life, choose a less dramatic compromise. Nevertheless (as we noted in

Chapter IV), the change in the status of women—legally, politically, economically, and educationally—has presented her with necessary role choices. No longer is she bound by a single option, that of housewife and mother. Though societal values still stress her role within the home, the interplay between mass education for women, the possibility of economic independence, and depreciation of the role of housewife as well as the expectation that the woman will assume this role have intensified the problematic aspects of her role choices.

Much of the literature on the contemporary female poses the issue dichotomously as one strictly between working and staying home. Popular books such as Betty Friedan's *The Feminine Mystique* and Phyllis McGinley's *Sixpence in Her Shoe* do not necessarily clarify the choice; in fact, they may make it more difficult by overstating the advantages of one or the other alternative.[30] This is, however, an area that has been studied so intensively by sociologists as to provide a ready-made laboratory for understanding both the issues involved in the contemporary role choices confronting both sexes, as well as the effects of different patterns upon the marriage and the children. Thus, we shall look in some detail at the working wife and her more traditional counterpart.[31]

Modern industrial society is the first in which women have had the right to enter the labor market on their own, to obtain jobs and promotions independently. It seems that, in 1890, when the labor force of the United States was one-sixth women, few of them worked for reasons other than economic necessity. Today, however, when women comprise about one-third of the labor force, many work because they want to, either to increase the family's standard of living or for a creative outlet.[32] At one time, it was assumed that if the wife worked, the result would necessarily be a poorer marital adjustment between herself and her husband. Were this view correct, it would still be incumbent upon the writer to answer the following question: Did the marriage become maladjusted because she began working or did she begin working because her home was already maladjusted?[33] Yet even this statement of the dilemma, Lois Hoffman feels, is unsatisfactory. The dichotomy between working and non-working is itself too grossly stated; it needs to be broken down and examined in terms of certain test variables. Following her advice, we shall examine the marital adjustment of working and non-working wives, using the following variables: (1) Role consensus, or how do the wife and husband feel about her particular role choice? (2) Motives, or why is she doing what she is doing? and (3) Social class differences in marital adjustment according to the work status of the female. In each case we shall attempt to discern from the literature what effect the "test variable" has upon her husband's and her marital adjustment.

Role Consensus

What does the wife desire for herself, and what does her husband expect of her, in terms of her working or not? There are four possibilities. First, she works because both she and her husband agree that she should. Second, she stays home because both she and her husband think she should. Third, she works despite the fact that her husband thinks she should be at home. Finally, though less likely in view of Motz's findings, she doesn't work, although her husband thinks she should. In general, either of the first two alternatives is considerably more satisfactory than the third and fourth. Does working, therefore, have a detrimental effect upon marital adjustment which is independent from role consensus? The crucial test of this question is in the comparison of the first two types, in which role consensus is controlled. Ivan Nye's answer is *yes:* When only those husbands who approve of what their wife is doing are compared, those whose wives are unemployed manifest a better marital adjustment.[34] One reason is that, even if the husband expresses a willingness for his wife to work, he may still define this as threatening or as undermining his dominant role as economic provider.

Motives

Without considering the issue of role consensus, Orden and Bradburn, in a study of 1,651 married persons, conclude that the wife who works by choice tends to have the best marital adjustment, followed by the wife who stays home, and then by the wife who works out of necessity.[35] Although this finding is interesting, it does not deal with the issue of husband-wife consensus, or with those questions involving general orientation and perception. In their study of 25 working-wife and 25 non-working-wife families in Champaign, Illinois, Hafstrom and Dunsing find that of the ten who say they are working out of necessity, seven indicate that they would continue working even if it were not necessary. The fact that a wife works, according to Hilda Krech, still has negative connotations regardless of her motivations:

In the eyes of many people, saying that a woman *must* work for financial gain casts a reflection on her husband. The question is raised: "Can't he support her?" Ironically, reflections are also cast on the woman who has chosen to work. The question is raised: "Does she really love her children?"[36]

What, then, does it actually mean for her to be "working out of necessity"? The important fact, it would seem, is that she *perceives* it to be necessity rather than choice. If she perceives and defines it as necessity, all the negative intimations that her working still arouses regarding her and her husband are heightened, and her marital adjustment suffers.

Yet why consider motives separately at all? Krech, for example, points out that "Making a sharp distinction between women who must work and those who have decided to work leaves out of account the powerful but often ignored phenomenon of 'mixed motivations.'"[37] Furthermore, to say that one is working "from necessity" is actually to describe a particular instance of role dissensus: she prefers to stay home but is forced to work. For, as Hafstrom and Dunsing report, if many who say they are working out of necessity would work anyway, what is the significance of necessity?[38] In short, then, much of the discussion of motivation, in terms of its influence upon adjustment, can be subsumed (with one extension) under the fourfold typology presented above: She stays home or works because she and her husband agree that she should. In such instances adjustment is satisfactory; but it is a little more so (perhaps because of social pressure) when the more conventional or traditional role pattern is agreed upon. She stays home although her husband wishes she would work. This is perhaps the least frequent option empirically, but it could result in marital maladjustment. Finally—and here is the extension—she works, but either her husband wants her to stay home or else *she wishes she could stay home*, the result being a substantial likelihood of marital maladjustment.

Social Class, Wife's Work Status, and Marital Adjustment

The several studies of working wives which take into consideration social class level tend to agree with Nye that "any net *adverse* effect of employment on marital adjustment is less in the higher socioeconomic families than in the lower."[39] Why this should be so is clarified by Orden and Bradburn and by Mirra Komarovsky's study, *Blue-Collar Marriage*. The former authors report that "the proportion of employed women who are in the labor market by choice increases with education from 34 per cent among those with an eighth-grade education or less to 77 per cent among college graduates."[40] Komarovsky, noting that wives work for different reasons, adds that working-class husbands seem a bit more ambivalent than middle-class. The former tend to hold the traditional ideology that woman's place is in the home, though they appreciate the higher standard of living that her income provides.[41]

Thus, the greater marital problems caused by the wife in the lower-status family working are a direct function of the fourth alternative presented at the close of the discussion of motives. That is, more low-status wives work out of necessity, wishing they could stay home (or at least that they had the option of doing so), and more low-status wives work whose husbands would prefer, on traditional ideological grounds, that they stay home. It is in the middle-class family that the combination of an equalitarian ideology and choice increases the likelihood that husband and wife can reach a consensus regarding her role choices based upon preference. A part of this consensus involves the couple's perception of what is best for the children.

Wife's Work Status and Child Adjustment

In general, the situation of the mother who is working for self-fulfillment or to raise an already adequate standard of living while the couple is young enough to enjoy it[42] (and whose husband wholeheartedly agrees with her choice), is neither inherently worse nor inherently better for the children than her not working.[43] In fact, in terms of satisfaction, control, and other aspects of child-rearing, the worst adjustment is found among those non-working mothers who prefer to work (perhaps as an escape from deficiencies as mothers).

But do the children not feel deprived when their mother works? Yarrow *et al.* indicate that employed women may actually spend more time with their children doing what the *children* enjoy than do unemployed mothers. They may even show more love toward their children, either because they are happier working and miss their children, or perhaps because they feel a certain amount of guilt at working in the face of the lingering conventional ideology.[44] Once again, it is not so much the fact of working as the attitudinal dimensions that determine her relation to her children, and their adjustment as well.

Two qualifications upon the foregoing generalization can be found in articles by Lois Hoffman and Aase Skard. Part-time employed mothers seem to have better adjusted children than do mothers employed full-time. Perhaps the reason for this is that the mother feels less guilt; but the most direct advantage of part-time employment over full-time is that the former is less likely to communicate to the children that the father is a failure, or is not the primary breadwinner.[45] In addition, no matter how much she works, it is best if her hours are relatively regular and if she works from the early months after the child's birth or else waits until he starts to school. In other words, the child's feelings of maternal deprivation, which are of great concern to those who argue against the mother working, are most apt to appear if the mother starts to work while the child is between ages two and five. And, of course, adequate help in the form of daytime care is necessary for the child's adjustment to remain satisfactory.[46] Thus, given the qualifications of part- vs. full-time employment, regularity and permanence, and adequate help, Skard is able to summarize the effect of mother's employment upon the child as follows: "Children develop best and most harmoniously when the mother herself is happy and gay. Whether she has work outside the home or not seems rather unimportant from the child's viewpoint."[47]

Conclusion

"To work or not to work" is obviously an oversimplified depiction of the home vs. community choice confronting the contemporary female. Many women who are unemployed spend as much time as they would at an occupation in various volunteer community activities. These, too, can be a source of strain or a source of pride for her family, depending upon their orientations. Nor, as we indicated in the early part of this chapter, do adjustments remain unchanged. There are many husbands, for example, who agree with their wife's role choices but who eventually find themselves annoyed by the amount of time that their talented and busy wives are spending in various sorts of community activity. Couple members cannot decide such matters prior to marriage, or even when role decisions are first made; therefore, a concomitant of role choice in the contemporary U.S. family is the necessity of continuing communication.

By this point it should be apparent that family adjustments are determined, not by the structural arrangements themselves, such as the wife's working or not working, but by the attitudinal and expectational components of role choices.

> "Fräulein Spöckenkieker is a divorced woman, so I have heard," said Frau Rittersdorf. "She is, I am given to understand, a woman of business—a lingerie business of sorts, she has three shops and has kept her maiden name in all circumstances. No wonder she no longer has a husband. It may also account for her manners, or lack of them."
> "I wished to continue with my teaching after marriage," said Frau Hutten, with wifely pride, "but my husband would not hear of it for a moment. 'The husband supports the family,' he told me, 'and the wife makes a happy home for them both. That is her sacred mission,' he said, 'and she must be prevented at all costs from abandoning it.' And so it was. From that day to this. I have done only housework, except to act as secretary to my husband."
> Frau Schmitt blushed. "I taught for years," she said, "in the same school with my husband, who was in poor health, almost an invalid, after the war. He could not carry a full professorship; it was important for him not to be too heavily burdened. We had no children, what else should I have been doing? There was not enough to do in our simple little house to keep me occupied. No, I was glad to help my husband. And we had a happy home as well." Her tone was gently defensive and self-satisfied.[48]

Thus does Katherine Anne Porter portray the subtle dominance of traditional roles among the available options. Family maladjustment, we have found, is most likely if there is no choice available at all, or if the husband and wife have differing expectations, or if the choice is interpreted as disparaging one or more family members (such as the husband's role as breadwinner).

In discussing the general issues regarding marital roles in the contemporary United States, we have passed over the more specific interactional and adjustment problems that must be faced by the married couple. How do they make day-to-day decisions? Who does what tasks in the household? What about the economic and sexual adjustments of husbands and wives? These and other such issues comprise the subject matter of Chapter XII.

NOTES

[1] Willard Waller and Reuben Hill, *The Family: A Dynamic Interpretation* (New York: Holt, Rinehart and Winston, 1951), p. 254. On the honeymoon, see Rhona Rapoport and Robert Rapoport, "New Light on the Honeymoon," *Human Relations,* 17 (1964), 33–56.

[2] Waller and Hill, *The Family,* p. 254.

[3] Alice S. Rossi, "Transition to Parenthood," *Journal of Marriage and the Family,* 30 (1968), 27; Robert O. Blood, Jr., and Donald M. Wolfe, *Husbands and Wives* (New York: Free Press, 1960), p. 43; and Mirra Komarovsky, *Blue-Collar Marriage* (New York: Random House, Vintage Books, 1967), p. 31.

[4] Robert Rapoport and Rhona Rapoport, "Work and Family in Contemporary Society," *American Sociological Review,* 30 (1965), 388, 389.

[5] Bernice Neugarten, *Personality in Middle and Late Life* (New York: Atherton, 1964).

[6] *Ibid.,* p. xvi.

[7] *Ibid.,* p. 187.

[8] *Ibid.,* p. 198.

[9] *Ibid.,* p. 194.

[10] In addition to the work done by Neugarten and her research associates, work is now being done by John Clausen, Glen Elder, and others from a processual and age-oriented perspective on the Oakland Growth Study. We shall return to Neugarten's perspective once again in Chapter XIV—on aging.

[11] Talcott Parsons, "Youth in the Context of American Society," *Daedalus,* 91 (1962), 103.

[12] Morris Zelditch, Jr., "Role Differentiation in the Nuclear Family: A Comparative Study," in Talcott Parsons and Robert F. Bales, eds., *Family, Socialization, and Interaction Process* (Glencoe, Ill.: Free Press, 1955), pp. 307–42.

[13] For a good discussion of this, see Hyman Rodman, "Talcott Parsons' View of the Changing American Family," in Hyman Rodman, ed., *Marriage, Family, and Society: A Reader* (New York: Random House, 1965), pp. 273–74.

[14] Charles Winick, "The Beige Epoch: Depolarization of Sex Roles in America," *The Annals,* 376 (1968), 18; see also Winick, *The New People: Desexualization in American Life* (New York: Pegasus, 1968).

[15] Robert K. Leik, "Instrumentality and Emotionality in Family Interaction," *Sociometry,* 26 (1963), 144.

[16] Rossi, "Transition to Parenthood," p. 39.

[17] Zelditch, "Role Differentiation in the Nuclear Family," p. 338. Popular references on role blurring include the following: Bruno Bettelheim, "Fathers Shouldn't Be Mothers!" *This Week Magazine,* April 20, 1958; Dorothy Barclay, "Trousered Mothers and Dishwashing Dads," *New York Times Magazine,* April 28, 1957; and Mike Wallace and John A. Schindler, "Are the Two Sexes Merging?" *New York Post,* October 17, 1957.

[18] Annabelle Bender Motz, "Conceptions of Marital Roles by Status Groups," *Marriage and Family Living,* 12 (1950), 136, 162, and Ernest W. Burgess, Harvey J. Locke, and Mary Margaret Thomes, *The Family,* 3rd ed. (New York: Litton Educational Publishing, 1963), pp. 3–4.

[19] Motz, "Conceptions of Marital Roles," p. 136.

[20] Robert S. Ort, "A Study of Role-Conflicts as Related to Happiness in Marriage," *Journal of Abnormal and Social Psychology,* 45 (1950), 691–99.

[21] Robert P. Stuckert, "Role Perception and Marital Satisfaction—A Con-

figurational Approach," *Marriage and Family Living,* 25 (1963), 415–19.

[22] *Ibid.,* p. 418.

[23] Burgess, Locke, and Thomes, *The Family,* p. 204. Copyright © 1963, by Litton Educational Publishing; Reprinted by permission of Van Nostrand Reinhold Company.

[24] Myron Brenton, *The American Male* (New York: Coward-McCann, 1966), p. 13. Copyright © 1966 by Myron Brenton; Reprinted by permission of Coward-McCann, Inc.

[25] Robert F. Winch, *The Modern Family* (New York: Holt, Rinehart and Winston, 1963 ed.), pp. 399–400.

[26] For additional ideas regarding the relationship between work and the family, see Rapoport and Rapoport, "Work and Family in Contemporary Society."

[27] Brenton, *The American Male,* pp. 28–29. On the decline in male authority, see J. M. Mogey, "A Century of Declining Paternal Authority," *Marriage and Family Living,* 19 (1957), 234–39.

[28] Brenton, *The American Male,* p. 135.

[29] On conjugal role relationships, see Lee Rainwater, *Family Design: Marital Sexuality, Family Size, and Contraception* (Chicago: Aldine, 1965), pp. 28–60. On family patterns and their effect on offspring, see J. W. Getzels and P. Jackson, *Creativity and Intelligence* (New York: Wiley & Sons, 1962).

[30] For a review of the debate on women's roles, see Hilda Sidney Krech, "Housewife and Woman? The Best of Both Worlds?," in Seymour M. Farber, Piero Mustacchi, and Roger H. L. Wilson, eds., *Man and Civilization: The Family's Search for Survival* (New York: McGraw-Hill, 1965, pp. 136–52. See also Betty Friedan, *The Feminine Mystique* (New York: Dell, 1963); Phyllis McGinley, *Sixpence in Her Shoe* (New York: Macmillan, 1964); Simone de Beauvoir, *The Second Sex* (New York: Knopf, Bantam, 1961); and Ferdinand Lundberg and Marynia Farnham, *Modern Women: The Lost Sex* (New York: Harper & Row, 1947).

[31] For some of the sociological literature on working wives, see F. Ivan Nye and Lois Wladis Hoffman, *The Employed Mother in America* (Chicago: Rand McNally, 1963), and *Marriage and Family Living,* 23 (1961), an issue which is devoted almost entirely to working wives.

[32] William J. Goode, *World Revolution and Family Patterns* (New York: Free Press, 1963), p. 61, quotes these figures on women's employment.

[33] This same issue is raised by Leland J. Axelson, "The Marital Adjustment and Marital Role Definitions of Husbands of Working and Non-Working Wives," *Marriage and Family Living,* 25 (1963), 195, and F. Ivan Nye, "Marital Interaction," in Nye and Hoffman, *The Employed Mother in America,* p. 272.

[34] Nye, "Marital Interaction," p. 279. See also Artie Gianopoulos and Howard E. Mitchell, "Marital Disagreement in Working Wife Marriages as a Function of Husband's Attitude Toward Wife's Employment," *Marriage and Family Living,* 19 (1957), 373–78.

[35] Susan R. Orden and Norman M. Bradburn, "Working Wives and Marriage Happiness," *American Journal of Sociology,* 74 (1969), 407.

[36] Krech, "Housewife and Woman?" pp. 146–47.

[37] *Ibid.*

[38] Jeanne L. Hafstrom and Marilyn M. Dunsing, "A Comparison of Economic Choices in One-Earner and Two-Earner Families," *Journal of Marriage and the Family,* 27 (1965), 409.

[39] Nye, "Marital Interaction," p. 280.

[40] Orden and Bradburn, "Working Wives and Marriage Happiness," p. 398.

[41] Komarovsky, *Blue-Collar Marriage,* p. 65.

[42] This is noted in Hafstrom and Dunsing, "A Comparison of Economic Choices," p. 409.

[43] Marian Radke Yarrow *et al.*, "Child Rearing in Families of Working and Non-Working Mothers," *Sociometry*, 25 (1962), 122–40.

[44] *Ibid.*

[45] Lois Wladis Hoffman, "Effects on Children: Summary and Discussion," in Nye and Hoffman, *The Employed Mother in America*, p. 197.

[46] Aase Gruda Skard, "Maternal Deprivation: The Research and Its Implications," *Journal of Marriage and the Family*, 27 (1965), 333–43.

[47] *Ibid.*, p. 343.

[48] Katherine Anne Porter, *Ship of Fools* (Boston: Little, Brown, 1945), pp. 155–56. Copyright 1945, 1946, 1947, 1950 © 1956, 1958, 1959, 1962 by Katherine Anne Porter; reprinted by permission of Atlantic-Little, Brown.

XII

Marriage:
Interactions and Adjustments

MANY INTERACTIONS OF HUSBANDS AND WIVES THAT OCCUR IN THE COURSE OF PERFORMING THEIR ROLES INVOLVE EITHER THE MAKING OF DAY-TO-DAY DECISIONS OR THE CARRYING OUT OF TASKS IN THE HOUSEHOLD DIVISION OF LABOR. EXPECTATIONS CONCERNING DECISION-MAKING HAVE BECOME INCREASINGLY EQUALITARIAN, THOUGH THERE ARE DIFFERENCES BETWEEN EXPECTATIONS AND ACTUALITY WHICH ARE APPARENT WHEN MIDDLE-CLASS AND LOWER-CLASS COUPLES ARE COMPARED. HOUSEHOLD TASKS, WHILE NO LONGER CENTRAL TO ECONOMIC PRODUCTIVITY NOR CAREFULLY DELINEATED BY SEX, STILL COMPRISE A CENTRAL CONCERN OF MARITAL ROLES. TWO AREAS OF MARITAL ADJUSTMENT—FINANCES AND SEX—ARE ASSUMED BY MANY OBSERVERS TO HOLD A UNIQUELY IMPORTANT PLACE WITHIN AMERICAN MARRIAGE; WE EXPLORE SOME OF THE REASONS FOR THIS ASSUMPTION. DISCUSSION OF THREE ISSUES—MARITAL PREDICAMENTS, COMMUNICATION, AND THE DESIRABILITY OF CHOICE—IS USED TO SUMMARIZE CHAPTERS XI AND XII.

Roles and transitions are the central axes of marriage; around them revolve the daily decisions, the household tasks, and the financial and sexual adjustments that give each marriage its particular character. This chapter concerns the day-to-day interactions and adjustments of modern marriage, with some assessment of the way in which these aspects of marriage have changed since colonial days. We begin with decision-making and the division of labor.

SECTION ONE

HUSBAND–WIFE INTERACTION: RUNNING THE HOUSEHOLD

Decision-making and Power

"No change in the American family," say Blood and Wolfe, "is mentioned more often than the shift from one-sided male authority to the sharing of power by husband and wife."[1] The point is not that the wife had no influence over what went on within the colonial family; she did resort frequently to subtle means in order to get her way, for the expectations of the agrarian, pre-industrial family were that the husband should dominate.[2] Nevertheless, one cannot speak of a straightforward, society-wide, normative and behavioral change from husband dominance and subtle female power to conscious equalitarianism. The complexities include such specifying factors as perceived and actual roles, social class differences, various decision-making areas, and whether or not the wife works.

Several authors, including William Kenkel and Fred Strodtbeck, have noted the distinction between perceived and actual decision-making patterns within the home.[3] There is a tendency for husbands and wives to perceive the husband as having the dominant role, with the wife's opinion solicited but the final decision being his. Yet, observation of actual decision-making among numerous married couples showed that well over half of them were actually equalitarian, coming to decisions together. Other research has found a correlation between social class position and the perceived and actual authority of the male. Goode describes these tensions thus:

> Lower-class men concede fewer rights *ideologically* than their women in fact *obtain*, and the more educated men are likely to concede *more* rights ideologically than they in fact grant. One partial resolution of the latter tension is to be found in the frequent assertion from families of professional men that they should not make demands which would interfere with his *work:* He takes precedence as *professional, not* as family head or male; nevertheless, the precedence is his. By contrast, lower-class men demand deference as *men*, as heads of families.[4]

On the one hand, the lower-class male claims authority on the basis of traditional or ideological patriarchy (he is "supposed" to be the boss), while in actual decision-making the lower-class wife wields substantial authority. On the other hand, Goode is saying, the middle-class or educated male ordinarily expresses the *norm* of equalitarianism, but in authority situations he manages to have more power anyway. At least a partial explanation for the divergence between both perceptions and expectations and actuality is found in the "resource" theory propounded by Blood and Wolfe. They argue that higher-status husbands have more resources at their disposal, or control more resources—financial and intellectual, than do lower-status husbands. The middle-class wives, even if they do work, still contribute a smaller proportion of the total family income. Thus, the higher the family's social and economic position, the greater is the husband's bargaining position for actual power, despite the fact that higher-status families tend to have moved further away from traditional patriarchal ideology toward equalitarian expectations.[5]

A second factor that complicates the simple change from patriarchal to equalitarian marriage concerns areas of influence. William Dyer and Dick Urban report in a predominantly middle-class sample that decision-making has been virtually institutionalized as equalitarian, with the exception of finances, where women prefer to make mutual decisions, while the men would rather divide up the various consumption areas and decide unilaterally.[6] Blood and Wolfe divide the decision-making areas into eight categories: husband's occupation, car, insurance, vacation, housing, whether or not the wife should work, choice of a doctor, and food budget. They find that high-status husbands do not exercise authority equally in all eight areas. Rather, they

> make more decisions in only three areas: whether to buy life insurance, what house or apartment to get, and especially whether the wife should go to work or quit work. Actually what happens is not that more high-status husbands make these decisions unilaterally, but that fewer wives do. In other words, high-status husbands take a more active part rather than the wife making the decisions by herself.[7]

Why do high-status husbands take a greater part in these three areas specifically? The reason is related to the issue of surplus income, Blood and Wolfe feel. Both insurance and housing are likely to be more important and costly to the middle-class family than to those at the lower end of the socioeconomic continuum. Furthermore, the wife works, not out of economic necessity, but to supplement the standard of living, and the middle-class husband therefore plays a greater role in the optional decision concerning his wife working.

A third study dealing with areas of influence is based on a sample of skilled workers and college professors in a southern city. Combining specific decisions into four areas—child-care, purchases and living standards, recreation, and role attitudes—Russell Middleton and Snell Putney find a general tendency toward equalitarianism. The working wife, however, plays a somewhat greater role in financial decisions, or those regarding purchases and living standards, than does the non-working wife, but a lesser role in the other three areas.[8] Lois Hoffman, studying 89 matched pairs of working and non-working wives, adds that the working wife makes fewer decisions about routine household matters than the non-working wife, and that the husband of the working wife makes more.[9] These findings are consistent with the economic contribution made by the working wife and the smaller amount of time she spends in the home.

What is the *total* effect of the wife's working or not working upon husband-wife power relations? On this point, the various studies are in disagreement. Blood and Wolfe observe, as had authors of earlier studies, that not only does the working wife have substantially more power than the non-working wife at all status levels, but that the "more years the wife has worked since marriage, the more power she has." In opposition to this is Middleton and Putney's conclusion, which they admit contradicts the findings of previous studies, that families in which the wife works are significantly *more* patriarchal in decisions than are those in which the wife does not work. Perhaps Hoffman is most accurate when she reports that *in toto* there is "no difference in husband-wife power between working and non-working women in the matched sample."[10] Such a conclusion is warranted, at least until further evidence appears.

To summarize the issue of family decision-making, we can say that, to a great extent, companionate or equalitarian expectations have been institutionalized in the U.S. family, though less so in the lower class. Extensions of this discussion include the consideration of social class, areas of influence, and women's roles, plus the fact that the manner in which a couple perceive themselves to make decisions and the manner in which they actually do are frequently two different things. There are some groups, however, such as the individualistic Texans of whom Strodtbeck wrote, which make a conscious or rational effort to be equalitarian in the family.[11] Such conscious equalitarianism is at present more characteristic of the middle class than of the lower class.[12]

The Sexual Division of Labor

Once decisions are made regarding child-care, financial expenditures, or other family matters, they must be implemented.

Someone must *do* the various household tasks, write the checks, and take care of the children. Traditionally, the man's work involved running the productive machinery of the family and supervising the family economic division of labor, while the woman's work was to handle the day-to-day tasks of cooking, sewing, and caring for the children. With the removal of the economic productive function from the home, the husband-father was confronted with two alternatives: He could leave the running of the household to the wife and restrict himself to making the living, or he could take a hand in the heavier, dirtier household tasks and play a supportive role in child-rearing with the realization that his would be a helping role in the household. In the United States, the former pattern has been most characteristic of lower-class families, while the latter has been predominantly a middle-class pattern.

The best single study showing social class differences in the distribution of household tasks was carried out by Marvin Olsen in Omaha, Nebraska. The sample included 391 housewives, who were asked "who does what" in the home, with the following major findings.[13] Amount of household responsibility assumed by the husband increases as status increases up through the upper middle class, or business and professional families. In the wealthy, or upper-class, families, help is hired to do many of the tasks that husbands perform in the middle class. The responsibilities that middle-class husbands assume at home are in those tasks ordinarily believed to be men's work. There is joking and practical concern about the middle-class husband in an apron, but he is much more likely to lend a hand in painting, putting up screens or storm windows, snow shovelling, cleaning out the garage, assembling a swing set, helping with lawn and garden care, and so on. Joint tasks in the middle class include budgeting, supervising children's schoolwork, planning vacations, while these tasks are avoided by working- and lower-class husbands to a marked degree. Blood and Wolfe's description of the division of labor in middle-class families agrees substantially with that of Olsen. Husbands predominate in household repairs, snow shovelling, and lawn mowing. Wives handle meal fixing, housecleaning, and dishwashing. Neither predominates in grocery buying or paying bills, with the latter being the most evenly divided.[14] Thus, while decision-making is consciously equalitarian, the division of labor still tends to be somewhat specialized by sex in the middle-class family. The role of the middle-class husband in household tasks, like that of the working wife in the occupational sphere, is considered to be a subordinate and helping role, rather than based upon complete equality of responsibility.[15]

As reported in an earlier chapter, the middle-class wife generally wants her husband to be supportive of their children, especially of sons, and the husband is ordinarily satisfied to play such a role. Working- and lower-class mothers, in contrast, tend to want their husbands to be directive, setting limits and structuring their children's lives, but the husbands are often unwilling to play such a role, feeling that their wives can do this as well as they.[16] The net consequence is less differentiation between the child-rearing roles of husbands and wives in the middle class than in the working and lower class, with a more intensive involvement of middle-class wives than husbands. The working- and lower-class father is likely to play little role at all.

At this point, much of what we have learned of marital roles and interactions from Motz, Blood and Wolfe, Olsen, Kohn, and other researchers can be brought together. Middle-class husbands and wives may or may not both work, but in any case they tend to strive for equalitarianism in decision-making. Compared to the working- and lower-class husband, the middle-class husband takes a greater hand in household tasks and child-rearing. Yet, despite the companionate nature of the home, the middle-class husband as a "good provider" is accorded considerable status and authority by his family. The lower-class father, on the other hand, plays a minor role in child-rearing and household tasks; he thus perceives himself to be running the family, having delegated responsibility in these areas to his wife. But, because he has fewer resources at his disposal (and for other reasons as well), he finds it difficult to actually assert *consistent* and *acceptable* authority within the home. Some of the comparatively more frequent marital difficulties found in lower-class—and, to some extent, working-class—homes may be due to this differential between expected and actual roles on the part of the male.

SECTION TWO

FINANCIAL AND SEXUAL ADJUSTMENTS IN MARRIAGE

We have discussed husbands' and wives' role choices and commented briefly upon decision-making, household tasks, and socialization. Two further aspects of husband-wife relations deserve attention: financial and sexual adjustments. Lee Rainwater comments concerning the black lower-class family that the "precipitating causes of marital disruption seem to fall mainly into economic or sexual categories."[17] One gets the distinct impression from many popular marriage manuals that this is not a lower-class phenomenon, but that about half of all marital difficulties are traceable to financial disagreements and the rest to sexual maladjustment. While this may be an overstatement, it does indicate that once a couple determines each member's major roles and the decision-making and household division of labor, all their problems have not yet been solved.

Financial Adjustment

Of eight possible areas of husband-wife disagreement—children, recreation, personality, in-laws, roles, values, sex, and money—*money* causes the greatest number of problems, according to Blood and Wolfe's study.[18] Finances are, of course, crucial in the lower-class family with limited resources. In a few instances the welfare system of the United States has made it necessary for the husband to absent himself from the home so that the wife and children may acquire a steady income from welfare. Or the financial burden of the lower-class family may be aggravated by the husband who dissipates what surplus income he has in the attempt to solve his personal problems or failures by means of alcohol. Such isolated examples are not, however, meant to convey the impression that financial adjustment is strictly a low-status problem. It involves the day-to-day explicit and implicit budgeting of family expenditures as they relate to general norms or expectations with regard to how families should live and what they should have. As Hadden and Borgatta point out, "failure to handle this problem may spell disaster for young families," not just in the lower class but in any portion of the society.[19]

Differing orientations toward money, as typified by the man who hoards and the wife who spends, may derive from the very same economic conditions, such as an economic depression. But why should financial orientations, and the disagreements that arise from divergences in outlook, be as problem-producing as Blood and Wolfe, Rainwater, and others find them to be? Let me mention three factors that make money more of a problem in U.S. society than it might otherwise be. First, money and *economic values* are at the heart of the American value system. The standard of living and "things" are crucial elements in the American definition of personal happiness, and personal happiness is, in turn, a focal concern of marriage.[20] The reader may wish to argue whether or not monetary and material values *should* be central, but it is difficult to contend convincingly that they are not. Second, *deferred gratification,* or putting off immediate desires for goals perceived to be of greater value in the future, *can continue for only so long.* In the lower-class family, the personal frustrations that may result from being unable to get ahead in a society that values affluence may be vented against the marital partner. In the middle-class family, a more likely occurrence is that the wife simply runs out of "deferments" before her husband does. She begins, often gradually, to want things now, while he is still establishing his career. And, of course, the economic system is consciously geared to the fostering of these wants in individuals and families. There are numerous other ways in which either the frustration or deferment of material gratifications may result in marital difficulties. The third factor that increases the probability of conflict regarding finances in the U.S. family is that *it is extremely difficult to talk about and reconcile differences in financial attitudes prior to marriage.* Dating couples infrequently discuss their financial orientations, but even if they did, it would be hard to foresee how one might be reacting ten years later to the added pressure of an occupation, a home, children, and perhaps aging parents. This is another of those issues in marriage which seems to require continuing communication on the part of the spouses if an adequate adjustment is to be perpetuated.

Sexual Adjustment

The understanding of sexual adjustment as an issue in contemporary marriage is facilitated by historical comparison. The biggest change has to do with the term itself: sexual adjustment. Not too many years ago—and still today in many lower-class families—the husband sought sexual gratification, and the wife was expected to provide it. Accompanying this asymmetry was an inhibition and feeling of sinfulness that *increasingly* pervaded U.S. and British society during the nineteenth century. These historical factors, asymmetry and guilt, form the backdrop against which today's sexual adjustments in marriage must be understood.

Beginning with the Kinsey reports and continuing into the 1960's, researchers have found a relationship between sexual adjustment and total marital adjustment.[21] In Bruce Thomason's study of young well-educated couples, for example, mutuality of orgasm was related to marital adjustment. In addition, Thomason reported that both sexual and marital adjustments tended to be better if the spouse was perceived to be sexually attractive, if sexual intercourse was by mutual desire, and if mates were willing and able to have intercourse as often as they wished it.[22] Such results, when coupled with the influence of Freud and the Kinsey reports, caused some to overcompensate for earlier inhibitions by feeling that sexual adjustment is the central fact of marriage, rather than being but one element among others. An immediate problem with the Kinsey, Thomason, and other research conclusions is that even when a correlation is found, as between sexual and overall adjustment, one must be cautious about arguing that sexual adjustment is causative. An equally plausible conclusion would be that marital maladjustment results in an unsatisfactory sexual experience, including the inability of the wife to achieve orgasm. However, later researchers have called the correlation itself into question. Komarovsky finds that the relation between sexual adjustment and total marital adjustment in her working-class couples is low. Many unhappy women had a satisfactory sex life; yet, she finds, as the wife's educational level increases, so does the relation between sexual and other adjustments.[23] John Cuber and Peggy Harroff's study of the marriages of professional and managerial men offers insights into the sexual adjustments of the highly educated. Their study, which included 235 upper-middle-class men and 202 women, indicated that

> many remain clearly ascetic where sex is concerned. Others are clearly *a*sexual. For still others, sex is overlaid with such strong hostility that an *anti*sexual orientation is clear. In sum, we found substantial numbers of men and women who in their present circumstances couldn't care less about anything than they do about sex.[24]

For some of Komarovsky's working-class couples, then, sex was still so segregated from the rest of marriage as to make the correlation between it and marital adjustment negligible. For some of Cuber and Harroff's middle-class couples, sex had simply become a matter of mutual non-salience, with the marriage left to revolve around the other aspects of their busy lives. Can the sexually exploitative or asexual marriage be truly well-adjusted? Perhaps it is only the expectations and overcompensations born of the post-Victorian era which cause us to feel that this is impossible.

But what of these expectations? The fact that wives as well as husbands are increasingly expected to find gratification in the sex act is at the heart of the problem of sexual adjustment today. "The contemporary male," says Myron Brenton,

> faces sexual responsibilities far exceeding those of men in earlier times. He must gratify himself *and* his sexual partner. He has to make sure he's a better lover—or at least no worse—than other men. He has to cope with the sexually liberated woman, something that can require a considerable amount of coping.[25]

This has resulted in some men tending to question their masculinity, or their ability to "satisfy" the female. This theme has, of course, been picked up and played upon prominently in American advertising.

On the female's part, the problem is likely to be that she is still sexually inhibited by her socialization, yet in marriage she is expected—and expects hereself—to be able to give herself to a man and gain personal satisfaction from it. Even engagement in premarital sex, as long as it includes lingering overtones of guilt, will do little to prepare the female for sexual responsiveness in marriage. Thus, the combination of overtones of guilt, plus overemphasis on the importance of sex, plus new expectations of mutuality, serve to intensify the problem of sexual adjustment in the contemporary U.S. family.

SECTION THREE

A SUMMARY OF MARRIAGE: PREDICAMENTS, COMMUNICATION, AND CHOICE

By now it should be evident that there are some serious and crucial adjustments and choices confronting the married couple in a day when the nuclear family is but slightly embedded in the kin network and when the other institutions operate, for the most part, apart from the family unit. Today's increasingly equalitarian U.S. couples are still ordinarily composed of persons who *believe* their commitment at marriage to be for life. Yet, because of the loss of many cultural supports for the permanence of the individual unit, the nuclear family has fewer resources at its disposal which differentiate it from the short-term relationship and which insure permanence. Some of the issues confronting married couples today are well summarized in four predicaments that we shall paraphrase from Bernard Farber.[26]

Marital Predicaments

Each of the four predicaments, or issues, that married couples must resolve, can be derived, from one or more portions of the two preceding chapters. The first concerns *instrumental and social-emotional roles* in marriage. Women's roles, decision-making, the family division of labor: all these are aspects of role differentiation or role similarity. Blood and Wolfe find that joint decision-making, confiding in one another, and having mutual friends are all related to the wife's satisfaction with her marriage, but the husband's performing household tasks is not. This may be the explanation of Motz's finding that the companionate role is desired for the husband and the conventional role for the wife. A possible interpretation is that the husband should be willing to allow his wife to have a major role in decisions and to work if she desires, but the wife is still expected by both herself and her husband to handle the majority of the household tasks, so that he can focus his attention on his economic role.

The last phrase of the preceding sentence indicates that, while there are role choices available to husbands and wives, these choices are still governed somewhat by the traditional ideology. Role blurring has not yet proceeded to the point that the husband who loves children can stay home and take care of them while the aggressive wife pursues a career and provides for the family's financial needs. This is not yet considered a viable option, although some feminists have argued that it should be legitimated as a cultural alternative. At present, the alternatives along the instrumental–social-emotional dimension tend to be variations in the theme of husband dominance in the economic-occupational-financial (instrumental) area and wife dominance in the home-children-kin (social-emotional) area.[27]

A second predicament, which is closely related to the first, concerns *internal versus external commitment*, or involvement in family versus community. How much of himself or herself should the husband or wife invest in the family and how much in the environment away from home? Farber notes that in a society in which the norms reinforce orderly replacement of family culture, the male can give himself to his work with little worry that his family will disintegrate for lack of his attention. However, if the family subsists on the personal involvement of its members, the father who is devoted entirely to his occupation may, in fact, be a disintegrative element in the family. Familism, or the investment of self in the family, is a likely aspect of both husbands' and wives' roles if the satisfactions expected from the family are to materialize.

Yet "family versus community" orientation only becomes a predicament when the community does not support, or is in competition with, family values. In many aspects of community life, including motion pictures, literature, and certain forms of recreation, there is at least a tension—if not an antagonism—between family and community values. Certain industries, however, instead of opposing family values, have begun to stress husband-wife togetherness and the socializing of their employees as family units. These companies are not fostering happy marriages as ends in themselves, but because the happily-married man is a more efficient worker. Furthermore, many businesses and advertisers stress the home because families are the central units of economic consumption. Yet, despite the fact that elements of the community support family values—for whatever reason—the predicament of how much time and energy should be invested in the family and how much outside the family still must be resolved by each married couple.

Short-term versus long-term planning and gratification within the family is the crux of the third predicament.[28] Short-run, or short-term, gratification is epitomized (or perhaps overstated) in the little popular folk song of several years back: "We'll sing in the sunlight, we'll laugh every day . . . and be on our way." When a couple's solidarity is based upon common interests, immediate physical gratification, or an ideal image of the kind of person the spouse is or is going to be, then a change in roles or interests may void the relationship. Long-range planning demands that the couple members regard their relationship as relatively stable and orderly. Farber, however, feels that the tendency today is toward more short-run gratification in marriage and less emphasis upon long-run planning; this tendency is consistent, he feels, with the movement of U.S. society toward *permanent* availability, i.e., the voidable relationship. Yet, it should be added that as long as deferred gratification and long-term planning are found to be strong in families, the pendulum cannot be said to have swung all the way to permanent availability.

The fourth predicament is an issue with which we have been

concerned throughout the volume: *individualism versus familism.* Closely linked to the third predicament, the issue here is whether the adjustment and happiness of the individual is primary, or whether it is subordinated to the needs of the family unit. Farber, who labels this issue "parent vs. children orientation," states that there is a tradition, especially among wives, of subordinating personal needs to those of the children. Once again, any tendency toward the spouses' gratifying their own needs, especially when this is coupled with short-term orientation, is linked with movement away from orderly replacement—since the parents are less concerned about the consequences of their behavior for their children—and toward permanent availability. Not only is socialization not put before personal gratification, but the family unit is less likely to be kept intact because of the presence of children in the home. One purpose of singling out these four predicaments is to remind the reader just how far the U.S. family still is from permanent availability, or serial monogamy, as normative or expected. In fact, many attributes of the equalitarian or companionate marriage —including familism, long-term orientation, and freedom to choose marital roles—go toward stabilizing family life and culture. Much of the stabilizing efficacy of such factors, however, seems to be a function of communication between husbands and wives.

Communication in Marriage

Throughout Chapters XI and XII we have hinted that many of the interactional and adjustment problems of modern marriage can be resolved if only couples will keep the communication channels open between them. Several years ago Harvey Locke, Georges Sabagh, and Mary Margaret Thomes reported that primary communication, or communication "which is intimate, free-flowing, and unrestricted," is correlated positively with marital adjustment in their sample of 126 California couples.[29] More recently Goodman and Ofshe have confirmed again that communication and understanding are central to marriage.[30]

Yet to assert that open communication results in a happy marriage would be an oversimplification. Cutler and Dyer, for example, note that among newly-married couples

> nearly half of the non-adjustive responses for both husbands and wives came as a result of an open sharing of the feelings about the violation of expectations. Contrary to what might be expected, an open talking about the

violation of expectations does not always lead to an adjustment.[31]

Likewise, Komarovsky reports that among her working-class couples there is no perfect correlation between self-disclosure and marital happiness. Some men don't want to be told too much; some achieve happiness precisely because they achieve some privacy. The better educated tend to communicate more, and in general the wives are less satisfied than the husbands with what they believe to be too little communication.[32]

Communication, therefore, can be problem-producing rather than integrative if the husband desires less or if conflict is defined as aberrant behavior or as a sign of the incipient breakup of the marriage. Communication often leads to conflict and, unfortunately, many married couples are afraid of conflict—having been socialized to the value of cooperation and "getting along," thus being unable to cope with open disagreement.[33] Many couples would rather seal off an area of life such as finances and avoid discussing it than to take the chance that disagreement will lead to marital disruption.

In summary, then, communication may help to resolve interactional and adjustment problems in marriage, but not if conflict is defined strictly in negative terms. It seems a bit ironic that the individuals who are most likely to communicate openly, i.e., middle-class persons, are also likely to define conflict as a purely negative phenomenon.

Summary and the Value of Choice

Differences between the traditional and equalitarian family types may be catalogued in absolute terms, but one should keep in mind the fact that most families operate somewhere between the two types (see Table 7). How do these types look when they are placed upon the "Marital Role" Continuum of Chapter V? (See Figure 12.) Unquestionably, the middle-class family is closer to the "choice-blurred-equalitarian" end of the continuum than is either the working- or lower-class family. Yet even middle-class marriage cannot be considered entirely open and choice-based as long as the traditional ideology defines certain options as deviant and unacceptable—an example being the aforementioned husband-homemaker, wife-breadwinner choice.

A final comment concerns the vocabulary employed to describe the equalitarian marriage—both in the popular press and in

TABLE 7

A Summary of Traditional and Equalitarian Roles of Husbands and Wives

Type of Marriage	Husband	Wife
Traditional (Conventional)	Legal authority and disciplinarian at home. Breadwinner. Economic coordinator and decision-maker.	Homemaker and child-rearer. Normatively subordinate in virtually every area of marriage.
Equalitarian (Companionate)	Subordinate role in socializing and home tasks. Breadwinner. Equalitarian decision-making.	Works if wants to, or does volunteer service. Shares overtly in decision-making. Dominates homemaking and child-rearing.

sociological writings. We have, throughout Chapters XI and XII, used the language of the literature at our disposal: "predicaments," "dilemmas," "ambiguities," "problems," "ill-defined." Yet these very terms that relate to choice are loaded with negative connotations. The same historical changes that have given rise to ambiguity could be described in terms of freedom, emancipation, and opportunity—but seldom are. The human being, it has been pointed out, whether he be sociologist or magazine writer, prefers tradition over choice, predetermination over ambiguity.[34] Furthermore, when the writer is male, or has been trained in a male-dominated society, the desirable pattern should obviously be in favor of male control. Perhaps Charles Winick is correct; too much uncertainty is unhealthy.[35] On the other hand, it is at least possible that once the contemporary family has escaped its midstream position, abandon-

FIGURE 12

The Author's View of Marital Roles in the Contemporary United States in Relation to the Marital Role Continuum.

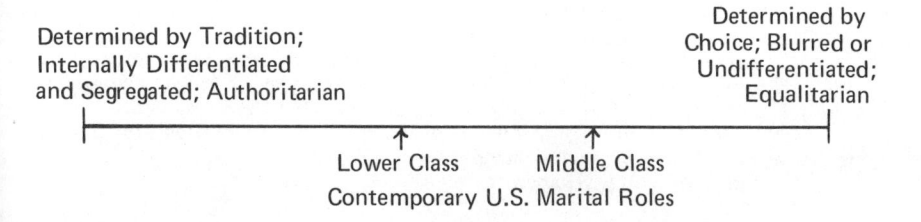

Determined by Tradition; Internally Differentiated and Segregated; Authoritarian

Determined by Choice; Blurred or Undifferentiated; Equalitarian

↑ Lower Class   ↑ Middle Class

Contemporary U.S. Marital Roles

ing the lingering elements of a traditional patriarchy, the freedom to choose for oneself may result in fulfillment and the development of the unique potentialities of each person and marriage.[36] *Regardless of whether one sees freedom and blurring as opportunity or problem, he should be cognizant of the subtle value implications of the terms being used to describe contemporary family roles.*

NOTES

[1] Robert O. Blood, Jr., and Donald M. Wolfe, *Husbands and Wives* (New York: Free Press, 1960), p. 11.

[2] Herman Lantz et al., "Pre-Industrial Patterns in the Colonial Family in America: A Content Analysis of Colonial Magazines," *American Sociological Review*, 33 (1968), 419.

[3] William F. Kenkel and Dean K. Hoffman, "Real and Conceived Roles in Family Decision-Making," *Marriage and Family Living*, 18 (1956), 308–14; William F. Kenkel, "Observational Studies of Husband-Wife Interaction in Family Decision-Making," in Marvin B. Sussman, ed., *Sourcebook in Marriage and the Family* (Boston: Houghton Mifflin, 1963 ed.), pp. 144–56; and Fred L. Strodtbeck, "Husband-Wife Interaction Over Revealed Differences," *American Sociological Review*, 16 (1951), 468–73.

[4] William J. Goode, *World Revolution and Family Patterns* (New York: Free Press, 1963), pp. 21–22. See also Lee Rainwater, *Family Design: Marital Sexuality, Family Size, and Contraception* (Chicago: Aldine, 1965), p. 54.

[5] Blood and Wolfe, *Husbands and Wives*. A variation on the resource theory, David Heer's exchange theory, is discussed in David M. Heer, "The Measurement and Bases of Family Power: An Overview," *Marriage and Family Living*, 25 (1963), 133–39, and "Rejoinder," pp. 475–78.

[6] William G. Dyer and Dick Urban, "The Institutionalization of Equalitarian Family Norms," *Marriage and Family Living*, 20 (1958), 58.

[7] Blood and Wolfe, *Husbands and Wives*, p. 33.

[8] Russell Middleton and Snell Putney, "Dominance in Decisions in the Family: Race and Class Differences," *American Journal of Sociology*, 65 (1960), 605–9.

[9] Lois Wladis Hoffman, "Parental Power Relations and the Division of Household Tasks," in F. Ivan Nye and Lois Hoffman, eds., *The Employed Mother in America* (Chicago: Rand McNally, 1963), pp. 229–30.

[10] Blood and Wolfe, *Husbands and Wives*, pp. 40–41; Middleton and Putney, "Dominance in Decisions in the Family"; and Hoffman, "Parental Power Relations and the Division of Household Tasks."

[11] Strodtbeck, "Husband-Wife Interaction."

[12] A further issue in family power concerns different *kinds* of power. This is discussed in Phyllis N. Hallenbeck, "An Analysis of Power Dynamics in Marriage," *Journal of Marriage and the Family*, 28 (1966), 200–3.

[13] Marvin E. Olsen, "Distribution of Family Responsibilities and Social Stratification," *Marriage and Family Living*, 22 (1960), 60–65.

[14] Blood and Wolfe, *Husbands and Wives*, p. 50.

[15] Dyer and Urban, "The Institutionalization of Equalitarian Family Norms," and Ruth E. Hartley, "Some Implications of Current Changes in Sex-Role Patterns," *Merrill-Palmer Quarterly*, 6 (1959–1960), 153–64.

[16] Melvin L. Kohn, "Social Class and Parent-Child Relationships: An Interpretation," *American Journal of Sociology*, 68 (1963), 476.

[17] Lee Rainwater, "Crucible of Identity: The Negro Lower-Class Family," *Daedalus* (Winter, 1966), 192.

[18] Blood and Wolfe, *Husbands and Wives*, p. 192.

[19] Jeffrey K. Hadden and Marie L. Borgatta, "The Economics of Family Living," in Hadden and Borgatta, eds., *Marriage and the Family* (Itasca, Ill.: Peacock, 1969), p. 449.

[20] On economics in the value system of the U.S., see Shepard Clough, *Basic Values of Western Civilization* (New York: Columbia University Press, 1960), p. 15, and Robin M. Williams, Jr., *American Society: A Sociological Interpretation* (New York: Knopf, 1960 ed.), Chaps. 10–14.

[21] Alfred C. Kinsey et al., *Sexual Behavior in the Human Male* (Philadelphia: Saunders, 1948); Kinsey et al., *Sexual Behavior in the Human Female* (Philadelphia: Saunders, 1953); Bruce Thomason, "Marital Sexual Behavior and Total Marital Adjustment: A Research Report," in J. Himelhoch and Sylvia F. Fava, eds., *Sexual Behavior in American Society* (New York: Norton, 1955), pp. 153–63; and Robert A. Dentler and Peter Pineo, "Sexual Adjustment, Marital Adjustment and Personal Growth of Husbands: A Panel Analysis," *Marriage and Family Living*, 22 (1960), 45–48.

[22] Thomason, "Marital Sexual Behavior."

[23] Mirra Komarovsky, *Blue-Collar Marriage* (New York: Random House, Vintage Books, 1967), p. 111.

[24] John F. Cuber and Peggy B. Harroff, *The Significant Americans* (New York: Appleton-Century-Crofts, 1965), p. 172.

[25] Myron Brenton, *The American Male* (New York: Coward-McCann, 1966), p. 29. Copyright © 1966 by Myron Brenton; reprinted by permission of Coward-McCann, Inc.

[26] Bernard Farber, *Family: Organization and Interaction* (San Francisco: Chandler, 1964), pp. 285–332.

[27] Some have argued that there is in fact a more insidious form of discrimination against women today than ever before, in that we speak of equality between the sexes at a time when women's empirical position in the society is becoming increasingly worse. On this, see Dean D. Knudsen, "The Declining Status of Women: Popular Myths and the Failure of Functionalist Thought," *Social Forces*, 48 (1969), 183–93.

[28] Farber, *Family: Organization and Interaction*, talks of "role versus career orientation" at this point. However, with the other common uses of the terms "role" and "career" we have decided to stick to the terms "short-run" and "long-run" planning and gratification.

[29] Harvey J. Locke, Georges Sabagh, and Mary Margaret Thomes, "Correlates of Primary Communication and Empathy," *Research Studies of the State College of Washington*, 24 (1956), 116–24.

[30] Norman Goodman and Richard Ofshe, "Empathy, Communication Efficiency, and Marital Status," *Journal of Marriage and the Family*, 30 (1968), 597–603.

[31] Beverly R. Cutler and William G. Dyer, "Initial Adjustment Processes in Young Married Couples," *Social Forces*, 44 (1965), 201.

[32] Komarovsky, *Blue-Collar Marriage*, pp. 142f.

[33] On this issue, see Gibson Winter, *Love and Conflict* (Garden City, N.Y.: Doubleday, 1958).

[34] See Erich Fromm, *Escape From Freedom* (New York: Rinehart, 1941).

[35] Charles Winick, "The Beige Epoch: Depolarization of Sex Roles in America," *The Annals,* 376 (1968), 24.

[36] A more positive view is stated by Goode, *World Revolution and Family Patterns,* 57, and Robert and Rhona Rapoport, "Work and Family in Contemporary Society," *American Sociological Review,* 30 (1965), 394. Likewise, Dennis H. Wrong, "The 'Break-Up' of the American Family," *Commentary,* 9 (1950), 380, speaks of changes in the family as increasing the freedom of the individual rather than breaking up the family.

XIII

Kinship Relations

KINSHIP UNITS AMONG CERTAIN SOCIETIES, SUCH AS THAT OF THE PAPAGO, SERVE ECONOMIC, POLITICAL, RELIGIOUS, AND OTHER INSTITUTIONAL FUNCTIONS. OTHER FUNCTIONS PERFORMED BY THE LARGER KIN UNITS IN SOME SOCIETIES INCLUDE: PROPERTY-HOLDING AND INHERITANCE, HOUSING, NEED-OBLIGATION, AND AFFECTIVE OR EMOTIONAL TIES. THERE IS, HOWEVER, NO SIMPLE LINEAR REMOVAL OF THESE FUNCTIONS AS ONE MOVES FROM DURKHEIM'S MECHANICALLY SOLIDARY SOCIETY TO THE "ORGANICALLY SOLIDARY" MODERN INDUSTRIAL STATE. YET, COMPARED TO THE PAPAGO, THE KINSHIP UNITS OF THE UNITED STATES ARE LESS CENTRAL TO THE SOCIETY'S OPERATION, PERFORMING A PRIMARY AFFECTIVE FUNCTION, A SECONDARY NEED-OBLIGATION FUNCTION, AND PERFORMING IDIOSYNCRATICALLY IN THE AREAS OF INHERITANCE AND HOUSING. IN THIS CHAPTER WE CONSIDER THE MEANINGS OF "DISTANCE" WITH RESPECT TO KIN, THE SIGNIFICANCE OF KIN TERMS, AND THE KINSMAN AS A PERSON. THE LAST PORTION OF THE CHAPTER IS GIVEN TO A CHARACTERIZATION OF RELATIONS BETWEEN THE FOLLOWING KIN: PARENTS AND ADULT OFFSPRING, ADULT SIBLINGS, SECONDARY KIN, AND IN-LAWS.

The maturing individual in modern industrial society ordinarily lives with his parents, brothers and sisters. He is also likely to be acquainted with aunts, uncles, cousins, and grandparents who do not live with him, but who are nevertheless considered important because of their status as kinfolk or relatives. Upon reaching adulthood and marrying he does not terminate his relationship with his family of orientation, i.e., parents and siblings, but they, too, become a part of his kin network—his "kin of orientation." It is this network, involving parents and adult offspring, siblings, grandparents, aunts, and uncles, as well as in-laws, that concerns us in the present chapter. The very fact that kin outside the individual's nuclear family have been virtually ignored since the early chapters of this volume should perhaps indicate to the reader something of the author's perspective on the importance of kin in the United States. But in order to understand U.S. kinship we shall once again resort to cross-cultural and historical comparison.

SECTION ONE

KIN FUNCTIONS IN CROSS-CULTURAL PERSPECTIVE

There are societies, such as the Papago of Arizona and northern Mexico, in which both institutions and personnel are embedded within the larger kin unit, so that most of the activities and interactions that occur are predicated upon kin ties of one sort or another. David Schneider characterizes the difference between kinship in such a society and in a modern, Western society thus:

> The kinship systems of modern, western societies are relatively differentiated as compared with the kinship systems found in many primitive and peasant societies. By "differentiated" I mean simply that kinship is clearly and sharply distinguished from all other kinds of social institutions and relationships. In many primitive and peasant societies a large number of kinds of institutions are organized and built as *parts of the kinship system itself*. Thus the major social units of the society may be kin groups—lineages perhaps. These same kin groups may be property-owning units, the political units, the religious units, and so on. Thus, whatever a man does in such a society he does *as a kinsman of one kind or another*.[1] (Italics added.)

The institutionally-embedded Papago, for example, have no political institutions beyond the village council, which consists of the elders in the various family units. These same village elders perform the major religious rituals on behalf of their kin. Even the economic division of labor is coterminous with the kin networks, there being no separate market functionaries.

One of the major variations described in Chapter IV is in institutional embeddedness within the kin network and nuclear family. It was noted that the society of classical China differed from that of the Papago in being characterized by a small number of powerful, institutionally-embedded and personnel-embedded patrilineages over against the state, but with the majority of non-affluent kin networks functionally separated into nuclear families. The description of the colonial U.S. showed the major institutional functions somewhat embedded in the nuclear families, but not in the kin networks. Finally, a crucial change between colonial days and the present was seen to be in terms of the increasing differentiation of institutional functions from the nuclear family—the larger kin group already having lost most of its institutional significance. There are, however, other specific functions that have been performed by the kin groups of some societies, but whose change cannot be traced in a linear fashion. These functions include: (1) property-holding and inheritance; (2) housing and residential proximity; (3) obligation, or helping in time of need; and (4) affection, emotional ties, or primary relationships.[2] The first of these, *inheritance*, is clearly a kin function in those societies with corporate lineages. But in both the small band, such as the Andaman Islanders, and in colonial America, the property-holding unit through which inheritance is controlled is the nuclear family represented by its male head, whose socially-determined prerogative may be to pass the inheritance to one offspring or to divide it among them all.[3] Thus, one change since colonial days is a result of the fact that the wife can hold property separate from that of her husband, and can distribute it to her offspring separately if she so desires.

The *housing-residential proximity* function, which is in reality two functions, is most difficult to place on a change continuum. For one thing, there are multiple forms of household sharing. In one society it may be the "long house," in which the men live apart from the women and children. In another it may be a joint family of brothers and their wives and children. A third may find an aged parent or parents living with one of their married offspring. Furthermore, although the norms of certain societies include household sharing, residence may actually be proximate rather than shared—with the kin group functioning as a unit. Finally, housing may be temporarily shared with kin in virtually any society, including the contemporary United States.[4] Thus, if the issue here is simply kin proximity, one might argue that there is a progressive change toward greater dispersion from the small, undifferentiated society to the modern industrial society.[5] But, if the same issue is stated as one of kin providing housing for each other, this is about as likely in rural-to-urban migrant groups in the U.S. as it is in the Hindu joint family of India. The difference is in the lack of specification, in the former case, of the relative with whom one *should* share his residence, and in the lack of an expectation of permanence.

The *obligatory* function, based on the expectation that one will help kin under certain circumstances, varies greatly from one society to another. In one society, the strongest obligation may be to the mother's brother; in another, to the grandfather; and in still another, to one's own parents. Also, the obligations range from warrior allegiance and a proper burial to finances or simply keeping in touch. The strongest sense of obligation in contemporary U.S. kinship seems to be between aging parents and their adult offspring, but even this is mitigated by the equally powerful societal value of nuclear family independence and self-sufficiency.

The final function, providing affectional or *emotional ties* for the individual, operates as a matter of choice in most kinship systems. Though each society has an expectation that certain kin will provide such ties, the actual strength of relationships is extremely varied. Societies in which institutions are embedded in the kin network, so that one kin line has jural and economic power over the individual, are often characterized by one's closest ties being with members of the other line. For example, in some patrilineal societies, the closest feelings are towards members of the mother's kin group.[6] Perhaps the most outstanding example in U.S. kinship of functional ties standing in the way of affect is the situation in which brothers and their father work together in the same business, with the result that they seek emotional gratifications elsewhere among their kin.[7]

To conclude this section, then, one can say that the greatest single difference in kinship between, say, the Papago and the contemporary U.S. is the removal of institutional functions so that the kin network *qua* kin network seldom performs economic productive, political, religious, or educational functions. Apart from that change, however, it is difficult to summarize briefly the changes in specific functions performed by kin in one society or another. It is better, rather, to stop with the assertion that, in the contemporary United States, kin perform a general affective function, a particular obligatory function, and operate idiosyncratically in the areas of inheritance and housing. Yet, this type of summarization only hints at many crucial issues that must be confronted before an adequate characterization of kinship in the United States can be effected. Some of these issues in kinship analysis are presented in Section Two.

SECTION TWO

SOME ISSUES IN KINSHIP ANALYSIS

From the many issues regarding kinship which could be reviewed in a book on the family, we have chosen five which seem most essential to understanding kin relations in the United States. These include the general issue of the significance of *kin terms,* the idea of the *kinsman as a person,* the meanings of kin *"distance,"* and the specific issues of kin *unimportance* and nuclear family *isolation* in urban-industrial society.

Kin Terms

For many years, the significance of kin terms has been debated in the literature on kinship. Do the terms used—such as mother's brother, parallel cousin, or aunt—have direct behavioral connotations, so that the compilation and comparison of terminological systems can be used to symbolize the kinship systems of different societies? Or are the terms psychologically grounded cultural constructs, or are they anachronistic and therefore only partially correlated with actual kinship norms, behaviors, and roles in a given society? Lewis Henry Morgan, says Robin Fox, "saw in the study of terminology the royal road to the understanding of kinship systems." Fred Eggan states plainly that "the verbal behavior symbolizes the socially defined relationships. . . ." Radcliffe-Brown shows that Choctaw and Omaha kin terms are as reasonable for their kinship systems as are our terms for our system. Roger Davies likewise points out that, among the kin-based Syrian Arabs, there are terms that distinguish between five generations.[8] This approach, which stresses the sociological significance of terminology, is epitomized in George P. Murdock's book, *Social Structure,* in which various types of kinship systems are classified and distinguished from each other primarily on the basis of terms.[9]

On the other side of the question are those such as A. L. Kroeber, who claims that terms reflect psychology, not sociology. In fact, he says, kinship systems are "linguistic patterns of logic, and their uncritical and unrestrained use as if they were uncontaminated reflectors of past or present institutions" is unsound and dangerous.[10] And, as Robin Fox notes, Malinowski, unlike Radcliffe-Brown, had little use for the study of kin terms, feeling that time would be better spent in the study of norms and actual relationships rather than language.[11]

While the debate has not been completely resolved, it seems that Robin Fox's conclusion is valid. Kinship systems, he says, are many-sided, and terminology may not reflect every side of them. What a system of terms may tell us "is *how the people themselves* see their world of kin. Who do they distinguish from whom and on what basis? It is often the case that they regard a certain distinction as crucial which has no meaning for us in terms of *our* analysis of the system of groups, alliances, etc."[12] There is, then, a correlation between terminology and behavior, but it is simply not perfect.

A part of the discussion of kin terms has concerned the European and U.S. system and its peculiarities. Fox, for example, points out that, in this system, "the terms for members of the nuclear family (father, mother, son, daughter, brother, sister) are *not used for anyone outside the family*. This is very different" from all those terminological systems in which the nuclear family receives little or no stress.[13] Among the Papago, for example, "all cousins of every degree, on both sides, are called brothers and sisters," although the Papago can, if need be, use words that mean a "near brother" (his own) and a "far brother" (a cousin).[14] Thus, the European-American terminological system (which Murdock classifies with the "Eskimo") manifests both the bilateral nature of our kin relations— i.e., our normatively equal relation to both mother's and father's kin—and the special importance attached to members of the nuclear family.

The above-mentioned studies are concerned with comparative differences in kin terms. A few authors have tried to determine the significance of American kin terms. David Schneider and George Homans assert that one of the more fundamental and interesting characteristics of American terminology is the wide variety of alternatives for the same individual.

> Mother may be called "mother," "mom," "ma," "mummy," "mama," by her first name, nickname, diminutive, "old woman," and a variety of other less commonly used designations.
> Father may be called "father," "pop," "pa," "dad," "daddy," by his first name, diminutive, "old man," "boss," and a variety of less commonly used designations. Uncles

may be addressed or referred to as uncle-plus-first name, first name alone, or uncle alone. Similarly for aunts.[15]

Beginning with these terms, Schneider and Homans proceed to report the relationship between terms and behavior. Among their findings are the following: (1) On the assumption that parental terms can be ranged on a continuum from most formal, "father" and "mother," to least formal, first name only, there is a tendency for both sexes to become relatively more formal with their same-sex parent. (2) Use of the terms "father" and "mother" for one's parents symbolizes a more formal and less close relationship with them. (3) Females use a wider variety of terms for their parents than males do for theirs. (4) The tendency is "for more first-name-alone designations to be applied to aunts and uncles on the mother's side than on the father's." (5) Males are more likely than females to address aunts and uncles by first name alone. In cases of either strong positive or negative sentiment the formal terms "aunt" and "uncle" are dropped and first-name-only is used.[16]

Since Schneider and Homans' article appeared, there have been attempts at replication by Lionel Lewis and by Hagstrom and Hadden.[17] These later investigations—which, like Schneider and Homans' study, have employed accidental or non-random samples —have verified findings (3), (4), and (5), but not the others. Hagstrom and Hadden interpret these findings to mean that females are generally more involved in kinship and people tend to be somewhat closer to maternal kin. However, neither of the findings regarding sentiment and parental terms is confirmed by Hagstrom and Hadden and, with the exception of females and their father's siblings, aunt and uncle terminology and sentiment were found to be unilinear rather than curvilinear, i.e., the closer the individual feels to his aunt or uncle the more likely he is to use first name only.[18]

Besides cross-cultural comparisons and analysis of the significance of kin terms in the U.S., a third portion of the study of kin terms is concerned with the naming of children. Alice Rossi, in a sample of 384 primarily middle-class women in the Chicago area, noted that there was a tendency between 1920 and 1950 away from naming offspring for mother's mother and father's father and toward naming them for mother's father and especially father's mother.[19] This, she feels, may indicate a greater equalitarianism within the family and the lessening role segregation between males and females and between maternal and paternal kin.

Rossi's article has, of course, but scratched the surface of what might be discovered from a study of names and naming. In fact, there is much left to be done in the analysis of kinship terms in a single society such as that of the United States. Hagstrom and Hadden indicate the current state of such research in their summary comments:

> It is not yet possible to know to what extent the selection among alternative kin terms depends on sentiment. . . .
> The analysis of kinship terminology has already proved its usefulness in comparing the social structures of different societies. It may also be useful in the analysis of kinship within single societies.[20]

Kinsman as a Person

The kinship network does not consist of terminological distinctions, or of roles and functions, but of people. These people have various personalities, behave in various ways, and view their social worlds from diverse perspectives. The kinship component of a relationship gives it an enduring quality, as distinct from the contingent solidarity of friendship; but, within this difference, the unique character of a relationship results from the involvement of the people with one another. There are, as Schneider points out, "Famous Relatives" who hold a particularly honored place among their kin.[21] Whether they are dead or alive, they are referred to with pride. Or a cousin with whom one enjoys doing things may be described as "more of a friend than a relative," the meaning being that the term "cousin" ordinarily connotes little affection or interaction, while this particular person is of greater significance than that. On the other side of this coin are the friends who are referred to as "Uncle Roald" and "Aunt Maureen," though they are in actuality not relatives at all. The kin terms indicate that a relationship is based on more than the fleeting interests and activities of the typical friendship, but is enduring and intimate to a degree usually present in relationships with certain kin.[22]

It is very likely that the fuzziness of kinship designations in the United States, and the flexibility with which kin ties are interpreted by specific people, are related to the great emphasis that is placed on personal achievement rather than on ascription. This emphasis is related both to the restricted terminological system referred to above and to the great variability in the actual relations between people holding the same structural positions within the kinship system, such as mother-son, or uncle-niece. This variability is made clearer by examining the three meanings of "distance" in kinship, especially as these pertain to U.S. kin relations.

Kin "Distance"

Distance, says David Schneider, means three things in American kinship.[23] First, it signifies *genealogical* distance, so that we may speak of a second cousin as being a more distant kinsman than an uncle. Some have tried to delineate the various circles of relatives in American society according to genealogical distance. Thus, the inner circle of relatives includes only those from Ego's family of orientation, i.e., his parents and children, brothers and sisters. The outer circle of relatives includes those from Ego's parents' family of orientation, including aunts, uncles, and grandparents. Finally, outside this outer circle are cousins, great aunts, and so on.[24] The position of affinal relatives, such as one's in-laws or aunts and uncles by marriage, has not been fixed in analyses of this kind, except Goodenough's.

The terms "closeness" and "distance" immediately elicit a second interpretation that Schneider calls *socioemotional* distance. Feelings toward kin may or may not be governed by genealogical distance. Thus, Robins and Tomanec report the following findings regarding affective closeness or distance: "Grandparents were closer to Ego than aunts and uncles, who were in turn closer than cousins. . . . Within kinship roles, maternal relatives were found to be closer than paternal relatives, female relatives closer than male relatives. . . ."[25] This type of distance or closeness is governed as much by the interactions and experiences shared or not shared with certain relatives as it is by the simple fact of genealogical distance.

This "sharing or not sharing" leads to the third type of distance that pertains to kinship: *physical* or residential distance. Intense interaction clearly requires proximity, and proximity in U.S. society is broadly related to genealogical closeness. However, the association between the three types of closeness or distance is far from perfect. Elizabeth Bott, for example, points out that proximity is a quasi-necessary, but not sufficient condition for intimacy or socioemotional closeness. Parents, on the one hand, are considered intimate relatives even when not physically accessible.[26] Aunts, uncles, and cousins, on the other hand, may be quite proximate and still not be objects of either great affection or frequent interaction. Schneider puts the same point thus: "A person who is genealogically close may be physically distant and neutral on the socioemotional dimension. Or a person may be close socioemotionally and physically but distant genealogically."[27] The same functional character of American kinship which gives rise to a system of terminology stressing the nuclear family and which allows for fuzzy boundaries and idiosyncratic personal relationships within the kin network also makes for a relatively low correlation between the three types of closeness or distance in U.S. kinship. But what, precisely, is the "functional" character of American kinship? Although this subject was roughly summarized in Section One, let us return to this important question.

Unimportance, Isolation, and Consistency

A generation ago, Talcott Parsons wrote an article on kinship in the United States in which he made three major points. First, compared to many other societies, kinship in the U.S. is relatively unimportant to the ongoing of the society. With the parcelling out of institutional functions to other settings—institutional differentiation—the kinship network has little role to play in societal maintenance, particularly compared to the role it played in the past (one that it still plays in other cultures). Second, the nuclear, conjugal family is the normal household unit, living "in a home segregated from those of both pairs of parents (if living) and . . . economically independent of both. In a very large proportion of cases the geographical separation is considerable."[28] Third, this isolated, open, bilateral kinship system with nuclear household units is most functional, or best suited, for the U.S. occupational system and urban living. It makes residential mobility in pursuit of occupational opportunities much easier than if one's corporate kin group had to be carried along on each move.

From this article, which echoes the sentiments of Louis Wirth and others regarding contemporary urban life,[29] could thus be drawn three conclusions: (1) Compared to other times and places, U.S. kinship is functionally unimportant. (2) The nuclear family is generally isolated from kin, economically and otherwise. (3) This system fits well with the other characteristics of the society. However, this article and the conclusions drawn therein have been a favorite target of kinship researchers since the 1950's. Among other things, these researchers have discovered that adult offspring are more likely to live close to their parents and other kin than "considerably separated" from them. Noting that Parsons was writing about the middle classes, specifically excluding farmers, matrifocal lower-class families, and the upper classes, Marvin Sussman and Paul Reiss find that even among middle-class families the separation from kin is not likely to be great.[30]

Even more important, the researchers have noted that the kin network does "function" in several ways; providing affectional ties, help when needed, and even supports for or deterrents to residential mobility.[31] The functionality of the kin network, demonstrated in study after study, leads Marvin Sussman to conclude that "the evidence on the viability of an existing kinship structure carrying on extensive activities among kin is so convincing that we find it unnecessary to continue further descriptive work in order to establish the existence of the kin network in modern urban society."[32]

Therefore, although Parsons claimed that kinship is relatively unimportant in U.S. society, and that this is consistent with the economic-industrial structure of this society, his critics have rightly responded: "Yes, but nuclear families are not isolated, kin networks do function, and many of their functions are perfectly consistent with the economic structure of the society."[33] Parsons himself has sought more recently to reemphasize his comparative perspective, while at the same time acknowledging the findings of his critics. The view of the "isolated nuclear family" and that of its critics, Parsons claims,

> are not contradictory but complementary. The concept of isolation applies in the first instance to kinship structure as seen in the perspective of anthropological studies in that field. In this context our system represents an extreme type, which is well described by that term. It does not, however, follow that all relations to kin outside the nuclear family are broken. Indeed, the very psychological importance for the individual of the nuclear family in which he was born and brought up would make any such conception impossible.[34]

Thus, it may be concluded that neither institutions nor personnel are as embedded in the kin networks of the United States as they have been in many other societies. This is not to say, however, that kinship performs no functions in the U.S. Nor is it to say that its performance of certain functions is inconsistent with the achievement-based institutions of that society. Nor, finally, is it to say that the absence of personnel embeddedness in a residential and solidarity sense means that kin are isolated from each other, either interactionally or emotionally. It does mean that the volitional element, the flexibility and variety that comes with choice, is heightened in American kinship. It also means that generalizations about kin are risky, and when they are based simply upon "the kin network" they are clearly overgeneralizations. One must, instead, speak of the relations between specific categories of kin—parents and offspring, siblings, in-laws, and so on—as we shall do in Section Three.

SECTION THREE

CATEGORIES OF U.S. KIN AND THEIR CHARACTERISTICS

Kin might be subdivided into large numbers of categories, including cousins, grandparents and grandchildren, mothers-in-law, and many others. Yet for the purposes of the present summary, four divisions seem sufficient. These include: parents and their adult offspring, siblings, secondary kin (which is all blood kin and their affines outside the nuclear family of orientation), and in-laws.

Parents and Adult Offspring

The relationships between parents and their adult offspring can be characterized by the phrase *positive concern*. This positive, or active, concern is manifested in several ways. First, there is extremely frequent contact between these intergenerational kin. When they live close to each other, weekly or more frequent interaction is the rule. But even when the parents and their offspring are separated by a substantial geographic distance, contact by mail or telephone tends to be monthly or more. A second characteristic of positive concern is a great amount of mutual aid. Immediately after the marriage of the young adult, the aid tends to flow primarily from the parents—taking the form of loans or cash, large gifts for the new household, and, if the parents are proximate, babysitting and other services when children are born. Later, as the parents age and become infirm, the direction of aid begins to reverse, so that the middle-aged adult cares for his own offspring and helps his aging parents as long as they live.[35]

A third characteristic of the positive concern between adult offspring and their parents is a social psychological bond that includes a strong affectional tie and a secondary obligatory element

—with the latter subsuming both the general duty to keep in frequent touch and the specific obligation to help out in time of need. The obligatory element, which is quite evident in parent-offspring relations, does not seem to stand in the way of affectional closeness, or to be dysfunctional, except when it becomes the primary factor in continued contact. An example of this is the young adult male who has few interests in common with his widowed mother, but who feels the need to help her tangibly or in other ways.[36] Yet, for the most part, frequent contact, mutual aid, affectional closeness and a feeling of obligation result in a close adult relationship between these kin from the same nuclear family. Nor do parents and their offspring, even in the middle class, fit the residential pattern of "considerable separation," which Parsons claimed was true of kin in general.

Of the four possible parent-offspring relationships: mother-daughter, mother-son, father-daughter, and father-son, the closest, both affectionally and interactionally, tends to be that between mother and daughter. This is true regardless of the socioeconomic, or social class, positions of the two individuals. A partial explanation for this closeness is the female role convergence of which Willmott and Young speak.[37] If we can assume that the major life role of the majority of women is wife-mother, while men's is occupational, then we can say that more mothers and daughters play the same major roles in adulthood than fathers and sons, mothers and sons, or fathers and daughters. In this author's Greensboro study, many young females explained their current positive feelings toward their mothers with some version of the following: "Now I know what my parents went through in raising me." The words "realize," "know," "appreciate," and "understand" appear over and over in the female responses. Thus, when role convergence is coupled with the generally greater social-emotional involvement of females with all sorts of kin, you have the basis for an extremely close relationship between adult daughters and their mothers. Yet, all four parent-offspring relationships tend to be closer than relations between any other two relatives in U.S. kin networks. Most of the exceptions to this are found among sibling relations, to which we now turn.

Adult Sibling Relations

The terms that seem to summarize best the relations between adult siblings are *interest* and *comparison/identification*. Interest simply means a general feeling that one should keep up with his sibling, keep posted on his activities, without the necessity of as frequent contact as that with parents or of as much mutual aid except in extreme circumstances. In fact, apart from the exchange of babysitting between proximate sisters, the sharing of financial or other forms of aid between siblings is likely to become a bone of contention or even a basis for alienation between them. Interest, then, is just that: the individual is "interested" in how his brother or sister is getting along.

The notion of sibling rivalry has been a topic of discussion for some time in the socialization literature. It must now be added that such rivalry does not end, but is transformed, when brothers and sisters leave home. In a success- and achievement-oriented society, with substantial emphasis on individualism within the family, brothers and sisters are the comparative reference group *par excellence*. That is, the question: "How am I doing?" can well be answered by noting how one's achievements compare with those of his siblings. Siblings, unlike friends, are "givens" in the individual's social network. He cannot (as he can with friends) drop them if he becomes dissatisfied with them. And when the kin of orientation (adult offspring and their parents) get together, conversation is likely to turn—sometimes subtly, sometimes openly—to how well George is doing in his business, or to what a good marriage Susan made. Therefore, there may be a considerable emotional alienation between brothers whose occupations diverge greatly in prestige. In the case of the other sibling combinations, a prestige divergence generally results in a one-way, or unreciprocated, identification. That is, the lower-status sibling expresses affection for and wants to be like the higher-status sibling, but these feelings are not mutual. This is, then, one point at which the economic success values of the society impinge upon and help to determine the social psychology of kin involvement. It is noteworthy, however, that these variations in feeling are not very evident in the area of interaction. Females especially seem to have little control over frequency of contact with siblings, and are thus unable—due to obligation—to bring contact frequency into line with their feelings. This is, of course, another indication of the greater obligatory burden that females bear in kinship relations.[38]

A few pairs of brothers or sisters evolve over the years the type of activity pattern that results in their being extremely close friends in adulthood. "Best friend" status for a sibling is, however, the exception rather than the rule. Yet, activity-based relationships are even less prevalent between secondary kin, such as cousins.

Secondary Kinship

Secondary kin are all those relatives who were not at some time in the past a part of Ego's family of orientation: aunts, uncles, cousins, grandparents, and so on. Contacts occur between many such kin in U.S. society, but the best terms to use in describing them are *circumstantial* or *incidental*. That is, such relations seldom involve frequent contact, common interests, mutual aid, or strong affectional and obligatory concern. Yearly contact—the Christmas card, for example, or perhaps a kin reunion at holidays or during a vacation—frequently suffice. The incidental nature of such kin relations may be seen in those instances in which, while one is visiting his parents, his aunt and uncle drop in. Or he goes home for the purpose of visiting his parents and siblings, but, while there, goes to see a cousin. The circumstantial side of secondary kin contact is well depicted in the "wakes and weddings" relatives of whom Schneider speaks. These are kin brought together by circumstances such as the marriage or death of a mutual kinsman.[39]

The notion of incidental or circumstantial contact is opposed to intentional or volitional, and fits quite well the character of most secondary kin in the U.S. In the Greensboro study (see note 38), a few respondents were troubled by the weakness of secondary kin ties. The wife of a clerk explained: "It is distressing that distance is pulling families apart so. Seeing relatives was very important when I was young and I miss it now. It bothers me that my children don't know their cousins and play with them like I did." However, a much greater proportion of respondents made comments such as: "My parents and sister mean a lot to me, but I simply don't have time to spend keeping up with a lot of kinsfolk that don't mean anything to me anyway." Or even more pointedly: "I have an aunt and one cousin besides my mother and brothers that mean a lot to me; as for the others—phooey!"

It should be noted that there are two prime exceptions to circumstantiality. One is the young adult whose grandparents are still alive. It is, in fact, those aging grandparents who, along with the females, form the hub of kin activity and involvement. However, by the time the young person reaches adulthood and marries, his own grandparents are often no longer alive. The second exception to circumstantiality is the activity and mutual concern of the secondary kin of many ethnic groups in the United States. Their activities—originally means for ensuring mutual survival—are now more likely to be means for achieving individual success. Leichter and Mitchell, for example, report a phenomenon that is somewhat prevalent among the Jewish families they studied in New York City:

> Family circles and cousin clubs may also support occupational achievement by giving instrumental help as an organization: the group's loan fund may help to support children's education, or special collections may be taken up when there is particular need on the part of one member.[40]

Such examples of secondary kin support have not necessarily or automatically disappeared as the various ethnic groups have been incorporated into the dominant structures of U.S. society. Yet these exceptions do not alter the overriding generalization to the effect that, even in the lower and working classes, secondary kin ordinarily play a relatively minor role in the individual's social network.[41]

In-law Relations

"If I had it to do over again," remarks the weary American husband, "I'd marry a Japanese girl. They're pretty, graceful, obedient—and your mother-in-law's in Yokohama." So goes one of the many inlaw jokes with its typical focus on mother-in-law troubles. As is often the case, the jokes have in them an element of truth, but the picture they present is incomplete and exaggerated as well. We shall, therefore, summarize what is known about in-law relationships in the United States, and in so doing perhaps clarify some popular impressions.

The discussion of in-laws, or those relatives one gains by marriage, requires that several distinctions be made. First, it is not always made clear by writers whether they are referring to the individual's relationship with his or her in-laws, or whether they are concerned with the influence of the in-laws upon relations between the spouses. We shall attempt to deal with both. Second, investigations of in-law relationships often distinguish between specific in-laws, such as the husband's mother and the wife's mother, sisters-in-law, and so on. Such specification is as necessary as it is in the discussion of blood kin. Third, while the majority of in-law studies have focussed on trouble or conflict, a few have noted the conditions that make for satisfactory relationships; we shall do the same.

In her classic article on sex roles, Mirra Komarovsky hypothesized that the female's closer ties to her parents would result in in-law troubles more often involving the husband and the wife's parents than the wife and the husband's parents.[42] Later studies of working-class families by Komarovsky and by Young and Willmott have in fact discovered a substantial amount of conflict between the husband and the wife's parents. According to Young and Willmott, this relationship is *ordinarily* one of conflict; Komarovsky, in *Blue-Collar Marriage*, adds: "It now seems likely that when the mode of life forces husbands to associate closely with their in-laws regardless of personal congeniality, the chances of strain can be as great as for their wives."[43] Yet, despite these studies indicating a considerable amount of husband–in-law trouble, the majority of studies since Komarovsky's hypothesis was formulated have concluded that in-law troubles are generally more frequent between the wife and the husband's mother than *vice versa*.[44] This is in spite of the tendency of married couples to interact somewhat more often with the wife's parents than with the husband's.[45]

The specification of factors that give rise to in-law conflict or peace is not complete, but several factors have been tentatively isolated. Duvall finds that older women have less in-law trouble than *younger* ones. Blood and Wolfe phrase it thus: "As young adult men and women transfer their loyalties from their parents to each other, some stress is inevitable and it shows in the concentration of in-law problems at the beginning of youthful marriages." Stryker adds that the presence of offspring in the home is likely to improve relations, particularly between the two mothers.[46] Thus, the fact that younger marrieds appear to have more in-law troubles than older marrieds can be explained partially by the independence struggle that is completed during the early years of marriage and partially by the strengthening of bonds resulting from the presence of grandchildren.

A second apparently necessary, but not sufficient, condition for in-law trouble is *proximity*. Young and Willmott report that, among working-class Londoners, there is likely to be trouble between the young husband and his mother-in-law unless one of three conditions is met—one of which is for the young couple to move away. Americans, Duvall claims, "really believe that the way to get along with our in-laws is to keep as far away as possible."[47]

While this is an overstatement, it does point up the fact that few married couples have trouble with in-laws who are *in absentia*.

Dependence upon parents is a third factor which, though not entirely separate from either age or proximity, seems to account for a portion of in-law conflict. While young adult females are more likely to manifest an emotional dependence upon their parents than males are upon theirs, a certain amount of female dependence seems to be acceptable in U.S. society. Thus, though female dependence is more prevalent, male dependence is more sure to cause trouble between the wife and his parents when it does occur.[48] The very involvement of females in kin relations means that the wife and the husband's mother may very easily come into conflict over the young husband's time and interest. Another reason why wife–mother-in-law conflict is more prevalent is that the husband is very often incorporated into the wife's family as a virtual offspring. Komarovsky, for example, points out the positive value of the "ability of some in-laws to play the role of parent-substitutes to a man who has been deprived of parental affection."[49] In many families, says Wallin, the husband is more attached to his wife's parents than she is.[50]

Treating a daughter- or especially a son-in-law as one's own offspring is not the only mechanism for avoiding in-law conflict, particularly that with the mother-in-law. Irwin Deutscher points out that today the myth of the meddlesome, troublesome mother-in-law causes many mothers-in-law to resolve *not* to be that way, but rather to do everything they can to stay out of the way.[51] Alice Rossi, furthermore, feels that adult-to-adult relationships with parents may "be difficult to achieve even after marriage, while parents-in-law are met as adults, so that relations with them may take on some of the quality of relations with a friendly peer." Thus, the increased equalitarianism of the family may have improved in-law relations and weakened parent–grown-child relations.[52] Treatment as a blood offspring, efforts to disprove the mother-in-law myth, and equalitarianism may all have gone to improve in-law relations in recent years.

Age, proximity, and dependence, which were all discussed in relation to in-law troubles, are also related to husband-wife conflict about kin.[53] And, of course, conflict *with* and conflict *about* kin are both related to marital adjustment, according to the Landises. In a sample of 544 couples in the early years of marriage, they find that 67 per cent of those who reported excellent adjustment to in-laws also reported very happy marriages, while only 18 per cent of those who had fair or poor adjustments to their in-laws indicated that their marriages were very happy.[54] As we have noted so often in this volume, however, a simple relationship may be causatively interpreted only with great caution. Although it is easy to jump to the conclusion that in-law trouble causes marital difficulties, an equally plausible interpretation would be that when couples are having marital difficulties it disrupts their relations with other members of their social network—including in-laws—as well. Yet, however, one explains the relationship between in-law trouble and marital conflict causally, it is to be expected that there will be a relation between them.

The least disrupted marriages, in terms of kin relationships, are those in which there are children and in which the couple lives some distance from the two kin networks and manifests little emotional dependence upon kin, so that attention is focussed upon their own family of procreation rather than upon their kin of orientation or other relatives. Yet, such a conclusion assumes that a great amount of value is placed upon simply avoiding conflict, with the positive functions of kinship involvement considered insignificant. The literature on kinship in the United States seems to show that most people disagree with Barrington Moore's assertion that kinship is nothing more than a barbaric "obligation to give affection as a duty to a particular set of persons on account of the accident of birth."[55] Despite the emphasis society places on individualism and independence—which make the relations of couples with their parents, in-laws, and other kin tenuous at times—most people seem to prefer the emotional support, visiting, and emergency help that genealogically close kin provide, rather than the total independence and isolation that might be achieved if the couple truly desired it.

Compared to other societies, cross-culturally and historically, kinship ties in the U.S. appear insignificant and weak. There is almost no institutional embeddedness in the kin network, and personnel embeddedness in terms of solidarity exists only with the kin of orientation in most middle-class and some working- and lower-class families. But U.S. kin ties do have their own form of viability that is positively valued by most people. Whether kin ties *should* "wither away" for the sake of other, more individualistic values, as Moore believes they should, is a question the reader may decide for himself.

NOTES

[1] David M. Schneider, *American Kinship: A Cultural Account* (Englewood Cliffs, N.J.: Prentice-Hall, 1968), p. v.
[2] Bert N. Adams, "Kinship Systems and Adaptation to Modernization," *Studies in Comparative International Development*, Vol. IV (1968–1969), 55.
[3] A. R. Radcliffe-Brown, *The Andaman Islanders* (Cambridge: Cambridge University Press, 1922); on this, see Meyer F. Nimkoff and Russell Middleton, "Types of Family and Types of Economy," *American Journal of Sociology*, 66 (1960), 215–25.
[4] An interesting discussion of the "branch family" is found in James S. Brown, Harry K. Schwarzweller, and Joseph J. Mangalam, "Kentucky Mountain Migration and the Stem-Family: An American Variation on a Theme by Le Play," *Rural Sociology*, 28 (1963), 48–69.
[5] Even this has been questioned in A. O. Haller, "The Urban Family," *American Journal of Sociology*, 66 (1961), 621–22.
[6] Examples of close affectional ties to non-corporate kin are found in William J. Goode, *World Revolution and Family Patterns* (New York: Free Press, 1963).
[7] Bert N. Adams, *Kinship in an Urban Setting* (Chicago: Markham, 1968), p. 132.
[8] Robin Fox, *Kinship and Marriage* (Baltimore: Penguin Books, 1967), p. 240; Fred Eggan, *Social Organization of the Western Pueblos* (Chicago: University of Chicago Press, 1950), p. 295; Radcliffe-Brown, "The Study of Kinship Systems," *Journal of the Royal Anthropological Institute*, 71 (1941), 3f; and Rodger P. Davies, "Syrian Arabic Kinship Terms," *Southwestern Journal of Anthropology*, 5 (1949), 249.
[9] George P. Murdock, *Social Structure* (New York: Macmillan, 1949).
[10] Alfred L. Kroeber, *The Nature of Culture* (Chicago: University of Chicago Press, 1952), pp. 172, 181.
[11] See Fox, *Kinship and Marriage*, p. 240, on this.
[12] *Ibid.*, p. 243.
[13] *Ibid.*, p. 258.
[14] Ruth M. Underhill, "The Papago Family," in Meyer F. Nimkoff, ed., *Comparative Family Systems* (Boston: Houghton Mifflin, 1965), p. 150.
[15] David M. Schneider and George C. Homans, "Kinship Terminology and the American Kinship System," *American Anthropologist*, 57 (1955), 1195.
[16] *Ibid.*
[17] Lionel S. Lewis, "Kinship Terminology for the American Parent," *American Anthropologist*, 65 (1963), 649–52, and Warren O. Hagstrom and Jeffrey K. Hadden, "Sentiment and Kinship Terminology in American Society," *Journal of Marriage and the Family*, 27 (1965), 324–32.
[18] Hagstrom and Hadden, "Sentiment and Kinship Terminology."
[19] Alice S. Rossi, "Naming Children in Middle Class Families," *American Sociological Review*, 30 (1965), 512.
[20] Hagstrom and Hadden, "Sentiment and Kinship Terminology," p. 332.
[21] Schneider, *American Kinship*, p. 67.
[22] Bert N. Adams, "Interaction Theory and the Social Network," *Sociometry*, 30 (1967), 75–76.
[23] Schneider, *American Kinship*, p. 73.
[24] Lee N. Robins and Miroda Tomanec, "Closeness to Blood Relatives Outside the Immediate Family," *Marriage and Family Living*, 24 (1962), 340–46; Talcott Parsons, "The Kinship System of the Contemporary United States," *American Anthropologist*, 45 (1943), 22–38; Ward H. Goodenough,

"Yankee Kinship Terminology: A Problem in Componential Analysis," *American Anthropologist,* 67 (1965), 259–87.
[25] Robins and Tomanec, "Closeness to Blood Relatives," pp. 342–43.
[26] Elizabeth Bott, *Family and Social Network* (London: Tavistock, 1957), p. 129.
[27] Schneider, *American Kinship,* p. 73.
[28] Parsons, "The Kinship System," p. 27.
[29] See especially Louis Wirth, "Urbanism as a Way of Life," *American Journal of Sociology,* 44 (1938), 1–24.
[30] Marvin Sussman, "The Isolated Nuclear Family: Fact or Fiction?" *Social Problems,* 6 (1959), 333–40, and Paul J. Reiss, "The Extended Kinship System: Correlates of and Attitudes on Frequency of Interaction," *Marriage and Family Living,* 24 (1962), 333–39.
[31] Eugene Litwak, "The Use of Extended Family Groups in the Achievement of Social Goals," *Social Problems,* 7 (1959–1960), 177–87; Marvin B. Sussman and Lee Burchinal, "Kin Family Network: Unheralded Structure in Current Conceptualizations of Family Functioning," *Marriage and Family Living,* 24 (1962), 231–40; Hope Jensen Leichter and William E. Mitchell, *Kinship and Casework* (New York: Russell Sage Foundation, 1967); Robert F. Winch, Scott Greer, and Rae Lesser Blumberg, "Ethnicity and Extended Familism in an Upper-Middle-Class Suburb," *American Sociological Review,* 32 (1967), 272; and Marvin B. Sussman, "Relationships of Adult Children with Their Parents in the United States," in Ethel Shanas and Gordon F. Streib, eds., *Social Structure and the Family: Generational Relations* (Englewood Cliffs, N.J.: Prentice-Hall, 1965), p. 73.
[32] Sussman, "Relationships of Adult Children," p. 63.
[33] Where kinship and economics are in conflict is ordinarily where kinship and the economic productive function are linked directly. Yet even this does not automatically cause trouble. See Leichter and Mitchell, *Kinship and Casework,* pp. 138, 145, and Adams, *Kinship in an Urban Setting,* p. 132.
[34] Talcott Parsons, "The Normal American Family," in Seymour M. Farber, Piero Mustacchi, and Roger H. L. Wilson, eds., *Man and Civilization: The Family's Search for Survival* (New York: McGraw-Hill, 1965), p. 35.
[35] Reuben Hill, "Decision Making and the Family Life Cycle," in Ethel Shanas and Gordon F. Streib, eds., *Social Structure and the Family: Generational Relations* (Englewood Cliffs, N.J.: Prentice Hall, 1965), p. 125.
[36] Bert N. Adams, "The Middle-Class Adult and His Widowed or Still-Married Mother," *Social Problems,* 16 (1968), 50–59.
[37] Peter Willmott and Michael Young, *Family and Class in a London Suburb* (London: Routledge and Kegan Paul, 1960), p. 84.
[38] See Adams, *Kinship in an Urban Setting,* pp. 93–132, for more on adult sibling relations.
[39] Schneider, *American Kinship,* p. 70.
[40] Leichter and Mitchell, *Kinship and Casework,* p. 156.
[41] Jacquelyne Jackson, at Duke Medical School, is currently studying the kin involvements of blacks in Durham, North Carolina. This research should shed some light on another too-little-studied aspect of family relations in the contemporary United States.
[42] Mirra Komarovsky, "Functional Analysis of Sex Roles," *American Sociological Review,* 15 (1950), 508–16.
[43] Michael Young and Peter Willmott, *Family and Kinship in East London* (Baltimore: Penguin Books, 1964), p. 62, and Mirra Komarovsky, *Blue-Collar Marriage* (New York: Random House, 1962), p. 279.
[44] Mirra Komarovsky, "Continuities in Family Research: A Case Study," *American Journal of Sociology,* 62 (1956), 46; Paul Wallin, "Sex Differences in Attitudes to 'In-Laws': a Test of a Theory," *American Journal of Sociology,*

59 (1954), 466–69; Evelyn Millis Duvall, *In-Laws Pro and Con* (New York: Association, 1954), p. 187; Peggy S. Marcus, "A Study of In-Law Relationships of 79 Couples Who Have Been Married Between 2 and 11 Years" (Master's thesis, Cornell University, 1950); and Leichter and Mitchell, *Kinship and Casework*, p. 174.

[45] Reiss, "The Extended Kinship System," p. 334; Leichter and Mitchell, *Kinship and Casework*, p. 174.

[46] Duvall, *In-Laws Pro and Con*, p. 219; Robert O. Blood, Jr., and Donald M. Wolfe, *Husbands and Wives* (New York: Free Press, 1960), p. 248; and Sheldon Stryker, "The Adjustment of Married Offspring to Their Parents," *American Sociological Review*, 20 (1955), 153.

[47] Young and Willmott, *Family and Kinship in East London*, pp. 62f; Duvall, *In-Laws Pro and Con*, p. 291.

[48] Komarovsky, *Blue-Collar Marriage*, p. 258; Komarovsky, "Continuities in Family Research," p. 46.

[49] Komarovsky, *Blue-Collar Marriage*, p. 278.

[50] Wallin, "Sex Differences in Attitudes to 'In-Laws.'"

[51] Irwin Deutscher, "Socialization for Postparental Life," in Arnold Rose, ed., *Human Behavior and Social Processes* (Boston: Houghton Mifflin, 1962), p. 520.

[52] Rossi, "Naming Children in Middle Class Families," p. 512.

[53] Blood and Wolfe, *Husbands and Wives*, p. 248, indicate that "In-laws are an issue when the partners are young—indeed the younger the wife, the more often conflicts over relatives are mentioned." Adams' Greensboro study found that both proximity and dependence are quasi-necessary, but not sufficient, conditions for conflict between husbands and wives about their kin.

[54] Judson T. and Mary G. Landis, *Building a Successful Marriage* (Englewood Cliffs, N.J.: Prentice-Hall, 1963), pp. 331–35.

[55] Barrington Moore, *Political Power and Social Theory* (Cambridge, Mass.: Harvard University Press, 1958), p. 163.

XIV

Aging and the Family in the United States

AGING IN THE UNITED STATES USUALLY INVOLVES THE RELINQUISHING OF TWO KEY ROLES IN THE LIVES OF MARRIED COUPLES: PARENTAL AND OCCUPATIONAL. IT REQUIRES THAT NUMEROUS DECISIONS BE MADE AND THAT A SUBSTANTIAL REORIENTATION OF ACTIVITY PATTERNS TAKE PLACE. THE DISCUSSION OF AGING IN THIS CHAPTER HAS FOUR MAJOR FOCI. THESE ARE: THE THEORY OF DISENGAGEMENT, SOCIALIZATION INTO OLD AGE, THE ISSUE OF AGE GRADING AND THE SOCIAL NETWORK, AND DISENCHANTMENT WITHIN THE MARRIAGE ITSELF. IN THE CONCLUDING SECTION, FOUR ACTIVITY PATTERNS IN OLD AGE ARE SUMMARIZED, AND A BRIEF COMPARISON IS DRAWN BETWEEN OLD AGE AND ADOLESCENCE.

The typical couple of two generations ago had a life expectancy which enabled them to survive together for 31 years after marriage, two years short of the time when their *fifth* child was expected to marry. But, "the decline in size of family and the improved survival prospects of the population since 1890 not only have assured the average parents of our day that they will live to see their children married but also have made it probable that they will have one-fourth of their married life still to come when their last child leaves the parental home."[1]

Throughout the history of mankind, aging has always meant losing hair, friends, illusions, and strength; and dealing with senescent or senile fellows has always been a problem for families and communities. However, in most known cultures, some sort of compensation to their inevitable losses and decrements had been devised and were available to the aging individuals. The aged have indeed very often been considered the more wise, influential, and honored people. We have within a few decades almost ruined such a conception of life. In the same time we have made old age a common and lengthier experience, and made it a period of isolation, anguish, boredom, and uselessness.[2]

These two statements, the first by Irwin Deutscher quoting Paul Glick, and the second by Michel Philbert, introduce us to the dilemmas of a period that has decreased in honor as it has increased in prevalence in U.S. society: old age. Longevity is currently approaching 70 for men and 75 years of age for women in a society that emphasizes the achievements of those in the young adult years and glorifies the period of youth. What is happening to these ever-increasing numbers of aged? Are they adjusting easily or with difficulty to this stage of the life cycle; and what does that adjustment require? According to one recent theory, the adjustment is effected by the process of *disengagement*.

SECTION ONE

DISENGAGEMENT THEORY AND ITS CRITICS

Disengagement theory was first set forth by Elaine Cumming and her coworkers in a 1960 *Sociometry* article, and was developed further in a book published the next year entitled *Growing Old: The Process of Disengagement*. The study upon which the theory is based involved 279 old people in the Kansas City area, ranging from working-class to upper-middle, and is the same sample that forms the basis for Bernice Neugarten's studies described in Chapter XI.[3] Very simply, disengagement is a universal theory of the reduction of one's life space and orientation toward death in old age. But let us delineate further the various aspects of the process.

At the heart of disengagement is the forfeiting of the individual's major life role: for the female this ordinarily means the parental role, and for the male, the occupational role. "On the whole, men make an abrupt transition from the engaged to the disengaged state, but it is soon resolved; women have a smoother passage, which lasts longer."[4] A concomitant of the role loss at the launching of offspring and at retirement is the "decreased interaction between the aging person and others in the social systems he belongs to. . . . His withdrawal may be accompanied from the outset by an increased preoccupation with himself."[5] There are changes, say the authors, in the number of people with whom there is interaction and in the amount of interaction. There are qualitative changes in interaction commensurate with decreased involvement. And there are changes in personality that cause decreased interpersonal involvement and result in increased preoccupation with self.[6] Preoccupation with self includes facing the inevitability of death. Any demoralization that results from the combination of role loss, withdrawal, and facing death, the authors feel, is only temporary. Older people eventually begin to appreciate the disengaged state, and to orient positively to it.[7] One reason for this positive orientation, pointed out by Deutscher in his discussion of the postparental period, is that it is "a time of new freedoms: freedom from the economic responsibilities of children; freedom to be mobile (geographically); freedom from housework and other chores. And, finally, freedom to be one's self for the first time since the children came along."[8] Thus, disengagement theory is, according to its proponents, a cross-culturally applicable theory that includes a generally positive orientation on the part of the aged to the loss of their major roles, to their withdrawal from the social world, and to their increasing preoccupation with self and death.

Criticism of disengagement theory has been both direct and indirect. The best single example of direct criticism is a volume edited by Arnold Rose and Warren Peterson, *Older People and Their Social World*. Using the concept of "aging group consciousness," the authors assert that "aging group conscious persons have not become disengaged from social roles as a result of aging or retirement. Rather, for most of them, aging and retirement have opened up new roles, because of the increase of leisure time *and* because of their aging group consciousness."[9] In order to criticize it, Rose and Peterson first describe disengagement theory as follows:

> The Cumming and Henry theory of disengagement is that the society and the individual prepare *in advance* for the ultimate "disengagement" of incurable, incapacitating disease and death by an *inevitable, gradual, and mutually satisfying process of* disengagement. . . . Cumming and Henry say that the values in American culture of competitive achievement and of future orientation make this society especially negative toward aging and hence encourage disengagement. But the process itself must be understood to be inevitable and universal, according to the theory, and not limited to any one group in a society or any one society.[10]

The three most direct criticisms made by the authors are that disengagement is not cross-culturally applicable as a theory of aging, nor is it universally applicable even in the United States, nor is it necessarily of positive value when it does occur.[11] The U.S.

culture and economic structure have created the conditions that lead to the disengagement of large numbers of aged. Although disengagement may make for a sense of freedom (as Deutscher claims), Rose and Peterson cite the evidence provided by Robert Havighurst and his associates "that the engaged elderly, rather than the disengaged, are the ones who generally, although not always, are happiest and have the greatest expressed life satisfaction."[12] Retreat, disintegration, devastation, threat, desolation: these are some of the terms used by various authors to describe the transition into old age. Disengagement, according to Ethel Shanas, is based upon bereavement. "The kind of theory we need is one that suggests not the image of erosion but, rather, that of sudden, if partial, disintegration and patched-up reconstruction."[13]

How, then, did Cumming and her associates arrive at the conclusion that aging and disengagement were actually considered of positive value? It is partially a result of the fact that they sampled primarily healthy people. Once the old person finds himself staying well and outliving his peers, his satisfaction increases as he compares himself with others. He is grateful to be alive and well, disengaged or not. A more subtle reason, Rose and Peterson feel, is that this theory draws the functionalist conclusion that "what is, must be," or, to change it slightly, "what is, is good."[14]

If this theory is not only *not* cross-culturally valid, but unable even to account for old age in U.S. society, how might it be corrected or expanded? For one thing, disengagement is psychologically continuous and gradual; early social attitudes are manifested behaviorally in the way one accepts children leaving and retirement.[15] Thus, the woman who is socially active, but who wishes she could escape the entertaining and other responsibilities which are demanded by her husband's occupation, may be positively oriented toward disengagement for many years before she can manifest this attitude in her behavior. Or the man who finds no inherent meaning in his occupation may be oriented positively toward disengagement virtually throughout his work career. "In the working class," Rosow finds, "there is initially more acceptance of aging."[16] While this acceptance may be partially explained by the greater residential density of aged working-class persons, it may also be a result of the more negative attitudes that working-class persons hold throughout their lives toward their dominant life roles. Thus, in terms of roles, there may actually be three categories of persons in U.S. society: (1) the positively oriented disengaged, who are more frequently working-class and who may have experienced "anticipatory disengagement" for many years prior to old age. (2) There are the negatively oriented disengaged, who, in relinquishing their dominant life roles, have given up a highly valued part of their lives, or who may have found old age to be a period of sickness, bereavement, and loneliness, rather than one of freedom. (3) There are those aged who have not become disengaged at all. The self-employed male who never retires exemplifies the still-engaged aged. Nevertheless, the numbers of still-engaged aged in the U.S. are small compared to the numbers of positively and negatively oriented disengaged.

Thus far, we have referred to the critics who have questioned the cross-cultural applicability of disengagement theory, and who, while admitting that most U.S. aged become disengaged from their major life roles, have noted that some react positively and some negatively to this. A further criticism of the theory concerns the issue of withdrawal from the social network. While many do become cut off from other people and preoccupied with themselves, two other patterns also recur. Shanas *et al.* report that the aged tend to find themselves "nearer one of two extremes—experiencing the seclusion of the spinster or widow without children and surviving brothers and sisters, or pushed towards the pinnacle of a pyramidal family structure of four generations."[17] The pyramidal kinship structure, characterized by substantial contact with children and grandchildren, nephews and nieces, and other kin, is more prevalent among working-class aged.[18] A third category of aged, described by Rose and Peterson, Rosow, and Mark Messer, are the aging group-conscious, who are neither isolated and withdrawn nor highly involved with kin or other members of the descending generation, but are age-segregated and in frequent contact with other aged.[19] Both Rosow's study in Cleveland and Messer's in Chicago indicate that age-segregation is not necessarily negative in its effect on the individual's sense of social integration. Messer, for example, finds that:

> (1) age grouping is associated with less dependence on the family as a source of morale, (2) this is not accompanied by a feeling of familial neglect, and (3) age grouping serves as a mediator between the older individual and the overall society, providing a greater sense of social integration.[20]

Rosow, agreeing that residential concentration of older people appears to be functional for their integration and support, admits that "some gerontologists strenuously object to such concentration as segregation which is implicitly invidious and anti-democratic."[21] Yet the main point at this juncture is that many elderly people do not simply withdraw from social contact, but either continue (and even intensify) their contacts with kin and friends, or else become active in groups whose members are aware of their common age bond.

In conclusion, we can say that Cumming and Henry have isolated an important aspect of aging in the United States: the relinquishing of the crucial parental and occupational roles in old age. This role loss, however, may be viewed positively or negatively by the individual, and it may or may not be accompanied by a withdrawal from social interaction, a reduction of one's life space, and a preoccupation with oneself. The debate regarding disengagement theory is reminiscent of the "isolated nuclear family" debate discussed in Chapter XIII. Parsons said that kin are less functional in industrial society, and his critics responded: "But they do function." Cumming *et al.* say that the aged are functionally unimportant and their critics answer: "Yes, but they do things." The variety of responses to old age in the U.S. makes it highly questionable whether one should generalize a theory that claims that disengagement is a universal, positive fact of old age which includes role loss, social withdrawal, and the facing of death. The various responses to old age are the result of a series of decisions that must be made as old age, particularly retirement, is reached.

SECTION TWO

SOCIALIZATION: THE DECISIONS OF THE AGED

Children leaving home and retirement from one's occupation are the kinds of changes in life situation which demand substantial reorientation on the part of individuals and married couples. According to Deutscher, there are several aids to parents in their preparation for the change that takes place when children leave home and postparental life begins.

> There is the underlying value in our society on change for its own sake—a value which can be applied to the particular case of change in the family structure; there are the temporary departures of children during the adolescent years for college, service in the armed forces, and

a variety of other reasons; there is the modern complex of urban high school life, which can move children into a world which is foreign to their parents; there are the exigencies of the work situation which often remove the middle-class father from the family during the years when the children are growing up; there is the myth and the reality of the mother-in-law which some mothers internalize as lessons for themselves. In addition, remnants of the older extended family pattern which tend to reduce the impact of the transition cannot be ignored.[22]

This description, while indicating the societal supports for child departure, ignores the fact that many parents are *never* really prepared for the postparental period. Nor, for that matter, are they prepared for many of the other changes that must be made in middle and old age. Nor is enough known about the actual transitions or processes of movement into old age. Rosow, for example, feels that a major focus for further study of the elderly should be socialization into old age. Old age, he says,

represents a devalued, unstructured role with sharp discontinuities from middle age. Hence, the individual enters the situation with little incentive, role specification, or preparation. Effective socialization under these conditions is problematic and it is necessary to clarify both the conducive and inimical forces at work in the situation.[23]

How difficult are the adjustments into old age? They are most certainly made more difficult by the fact that roles and norms, or expectations concerning what the aged should do and be, are so poorly spelled out. The greatest amount of trouble, however, is likely to be experienced by two specific types of persons. The wife who has poured body and soul into her children, who had few outside interests except those that went to the furtherance of her children's development, can very easily shrivel up personality-wise and even physically when her children have achieved independence and as she finds herself "attached to her absent children's apron strings." Their very independence may drain the meaning from her life, which was sustained by the nurturing of her family. Likewise, many a man has lived but a few months into the retirement years during which he planned to do so many things. If the entire significance of his life was wrapped up in working and earning, the physical and psychological adjustment necessitated by retirement may be too much for him. Thus, neither the family-oriented woman nor the occupation-oriented man who have no alternative values to fall back on is likely to be well prepared for a *positive* disengagement from these major life roles.

In this problematic atmosphere, and with all-too-little information on the decision-making processes and outcomes in old age, what are some of the decisions that the elderly must make? First, they must make *residential* decisions. These include that of whether to stay in the same home in which they have reared their children, for the sake of periodic family reunions, or whether to change residence completely.[24] Furthermore, change of residence may mean deciding whether to move into an apartment, trailer, or smaller house in the same community (perhaps closer to the business district) in which they have previously lived; whether to move to a retirement, or age-segregated community; or whether to move to another community in which their children or other kin are located. Second, they must make *activity* decisions. They may continue the same activities, or take up new ones. They may join new, perhaps age-graded organizations, such as golden age clubs, or continue their current memberships in religious and other groups, or simply drop many of the old activities and organizations. Another set of decisions which is not unrelated to the two already introduced has to do with relating to their *social networks*. How do they relate in terms of proximity and contact to age companions, children, and other friends and kin—or do they simply disengage from most social contacts?

The final set of decisions concerns *marital relations* (if, of course, the marriage is still intact). What activities should they participate in as a couple, and which ones as individuals? How should household responsibilities be divided up, now that the husband no longer goes off to work each morning? These last two decision areas—social network relations and marital relations in old age—have been the objects of substantial research. They are complex and important enough for us to take a more intensive look at them in Sections Three and Four.

SECTION THREE

THE SOCIAL NETWORK AND AGE SEGREGATION

The social networks of the elderly consist of two categories of persons: *kin,* who are primarily children and others of the descending generation, and *non-kin*, who are for the most part of the elderly individual's own generation.

Kin Relations of the Elderly

The elderly are likely to keep in touch with whatever kin they have available. This may mean considerable contact with their own aging brothers and sisters,[25] but more often it has its focus in children and grandchildren—their family of procreation. Shanas and her associates, in their excellent study of 2,500 aged in each of three countries—Denmark, Britain, and the United States—report that there are some significant differences in contact with adult offspring, which are related to social class position.

> Middle class, white collar persons in both Britain and the United States are more likely than working class persons to have only a few children and to live at a greater distance from their children. The married children of middle class families, both sons and daughters, tend to live apart from their parents, not only in separate households, but also at a greater distance from them. In some degree this physical separation of parents and children is compensated for by more overnight visiting on the part of white collar families. The average old person of white collar background maintains strong relationships with his children. He is more likely than his blue collar counterpart, however, to see his children infrequently or not at all. In the case of white collar parents, the patterns of help in old age flow from parents to children; in the case of blue collar parents, they flow from children to parents.[26]

The author's own study of young adults and their aging parents, which corroborates most of the above conclusions, adds a few observations to the picture. When adult offspring—particularly middle-class—are spatially separated from their parents, they keep in touch not only by periodic visits but also by telephone and letter. These forms of frequent contact are one reason why Shanas *et al.* can say that the white-collar aged "maintain strong" ties with their children, and in the next sentence indicate that they may see them "infrequently or not at all." Also, the pattern of white-collar aid does move increasingly toward equality, and, in many cases, changes over time so that services and even finances flow primarily from the middle aged white-collar adult to his elderly parents.[27] The effect of the need of the aged for care in sickness and for monetary assistance is a function, to some extent, of historical changes in relations between the generations. In 1900, says Meyer Nimkoff, the elderly were still more authorities and less playmates for their adult offspring than they are today.[28] But today, according to the Glassers, there is a role reversal, with the aging parents becoming dependent upon their adult offspring, with no power or authority base to offset their dependence. The result is conflict and psychological threat to the aged.[29]

Other authors have also found that dependence on children in old age is alienative,[30] but Gordon Streib's early report on the Cornell study of aging and retirement agrees with Shanas' report that solidarity is generally quite strong between the generations.

> Our analysis of around 1,500 cases has indicated that there is a higher degree of family solidarity as measured by our indices than has been noted by other writers. . . . The high degree of family cohesion between older parents and their children is . . . shown by the fact that there is a high degree of congruity between parental expectations for their children and the children's behavior. In the minds of older parents, affectional ties are more important than financial assistance, although, as one might expect in view of their greater economic deprivation, retirees tend to stress the importance of financial assistance more than older parents who are still working.[31]

Seven years later, however, in reporting on the panel phase of the same study, Streib noted that, while the retired stress affectional ties between themselves and their offspring, their offspring see the relationship as dependent upon both affection and their aged parents' need of help. "It appears," Streib concludes, "that from the standpoint of the adult child, family relations within the family of procreation take precedence over linkages to the family of orientation."[32]

In summary, then, relations between aging parents and their adult offspring are clearly based more upon friendship than upon authority; it is those instances of aged dependence that are most likely to cause intergenerational strain.

The grandparent role, which has been more discussed than studied, is of course intertwined with the intergenerational relationships just discussed. When relationships between parents and their offspring are authoritarian and formal, the alliance between grandparent and grandchild is likely to be quite strong. The reason for this is that the child in this situation, when he is disciplined by or in conflict with his parents, can look for an ally in his grandparents. In the United States, however, the grandparent role is actually a grandmother role.[33] "Interaction includes visits, gifts, communication, interest in the progress of the young, and sharing of wisdom by the grandparents."[34] While the grandparents may interfere in conflicts between parents and children, this is not as likely as it is in societies in which the family is more authoritarian. In the United States, Cumming and Henry assert,

> where the bonds between children and parents are defined as friendly rather than hierarchical, and where the generational difference is minimized, not only does the child not need a friendly ally but the grandparent presumably has maintained an unbroken friendly relationship with his own child, and thus does not need a mediating relationship.[35]

The position of grandparent, therefore, may involve any of four possibilities: authority, friendship, dependence, and inheritance. In working-class and lower-class families, the aging parents are apt to provide important friendship relations for their descendants, but their likely dependence upon their adult offspring strains the friendship to some extent. In the middle class, the aged are less likely to be dependent and more apt to control an inheritance; but their adult children tend to have more age-peer friends and to be more residentially separated from their parents than working- and lower-class offspring, and thus they need their parents' friendship less. Even the inheritance does not necessarily strengthen the friendship between the generations, but may instead give the relationship economic overtones. In other words, whatever role the aged play in the lives of their children and other kin is ordinarily based upon social-emotional centrality; but this role is often tenuous and the aged are simply not defined as *necessary* by their descending kin.

Non-kin and Age-grading

Members of the younger generation tend to exclude from society, not only their kin, but all aged. This exclusion is based upon the devaluation of the aged's loss of efficiency and the lack of any special prestige marks for them. Devaluation by society in general and their "surplus" character in the eyes of kin result in the aged's increasingly becoming a subsociety, with a few distinctive cultural elements. "Those in retirement communities, in rural communities from which younger people are rapidly emigrating, and in the central parts of big cities are most age-separated and hence are most likely to develop a subculture."[36]

One of the constraints upon assimilation into the aged peer group is a function of one's marital status. Some aged subcommunities consist of widows, especially in big cities, while others, such as retirement communities, are likely to involve couples. Zena Blau points out, in her study of the elderly in New York City and Elmira, New York, the effect that a change in one's marital status has upon his peer group affiliations.

> Since friends tend to be of the same sex and in a similar age group, a change in marital status that places an individual in a deviant position among his age and sex peers and differentiates his interests and experiences from theirs is likely to have an adverse effect on his friendships. When, on the other hand, widowhood becomes prevalent among others similarly located in the social structure it is the individual who is still married who occupies a deviant position and who, therefore, often sees less of his old friends.[37]

Thus, one of the bases for a residential or activity decision in old age may very well be the death of one's spouse, as he seeks out age companions whose marital status is the same as his.

Both Messer and Rosow have found that the age-graded elderly tend to feel a greater sense of integration into society than those who depend for social contact on kin of the descending generation. In fact, if children and other kin are not located nearby, the aged generally do not even feel dependent upon them or greatly deprived by their absence. Messer puts it this way: "Older people living in a situation which lends itself to age-peer formation rely less on the family for social support, but at the same time do not feel more alienated from their families." And, speaking functionally, Messer concludes that this "situation seems appropriate for the predominant system of conjugal family organization in complex societies."[38]

The middle-class elderly fit Messer's picture of the ideally age-segregated more closely than do the working-class and lower-class aged. Their kin tend to be more scattered, and they have more friends than the blue-collar aged.[39] While those friends are more scattered, the middle-class aged have a greater number of options open to them in terms of socialization into old age, due to their generally greater economic resources and their more cosmopolitan life orientations. This, however, does not necessarily mean a smoother transition into old age for middle-class persons, because they are most likely—as indicated above—to have a strong positive orientation toward those major life roles which they must give up, and are therefore negatively oriented toward disengagement.

SECTION FOUR

HUSBAND-WIFE RELATIONS IN OLD AGE

The marital complement of personality simplification and deterioration, and the other gradual transitions of which Neugarten speaks (p. 236), is *disenchantment*. By "disenchantment" Peter Pineo means the lessening of marital satisfaction, a decrease in intimacy, and even some second thoughts about the individual one has married.[40] Why, asks Pineo, do the unforeseen changes and gradual transitions of marriage result in these various signs of disenchantment? Why do the changes not result as often in increased marital satisfaction? The reason is, of course, because mating is not random, but by personal choice. If it were random, the "fit" between the two individuals might become better as often as it becomes worse. Choice, to whatever extent it is based upon perceived attributes of the other person, will usually find its basis eroded away rather than strengthened. "Couples, for example, who might marry because of identical religious attitudes could only retain or lose this characteristic; they could not become more identical."[41] Furthermore, according to Pineo, husbands experience disenchantment earlier than do their wives. The reason for this, based upon evidence from Hobart and Kephart (see Chapter X), is that men tend to romanticize their wives more than wives do their husbands, with the result that the wives may fall faster and further from their husband's idealizations. Thus, using data from Burgess and Wallin's longitudinal study of engagement and marriage, Pineo has concluded that marriage is a process of gradual disenchantment.

Moving from the general character of marriage to some of its specific characteristics in old age, we recall Ruth Cavan's point, as summarized by Ballweg, that retired husbands are more apt to take on a heightened role in household responsibilities rather than a "playboy" or social activity role.[42] Yet the home is presumably the wife's domain, and one might assume that the sudden availability of the husband might make for substantial marital conflict. Several reasons why this is not the case are indicated by Meyer Nimkoff and by Ballweg. Noting historical changes, Nimkoff asserts that, in 1900, the division of labor between the sexes was such that the "home was more exclusively the wife's domain," than it is today.[43] Thus, while retirement is more likely to be compulsory today than it was in 1900, it is compensated somewhat by a normative change, especially in the middle class, toward greater acceptance of male involvement in household tasks. There are, according to Ballweg, two factors that lessen the possibility that the husband's involvement in household tasks will disturb the family equilibrium. Results of his small scale research showed that:

> the retired husband did not share tasks with his wife to any greater extent than was the case during his work career. Rather than shared activities with the wife, the retired husband was more likely to assume full responsibility for a select group of tasks. Secondly, these tasks which the retired husband carried out appeared to be masculine or marginal in orientation, [such as burning trash, moving furniture, fixing faucets, or administrative tasks such as paying bills,] rather than those which would have a significant influence on the self-conception of the wife. The supposed invasion by the retired husband thus became more of an emancipation from tasks which the wife could have relinquished at any time the husband was willing to accept them.[44]

When we turn from tasks to husband-wife power relations, we find an apparent contradiction in the literature. Harold Smith, on the one hand, asserts that, due to the scarcity factor, the wife whose husband has survived into old age tends to show deference to him. Nor does the husband's withdrawal from his work role alter husband-wife power. Reuben Hill, on the other hand, finds in his three-generational study that there is "both a decline in husband dominance from the early stages represented by the married child generation and an increase in wife dominance into the last stage of the cycle."[45] It is at least possible that both are correct, but that they are in fact talking about different phenomena. It may be, for example, that the husband makes the major decisions in old age, such as residential location, and perhaps has a greater say-so in the running of the household, while the wife runs the social-emotional machinery of the couple, particularly as it relates to the social network. Yet, further work on the power, influence, and dominance of elderly husbands and wives needs to be done before this issue can be completely resolved.

SECTION FIVE

SUMMARY AND CONCLUSIONS

Socialization into old age includes decisions about residence, activity, the social network, and couple relations. Wayne Thompson and Gordon Streib, in their article, "Meaningful Activity in a Family Context," summarize much of the foregoing discussion by means of a useful fourfold typology (see Table 8), focussing primarily upon the social network and upon marital relations.[46]

TABLE 8
Four Ways That the Aged May Relate to Their Spouses and to Their Social Networks

Types	Marriage (Cohesion)	Social Network (Ties)
I	High	Close-knit
II	High	Loose-knit
III	Low	Close-knit
IV	Low	Loose-knit

First (Type I), an aged couple may be characterized by high cohesion to one another and by close ties to their social networks. This couple finds meaning in shared activities and in continued contacts with persons outside the home, including friends and/or kin. Many of the couple's former role adjustments are maintained as they move together through their various activities, as well as separately within their own networks.

The second possible adjustment of the aged couple (Type II) involves high marital cohesion and a loose bond to extra-familial persons. This is the prototype of what the popular press calls "togetherness." They not only share goals—a bond that may have characterized their earlier lives—they share activities as well. This is a likely pattern for successful and striving couples who were too busy during their adult careers to spend much time or energy developing strong ties to other persons.

The third possibility (Type III) is low couple cohesion and close ties to members of the social network. This relationship is exemplified by the old man who spends the majority of his time with his cronies and the wife who is always busy with her clubs. The peer group has reasserted itself, perhaps as marital disenchantment has resolved itself into a kind of mutual avoidance. Network relations may involve kin instead of friends; this type of adjustment in old age is most apt to be found among those couples who have had the greatest amount of role segregation or differentiation during their adult lives, i.e., the working and lower classes.

Finally, there is the low cohesion couple that is loosely tied to the social network (Type IV). This situation is especially a problem for the retired male, who must find hobbies, such as the basement workshop or the garden, to occupy himself during his declining years. The wife, under these circumstances, may vigorously pursue a speck of dust in the home, and may actually find the husband in the way. The couple live together, but are not really together.

In which of the four types is the desolation of one spouse likely to be the greatest at the death of the other? A spouse of Type II, whose activity patterns in old age have involved doing things with his spouse, is obviously going to find the death of his spouse a severe blow. However, substantial desolation also occurs when a member of a Type IV couple dies. For, while their old age may have been spent in conflict and avoidance, their habit patterns are almost as dependent upon each other as in the case of Type II's. Thus, the bereavement of the surviving spouse, regardless of the specific character of the husband-wife bond, is likely to be greatest in those cases in which the individual is not closely tied to social relationships not involving his spouse. Shanas *et al.* reported that "some of those who have experienced severe social loss are relieved by substitute or remaining contacts and relationships, particularly with members of their families. Companionship may thus prevent or mitigate loneliness," although the precondition for loneliness in old age is more often the loss of a spouse than it is simply the lack of extra-familial companions.[47]

In this chapter we should by now have become aware that, even without the inevitabilities of sickness and death, old age is a period of uncertainty and loss in the United States, with few positive compensations. According to Leo Simmons,

> while we have made much ado over the discovery of adolescence as a unique stage in life experiences, and recognized it as quite different from adulthood, we are

continuing—mistakenly—to regard aging as little more than a somewhat discredited extension of mid-adulthood. . . .

There are some quite justifiable reasons to assume that a shift from mid-life to old age can be as significant a change as that from adolescence to adulthood, and the range of variations in the successful fruition of life in old age may really be much wider than it is for youth.[48]

If one looks back over Chapter XIV, at least three points of similarity between old age and adolescence in the United States become apparent. First, the multiple decisions that the aged must make parallel the decisions of adolescence and demonstrate that a vast amount of *socialization* takes place during each of these periods. Granted, the decisions of adolescence are concerned with the "engagement" process, or the assumption of one's major life roles, while those of old age are related to disengagement, but the choices are numerous during both periods. Secondly, both the adolescent and the elderly person are presented with muddy or *unclear role options*. The question "how should the adolescent behave," posed in Chapter VIII, may appropriately be applied to the aged as well. For, in U.S. society, the behavioral expectations for both young people and old people are not clear-cut, but are up to individual decision. As long as adolescents and the aged stay out of the way, they may determine their own social behaviors. This condition, "staying out of the way," brings us to the final similarity between the elderly and the adolescents. In many ways both groups have increasingly taken on the character of *minorities*. They are increasingly age-segregated socially, they have little social power as a group, and they are tolerated as long as they keep to themselves. Even among the working classes, the aged are decreasingly embedded personnelwise in their kin networks. An important reason for treating these two categories of persons as subsocieties appears to be economic: both adolescents and the elderly must be kept out of the occupational market so that unemployment rates may be kept to a minimum.

Despite these similarities, old age is generally a more pessimistic and negative period than adolescence, for the adolescent has his adulthood to look forward to, while the elderly must look either to the past or to a future of decline and death. It would be nice if disengagement were the positive process described by Cumming and Henry, yet while some aged may find satisfaction in leisure and "a job well done," many others in the United States simply cannot make their peace with this period of ill-defined choices, separation, and loss.[49]

NOTES

[1] Irwin Deutscher, "Socialization for Postparental Life," in Arnold Rose, ed., *Human Behavior and Social Processes* (Boston: Houghton Mifflin, 1962), p. 507.

[2] Michel A. J. Philbert, "The Emergence of Social Gerontology," *Journal of Social Issues*, 21 (1965), 5.

[3] Disengagement theory was first presented in Elaine Cumming, Lois R. Dean, and David S. Newell, "Disengagement, a Tentative Theory of Aging," *Sociometry*, 23 (1960); see also Cumming and William Henry, *Growing Old: The Process of Disengagement* (New York: Basic Books, 1961). Neugarten's study is Bernice L. Neugarten, *Personality in Middle and Late Life* (New York: Atherton, 1964).

[4] Cumming and Henry, *Growing Old*, p. 159.

[5] *Ibid.*, p. 14. On role loss, see Cumming, "Further Thoughts on the Theory of Disengagement," *International Social Science Journal*, 15 (1963), 377–93.

[6] Cumming and Henry, *Growing Old*, p. 15.

[7] Cumming, "Further Thoughts," p. 385; Cumming and Henry, *Growing Old*, p. 142.

[8] Deutscher, "Socialization for Postparental Life," p. 524.

[9] Arnold M. Rose and Warren A. Peterson, eds., *Older People and Their Social World* (Philadelphia: Davis, 1965), p. 26.

[10] *Ibid.*, pp. 360, 361.

[11] *Ibid.*, pp. 362, 363.

[12] *Ibid.*, p. 363.

[13] Ethel Shanas, et al., *Old People in Three Industrial Societies* (New York: Atherton, 1968), p. 285. Copyright © 1968, Atherton Press, Inc.; reprinted by permission of the publishers. All rights reserved. See also Cumming and Henry, *Growing Old*, p. 159; and Paul H. and Lois N. Glasser, "Role Reversal and Conflict Between Aged Parents and Their Children," *Marriage and Family Living*, 24 (1962), 46–51.

[14] Rose and Peterson, *Older People and Their Social Worlds*, p. 366.

[15] Neugarten, *Personality in Middle and Late Life*, p. 193.

[16] Irving Rosow, *Social Integration of the Aged* (New York: Free Press, 1967), p. 291.

[17] Shanas et al., *Old People in Three Industrial Societies*, p. 172.

[18] *Ibid.*, p. 256.

[19] Rose and Peterson, *Older People and Their Social World*; Rosow, *Social Integration of the Aged*; and Mark Messer, "Age Grouping and the Family Status of the Elderly," *Sociology and Social Research*, 52 (1968), 271–79.

[20] Messer, "Age Grouping," p. 279.

[21] Rosow, *Social Integration of the Aged*, pp. 323–24.

[22] Deutscher, "Socialization for Postparental Life," p. 522.

[23] Rosow, *Social Integration of the Aged*, p. 326.

[24] This is referred to in Reuben Hill, "Decision Making and the Family Life Cycle," in Ethel Shanas and Gordon F. Streib, eds., *Social Structure and the Family: Generational Relations* (Englewood Cliffs, N.J.: Prentice-Hall, 1965), p. 130.

[25] Elaine Cumming and David M. Schneider, "Sibling Solidarity: a Property of American Kinship," *American Anthropologist*, 63 (1961), 498–507.

[26] Shanas et al., *Old People in Three Industrial Societies*, p. 256.

[27] Bert Adams, *Kinship in an Urban Setting* (Chicago: Markham, 1968), p. 46, and Adams, "Structural Factors Affecting Parental Aid to Married Children," *Journal of Marriage and the Family*, 26 (1962), 327–32.

[28] M. F. Nimkoff, "Changing Family Relationships of Older People in the United States During the Last Fifty Years," *The Gerontologist*, 1 (1961), 96.

[29] Glasser and Glasser, "Role Reversal and Conflict," p. 50.

[30] Robert M. Dinkel, "Attitudes of Children Toward Supporting Aged Parents," *American Sociological Review*, 9 (1944), 370–79, and Bert N. Adams, "The Middle Class Adult and His Widowed or Still-Married Mother," *Social Problems*, 16 (1968), 50–59.

[31] Gordon F. Streib, "Family Patterns in Retirement," *Journal of Social Issues*, 14 (1958), 60.

[32] Gordon F. Streib, "Intergenerational Relations: Perspectives of the Two Generations on the Older Parent," *Journal of Marriage and the Family*, 27 (1965), 475.

[33] Harold E. Smith, "Family Interaction Patterns of the Aged: A Review," in Rose and Peterson, *Older People and Their Social Worlds*, p. 156; see also Ruth Albrecht, "The Parental Responsibilities of Grandparents," *Marriage and Family Living*, 16 (1954), 201–4.

[34] Smith, "Family Interaction Patterns of the Aged," p. 156.

[35] Cumming and Henry, *Growing Old*, p. 61.

[36] Rose and Peterson, *Older People and Their Social Worlds*, p. 7.

[37] Zena Smith Blau, "Structural Constraints on Friendship in Old Age," *American Sociological Review*, 26 (1961), 438.

[38] Messer, "Age Grouping," p. 276.

[39] Rosow, *Social Integration of the Aged*, p. 293.

[40] Peter C. Pineo, "Disenchantment in the Later Years of Marriage," *Marriage and Family Living*, 23 (1961), 9–10.

[41] Ibid., p. 7.

[42] John A. Ballweg, "Resolution of Conjugal Role Adjustment After Retirement," *Journal of Marriage and the Family*, 29 (1967), 277, 281.

[43] Nimkoff, "Changing Family Relationships," p. 92.

[44] Ballweg, "Resolution of Conjugal Role Adjustment," p. 281.

[45] Smith, "Family Interaction Patterns," p. 151, and Hill, "Decision Making," p. 127.

[46] Wayne E. Thompson and Gordon F. Streib, "Meaningful Activity in a Family Context," in Robert W. Kleemeier, ed., *Aging and Leisure: A Research Perspective into the Meaningful Use of Leisure Time* (New York: Oxford University Press, 1961), pp. 177–211.

[47] Shanas et al., *Old People in Three Industrial Societies*, p. 285. In Willard Waller and Reuben Hill, *The Family: A Dynamic Interpretation* (New York: Holt, Rinehart and Winston, 1951), p. 482, the authors note that the desolation of the remaining partner is greatest when the couple's habit patterns are enmeshed, regardless of social network relations. They state it thus: "It is submitted that this account" of serious bereavement "is essentially correct whether the bereavement situation represents the loss of a person intensely loved or merely a greatly ramified loss entailing necessary readjustments in a number of phases of life."

[48] Leo William Simmons, "Social Participation of the Aged in Different Cultures," *The Annals,* 279 (1952), 51.

[49] For more on the demographic characteristics of the aged, see Maria Davidson, "Social and Economic Characteristics of Aged Persons (65 Years Old and Older) in the United States in 1960," *Eugenics Quarterly,* 14 (1967), 27–44.

XV

Response of the Family to Change and Challenge

FAMILY LIFE INVOLVES BOTH PATTERN AND CHANGE. THUS FAR WE HAVE CONCENTRATED PRIMARILY UPON THE PATTERNS THAT DEVELOP AND PERSIST IN THE MODERN FAMILY. IN THIS CHAPTER THE FOCI OF ATTENTION ARE THE ACTS, EVENTS, AND PROCESSES—SUCH AS UNEMPLOYMENT, MENTAL ILLNESS, ALCOHOLISM, AND DEATH—THAT REQUIRE SOME FORM OF ADJUSTMENT ON THE PART OF THE FAMILY. THESE TOPICS AND OTHERS LIKE THEM ARE OFTEN DISCUSSED UNDER SUCH HEADINGS AS CRISIS, DISORGANIZATION, AND DISSOLUTION. WE SHALL ATTEMPT TO DEVELOP A FRAMEWORK FOR DISTINGUISHING AMONG THE VARIOUS CHANGES AND CHALLENGES THAT CONFRONT FAMILIES AND TO SUMMARIZE THE CONDITIONS THAT DETERMINE DIFFERENT FAMILY RESPONSES. FINALLY, FOUR SPECIFIC EVENTS THAT AFFECT FAMILIES ARE DISCUSSED IN SOME DETAIL. THESE ARE ILLEGITIMACY, UNEMPLOYMENT, DIVORCE, AND DEATH.

Life in the family is not just many years of habit and routine. Although some married people may complain that "nothing exciting ever happens," the fact is that transition and change are as central to family experience as are continuity and pattern. The gradual and abrupt transitions of parenthood, departure, decline, and eventual death are expected and inevitable; in addition to these transitions, most families face one or more unexpected challenges along the way.

The literature on these expected and unexpected acts, events, and processes as they relate to the family is voluminous. It includes studies of parenthood, infidelity, illegitimacy, departure, unemployment and economic setback, physical and mental illness, disability, retardation, alcoholism, divorce, and death.[1] The vocabulary that has been used to describe family responses to these changes and challenges is multifaceted and often vague; it has included, among other concepts, those of trouble, problem, crisis, stress, demoralization, deviance, disorganization, breakdown, maladjustment, disintegration, dissolution—and their opposites, such as organization, adjustment, and integration. William J. Goode, John Scanzoni, Jetse Sprey and others have met with some success in their attempt to clarify this series of concepts by means of definitional distinctions.[2] Sprey, for example, distinguishes between deviance and disorganization in terms of the family's mutual role expectations. If a family member violates his generally understood and accepted role in the family, this is deviance. But if the family lacks a set of understood and accepted roles, or "rules of the game," that family can be said to be disorganized.[3] Yet, important as terminological clarity is, the present author will focus instead upon: (1) a framework for organizing the various changes and challenges that may confront families, and (2) specification of the conditions for various family responses. Perhaps a by-product of these two concerns will be an increase in conceptual clarity as well.

SECTION ONE

A FRAMEWORK FOR ANALYZING CHALLENGES AND FAMILY RESPONSES TO THEM

Several authors have developed frameworks to deal with the process of family reaction to various stimuli. Some have been derived from research on a specific problem. For example, E. Wight Bakke described the stages of the family's response to unemployment during the Depression as follows: (1) momentum stability; (2) unstable equilibrium; (3) disorganization; (4) experimental readjustment; and (5) permanent readjustment. Likewise, Joan Jackson traces the family's reaction to alcoholism through denial, admission, attempts to eliminate the problem, strain and disorganization, exclusion of the alcoholic, and reorganization of the family.[4]

Other frameworks, however, are not problem-specific, but are general descriptions of the process of family adjustment to crisis. According to Reuben Hill, the parts of the process are: "crisis—disorganization—recovery—reorganization" (see Figure 13). Hill discusses the conditions that make it possible for some families to react to a stressor, or crisis-provoking event, without disorganization.[5] Although Hill treats both the stressor and the family adjustment as variables and spends considerable time discussing the factors that are conducive to a good adjustment to crisis, Bernard

FIGURE 13

Hill's "Roller-coaster Profile" of Family Reaction to a Crisis-provoking Even

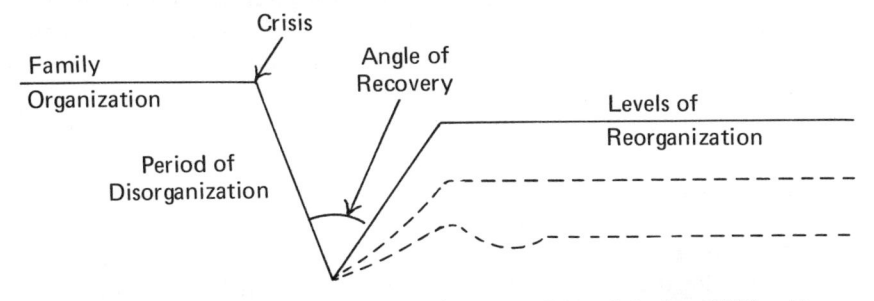

SOURCE: Reuben Hill, *Families Under Stress* (New York: Harper & Brothers, 1949), p.14.

Farber feels that Hill's major attention is devoted to the period of disorganization. Thus, Farber indicates that an alternative to viewing crisis as producing disorganization and a new equilibrium is viewing it as setting in motion a lengthy process of adaptation and reorganization. This process he labels the "Crisis Process," though it is in reality the "Family Adjustment, or Reorganization, Process."[6] Changes that affect one family member, says Farber, affect the others as well. Drawing upon Bakke, Jackson, and others who have described family response to specific crises, Farber defines the stages of family adjustment as follows. First, the attempt is made to handle the challenge within existing role structures—combining the ideas of denial and momentum stability. A part of the rationale behind this approach is the hope that the condition is temporary and that restoration will soon occur. Unless the situation is righted, a second stage is reached when the problem is faced—the result being a test of former family commitments. Next, the problem becomes public and extra-familial ties are altered. Fourth, there is role reorientation or, using the term in Sprey's sense, reorganization. That is, a new set of mutual expectations is developed and accepted by the family members. The final stage of the crisis process is "freezing out," or the removal of the crisis-causing individual from the home, so that the family unit can get on about the business of passing on its culture.

Although Farber's process furnishes excellent conceptual tools with which to tackle the vast literature on family response, it has limitations in applicability that become apparent as one attempts to relate it to the various acts, events, and processes listed at the beginning of this chapter. Many crises never advance beyond stage one; that is, the crisis *is* temporary and the family is reconstituted pretty much in its former state. Also, stages two and three may frequently occur in reverse order, with a problem becoming public knowledge while the family continues to deny its existence. In fact, being confronted by a member of one's social network may trigger the admission on the family's part that "We've got a problem." Finally, there are two ways in which "freezing out" may differ from Farber's view of it as the last stage of the crisis process. In some instances, such as the launching of an offspring or death of a family member, freezing out may be viewed as the *first* stage of the process, followed by admission and reorganization. Furthermore, instead of the individual being frozen out of the family unit, the behavior may be frozen out and the individual reinstated. This is a particularly appropriate response to deviant behavior, and will be illustrated in some detail when we discuss illegitimacy later in the chapter.

Farber's crisis process, as he presented it, does not, therefore, apply equally well to all the various types of changes and challenges that may confront the family. For that reason, we shall introduce a somewhat more complex framework for viewing family responses by first categorizing the stressors along two dimensions which, in light of the literature, seem to be crucial: Is the stressor temporary or permanent, and is it voluntary or involuntary? (See Figure 14.) With these two variables as the axes, it is possible to locate the stressor events within the quadrant in which they would typically appear. Two qualifications regarding the location of the stressors involve *variation* and *compounding*. Physical illness is usually both involuntary and temporary; however, there are psychosomatic elements in many illnesses which make it difficult to distinguish the involuntary from the voluntary, and the most serious forms of illness may result in a permanent disability. Other variations include the possibility of the alcoholic's becoming "dry"; although he is not cured, he may nevertheless be reinstated in the family if he responds to treatment. Even divorce is temporary in those few cases in which the same individuals remarry. Thus, many of the stressors actually cover a range of possibilities, and have been placed in Figure 14 according to their modal character as perceived by the author. The second qualification concerns the compounding of stressors. Infidelity on the part of one spouse might contribute to alcoholism on the part of the other, with the eventual outcome of the process being divorce.[7]

We have, however, isolated the specific stressors in Figure 14

FIGURE 14

A Categorization of Changes and Challenges (Stressors)

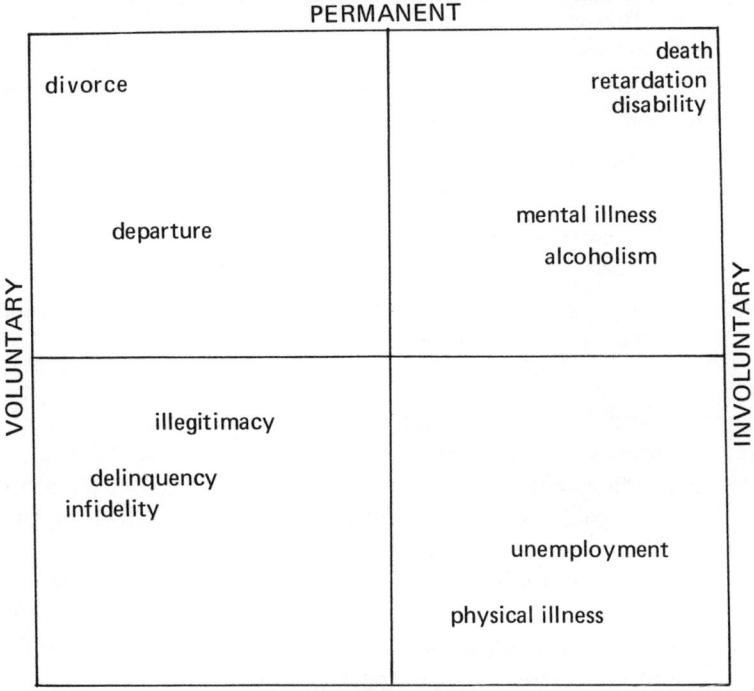

PERMANENT

VOLUNTARY		INVOLUNTARY
divorce		death retardation disability
departure		mental illness alcoholism
illegitimacy delinquency infidelity		
		unemployment physical illness

TEMPORARY

according to their modal character so that we may proceed to the more important question: How does the family typically respond to the various types of challenges (See Table 9.) A voluntary-temporary event (which would include most forms of deviant behavior) may simply be frozen out of the family's thoughts and lives and the individual reinstated on the assumption that it will never happen again. This would apply as well to the sorts of family conflict mentioned in Chapters XI and XII. It was stated, for example, that one way a married couple may resolve constant disagreements about family finances is to make a basic decision about the distribution of income each month and subsequently "freeze out" that area of life from family communication. If, however, a stressor such as infidelity persists, the result may be disorganization in the sense of a confusion of expectations, a loss of consensus on "the rules of the game."

An involuntary-temporary event, such as unemployment, is apt to be met first with the assumption that it will soon be over, and

TABLE 9

Most Likely Family Responses to Changes and Challenges (Stressors)

Type of Stressor (with Example)	Responses
Voluntary-Temporary (illegitimacy)	Freeze out behavior ⟶ reinstate person (if persists, other stressors may follow)
Involuntary-Temporary (unemployed)	Ignore or deny; or else admit ⟶ temporarily reorganize ⟶ reinstate
Voluntary-Permanent (divorce)	Reorganize
Involuntary-Permanent (retardation)	Admit ⟶ freeze out person ⟶ reorganize (death: admit ⟶ reorganize)

therefore requires no family adjustment except a tightening of the family budget. If it is not immediately remedied, the family may admit its predicament, may temporarily reorganize (perhaps by the wife getting a job), and subsequently reinstate the former family role structure when the husband is once again employed.

The two permanent stressors ordinarily involve a freezing out of the individual. In the case of divorce and departure, the freezing out is voluntary and requires the reorganization of the remaining family members. The involuntary forms of permanent stress include death, which requires admission and reorganization, and retardation and mental illness, which are ordinarily responded to by eventually recognizing the problem, freezing out the person, and reorganizing the family.

Thus, different challenges result in different typical responses: freezing out the behavior and reinstating the individual, or temporarily reorganizing and reinstating, or freezing out the individual and permanently reorganizing. However, this picture of different challenges resulting in different responses is oversimplified. It is quite possible that the same challenge may meet with different responses due to other variables besides the two primary axes of Figure 14. These additional variables that may alter the intensity of the family's response include: (1) whether the challenge was *expected or unexpected;* (2) whether the challenge originated outside of or inside the family, i.e., *externally or internally;* (3) how the *family* is *structured in* relation to *its environment*—is it embedded in a large kin network, is it a large or small nuclear family in which the individuals are highly embedded, or is it a nuclear family that is highly individualistic; (4) how the *family* is *organized internally*—is it well organized and adaptable prior to the challenge, or is it already disorganized or else too rigid; (5) *definition* of the stressor—is it defined as deviant, as a source of trouble, or not. Let us look briefly at each of these five as they affect the intensity of family crisis and disorganization in response to a challenge.

(1) Expected or Unexpected Challenges

"A crisis," says Burgess and Locke, "is any decisive change which creates a situation for which the habitual behavior patterns of a person or a group are inadequate."[8] Thus, E. E. LeMasters is able to speak of parenthood as a crisis, since it calls into play new role demands and alters a married couple's habitual interaction patterns.[9] Yet the crisis is not in the event but in the response, and the response to an expected event is likely to be substantially less severe and disorganized than the response to an unexpected one. Alice Rossi asserts that the birth of the first child is a more crucial marital transition than the marriage itself.[10] It is obvious, then, that the likelihood of crisis is substantially greater in the birth of a handicapped or retarded child (an unexpected event), than in the birth of a child (an expected event).[11]

(2) External Versus Internal Origin

When the stressor event originates outside the family, such as a natural disaster, a depression, or a war, the family may respond either by disorganization or by increased solidarity, depending upon its internal resources. If, however, the stressor event itself originates within the family, the likelihood of crisis and disorganization is great. Compare, for example, the family that loses its belongings in a flood with the family in which the husband gambles away its resources. Or compare the family in which the husband, like millions of others, loses his job in a depression with the family in which the husband loses his job because of excessive drinking. Or, again, compare the family disrupted by war with the family disrupted by the husband's desertion. In each of these instances, the latter is more likely to cause family difficulties since the blame cannot be placed outside the family.

(3) Family Structure in Its Network

"Compared with other associations in the society," says Reuben Hill,

> the average family is badly handicapped organizationally. Its age composition is heavily weighted with dependents, and it cannot freely reject its weak members and recruit more competent team mates. . . . This group is not ideally manned to withstand stress, yet society has assigned to it the heaviest of responsibilities: the socialization and orientation of the young, and the meeting of the major emotional needs of all citizens, young and old.[12]

The family is, however, better able to withstand internal stresses if it is embedded in a larger kin network that can absorb some of the shock. Researchers have found that, even when the family is not highly embedded in its kin network, it may call upon those ties in times of external threat.[13] There is likewise a difference, according to Thomas Dow, in the ability of non-embedded families to withstand various challenges. While admitting that further research is needed, Dow comments that "the affective, interpersonal, intrafamily crisis is better met by the large family structure, while the material, economic, instrumental crisis is more effectively avoided and/or coped with by the small family structure."[14] When the kin-embedded family (personnel-wise), the large nuclear family, the small nuclear family, and the individualistic family are compared, the small nuclear family appears to be most vulnerable to stressor events that originate within the family unit itself. The very intensity of emotional ties and the strength of mutual expectations in the small family make it quite likely that both deviant behavior and the freezing out of an individual will severely test its coping ability. While the least disorganization and crisis might characterize the response of a truly individualistic family to a stressor event, the fact remains that there are apparently few families in which the *laissez-faire* attitude regarding member behavior is carried to the point that the family has *no* mutual expectations whatsoever.

(4) Internal Family Organization

Hill states that the various researchers who studied the Depression concurred that it is "possible to explain the different reactions of crisis-proof and crisis-prone families to sharp decreases in income during the Depression by these twin factors of integration and adaptability, with a restudy [by Angell] suggesting the greater importance of family adaptability."[15] Thus, the family with mutual role expectations, common goals, flexibility, and a sense of satisfaction in family experience is adequately organized and less vulnerable to stressor events than are other families. While such variables are unquestionably important to family stability, there are two problems in their use as predictors of family response. First, they are somewhat *tautological* in their relation to the stressor events. For example, the family in which a member deviates from expectations can be said to have weak mutual expectations. Likewise, the family that is unable to adapt to the birth of a retarded child obviously lacks flexibility. In other words, the variable that is said to help the family withstand stress may also be considered part of the stressor syndrome itself. Second—and this is really inseparable from the first problem—these internal variables are almost inherently *post hoc*. How can it be determined whether a family is organized and adaptable until it has confronted an event that tests its organization and adaptability? Yet, despite these qualifications in their use, these internal characteristics of families are obviously important determinants of their responses to changes and challenges.

(5) Definition, or Perception, of the Stressor

Here is a variable that quite clearly overlaps with some of those already discussed. For example, when a family is able to define an external event as threatening many people, it may make it easier for that family to "ride it out." The condition under which this variable is best distinguished from the others, however, is one in which a particular act, event, or process is simply not defined as a stressor. Perhaps the best example of this would be the birth of an illegitimate child. When this is not defined by a family as deviant behavior, any crisis caused by the event will not be a result of internal stress but of the ostracism of people in the society who define the behavior as deviant.[16]

We have now catalogued both the stressors and the likely familial responses to them, and have subsequently outlined the conditions under which a family is apt to be more or less susceptible to crisis and disorganization. According to the variables that influence the *intensity* of family response, the *greatest threat* to the family is likely to result from the following combination of factors:

a *small,* non–kin-embedded, *nuclear family lacking flexibility* confronts an *unexpected, internal* challenge that is defined by that family as a stressor. The *least threat,* or greatest resilience, is likely to characterize the *adaptable, kin-embedded* families that face an *expected* event, an *external* challenge, or a situation not defined as crisis-provoking. This section has pointed out that to speak of *"the* crisis process" is to oversimplify a complex set of stimuli and responses; the purpose of the framework presented above is to help to order a wide variety of materials concerning the non-routine aspects of family life.

SECTION TWO

FOUR CHANGES AND CHALLENGES BRIEFLY CONSIDERED

Having developed a framework for understanding family responses to various stressors, we shall now describe briefly a few of the characteristics of illegitimacy and of family economics as stressor events, and then review at somewhat greater length the prevalence and significance of divorce and death in the contemporary United States family.

Illegitimacy

In the United States, pre-marital pregnancy is very likely to be defined by the girl's family as deviant behavior, and to be accompanied by strong feelings of guilt on her part. Some families that define it negatively have neither the resources nor the information necessary to guarantee being able to protect the family's "respectability." Other families handle illegitimacy within the existing family structure, and incorporate the newborn baby into the household. There are, however, substantial numbers of primarily middle-class families whose reaction to an extra-marital pregnancy is to try to freeze out the behavior; there are social agencies that provide these families aid in their efforts at privacy and secrecy. The female leaves home and lives at the agency, or in agency-approved housing, until the baby is born. The baby is then put up for adoption, and the female returns home (perhaps following a "Mediterranean cruise"). From that point on, the approach is apt to be simply to blot out this aspect of the past from the thinking and conversation of the family members. Thus, the behavior has been frozen out, while the individual has been reinstated with little or no role alteration. This, of course, makes it possible for the family to pursue the "orderly replacement" of its culture without major upheaval or readjustment. On the other hand, the approach of freezing out the behavior and reinstating the person does not necessarily resolve the individual's problem and guilt—it may only hide them. It seems quite likely that substantial numbers of females have lived for years under a cloud of unresolved guilt as a result of the family's freezing out of their deviant behavior. Keeping the baby; putting the baby up for adoption, but facing and working through the experience; freezing out the deviance entirely—each of these approaches is oriented to a specific set of societal, family, and individual values and needs. Here, then, is exemplified one of those situations in which concern for the *family*, with its members embedded in it and serving its needs, requires the freezing out of individual deviance; while concern for the *individual* and his development and well-being might very well necessitate a different strategy. While many facets of illegitimacy have been researched and discussed, the issue of family responses and their significance, which we have been addressing, needs much further research.[17]

Economics, Employment, and the Family

There is a close relation between rates of both marriage and divorce and the business cycle. Based on his analysis of the period from 1860 to 1956, Paul Jacobson asserts that

> the incidence of divorce, like that of marriage, closely follows the business cycle, running low in periods of depression and correspondingly high during years of prosperity. In general, however, the divorce rate is less sensitive to changes in economic conditions, due largely to the fact that a marriage cannot be dissolved as readily as it can be contracted.[18]

What it boils down to is that people can ill afford to change their commitments, either through marriage or divorce, when times are hard. For, the reorganization process itself costs money; therefore, such periods are characterized by individuals tending to maintain their present interpersonal affiliations as much as possible. Although figures are lacking, it is also possible that in times of economic hardship an intolerable situation is more likely to be escaped by desertion than by dealing with the costly system of legalized divorce.

How does the individual family react to an economic setback, whether it be unemployment during a depression or loss during a natural disaster? The vast majority of families tend to look to their kin at such times.[19] Yet the problems in thus utilizing kin are twofold. First, the poor and unskilled, who are in greatest economic jeopardy because they constantly live close to the subsistence level, are likely to have kin who are also struggling for subsistence. Thus, they may be forced to look to outside agencies for help. Second, members of the middle classes and stable working classes, who are more likely to have economically secure kin upon whom to call for help, are also likely to be characterized by values that stress individualism and independence. As we indicated in Chapter XIII, kin relations in U.S. society appear to operate most smoothly when the obligatory elements are kept in the background. Our family values do not give positive, but rather negative, sanction to such economic functions and obligations. Therefore, even though the kin network may provide a buffer against economic setback, there is still the likelihood of interpersonal strain and personal insecurity—an insecurity that results from the strain between one's value system and the necessities of existence.

A large number of significant research projects grew out of the Depression in the United States during the 1930's. This research showed that the same stimuli—unemployment and financial loss—affected different families in different ways. Some made temporary adjustments, such as moving in with relatives; other families disintegrated; and still others (e.g., 27 of the 100 families studied by Cavan and Ranck) reacted by rallying together and manifesting a new and more overt sense of family unity than ever before.[20] A portion of the explanation for the various reactions to this specific challenge is found in the family's value system. If the family's major goals and values have been economic, the undermining of their economic position will result in a severe disorganization of their values and norms, or behavior patterns. If, however, the family has other end values—perhaps religion, perhaps service to others, perhaps experience and adaptation—these may serve as rallying points at such a time. The ability to adapt and cope is seldom developed overnight; it either is or is not developed by a family as a result of many experiences, and as stated above, it is difficult to know whether a given family has developed this capacity until *after* it confronts a challenge and demonstrates its preparation or lack of it.

Unemployment and economic setback may, of course, be a consequence of internal rather than external challenge. If the husband loses his job due to excessive absence from work, or if he gambles away the family's resources, it is relatively easy to pinpoint him as the chief cause of the trouble; the likelihood of crisis, weakened solidarity, and at least temporary reorganization is much greater in this situation than in one in which the threat can be "externalized" or generalized.[21] Here, then, once again we see a range of possible outcomes that depends both on the nature of the challenge and on the family's structure and values at the time of impact.

Divorce in the United States

A brief legend from nineteenth century India may serve to introduce one of the most frequently debated aspects of the contemporary family.

> In the first year of the reign of King Julief, two thousand married couples were separated, by the magistrates, with their own consent. The emperor was so indignant, on learning these particulars, that he abolished the privilege of divorce. In the course of the following year, the number of marriages in Agra was less than before by three thousand; the number of adulteries was greater by seven thousand; three hundred women were burned alive for poisoning their husbands; seventy-five men were burned for the murder of their wives; and the quantity of furniture broken and destroyed, in the interior of private families, amounted to the value of three millions of rupees. The emperor re-established the privilege of divorce.[22]

Making divorce easy, some commentators would say, is just another compromise with the weakness of the flesh. To these authors, the rate of divorce in the United States is another sign of the imminent collapse of both the family system and the society. But how does divorce in the U.S. look in cross-cultural and historical perspective? Practically all societies, with the possible exception of the Incas, says George P. Murdock, have made some cultural provision for terminating marriage through divorce.[23] In a sample of 40 societies, 16 had a lower divorce rate than the contemporary U.S., and 24 had a higher rate. In some of these 24 societies, divorce is a private matter, with informal social pressure rather than legal restrictions or contracts keeping most couples together. However, in 19 of Murdock's sample of 40 societies, the rate of permanent separations appears to exceed that in the United States at present. Murdock therefore concludes that, despite "the widespread alarm about increasing 'family disorganization' in our own society, the comparative evidence makes it clear that we still remain well within the limits which human experience has shown that societies can tolerate with safety."[24]

In view of the cross-cultural evidence, why has the rate of divorce in the United States been viewed with alarm by many observers? The answer is that it has been so viewed, not by comparison with other countries, but in comparison with our own traditions and history. Max Rheinstein, for example, reports that the family and control of divorce in the West first came under increasing religious domination and has subsequently gone through a process of liberalization and secularization.[25] The Victorian nuclear family was simultaneously the end of the religious and institutional era and the beginning of the era of high expectations for families consisting of a small number of intensely involved persons. William O'Neill, in his book, *Divorce in the Progressive Era*, describes the close link between Victorian family expectations and the increase in the prevalence of divorce:

> When families are large and loose, arouse few expectations, and make few demands, there is no need for divorce. But when families become the center of social organization, their intimacy can become suffocating, their demands unbearable, and their expectations too high to be easily realizable. Divorce then becomes the safety valve that makes the system workable. Those who are frustrated or oppressed can escape their families, and those who fail at what is regarded as the most important human activity can gain a second chance. Divorce is, therefore, not an anomaly or a flaw in the system, but an essential feature of it. When the modern family came to dominate society in the nineteenth century, divorce became common.[26]

But doesn't divorce, even in a society whose family system appears to require it, eventually lead to the destruction of that society? To this question Morton Hunt responds:

> It is fairly well known that freedom to divorce has existed in certain deteriorating societies; this was the case in the later years of the Roman Empire. What is less well known, freedom to divorce has existed in certain stable and healthy societies—especially those which have mechanisms other than the father-mother family for insuring the well-being and socialization of the children.[27]

This latter concept is exemplified, according to Hunt, by the Hopi Indians. Yet he does not go on to compare the contemporary U.S. family with the Hopis in terms of its cultural mechanisms for coping with a high rate of divorce. We shall keep this issue in mind as we look more closely at divorce in the U.S., beginning with the *prevalence* to which so many authors refer.

The classic work on the prevalence of divorce in the United States is Paul Jacobson's *American Marriage and Divorce*. He traces the rate of divorce per 1,000 marriages from 1860 to 1956; Alexander Plateris has recently carried the data on through 1963. Thus, Figure 15 combines Jacobson's and Plateris' results and traces the rate of divorce from 1860 to 1963 by five-year intervals. The highest single period in U.S. history was from 1943 to 1950, during which time, the rate of divorces among wartime marriages reached a peak of 18.2 per 1,000 marriages (1946), subsequently dropping back to its present level of between 9 and 10 per 1,000 marriages each year.

As Figure 15 illustrates, rates of divorce declined during economic recession and rose during and after wars. It is also instructive to relate the divorce rate to death and desertion. While the divorce rate has risen in 100 years from one per 1,000 marriages to nine per 1,000 marriages, the death rate has declined during the same period by an even greater amount. Consequently, says Jacobson, "the annual rate of total marital dissolutions is lower now than it was 100 years ago; the combined rate has declined from an annual average of 33 per 1,000 in the 1860's to about 27 per 1,000 at present" (1956).[28] Jacobson, however, was comparing the 1860's

FIGURE 15

Divorce Rate per 1,000 Marriages in the United States between 1860 and 1963 by Five-year Intervals

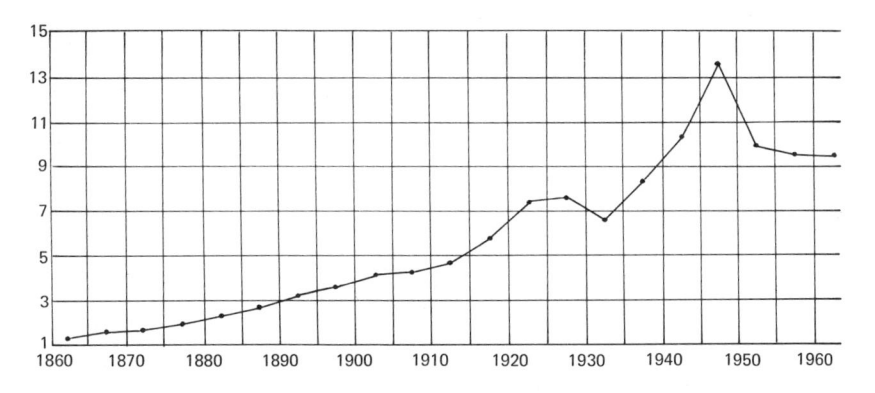

SOURCE: Computed from annual rates, by permission of the author, from Paul H. Jacobson, *American Marriage and Divorce* (New York: Rinehart, 1959), p. 90, Table 42; and Alexander A. Plateris, *Divorce Statistics Analysis (United States—1963)*, Department of Health, Education, and Welfare, Vital and Health Statistics, Series 21, No. 13 (1967).

—a wartime period—with the mid-1950's—a period without war. In Table 10 we compare four selected years: 1860, 1908, 1956, and 1963 in terms of their rates of death and divorce. It might seem reasonable to argue that one explanation for the rise in the divorce rate is that unhappy marriages that, a hundred years ago, would have been terminated by death, today last until a divorce. Yet the problem with this explanation is that more than half of today's

TABLE 10
Rates of Death, Divorce, and Total Marital Dissolution
per 1,000 Marriages for Selected Years, 1860–1963

Year	Death	Divorce	Total Dissolution	Per Cent Divorces
1860	28.4	1.2	29.6	4.1%
1908	24.4	4.4	28.8	15.4
1956	17.5	9.3	26.8	34.6
1963	19.1	9.6	28.7	34

SOURCE: Reprinted by permission of the author, from Paul H. Jacobson, *American Marriage and Divorce* (New York: Rinehart, copyright © 1959), p. 142, Table 70.

divorces occur during the first ten years of marriage; thus, the explanation is partial at best.

A second partial explanation offered for the rise in the divorce rate has to do with desertions. According to Freed and Foster, prior to 1900 "for the working man, desertion and heading west was the common way for husbands to escape from intolerable marriages."[29] To this, James Peterson adds:

> Whether, then, the increase in total divorce represents only the increased use of legal facilities by these classes we do not know. It is possible that a rising divorce rate may represent a more law-abiding population which signifies disruption with legal means, whereas, previously, the same disruption would have been accomplished by separation or desertion.[30]

Yet today, Freed and Foster indicate, the annual number of divorces and desertions are approximately the same; legalized divorce has not entirely replaced desertion as a means of marital separation. It seems most probable that a tendency to legalize marital dissolutions accounts for part, but not the majority, of the increase in the rate of divorce since the mid-1800's.

A final issue concerning the prevalence of divorce involves, not the yearly rate, but the number of U.S. marriages that eventually end in divorce. For some years following World War II it was thought that somewhere between one-third and one-fourth of all marriages were thus terminated. However, careful research by Thomas Monahan and others has concluded that a portion of that apparent rate is accounted for by the greater likelihood that second and subsequent marriages will not last. In fact, Monahan found in an Iowa study that 16.6 per cent of first marriages end in divorce, as compared to 34.9 per cent of second marriages and 79.4 per cent when both spouses have divorced twice or more.[31] Thus, the failure rate for first marriages is about one in six: this, says Peterson, does not indicate that we are moving toward serial monogamy (or even toward "permanent availability").

When we turn from the prevalence of divorce in the United States to its *causes*, we find two types of variables discussed in the literature. The first begins by dividing the married population into certain basic categories, such as by age and by socioeconomic level, notes where the divorce rates are higher or lower, and attempts to explain these differences. The second set of variables consists of the answers that divorced or divorcing persons give to direct questions about the causes of their marital difficulties. William J. Goode, Thomas Monahan, and J. Richard Udry all report that lower-status couples have higher rates of divorce than higher-status families. Monahan, for example, found in the mid-1950's that professionals, owners, and managers—who comprised 23.4 per cent of his sample—accounted for only 9.6 per cent of the divorces. Skilled craftsmen, 22.7 per cent of his sample, accounted for 21.2 per cent of the divorces; and unskilled laborers, who made up 9.9 per cent of his sample, accounted for 31.8 per cent of the divorces.[32] A partial explanation for these figures is that low status families are more susceptible to many of the stressors discussed above, including alcoholism and unemployment; a possible outcome of such stressors is disorganization and crisis and eventually divorce. In addition, "young marriages disproportionately involve persons from lower- or working-class backgrounds," and young marriages—specifically those in which one or both spouses are in their teens—are less stable than are those contracted later.[33]

"The divorce risk for teen-agers was said to be six times greater than that for adults," say Freed and Foster; because this is true at all status levels, the high divorce rate of teen-agers cannot be entirely explained by the association between low status and youthful marriage.[34] Why, then, are youthful marriages on the whole less likely to last? Three partial answers to this include: (1) divergence in marriage, (2) marriage as an escape, and (3) premarital pregnancy. Some have claimed that in a society that stresses both personal choice of a mate and deferred adulthood, young people are not psychologically and intellectually prepared to make sound mate selections. While this assumption can easily be questioned by noting the way in which both improved diet and the mass media serve to help young people mature (physically and mentally) earlier than ever before, the fact remains that the earlier a couple marries the greater is the likelihood that their careers, interests, and personalities will diverge during the first few years of their marriage.

A second possible explanation is that early marriage is often as much an *escape from* something as it is a *commitment to* something. Young people who find themselves increasingly unable to put up with an unhappy home may find in love and marriage the opportunity to escape; and, therefore, may not allow sufficient time for unstable or unworkable dating relationships to run their course and dissolve. The third and most often mentioned reason for the instability of young marriages is *premarital pregnancy.* There are two steps to the explanation. In the first place, a substantial proportion of teenage marriages involve a premarital pregnancy—35–45 per cent according to Freed and Foster and 30–60 per cent according to Peterson. Samuel Lowrie finds that, in an Ohio sample of 1,850 first marriages, "70.9 per cent of the premaritally pregnant brides were 18 or younger. . . ."[35] In the second place, most researchers agree that marriages characterized by a premarital pregnancy show a greater incidence of divorce than marriages not so characterized.[36] Why should such marriages be less stable? Though few writers attempt to explain why, it seems likely that many of the couples who become thus involved in marriage would have weeded themselves out if they had been free from the pressure to marry that was occasioned by the pregnancy. In other words, in such marriages the working of choice has been short-circuited.

This brings us to the second set of explanations given for divorces in the U.S.—the direct causes mentioned by divorced and divorcing persons. According to the wives interviewed by Goode, the causes of divorce were: non-support, arbitrary authority, complex reasons, drinking, personality problems, home life, value divergence, disagreements about consumption patterns, and the "triangle" or extra-marital affair, as well as a scattering of others. George Levinger, dividing his sample of 600 Cleveland applicants for divorce into lower-status and middle-status groups, reports the following differences by sex and socioeconomic status in reasons given for desiring a divorce.

. . . lower-status wives were considerably more likely than middle-status wives to complain about financial problems, physical abuse and drinking. Middle-class wives were significantly more prone to complain about lack of love, infidelity and excessive demands. Middle-class husbands paralleled the wives in their significantly greater concern with lack of love; on the other hand, they were significantly *less* likely than lower-class husbands to complain of the wife's infidelity.[37]

The difference is, very simply, that low-status marriages (and, therefore, complaints) are focussed in the areas of physiological needs for food and safety or protection, while higher-status marriages tend to take these matters for granted and are thus more concerned about forms of emotional and psychological expression.

With some understanding of the prevalence and causes of divorce in the United States, it is possible to look now at the *significance* and *effects* of divorce. First, what does divorce itself mean? As we stated above, the fact that 84 per cent of first marriages in the United States remain intact does not seem to indicate that that country is moving rapidly toward serial monogamy. Nor is the increase in the rate of divorce during the twentieth century necessarily a sign of moral degeneration. While it may be so interpreted, some writers would argue precisely the opposite. For example, Foster argues that "sexual dissatisfaction in marriage today is more apt to lead to divorce and remarriage than to the acquisition of a mistress or a visit to a prostitute. In this sense, it may be argued, divorce promotes public morality."[38] What it does unquestionably mean is that there is a lessened social stigma attached to divorce than there was in the earlier periods of U.S. history; divorce is more acceptable as a "cultural alternative" to an intolerable marriage.[39]

Does the increase in the divorce rate indicate either the breakdown of the U.S. marriage system or its decrease in popularity? "Despite the prevalence of divorce," say Freed and Foster, "marriage is more popular than ever before. In 1900 only a little more than half of all Americans above fourteen were married; today almost two-thirds are."[40] To this, Hunt adds that the "wide use of divorce today is not a sign of a diminished desire to be married, but of an increased desire to be happily married."[41] The effect of divorce upon the marriage and family system of the United States has, O'Neill claims, justified neither the expectations of the liberals, who thought it would act as a safety valve and solve all the internal inconsistencies in our family system, nor the fears of the conservatives, who believed that the availability of divorce would signal the disintegration of the family as we know it. What has happened is that what was "once a moral issue has become increasingly a clinical problem. That we have not solved it any more than the Progessives did" in the early 1900's "is probably less important than our abandonment of their utopian stance."[42] But the effect of divorce upon marriage and the family cannot be viewed apart from the issues of children and remarriage.

Divorces increasingly involve couples with children. "In 1948," according to Freed and Foster, "only 42 per cent of divorcing couples had children under 18, but in 1955, the figure was 47 per cent, and in 1962 reached 60 per cent, involving 537,000 children."[43] Goode, however, found that the divorced mothers he studied in Detroit were convinced that their children were better off in divorce than they would have been if their mothers had stayed married to their first husbands.[44] While this may be partially a rationalization of the decision that these divorced mothers had made, their belief is generally corroborated by Ivan Nye in his study of children from broken homes and from unhappy, unbroken homes. Using as his sample ninth through twelfth graders in three Washington schools, Nye discovers that

> in the areas of psychosomatic illness, delinquent behavior, and parent-child adjustment . . . children show better adjustment in broken homes. Children of homes broken by divorce in terms of the over-all adjustment picture do not have poorer adjustment than those from homes broken in other ways.[45]

One reason, Nye feels, that many studies have overemphasized the strain that divorce causes the children is that these studies have concentrated upon the period of the divorce process itself, rather than upon the subsequent period of readjustment and reorganization.

As far as the post-divorce adjustment of the divorcee is concerned, Goode and others have reported that the prevalence of remarriage following a premature (as opposed to a later breakup caused by death in old age) marital breakup is such that it could be considered institutionalized.[46] Both this fact, and the fact that there are greater economic opportunities for women today, present alternatives to the divorcee which were much less available a few years ago. Though second and subsequent marriages are less stable than first marriages, the significance of this lesser stability seems to be that selectivity has occurred, so that those who have been willing to divorce once are the subcategory of married persons who are most willing to accept divorce as a working alternative to an unhappy marriage.[47]

The tendency, in discussing the significance of divorce as we have, has been to minimize the tensions and problematic aspects of divorce in the U.S. At this point we shall review the three factors that serve to increase the *strain* of divorce today. The first and most important tension-producing factor is the law. The history of divorce law in the United States is one of plaintiff and defendant, of perjury and legal skirmishing—all of which may add to the pangs of a process that may in actuality signify the "decent burial" of a dead marriage. Love is presumably the basis for marriage, but the mutual cessation of love is not a legal grounds for divorce (see Table 11). The legal grounds in our fault-based system have changed over the years, but do not yet embody the mutuality of a

TABLE 11
Grounds for Divorce, by Per Cent

Year	Cruelty	Desertion	Adultery	All Others
1867–70	12.4	35.4	26.4	25.8
1950	58.7	17.6	2.7	21.0

SOURCE: Reprinted by permission of the author, from Paul H. Jacobson, *American Marriage and Divorce* (New York: Rinehart, copyright © 1959), p. 121, Table 58.

dead marriage—the exception being California's recent move in that direction. The statutory grounds for divorce and the causes of marital breakdown have little relationship; and both Rheinstein and Freed and Foster point out the difficulty in getting legislators to bring the laws into keeping with the times. Freed and Foster put it this way:

> Even if judges and lawyers are convinced, for the most part, that marital fault is a difficult, if not impossible, thing to assess, legislators are most apt to be committed to the fault concept. In other words, the breakdown theory is a radical departure from prior law, and is not likely to appeal to most state legislators.[48]

The ten per cent of American divorce cases that were contested in the 1950's and 1960's seldom involved an individual trying to save his marriage, but, more often, a spiteful, recalcitrant, or greedy spouse.[49] Eugene Litwak, Foster, and others have suggested ways in which the law might be made more consistent with the current individualism and concern with happiness that characterize marriage in the U.S. It is unquestionable that the present public, legal, and fault basis for the law serves to increase the strain of divorce rather than to alleviate it.[50] As Clifford Kirkpatrick asserts: "There is a good chance that persons seeking divorce under present-day provisions will have contact with legal confusion, collusion, perjury, degradation, humiliation, increased bitterness, and frustration, rather than professional help for the sickness of marital maladjustment." And laws are but a portion of the problem.[51]

A second factor increasing the strain of divorce involves the expectations and intensity that characterize the U.S. family. We tend to expect love, understanding, happiness, and companionship in our marriages. Lincoln Day, comparing Australian and U.S. marriages, finds that the Australian male, far more than his American counterpart, "appears to obtain his recreation in the company of other men." In "mateship" Australian husbands find "many of the satisfactions that a society characterized by more companionable marriages would expect them to obtain primarily in the company of their wives. . . . Compared with American couples, the Australian husband and wife seem to share fewer activities and to participate less often in joint decision-making."[52] The results are, thus, higher marital expectations on the part of the U.S. couple, greater emotional intensity invested in the marriage, more opportunities for friction due to interaction, and, finally, a greater sense of personal failure if the marriage goes wrong. As has been pointed out, we have not moved in U.S. society to universal, permanent availability; but only as far in that direction as the companionship family—i.e., the family based upon psychological involvement, adjustment, love, and so on. Therefore, the damage to that adjustment and the death of that love which are indicated by divorce are signs of individual failure, of one's inability to live up to current expectations for the family, that is, the happiness of its members.

Not only do divorce laws demonstrate a substantial lag, and our family system foster a sense of personal and corporate failure in divorce, but a third factor intensifies the strain of contemporary divorce. An increased divorce rate is a fairly recent phenomenon. Thus, the U.S. family system has not yet developed institutionalized supports for the individual going through this process. In fact, remarriage following divorce has been institutionalized in U.S. society more fully than has the divorce process itself. Not only is the legal aspect of the process complex and confusing, but the friends and kin of a divorcing couple are unlikely to be highly supportive at such a time. Burgess and Locke indicate the problem thus: "In our society divorced persons are presented with no socially sanctioned means of adjustment such as those available to the bereaved."[53] It may not, of course, be feasible to develop a divorce ritual similar to that surrounding death; yet it is significant that, while the frontier of death has been slowly receding, the rate of premature marital breakup by divorce has gradually risen.

Three factors, in summary, which make divorce more of a personal and social problem in the U.S. than it might otherwise be are: outmoded laws, the psychological intensity and expectations that U.S. family life entails, and the lack of institutionalized means for coping with the divorce process. Those who feel that the individual should be embedded in the nuclear family and serve its needs, assert that to lessen the strains by simplifying the laws and institutionalizing emotional support for the divorce is to invite more divorces. The strains, it is argued, are "functional" for keeping down the rate of divorce. The individualistically-oriented, on the other hand, feel that divorce is a valuable safety valve for the U.S. family system, and should be made as personally painless as possible. Regardless of one's personal value position, there are signs that changes in the law, such as that in California, are imminent—but when or how (or whether) the other strains will be reduced is highly problematic.

Death and the Family

Even in the 1960's, approximately two marriages were terminated by death to every one marriage that ended in a divorce. However, if statistical analysis is restricted to those marriages that are *prematurely* terminated by death or divorce, the ratio is much smaller. Traditionally, the response to death has been supportive of the bereaved in two ways. First, the institutionalized death ritual seeks to help the individual *face the fact* of death. This is extremely important in working through the grief process. The child, for example, who is allowed to retain fantasies about the return of a deceased father some day, may be in for serious mental difficulties. Granted, there has been a substantial furor in recent years over whether the removal of the critically ill from the home and current U.S. funeral practices are helpful or harmful to the individual in facing and admitting the death of a loved one. However, this is one of the points of greatest distinction between death and divorce: "We are divorced now" is considerably less convincing than "He is dead now"; this is particularly true when the ex-spouse remains nearby and interacts from time to time with the children.[54] In other words, working through the bereavement caused by divorce is more difficult than working through the bereavement that results from death.

A second difference between the responses to death and divorce is in the rallying of friends and kin to the support of the individual bereaved by death. Both material and emotional support may be forthcoming in the latter instance, while the effect of a divorce may be alienation from the members of one's social network. Burgess, Locke, and Thomes summarize these and other distinctions between the attitudes toward death and divorce as follows:

> In bereavement there is a tendency to concentrate on the best traits of the departed and to give assistance to the survivors; in divorce there is a tendency to condemn the defects of one or both spouses, and possibly ostracize those involved. In bereavement the individual secures comfort and group support by the rallying around of his friends and relatives; the divorced may be confronted with gossip, unfriendliness, and the taking of sides by relatives. In bereavement it is expected that the normal person will show some signs of emotional disturbance; a divorced person who shows signs of emotional disturbance is given little consideration—in fact, he may be thought of as emotionally unbalanced. . . . In bereavement, catharsis is secured through participation in religious ceremonies; the divorced may experience an increase in emotional disturbance through the necessity of resorting to legal advice and court procedures.[55]

A third aspect of the resolution of premature death in a family is that, following the death of a young parent, a long period of institutionalized mourning is no longer expected. Instead, the remarriage of the remaining parent or spouse is accepted within a reasonably short period of time following bereavement. This is, of course, the point of greatest similarity between responses to death and divorce.

The death of a young child or parent is less common and, therefore, likely to be more traumatic than it was in the past. The trauma may be greater in those cases in which the support of friends and kin is largely verbal and short-lived.[56] Ideally, however, society has devised a basic resolution consisting of assistance to the individual in facing or admitting the loss; support from one's social network; and, in the case of the death of a young parent, renewed courtship and remarriage for the remaining spouse.

SECTION THREE

CONCLUSIONS

In a totally non–personnel-embedded, or individualistic, family system, deviance would cause no family crisis and divorce and death no great grief. But the U.S. family is characterized by strong bonds and frequently strong norms as well. The embeddedness of individuals in the nuclear family has not yielded to individualistic pressures, with the result that the strains caused by many of the changes and challenges to which we have referred in this chapter are as great as they have been in the past. Even divorce is neither as prevalent nor confronted as nonchalantly as the pessimists and conservatives of the early twentieth century predicted.

But what of the future? Are the challenges to family stability to be viewed as indicators of the U.S. family's eventual disintegration, or is the contemporary family a highly adaptable and resilient unit in the face of current societal and cultural changes? In the closing chapter, we shall review several of the major themes of the preceding chapters and introduce several viewpoints regarding the future of the family in the United States.

NOTES

[1] *Parenthood:* E. E. LeMasters, "Parenthood as Crisis," *Marriage and Family Living,* 19 (1957), 352–55; Everett D. Dyer, "Parenthood as Crisis: A Re-study," *Marriage and Family Living,* 25 (1963), 196–201; Daniel F. Hobbs, Jr., "Parenthood as Crisis: A Third Study," *Journal of Marriage and the Family,* 27 (1965), 367–72; and Hobbs, "Transition to Parenthood: A Replication and an Extension," *Journal of Marriage and the Family,* 30 (1968), 413–17.

Infidelity: One of the best sources on this is a recently compiled book of readings, Gerhard Neubeck, ed., *Extra-Marital Relations* (Englewood Cliffs, N.J.: Prentice-Hall, 1969).

Illegitimacy: William J. Goode, *The Family* (Englewood Cliffs, N.J.: Prentice-Hall, 1964), pp. 19–30; Alice J. Clague and Stephanie J. Ventura,

Trends in Illegitimacy; United States—1940–1965, Department of Health, Education, and Welfare, Vital and Health Statistics, Series 21, No. 15 (1968); and Clark E. Vincent, *Unmarried Mothers* (New York: Free Press, 1963). For other sources, see note 17.

Departure: See Ernest W. Burgess, Harvey J. Locke, and Mary Margaret Thomes, *The Family,* 3rd ed. (New York: Litton Educational Publishing, 1963).

Unemployment and Economic Setback: Mirra Komarovsky, *The Unemployed Man and His Family* (New York: Dryden, 1940); Robert C. Angell, *The Family Encounters the Depression* (New York: Scribner's, 1936); E. Wight Bakke, *Citizens Without Work* (New Haven, Conn.: Yale University Press, 1949); Ruth Shonle Cavan and Katherine Howland Ranck, *The Family and the Depression* (Chicago: University of Illinois Press, 1938); see also parts of Earl Lomon Koos, *Families in Trouble* (Morningside Heights, N.Y.: King's Crown, 1946).

Physical and Mental Illness: Talcott Parsons and Renee C. Fox, "Illness, Therapy, and the Modern Urban American Family," *Journal of Social Issues,* 13 (1952), 31–44; Ezra F. Vogel and Norman W. Bell, "The Emotionally Disturbed Child as the Family Scapegoat," in Bell and Vogel, eds., *The Family* (New York: Free Press, 1960), pp. 382–97; and John A. Clausen and Marian Radke Yarrow, eds., "The Impact of Mental Illness on the Family," *Journal of Social Issues,* 11 (1955), No. 4.

Disability: Geoffrey Gibson and Edward G. Ludwig, "Family Structure in a Disabled Population," *Journal of Marriage and the Family,* 30 (1968), 54–63.

Retardation: Irving Tallman, "Spousal Role Differentiation and the Socialization of Severely Retarded Children," *Journal of Marriage and the Family,* 27 (1965), 37–42; and Bernard Farber, *Family: Organization and Interaction* (San Francisco: Chandler, 1964). See Farber's material in this book as well as his footnotes to his own and other works on the subject.

Alcoholism: Selden D. Bacon, "Excessive Drinking and the Institution of the Family," *Alcohol, Science, and Society* (New Haven, Conn.: Journal of Studies on Alcohol, 1945); Samuel C. Bullock and Emily H. Mudd, "The Interaction of Alcoholic Husbands and Their Non-Alcoholic Wives During Counselling," *American Journal of Orthopsychiatry,* 29 (1959), 519–27; Joan K. Jackson, "Alcoholism and the Family," *The Annals,* 315 (1958), 90–98; see especially Jackson, "Alcoholism and the Family," in David J. Pittman and Charles R. Snyder, eds., *Society, Culture, and Drinking Patterns* (New York: Wiley and Sons, 1962), pp. 472–92, for an excellent summary and other literature on the subject.

Divorce: Paul H. Jacobson, *American Marriage and Divorce* (New York: Rinehart, 1959); William J. Goode, *After Divorce* (Glencoe, Ill.: Free Press, 1956); and William L. O'Neill, *Divorce in the Progressive Era* (New Haven, Conn.: Yale University Press, 1967). For other sources on divorce, see notes 23f.

Death: Willard Waller and Reuben Hill, *The Family: A Dynamic Interpretation* (New York: Holt, Rinehart and Winston, 1951), and Burgess, Locke, and Thomes, *The Family,* pp. 460f.

[2] William J. Goode, "Family Disorganization," in Robert K. Merton and Robert A. Nisbet, eds., *Contemporary Social Problems* (New York: Harcourt Brace, 1961); John Scanzoni, "Family Organization and the Probability of Disorganization," *Journal of Marriage and the Family,* 28 (1966), 407–11; and Jetse Sprey, "Family Disorganization: Toward a Conceptual Clarification," *Journal of Marriage and the Family,* 28 (1966), 398–406.

[3] Sprey, "Family Disorganization."

[4] Bakke, *Citizens Without Work;* and Jackson, "Alcoholism and the Family."

[5] Reuben Hill, "Generic Features of Families Under Stress," *Social Casework*, 39 (1958), 139–50.
[6] Bernard Farber, *Family: Organization and Interaction* (San Francisco: Chandler, 1964), pp. 403–6.
[7] An article by Koos and Fulcomer, referred to in Hill, "Generic Features of Families Under Stress," p. 145.
[8] Burgess, Locke, and Thomes, *The Family*, p. 415. Copyright © 1963, by Litton Educational Publishing; reprinted by permission of Van Nostrand Reinhold Company.
[9] LeMasters, "Parenthood as Crisis."
[10] Alice Rossi, "Transition to Parenthood," *Journal of Marriage and the Family*, 30 (1968), 27.
[11] Hobbs, "Parenthood as Crisis," and Hobbs, "Transition to Parenthood," question whether becoming a parent for the first time very often causes a crisis in the family.
[12] Hill, "Generic Features," p. 140.
[13] Thomas E. Drabek and Keith S. Boggs, "Families in Disaster: Reactions and Relatives," *Journal of Marriage and the Family*, 30 (1968), 443–51.
[14] Thomas E. Dow, Jr., "Family Reaction to Crisis," *Journal of Marriage and the Family*, 27 (1965), 366.
[15] Hill, "Generic Features," p. 144.
[16] Hallowell Pope, "Unwed Mothers and Their Sex Partners," *Journal of Marriage and the Family*, 29 (1967), 555–67.
[17] Leontine Young, *Out of Wedlock* (New York: McGraw-Hill, 1954); Sarah Edlin, *The Unmarried Mother in Our Society* (New York: Farrar, Straus, & Young, 1954); see especially the articles in Robert W. Roberts, ed., *The Unwed Mother* (New York: Harper & Row, 1966).
[18] Reprinted by permission of the author, from Paul H. Jacobson, *American Marriage and Divorce* (New York: Rinehart, copyright © 1959), p. 95.
[19] Koos, *Families in Trouble*, p. 87; Drabek and Boggs, "Families in Disaster"; and Enrico L. Quarantelli, "A Note on the Protective Function of the Family in Disasters," *Marriage and Family Living*, 22 (1960), 263–64.
[20] Cavan and Ranck, *The Family and the Depression*.
[21] Koos, *Families in Trouble*, pp. 91–102.
[22] Nelson Manfred Blake, *The Road to Reno: A History of Divorce* (New York: Macmillan, 1962), pp. 80–81, quoted from 28 Niles Register 229, June 11, 1825.
[23] George P. Murdock, "Family Stability in Non-European Cultures," *The Annals*, 272 (November, 1950), 195.
[24] *Ibid.*, pp. 199, 197.
[25] Max Rheinstein, "Trends of Marriage and Divorce Law of Western Countries," *Law and Contemporary Problems*, 18 (1953), reprinted in Marvin B. Sussman, ed., *Sourcebook in Marriage and the Family* (Boston: Houghton Mifflin, 1968 ed.), pp. 543–54.
[26] O'Neill, *Divorce in the Progressive Era*, pp. 6–7.
[27] Morton M. Hunt, *The World of the Formerly Married* (New York: McGraw-Hill, 1966), p. 290.
[28] Jacobson, *American Marriage and Divorce*, p. 143.
[29] Doris Jonas Freed and Henry H. Foster, Jr., "Divorce American Style," *The Annals*, 383 (1969), 75.
[30] James A. Peterson, "Catastrophes in Partnership: Separation, Divorce, and Widowhood," in Seymour M. Farber, Piero Mustacchi, and Roger H. L. Wilson, eds., *Man and Civilization: The Family's Search for Survival* (New York: McGraw-Hill, 1965), p. 73.
[31] Thomas P. Monahan, "The Changing Nature and Instability of Remarriages," *Eugenics Quarterly*, 5 (1958), 81.

[32] Goode, *After Divorce*, Chap. V; Monahan, "Divorce by Occupational Level," *Marriage and Family Living*, 17 (1955), 322–24; J. Richard Udry, "Marital Instability by Race, Sex, Education and Occupation Using 1960 Census Data," *American Journal of Sociology*, 72 (1966), 203–9; Udry, "Marital Instability by Race and Income Based on 1960 Census Data," *American Journal of Sociology*, 72 (1967), 673–74.

[33] Lee G. Burchinal, "Trends and Prospects for Young Marriages in the United States," *Journal of Marriage and the Family*, 27 (1965), 249.

[34] Freed and Foster, "Divorce American Style," p. 83.

[35] *Ibid.*; Peterson, "Catastrophes in Partnership," p. 75; Samuel H. Lowrie, "Early Marriage: Premarital Pregnancy and Associated Factors," *Journal of Marriage and the Family*, 27 (1965), 48–56.

[36] Lowrie, "Early Marriage," p. 53; Burchinal, "Trends and Prospects," p. 252; Harold T. Christensen and Betty B. Rubenstein, "Premarital Pregnancy and Divorce: A Follow-Up Study by the Interview Method," *Marriage and Family Living*, 18 (1956), 114–23; Harold T. Christensen and Hanna H. Meissner, "Studies in Child Spacing III—Premarital Pregnancy as a Factor in Divorce," *American Sociological Review*, 18 (1953), 641–44. One researcher who disagrees is J. Ross Eshleman, who finds in a small Ohio sample that "contrary to most common notions about premarital pregnancies, the present study did not find pregnancy prior to marriage to be significantly related to either mental health or marital integration." See Eshleman, "Mental and Marital Integration in Young Marriages," *Journal of Marriage and the Family*, 27 (1965), 257.

[37] Goode, *After Divorce*, p. 123; George Levinger, "Sources of Marital Dissatisfaction Among Applicants for Divorce," *American Journal of Orthopsychiatry*, 36 (1966), 806.

[38] Foster, "The Future of Family Law," *The Annals*, 383 (1969), 142.

[39] Goode, *World Revolution and Family Patterns* (New York: Free Press, 1963), p. 81.

[40] Freed and Foster, "Divorce American Style," p. 82.

[41] Hunt, *The World of the Formerly Married*, p. 292.

[42] O'Neill, *Divorce in the Progressive Era*, p. 273.

[43] Freed and Foster, "Divorce American Style," p. 84.

[44] Goode, *After Divorce*, p. 329.

[45] F. Ivan Nye, "Child Adjustment in Broken and in Unhappy Unbroken Homes," *Marriage and Family Living*, 19 (1957), 361.

[46] Goode, *After Divorce*, Chap. XX. See especially Jessie Bernard, *Remarriage: A Study of Marriage* (New York: Holt, Rinehart and Winston, 1956).

[47] Hunt points out that simple figures such as those reported by Monahan should not necessarily be interpreted to mean that divorcees are unstable or "bad bets," but rather that they may have merely discovered that divorce isn't all that bad after all. See Hunt, *The World of the Formerly Married*, pp. 278–79.

[48] Freed and Foster, "Divorce American Style," p. 86.

[49] *Ibid.*, p. 79.

[50] Foster, "The Future of Family Law," pp. 137f; Eugene Litwak, "Three Ways in Which Law Acts as a Means of Social Control: Punishment, Therapy, and Education: Divorce Law a Case in Point," *Social Forces*, 24 (1956), 217–23.

[51] Clifford Kirkpatrick, *The Family as Process and Institution* (New York: Ronald Press, 1955 ed.), p. 547.

[52] Lincoln H. Day, "Patterns of Divorce in Australia and the United States," *American Sociological Review*, 29 (1964), 521.

[53] Burgess, Locke, and Thomes, *The Family*, p. 462.

[54] On this see Goode, *After Divorce*, Chap. XX; see also Hyman Rod-

man's brief summary of Willard Waller's *The Old Love and the New* (Carbondale: Southern Illinois University Press, 1967) in Rodman, *Marriage, Family and Society: A Reader,* New York: Random House, 1965, 91.

[55] Burgess, Locke, and Thomes, *The Family,* p. 468.

[56] For an interesting and insightful discussion of the problems of adjustment to widowhood, see Peter Marris, *Widows and Their Families* (London: Routledge and Kegan Paul, 1958).

XVI

The Family in the United States: Retrospect and Prospect

THE FAMILY IN THE UNITED STATES PROVIDES AFFECTIVE TIES FOR THE INDIVIDUAL AND THE PRIME MARKET FOR THE ECONOMIC SYSTEM, AS WELL AS PLAYING A DIRECTION-GIVING ROLE IN THE SOCIALIZATION PROCESS. IN ADDITION, INCONSISTENCIES IN AND VARIETIES OF U.S. FAMILY EXPERIENCE ARE CONSTANTLY IN EVIDENCE. ON EACH OF THE FIVE CONTINUA PRESENTED IN CHAPTER V, THE U.S. FAMILY CAN BE SEEN TO BE SOMEWHERE BETWEEN THE TWO EXTREMES. BUT WHAT OF THE DIRECTION AND SPEED OF CHANGE IN THE FUTURE? POSSIBILITIES FOR PREDICTING THE FUTURE OF THE FAMILY ARE BASED ON THE INTERPLAY BETWEEN INTRINSIC AND INSTRUMENTAL FAMILY VALUES AND INDIVIDUALISTIC VALUES. BY ADDING TO THESE PERSPECTIVES THE FACTOR OF TECHNOLOGICAL AND BIOLOGICAL DEVELOPMENTS, WE ARE PREPARED TO MAKE LONG-RANGE PREDICTIONS REGARDING THE FAMILY'S FUTURE.

The first step in peering into the future would seem to be a brief review of where we have been. Some aspects of the U.S. family system have either appeared for the first time, or increased in prevalence during the twentieth century, and have not yet produced institutionalized sets of expectations. Examples are the aged, the divorce process, and, to some extent, the dating system. Other aspects of the family were once institutionalized but have lost some of their predetermined character and are thus more open to individual choice. The best example of these aspects is marital-parental roles, especially in the middle-class family. In reviewing the characteristics of the contemporary family in the United States, it would seem profitable to return to the frameworks and continua developed in Chapter V, employing them as the bases for review.

SECTION ONE

THE CONTEMPORARY UNITED STATES FAMILY: A REVIEW

There are many kinds of family-kin systems in the world; the U.S. family is but one of them. It is impossible to assert that one type of family is inherently "better" than the others, unless one is willing to go on and point out the ways in which that particular system functions to solve problems for both the individual and the society, and the ways in which it avoids strains and inconsistencies. This book has been but a case study—a look at the inconsistencies and functions that characterize one of these systems: that of the United States. It will be for others to ask the comparative value question of "goodness of fit."[1]

We have seen repeatedly that the family in the United States performs an important function in providing *affective* or primary relationship ties for its members. In the middle-class family, these ties are likely to be quite intense within the nuclear family, but not to extend very far out into the kin network; while in the working and lower classes, the burden of love and understanding is more often shared by other kin as well. The same holds for the direction-giving function played by the family in *socialization:* much socialization takes place outside the U.S. home, but it is in the nuclear family that the individual acquires his cultural orientation, reinforced or contradicted by extra-familial influences. Lower- and working-class children are somewhat more likely than middle-class to be influenced considerably by other members of the social network as well as by parents and siblings. Thus, affection and direction, or strong bonds and norms, are produced by family experience, and may be viewed as important aspects of the family's functioning in contemporary U.S. society.

The economic system and values of U.S. society are also related in a crucial way to the nuclear family. This unit seldom operates as a productive segment of the economy, but it does serve as a basic *consumer* of the goods of the market. Thus, it is not unexpected that the larger society would stress simultaneously the easing of divorce restrictions and the desirability of marriage and a family, for "the happy family is a 'consuming' family." The high rates of divorce and marriage are quite consistent with the needs of the U.S. economic system and the materialistic values fostered thereby.

In the course of history, the various parts of any given social system do not change at the same rate of speed nor with the same degree of completeness. The result is that the same subsystem, such as the U.S. family, is simultaneously characterized by integration into the larger society and by inconsistencies and fragmentary changes. Such *inconsistencies* have been quite apparent in the present volume, noticeably in the middle-class family. They include the following: (1) The U.S. family, particularly in its middle-class variety, is currently walking a difficult line between stress upon ego struggle and upon conformity; parents teach the child to adapt and to assert his uniqueness, but also to comply with the strong family norms referred to above. That is, the family's attempt to "orderly replace" its culture in its offspring is somewhat inconsistent with the heterogeneous nature of the norms that the growing individual is likely to confront by the time he reaches adulthood. This is the socialization locus of the current struggle between individualism and nuclear family personnel embeddedness. (2) Young people are maturing earlier—in their awareness and even physiologically—and are, at the same time, being kept out of adult society longer than ever. Middle- and working-class young people are faced with other inconsistencies or fragmentary changes as well, such as the freedom from pregnancy fears accompanied by a still-substantial adult invoking of sexual absolutes. (3) In marriage, there is role choice without sexual equality. This is a partial change, leaving the wife's economic role and the husband's domestic role as supportive. One might say that having a door half-way open is more tension-producing than if it is shut or all the way open—and thus it is with marital roles. (4) In kinship relations, the norms of independence and filial obligation often run at cross purposes, serving to increase the ambivalence of kin toward each other. (5) Divorce laws are inconsistent with attitudes toward and causes of marital breakup. While the grounds for divorce have multiplied, the "fault" system still predominates. There is no positive or supportive ritual through which the divorcing couple passes. It may be neither advisable nor possible to resolve all the inconsistencies within the U.S. family system. Yet it seems to the present author that the resolution of some of them would aid the individual, both in his intrapersonal and interpersonal—especially his family—adjustments.

The *varieties* of U.S. families were the specific subject of

Chapter VI, and differences between middle-class, working-class, and lower-class families in the U.S. have been referred to in virtually every chapter. The racial and ethnic subsocieties, dealt with primarily in Chapter VI, mirror primarily the culture of the other families in the society which are of the same socioeconomic level. There is, however, some cultural distinctiveness based upon differences in traditions; in the case of the black family this distinctiveness is based upon both prejudice and discrimination against them as well as a current stress on ethnicity. It is worth noting that middle-class and working-class blacks seem to be as much or more concerned with the dominant forms of respectability and morality than white families of the same social status, since they must continually seek to overcome the distorted white stereotype regarding behavior in the black community.[2] Thus, the U.S. family system includes diversity, inconsistency, and several important functions that it performs for the individual and the society.

In Chapter V, five continua were presented upon which the characteristics of the U.S. family might be located. These continua pertain to mate selection, socialization, marital roles, institutional embeddedness, and personnel embeddedness. Each of these is, of course, a complex of variables; locating the contemporary U.S. family upon them is accomplished only by reducing its variations to zero. Thus, heeding the proper cautions regarding oversimplification, these continua may be profitably employed to summarize many of the findings reported in the preceding pages (see Figure 16). (1) *Mate choices* in the U.S. are based upon personal desires, but are restricted considerably by propinquity and the salient family values concerning such issues as religion and race. (2) *Socialization:* the individual is influenced by both familial and extra-familial socializing agents, with the direction-giving influence of parents still substantial. (3) *Marital roles:* there is modified role choice in marriage. Certain options are available to both sexes, though aspects of the old patriarchy and the economic-familial division of labor by sex are still operative openly in the working and lower classes and subtly in the middle class. (4) *Institutional embeddedness:* other institutions have become highly differentiated from the kin group and the nuclear family. The latter still specializes in primary relations, socialization, and economic consumption, and sometimes in recreation and religion. (5) Nuclear family *personnel embeddedness*—with the individual interacting intensely with family members, while being subservient to the family's norms and needs, and individualism—with the family

FIGURE 16

A Tentative Location of the Contemporary U.S. Family on Five Ideal-typical Continua Concerning the Family and its Characteristics

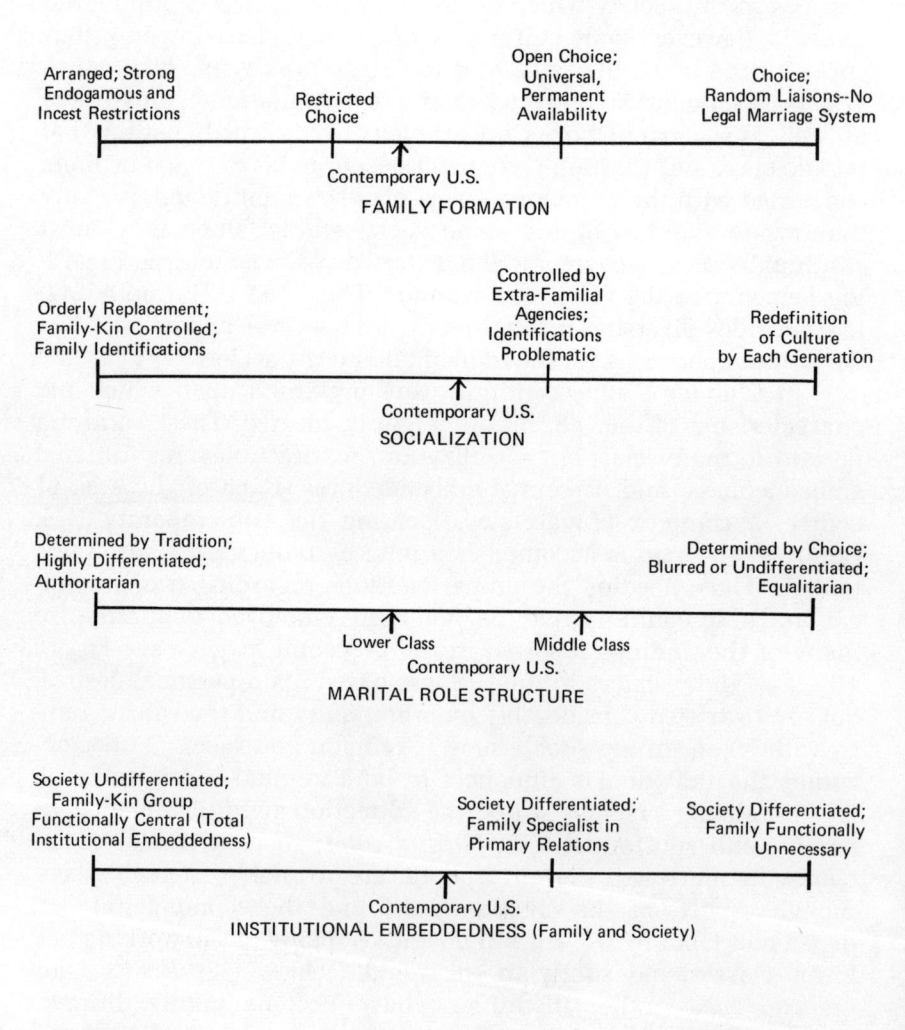

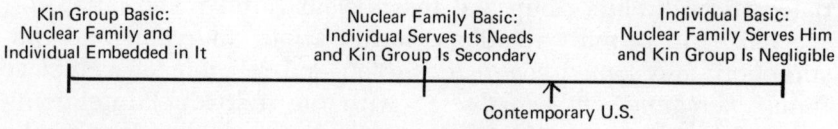

Arranged; Strong Endogamous and Incest Restrictions — Restricted Choice — *Contemporary U.S.* — Open Choice; Universal, Permanent Availability — Choice; Random Liaisons--No Legal Marriage System

FAMILY FORMATION

Orderly Replacement; Family-Kin Controlled; Family Identifications — Controlled by Extra-Familial Agencies; Identifications Problematic *Contemporary U.S.* — Redefinition of Culture by Each Generation

SOCIALIZATION

Determined by Tradition; Highly Differentiated; Authoritarian — Lower Class — Middle Class — Determined by Choice; Blurred or Undifferentiated; Equalitarian

Contemporary U.S.

MARITAL ROLE STRUCTURE

Society Undifferentiated; Family-Kin Group Functionally Central (Total Institutional Embeddedness) — Society Differentiated; Family Specialist in Primary Relations — Society Differentiated; Family Functionally Unnecessary

Contemporary U.S.

INSTITUTIONAL EMBEDDEDNESS (Family and Society)

Kin Group Basic: Nuclear Family and Individual Embedded in It — Nuclear Family Basic: Individual Serves Its Needs and Kin Group Is Secondary — Individual Basic: Nuclear Family Serves Him and Kin Group Is Negligible

Contemporary U.S.

PERSONNEL EMBEDDEDNESS

serving the individual's needs for personality development and uniqueness—are currently vying for value ascendency in U.S. society, with the kin network playing a supportive role in the background.

SECTION TWO

THE FUTURE PROSPECTS FOR THE U.S. FAMILY

During the 1930's and 1940's, Carle Zimmerman, Pitirim Sorokin, and others analyzed the changes that had occurred in the U.S. family since the nineteenth century, and concluded that its future was one of *disintegration*. Zimmerman summarized such predictions in 1949:

> The influence of these gradual developments during several centuries, and the recent upheavals, have given us a plethora of unusual family behavior in recent years. Some persons see these changes as "progress," or the breaking through toward a new and more interesting family system. Others, including the writer, look upon it as a polarization of values typical of the breakdown of a family system. . . .
> We must look upon the present confusion of family values as the beginning of violent breaking up of a system. The mores or social forces present when it rose to power now no longer exist. Negative polarization is here because the crisis is at hand.[3]

Just as Vance Packard speaks of changes in the sexual sphere as a "wilderness," and other authors describe today's marital role choices as "problems," "predicaments," or "dilemmas," so these earlier authors were convinced that changes in the nineteenth and twentieth centuries were negative in their import and signalled the disintegration of the family as we know it.

In the mid-1940's, Ernest Burgess and Harvey Locke responded to these dire predictions by asserting that the U.S. family is not disintegrating, but is *reorganizing* with characteristics that approximate the companionship family. "Family reorganization," the authors claimed,

> may be considered in its two aspects: (1) the checking of tendencies to disorganization in the individual family

and its reshaping through the redefining of attitudes and values of the husband and wife and parents and children; and (2) the development in society of a new conception of the family which its members individually and collectively attempt to realize.[4]

The family would stabilize, they felt, within 20 to 30 years, due to education, more security in the economy, and a slowing down of immigration and population increase. From the time of writing, this meant that stability should be reached between 1965 and 1975. In addition, Burgess and Locke saw certain trends of the early 1940's as continuing into the future, among them: (1) a declining birth rate and smaller sized families; (2) continuing increase in the proportion married among those of marriageable age; (3) a lowering of the age at marriage, coincident with family life education; (4) an increase in the employment of all women, including married women; and (5) continued decline in the family's historic functions in favor of emotional functions, such as happiness and companionship.

For some 20 years, the twin themes of disintegration and reorganization held sway within the family literature. During the 1960's, however, several authors took up once again the themes of projection and prediction, with the former based upon current statistical trends and the latter upon an informed survey of societal changes and their significance for the family. One of the more insightful recent projections was effected by Robert Parke and Paul Glick, working with 1960 census data. They agree with Burgess and Locke's projection of the proportion married, and continue it into the future; they find the age at marriage *increasing* and project this; and they find family size small and likely to remain at about the current level. In addition, they project other trends such as the following:

> Over and above any general decline in mortality, the declines in the difference between the ages of the husband and wife will reduce the frequency of widowhood and increase the proportion of couples who survive jointly to retirement age.
> . . . Declines in the relative frequency of divorce and separation should result to the extent that there are reductions in poverty and general improvements in the socioeconomic status of the population.[5]

While the projection of internal family trends performs a useful service for the student of the family, the more exciting and debatable (and perhaps foolhardy) predictions come from those who write about the future of the family on the basis of a holistic perspective and "informed conjecture." At times it is difficult to separate suggestions and criticisms from predictions, but we must attempt to do so. In the category of suggestions and criticisms would be the writings of neo-Freudians and Marxists, who decry the family's "corporate neurosis" and the "domestic slavery of the wife," as well as the family's barbarism and obsolescence.[6] In the same category, but vastly different in orientation, are appeals for scientific or government intervention on the family's behalf. Zimmerman and others wonder how the family can be kept from imminent disintegration without such intervention to strengthen familistic values.[7]

Such projections and suggestions form the backdrop against which predictions of the family's future have been attempted. Ivan Nye sees two possible value positions regarding the family which may be predictive of its future: one views the family as having *intrinsic* value and the other sees it as having *instrumental* value.[8] In the former case, the strengthening and preservation of the family is an end in itself. The purpose of the National Council on Family Relations, for example, is "to advance the cultural values now principally secured through family relations for personality development and the strength of the nation."[9] The maintaining of traditional family forms is inherently important to some members of society and to organizations such as the NCFR. Yet, despite the efforts of Carle Zimmerman, the NCFR, and other organizations and individuals, this intrinsic view hardly seems adequate as the basis for predicting the family's future in the U.S. Let us see why.

For many years the family has been considered important by many policy-makers, not because of its intrinsic worth as a social form, but because of the functions it performs for society and the individual—its instrumental value. Meyer Nimkoff, starting from such a perspective in his book *Comparative Family Systems*, draws several important conclusions regarding the future of the family in urban-industrial society. First, he says, the family has certain minimal functions that it is seemingly unable to yield to other societal institutions. These are reproduction and the early socialization of children. In societies such as that of early Communist Russia and the Israeli kibbutzim, in which institutional socialization has been attempted, the family as a system was seen to be necessary, says Nimkoff, and was, therefore, retained. Furthermore, he asserts, it is interesting that the family is so often blamed for the ills of society. One reason it is so blamed is that it is the primary social institution in virtually everyone's experience. Instead, it may actually be the most stable social insitituon of all. For, as Helmut Schelsky found in post-World War II Germany, when the economy and the state collapse, the family is frequently found to endure. When the rest of Germany was in a state of disintegration, the people retreated into their families and lived for them. In short, the family, Nimkoff asserts, persists and will persist because of its reproductive and socialization functions.[10]

If we grant Nimkoff's assumptions for the moment, we must still go on to ask him what sort of family is going to persist. A major influence in determining the family's character, he feels, will be abundant leisure for the masses. This will demand a reorientation of family values to include recreation and non-work activities as intrinsic values; whereas, until now, recreation has been looked upon—particularly by middle-class people—as preparation to work again. (The inability to find basic meaning in leisure is, of course, one fact behind a favorite term, "alienation," used to describe the modern industrial worker).[11] Some authors, as we noted in Chapter XI, even now decry the father who spends his at-home hours in playing with his offspring. However, if Nimkoff is correct in thinking that children must increasingly develop values in keeping with increased leisure time, so that they can "play without guilt," the "buddy" role on the part of the father may very well be one step in defining leisure as acceptable.

Nimkoff sees the developing play spirit of U.S. society as also extending to sex in marriage. Both males and females will increasingly seek gratification through sex in marriage. This prediction, made in 1964, is increasingly a "fait accompli" in middle-class families.[12]

Finally, because the economic function of the family is and will continue to be so minor, according to Nimkoff, the divorce rate will remain high. Although it is more difficult to sustain a modern marriage, the psychological rewards are probably greater for those who succeed, he feels. The family, therefore, plays an instrumental role in reproduction, socialization, leisure, and personality development; and, despite Nimkoff's comment regarding its minor economic role, the family's function as consumer must not be overlooked. A key reason why the family is valued by the politico-economic leaders of the society is that it is a focal point in consuming the goods of the market. In addition, many businesses have found that the happily-married man is a productive worker— that family life cannot be separated from work life. Thus, there are numerous instrumental functions performed by the nuclear family in contemporary society which give rise to efforts to conserve this system.

Besides the intrinsic or instrumental value of the family, a third basis for predicting the family's future derives from *individualistic* values. U.S. society, some would say, is increasingly concerned about individual development, individual adjustment, individual happiness—in short, about individual needs. What do I need; what works best for me? These are the sorts of questions being asked by many members of U.S. society today about the family and other institutions as well. It should be noted that the individualistic orientation is no more inherently destructive of the contemporary family than the "instrumental" viewpoint is inherently conservative of the family—a fact that will become more apparent below.

As we indicated in Chapter IX, with the absence of pregnancy fears, sexual adjustment prior to marriage is currently vying with sexual continence for value adherence. In fact, from an individualistic predictive standpoint, it seems probable that "the arrangement," or the sharing of domestic life between the unmarried, may become an increasingly popular way of engaging in sex before marriage. This, however, will be considered a "pre-marriage" and not as a replacement for the institution of marriage.

A more radical critique of the U.S. family has resulted in a small-scale movement toward the development of new *non-kin* communities. Sometimes urban, and stressing various kinds of experiences or social action; sometimes rural, resembling in many ways the old family-kin subsistence farm, the multifaceted communes of the late 1960's bespeak a substantial individual need for primary relationship experience beyond today's small nuclear family. At present, it seems unlikely that either the arrangement or the commune will have much immediate effect upon the family system, one reason being that this monogamous nuclear family is itself defined by the vast majority of persons as meeting many of their *individual* or personal needs for fulfillment.

There is, however, one further set of factors—that are not subsumed under the intrinsic, instrumental, or individual value approach—which may have a substantial long-range influence upon the family. In 1950 and again in 1960, Meyer Nimkoff previewed the advances in human biology that were being made at that time, in terms of their possible effects upon families. Improvements in contraception, artificial insemination, incubator birth (in which, after conception, the fetus resides outside the human body), control over the sex of the child, and work with sex hormones—although these processes are at different stages of development, all would seem to have implications for the family.[13] It is noteworthy that, when Nimkoff wrote about the persistence of the family for purposes of reproduction and early socialization, he ignored the possible repercussions of his earlier analyses of biological discoveries. If the preservation of the ovum were perfected, reproduction outside the family would become possible. And if it were found further that incubator fetuses were less likely to have birth defects and were more uniformly able to maximize the positive hereditary features of the two parents, then "instrumental" values might lead increasing numbers of society to a new view of "what works best."

Thus, on one side are those intrinsic, instrumental, and individual values that define the family as good: good in and of itself, good because of the functions it performs, or good for the individual. On the other side are those individualistic values that define the family as standing in the way of individual development or community, and those scientific discoveries that might alter the societal definition of what is instrumental or functional. At present, the strength of the former coalition of values is unquestionable. As Nye says:

> There is little doubt that the institution of the family is *here to stay*, not because this basic unit of social structure is valuable per se, but because it is instrumental in maintaining life itself, in shaping the infant into the person, and in providing for the security and affectional needs of people of all ages.[14]

In fact, the dominance of this value-set is likely to continue into the foreseeable future. However, one additional certainty is that scientific discovery does not "take a vacation" simply because people's values are unprepared for its implications. A second fact that is almost as certain is that value systems do, sooner or later, incorporate and utilize the discoveries of science.[15] In a segment of social life such as the family, which is infused with much positive value, the incorporation of these sorts of developments is likely to be a slow and painful process, but not postponed indefinitely.

The future of the family, therefore, will be a result of the interplay between three types of values and scientific discovery. The multiple definitions of the family as "good" give rise to continual attempts at consistency, though there will continue to be strains and inconsistencies within the family system as well. Barring a major historical upheaval,[16] the family as described herein is likely to persist over the next generation, making concessions (once thought to be signs of disintegration) here and there to new definitions of individual and societal need—in pre-marital sex, divorce law, even in the areas of abortion and extra-marital sex.[17] Yet, most readers of this volume will enter marriage, with all of its intensity, choices, and uncertainties, with the hope that the family they help to create will be a constant source of excitement, fulfillment, and satisfaction to all its members.

NOTES

[1] Functionalists, such as Talcott Parsons, have often written to show how well particular characteristics of U.S. family and kin behavior fit that society's needs. Three good examples are: Talcott Parsons, "The Kinship System of the Contemporary United States," *American Anthropologist*, 45 (1943), 22–38; Parsons and Renee C. Fox, "Illness, Therapy, and the Modern Urban American Family," *Journal of Social Issues*, 13 (1952), 31–44; and Elaine Cumming and William Henry, *Growing Old: The Process of Disengagement* (New York: Basic Books, 1961).

[2] This does not, then, disagree with the assertion made by Billingsley with which we concurred in Chapter VI to the effect that blacks are becoming increasingly an ethnic group and sub*society* in the United States.

[3] Carle C. Zimmerman, *The Family of Tomorrow* (New York: Harper and Brothers, 1949), pp. 200–10; see also Carle C. Zimmerman, *Family and Civilization* (New York: Harper and Brothers, 1947); and Pitirim A. Sorokin, *Social and Cultural Dynamics*, 4 vols. (New York: American Book, 1937).

[4] Ernest Burgess and Harvey Locke, *The Family: From Institution to Companionship* (New York: American Book, 1945), p. 708.

[5] Robert Parke, Jr., and Paul C. Glick, "Prospective Changes in Marriage and the Family," *Journal of Marriage and the Family*, 29 (1967), 256.

[6] Frederick Engels, *The Origin of the Family, Private Property, and the State* (New York: International Publishers, 1942), p. 65; and Barrington Moore, *Political Power and Social Theory* (Cambridge, Mass.: Harvard University Press, 1958), pp. 160–78. See also the writings of Norman Brown and Herbert Marcuse.

[7] Zimmerman, *The Family of Tomorrow*, pp. 234f.

[8] F. Ivan Nye, "Values, Family, and a Changing Society," *Journal of Marriage and the Family*, 29 (1967), 241–48.

[9] See the inside cover of *Journal of Marriage and the Family*.

[10] M. F. Nimkoff, ed., *Comparative Family Systems* (Boston: Houghton Mifflin, 1965), pp. 357–62; see also Helmut Schelsky, "The Family in Germany," *Marriage and Family Living*, 16 (1954), 331–35.

[11] For a lengthy discussion of alienation, see Kenneth Keniston, *The Uncommitted* (New York: Dell, 1960), Appendix.

[12] Nimkoff, *Comparative Family Systems,* pp. 365–69.

[13] Nimkoff, "Biological Discoveries and the Future of the Family: A Reappraisal," *Social Forces,* 41 (1962), 121–27.

[14] Nye, "Values, Family, and a Changing Society," p. 248.

[15] One of the more interesting cases in point is the discovery and eventual acceptance of anesthesia within the value system of modern man. For a generation after anesthesia was developed and usable, it was kept from the public by those who argued on Biblical and other grounds that it was an immoral creation.

[16] On historical upheavals and the difficulty of long-range forecasting, see Bernard Farber, *Family: Organization and Interaction* (San Francisco: Chandler, 1964), pp. 279–80.

[17] Besides those authors discussed in this chapter, many others have, during the 1960's, tried their hand at predicting the family's future. The following articles are both informative and helpful as supplements to the present analysis. Margaret Mead, "The Life Cycle and Its Variations: The Division of Roles," *Daedalus,* (1967), 871–75; Reuben Hill, "The American Family of the Future," *Journal of Marriage and the Family,* 26 (1964), 20–28; Otto Pollak, "The Outlook for the American Family," *Journal of Marriage and the Family,* 29 (1967), 193–205; Charles W. Hobart, "Commitment, Value Conflict, and the Future of the American Family," *Marriage and Family Living,* 25 (1963), 405–12; and John N. Edwards, "The Future of the Family Revisited," *Journal of Marriage and the Family,* 29 (1967), 505–11.

Author Index

Aberle, D. F. *et al.*, 100n
Abrahams, D'arcy, 201n
Adams, Bert N., 155n, 202n, 296n, 297n, 317n
Adams, Charles F., 61, 67
Adelson, Joseph and Douvan, Elizabeth, 161–63, 168, 170, 174n
Albrecht, Ruth, 317n
Angell, Robert C., 327, 344n
Ariès, Philippe, 57, 76n
Aronson, Vera, 201n
Axelson, Leland J., 257n

Bachofen, J. J., 4
Backman, Carl W., 231n
Bacon, Selden D., 344n
Bakke, E. Wight, 320–21, 344n
Bales, Robert, 241
Ballweg, John A., 311–12, 317n
Banks, Franklin, 231n
Barclay, Dorothy, 256n
Bardis, Panos D., 76n
Barth, Frederik, 34n
Bates, Alan, 184–85
Bayer, Alan E., 184, 188, 201n
Bee, Lawrence S. and Schellenberg, James A., 215, 232n
Bell, Norman W., 344n
Bennett, John W., 107–08, 131n
Benson, Purnell, 213–14, 232n
Berardo, Felix M. and Nye, F. Ivan, 14n
Berger, Bennett M., 155n, 164–65, 171, 174n
Bernard, Jessie, 117, 121, 123, 125, 132n, 229, 233n
Bessner, Arthur, 131n

Bettelheim, Bruno, 256n
Billingsley, Andrew, 119, 121, 123–26, 128–30, 132n, 133n, 233n, 359n
Blake, Nelson Manfred, 345n
Blau, Peter M., 196, 202n
Blau, Zena Smith, 123, 132n, 310, 317n
Blood, Robert O., Jr., 179, 200n
Blood, Robert O., Jr. and Wolfe, Donald M., 256n, 259–65, 269, 274n, 275n, 293, 298n
Blumberg, Rae Lesser, 101n, 297n
Boggs, Keith S., 345n
Bolton, Charles D., 214, 220–21, 223–24, 232n
Borgatta, Edgar, 175n
Borgatta, Marie L. and Hadden, Jeffrey K., 202n, 265, 275n
Bossard, James H. S., 9, 207, 230n
Bott, Elizabeth, 285, 297n
Bowerman, Charles E. and Day, Barbara R., 215, 232n
Bowlby, John, 154n
Bradburn, Norman and Orden, Susan, 251, 253, 257n
Brattrud, Audrey, 131n
Brenton, Myron, 246, 248–49, 257n, 268, 275n
Brim, Orville G., Jr., 142, 154n, 155n
Brody, Grace F., 151
Bronfenbrenner, Urie, 150–51, 155n
Broom, Leonard, 100n
Brown, James S., 296n
Bullock, Samuel C., 344n

AUTHOR INDEX

Burchinal, Lee G., 231, 297n, 346n
Burgess, Ernest W., 5, 83–84, 89–90, 99, 100n, 243, 256n, 257n, 344n, 345n, 346n
Burgess, Ernest and Locke, Harvey J., 325, 341–42, 353–54, 359n
Burgess, Ernest and Wallin, Paul, 215–17, 231n, 232n, 311
Butler, James E., 155n
Bynder, Herbert, 101n

Calhoun, Arthur W., 77n
Campisi, Paul J., 113–14, 132n
Caplow, Theodore and Kirkpatrick, Clifford, 183, 200n
Carmichael, Stokely, 133n
Catton, William R., 34n
Cavan, Ruth Shonle, 102–03, 107, 113, 131n, 229, 233n, 311
Cavan, Ruth Shonle and Ranck, Katherine Howland, 330, 344n, 345n
Cayton, Horace and Drake, St. Clair, 228, 233n
Chancellor, Loren E., 231n
Chilman, Catherine S., 125, 132n
Centers, Richard, 231n
Christensen, Harold T., 6–8, 14n, 78n, 100n, 131n, 346n
Christensen, James Boyd, 23, 33n
Clague, Alice J., 343n
Clark, Burton, 175n
Clausen, John A., 256n, 344n
Clough, Shepard, 275n
Coleman, James, 164–65, 174n
Cooley, Charles H., 5, 88, 138, 154n
Coombs, Robert H., 212, 231n
Cottrell, Leonard S., 100n
Cuber, John F. and Harroff, Peggy B., 267, 275n
Cumming, Elaine *et al.*, 300, 302, 304, 316n, 317n
Cumming, Elaine and Henry, William, 304, 309, 315, 316n, 317n, 359n
Cutler, Beverly R. and Dyer, William G., 271, 275n

Dai, Bingham, 154n
Darwin, Charles, 4
Davidson, Maria, 318n
Davies, Rodger P., 281, 296n
Davis, Alan and Kerckhoff, Alan, 219–22
Davis, Keith E. and Kerckhoff, Alan, 219–22, 232n
Davis, Kingsley, 27, 33n, 81, 83, 167, 175n, 225–29
Day, Barbara R. and Bowerman, Charles E., 215, 232n
Day, Lincoln H., 340, 346n
Dean, Lois R., 316n
Dentler, Robert A., 275n
Deutsch, Morton, 154n
Deutscher, Irwin, 294, 298n, 300–04, 316n
Dewey, John, 153
Dinitz, Simon, 231n
Dinkel, Robert M., 317n
Dorjahn, Vernon, 33n
Douvan, Elizabeth and Adelson, Joseph, 161–63, 168–70, 174n
Dow, Thomas W., Jr., 326, 345n
Drabek, Thomas E., 345n
Drake, St. Clair and Cayton, Horace, 228, 233n
Dunsing, Marilyn M. and Hafstrom, Jeanne L., 251–52, 257n, 258n
Durkheim, Emile, 79, 85, 87–90, 101n
Duvall, Evelyn Millis, 153, 155n, 293, 297n, 298n
Dyer, Everett D., 343n
Dyer, William G., 261, 274n, 275n
Dyer, William G. and Cutler, Beverly R., 271, 275n

Eckland, Bruce K., 209–10, 212, 215, 217, 231n, 232n
Edlin, Sarah, 345n
Edwards, Harry, 132n
Edwards, John N., 101n, 360n
Eggan, Fred, 281, 296n
Ehrmann, Winston, 190–91, 201n
Elder, Glen H., Jr., 175n, 186, 201n, 256n

Elkin, Frederick, 154n, 174n
Elkins, Stanley M., 116–17, 132n
Ellis, Albert, 194–95
Engels, Friedrich, 2, 4, 13n, 359n
Erikson, Erik, 236
Eshleman, J. Ross, 346n

Farber, Bernard, 14n, 77n, 82–84, 91, 93, 98, 100n, 150, 155n, 162, 174n, 175n, 177, 205, 211, 214, 222–23, 231n, 269, 271, 275n, 335, 344n, 345n, 360n
Farber, Seymour F., 77n, 257n, 297n, 345n
Farnham, Marynia, 257n
Fava, Sylvia F., 201n, 275n
Foster, Henry, 337
Foster, Henry H., Jr. and Freed, Doris Jonas, 334–39, 345n, 346n
Fox, J. Robin, 27, 29–32, 33n, 281–82, 296n
Fox, Renée C., 344n, 359n
Frazier, E. Franklin, 117, 120–24, 132n
Freed, Doris Jonas and Foster, Henry H., Jr., 334–39, 345n, 346n
Freedman, Maurice, 43ff., 51, 54n, 58, 64, 75, 89
Freud, Sigmund, 3, 29–30, 32, 33n, 38, 153, 267
Friedan, Betty, 250, 257n
Friedenberg, Edgar, 3, 171–73, 175n
Friesen, David, 165, 175n
Fromm, Erich, 275n
Furstenberg, Frank F., Jr., 77n

Geiger, H. Kent, 233n
Getzels, J. W., 257n
Gianopoulos, Artie, 257n
Gibson, Geoffrey, 344n
Glassers, Paul and Glassers, Lois, 308, 316n, 317n
Glick, Paul C., 300
Glick, Paul C. and Parke, Robert, Jr., 354, 359n

Goode, William J., 6, 8, 65, 77n, 81, 82, 96, 100n, 205–06, 230n, 257n, 260, 274n, 276n, 296n, 335–36, 338, 343n, 344n, 346n
Goodman, Louis Wolf, 101n, 200n
Goodman, Norman and Ofshe, Richard, 271, 275n
Goodman, Paul, 3
Gordon, Albert I., 231n
Gordon, Michael, 156n
Gorer, Geoffrey, 178, 182, 200n
Gottlieb, David and Ramsey, Charles, 164–66, 174n, 175n
Gough, Kathleen, 36–39, 54n
Gray, Horace, 232n
Gray, S. W., 155n
Green, Arnold W., 151–52, 155n
Greenfield, Sydney, 77n
Greer, Scott, 297n
Grinnell, G. B., 154n
Gross, Paul S., 108, 131n
Guyon, René, 195

Habakkuk, H. J., 77n
Hadden, Jeffrey K. and Borgatta, Marie L., 202n, 265, 275n
Hadden, Jeffrey K. and Hagstrom, Warren O., 283, 284, 296n
Hafstrom, Jeanne L. and Dunsing, Marilyn M., 251–52, 257n, 258n
Hagstrom, Warren O. and Hadden, Jeffrey K., 283–84, 296n
Hallenbeck, Phyllis N., 274n
Haller, A. O., 296n
Hamilton, Charles V., 133n
Hansen, Donald, 8–10
Hansen, Donald and Hill, Reuben, 14n
Harroff, Peggy B. and Cuber, John F., 267, 275n
Hartley, Eugene L., 155n, 174n
Hartley, Ruth E., 275n
Havighurst, Robert, 302
Heer, David M., 231n, 233n, 274n
Hefner, Hugh, 195
Heise, David, 192

AUTHOR INDEX

Henry, William and Cumming, Elaine, 304, 309, 315, 316n, 317n, 359n
Herberg, Will, 114, 132n, 231n
Herman, Robert D., 181–82, 200n
Herskovitz, Melville J., 117–18, 132n
Hill, Herma Kay, 77n
Hill, Reuben, 6, 8–10, 256n, 297n, 312, 317n, 320–21, 326, 344n, 345n, 360n
Hill, Reuben and Hansen, Donald, 14n
Hill, Reuben and Katz, Alvin, 207, 230n
Himmelhoch, Jerome, 201n, 275n
Hobart, Charles W., 360n
Hobart, Charles W. and Kephart, William, 311
Hobart, Charles and Kirkpatrick, Clifford, 217–18, 232n
Hobbs, Daniel F., Jr., 343n, 345n
Hoffman, Dean K., 274n
Hoffman, Lois Wladis, 250, 254, 257n, 258n, 262, 274n
Hollingshead, August B., 155n, 210–11, 231n
Homans, George C. and Schneider, David, 282–83, 296n
Hostetler, John, 108–09, 131n
Hunt, Morton M., 76n, 332, 337, 345n, 346n
Hunt, T. C., 231n
Huntington, Gertrude Enders, 131n

Irelan, Lola M., 131n
Irving, Washington, 77n

Jackson, Jacquelyne, 297n
Jackson, Joan K., 320–21, 344n
Jacobson, Paul H., 257n, 329, 333, 344n, 345n
Jones, Donald S., 154n
Jones, Jenkin Lloyd, 201n

Katz, Alvin and Hill, Reuben, 207, 230n
Keniston, Kenneth, 171, 174n, 175n, 359n

Kenkel, William F., 260, 274n
Kephart, William, 180, 200n, 201n, 223, 233n
Kephart, William and Hobart, Charles, 311
Kerckhoff, Alan and Davis, Keith E., 219, 220, 221, 222, 232n
King, Martin Luther, 129
Kinsey, Alfred C., 158, 174n, 189–90, 197, 201n, 267, 275n
Kirkendall, Lester, 194–95, 201n
Kirkpatrick, Clifford, 167–68, 175n, 340, 346n
Kirkpatrick, Clifford and Caplow, Theodore, 183, 200n
Kirkpatrick, Clifford and Hobart, Charles, 217–18, 232n
Klaus, R., 155n
Kleemeier, Robert W., 317n
Klemer, Richard, 201n
Knudsen, Dean D., 78n, 201n, 202n, 275n
Kohn, Melvin L., 146–47, 151, 155n, 264, 275n
Komarovsky, Mirra, 131n, 163, 174n, 253, 256n, 257n, 267, 272, 275n, 293–94, 297n, 298n, 344n
Koos, Earl Lomon, 344n, 345n
Krauss, Robert M., 154n
Krech, Hilda Sidney, 251–52, 257n
Kroeber, Alfred L., 281, 296n
Ktsanes, Thomas and Ktsanes, Virginia, 215, 232n
Kwan, Kian M. and Shibutani, Tamotsu, 113, 131n

Lambert, William W., 175n
Landers, Ann, 2
Landis, Judson T. and Landis, Mary G., 294, 298n
Lantz, Herman et al., 69, 77n, 112, 274n
Layard, John, 33n
Leach, Edmund, 2
Lee, S. C., 131n

AUTHOR INDEX 365

Leichter, Hope Jensen and Mitchell, William E., 292, 297n, 298n
Leik, Robert, 242, 256n
LeMasters, E. E., 325, 343n, 345n
Le Play, Frederic, 4
Leslie, Gerald, 14n, 76n, 133n, 191, 231n
Levinger, George, 336, 346n
Lewis, Lionel S., 283, 296n
Linton, Ralph, 131n
Litwak, Eugene, 297n, 339, 346n
Locke, Harvey J., 100n, 231n, 245, 256n, 271, 275n, 344n, 345n, 346n
Locke, Harvey J. and Burgess, Ernest, 325, 341–42, 359n
Lowie, Robert, 28, 33n
Lowrie, Samuel H., 183, 200n, 336, 346n
Luckey, Eleanor Braun, 232n
Ludwig, Edward G., 344n
Lundberg, Ferdinand, 257n
Lynn, David B., 142, 155n

Maccoby, Eleanor E., 155n, 174n
Mace, David, 194
MacIver, Robert, 13, 14n
Malinowski, Bronislaw, 201n, 282n
Mangalam, Joseph J., 296n
Mange, Arthur P., 109, 131n
Marcus, Peggy S., 297n
Marris, Peter, 346n
Marx, Karl, 3
Mazur, Ronald M., 77n
McDaniel, Clyde O., 182–83, 200n
McGinley, Phyllis, 250, 257n
Mead, George Herbert, 138, 154n
Mead, Margaret, 13n, 134–36, 154n, 158, 174n, 360n
Meissner, Hanna H., 346n
Merton, Don and Schwartz, Gary, 164, 168, 174n
Merton, Robert K., 100n, 344n
Messer, Mark, 303, 310, 316n, 317n
Middleton, Russell, 33n, 101n, 296n

Middleton, Russell and Putney, Snell, 261–62, 274n
Miller, Daniel and Swanson, Guy, 146, 155n
Mirande, Alfred M., 202n
Mitchell, Howard E., 257n
Mitchell, William E. and Leichter, Hope Jensen, 292, 297n, 298n
Mogey, J. M., 257n
Monahan, Thomas P., 335, 345n, 346n
Moore, Barrington, 3, 295, 298n, 359n
Morgan, Lewis Henry, 4, 281
Morioka, Kiyomi, 14n
Motz, Annabelle Bender, 244–45, 254, 256n, 264, 269
Moynihan, Daniel P., 120, 122, 126, 128, 132n
Mudd, Emily H., 344n
Murdock, George Peter, 17, 28, 33n, 36, 39, 81, 83, 189, 201n, 281, 296n, 331, 345n
Murstein, Bernard I., 233n
Musgrove, Frank, 101n, 155n, 157, 158, 166, 172, 174n, 175n, 233n
Mustacchi, Piero, 77n, 175n, 257n, 297n, 345n
Myrdal, Gunnar, 225–26, 228, 233n

Nass, Gilbert and Skipper, James, 180, 187, 200n, 201n
Neubeck, Gerhard, 343n
Neugarten, Bernice L., 236–39, 256n, 300, 311, 316n
Newcombe, Theodore M., 155n, 174n
Newell, David S., 316n
Nimkoff, Meyer F., 8, 33n, 77n, 101n, 296n, 307, 311–12, 317n, 355–58, 359n, 360n
Nisbet, Robert N., 54n, 344n
Nye, F. Ivan, 251–52, 257n, 258n, 274n, 338, 346n, 355, 358, 359n, 360n

Nye, F. Ivan and Berardo, Felix M., 14n

Ofshe, Richard and Goodman, Norman, 271, 275n
Ogburn, William F., 77n, 78n, 79, 83–84, 89–90, 99, 100n
Olsen, Marvin, 263, 264, 274n
O'Neill, William L., 199, 202n, 332, 337, 344n, 345n, 346n
Orden, Susan and Bradburn, Norman, 251, 253, 257n
Ort, Robert, 245, 256n

Packard, Vance, 196–97, 202n, 353
Parke, Robert, Jr. and Glick, Paul C., 354, 359n
Parsons, Talcott, 31–32, 33n, 241–43, 256n, 286–87, 296n, 297n, 304, 344n, 359n
Pasamanick, Benjamin, 231n
Pavela, Todd, 229, 233n
Peterson, James A., 334–36, 345n, 346n
Peterson, Warren A. and Rose, Arnold M., 301–03, 316n, 317n
Philbert, Michel A. J., 300, 316n
Pineo, Peter, 275, 311, 317n
Pittman, David J., 344n
Plateris, Alexander, 333
Poffenberger, Thomas, 201n
Pollak, Otto, 360n
Pope, Hallowell, 201n, 345n
Porter, Blaine, 202n
Porter, Katherine Anne, 255, 258n
Putney, Snell and Middleton, Russell, 261–62, 274n

Radcliffe-Brown, A. R., 281–82, 296n
Rainwater, Lee, 122, 125–26, 132n, 148, 155n, 257n, 265, 275n
Ramsey, Charles and Gottlieb, David, 164–66, 174n, 175n

Ranck, Katherine Howland and Cavan, Ruth Shonle, 330, 344n, 345n
Rapoport, Rhona and Rapoport, Robert, 236, 256n, 257n, 276n
Redlich, F. C., 155n
Reiss, Ira L., 6, 39, 54n, 81–83, 100n, 180, 190, 198, 200n, 201n, 202n
Reiss, Paul J. and Sussman, Marvin, 287, 297n, 298n
Rheinstein, Max, 332, 339, 345n
Richardson, Arthur H., 231n
Riesman, David, 146–47, 155n
Roberts, Robert W., 345n
Robins, Lee N. and Tomanec, Miroda, 285, 296n, 297n
Rodman, Hyman, 256n, 346n
Rose, Arnold M., 298n, 316n
Rose, Arnold M. and Peterson, Warren A., 301–03, 316n, 317n
Rosenfeld, Henry, 19, 33n, 59, 75, 95
Rosow, Irving, 302–03, 305, 310, 316n, 317n
Rossi, Alice, 243, 256n, 283, 294, 296n, 298n, 325, 345n
Rottman, Leon, 201n
Rubenstein, Betty B., 346n
Rubin, Isadore, 194, 197, 201n

Salinger, J. D., 159–61, 174n
Sarbin, Theodore R., 154n
Scanzoni, John, 320, 344n
Schellenberg, James A. and Bee, Lawrence S., 215, 232n
Schelsky, Helmut, 118, 122, 132n, 356
Schindler, John A., 256n
Schneider, David M., 11, 14n, 278, 285, 291, 296n, 297n, 316n
Schneider, David M. and Homans, George, 282–83, 296n
Schur, Edwin, 202n
Schwartz, Gary and Merten, Don, 164, 168, 174n
Schwarzweller, Harry K., 296n

AUTHOR INDEX

Sears, Robert et al., 150
Secord, Paul F., 231n
Seiden, Rita and Smigel, Erwin, 191–94, 201n
Shanas, Ethel et al., 297n, 302–03, 307–08, 314, 316n, 317n
Shaw, George Bernard, 213
Shibutani, Tamotsu and Kwan, Kian M., 113, 131n
Simmons, Leo William, 314, 318n
Sirjamaki, John, 9, 14n
Skard, Aase Gruda, 254, 258n
Skipper, James and Nass, Gilbert, 180, 187, 200n, 201n
Smelser, Neil J., 77n, 242
Smigel, Erwin and Seiden, Rita, 191–94, 201n
Smith, Anthony J., 231n
Smith, Harold W., 312, 317n
Snyder, Charles R., 344n
Snyder, Eloise C., 212, 216, 220, 232n
Sorokin, Pitirim A., 2, 353, 359n
Spock, Benjamin, 151, 153, 156n
Sprey, Jetse, 320–21, 344n
Stephens, William N., 42, 54n, 101n
Stiles, Henry Reed, 77n
Stokes, Walter, 194–95, 202n
Straus, Murray A., 175n
Strauss, Anselm, 215–17, 232n
Streib, Gordon F., 297, 308, 316n, 317n
Streib, Gordon F., and Thompson, Wayne E., 313, 317n
Strodtbeck, Fred L., 260, 262, 274n
Stryker, Sheldon, 293, 298n
Stuckert, Robert, 245, 256n
Sussman, Marvin B., 185, 201n, 274n, 297n, 345n
Sussman, Marvin and Reiss, Paul, 287, 297n
Swanson, Guy and Miller, Daniel, 146, 155n

Tallman, Irving, 344n
Talmon, Yonina, 101n

Tennyson, Alfred, 76n
Ternan, Louis, 190
Thomas, John L., 210–11, 231n
Thomas, W. I., 5
Thomason, Bruce, 266–67, 275n
Thomes, Mary Margaret, 100n, 271, 231n, 256–57n, 275n, 342, 344–46n
Thompson, Wayne E. and Streib, Gordon F., 313, 317n
Tomanec, Miroda and Robins, Lee N., 285, 296n, 297n
Trow, Martin, 175n

Udry, J. Richard, 215–17, 232n, 335, 346n
Underhill, Ruth M., 35, 54n, 296n
Urban, Dick, 261, 274n, 275n

Vernon, Glenn M., 231n
Ventura, Stephanie J., 343n
Vincent, Clark E., 91–92, 101n, 344n
Vogel, Ezra F., 344n

Wallace, Mike, 256n
Waller, Willard, 178–79, 182–83, 200n, 235, 256n, 317n, 344n
Wallin, Paul, 294, 297n, 298n
Wallin, Paul and Burgess, Ernest W., 215–17, 231–32n, 311
Walster, Elaine et al., 186, 201n
Warner, W. Lloyd, 24
Watson, John B., 153
Westermarck, Edward, 4, 28, 30, 32, 33n
Westley, William A., 174n
Wheeler, Stanton, 154n
Williams, Robin M., Jr., 154n, 275n
Willmott, Peter and Young, Michael, 289, 293, 297n, 298n
Wilson, Roger H. L., 77n, 175n, 257n, 297n, 345n
Winch, Robert F., 6, 8, 101n, 142, 155n, 180, 200n, 206, 214–

Winch, Robert F., (*continued*)
 15, 218–19, 230n, 232n, 246, 257n, 297n
Winick, Charles, 242, 256n, 273, 276n
Winter, Gibson, 275n
Wirth, Louis, 286, 297n
Wolfe, Donald M. and Blood, Robert O., Jr., 256n, 259–65, 269, 274n, 275n, 293, 298n
Wolfenstein, Martha, 153, 155n
Wrong, Dennis H., 154n, 276n

Yancey, William L., 132n
Yarrow, Marion Radke *et al.*, 253, 258n, 344n
Young, Frank, 29, 31–32, 33n
Young, Leontine, 345n
Young, Michael and Willmott, Peter, 289, 293, 297n, 298n

Zelditch, Morris, 78n, 87, 241–43, 256n
Zimmerman, Carle, 2, 353, 355, 359n

Subject Index

Absence of male in Afro-American family, 120, 122
Achievement in Afro-American family, 120
Adaptation, 92
    role of family in, 92
Adjustment in old age, 305–06
Adolescence, 157–74
    as a period of physical maturation, 157
    as a process, 161–70
    behavioral autonomy in, 162
    conflict with parents, 167–70
    definition of roles in, 165–66
    emancipation process in, 162–64
    emotional autonomy in, 162
    generation gap in, 167–70
    in college, 170–71
    in contemporary U.S., 158, 169–70, 172–74
    in Hutterite family, 111
    value autonomy in, 162
Adolescent as ideal-type, 159–61
    definition, 157
Affective function of family, 93
African family
    polygyny in, 117
African social organization, 117
Afro-American family
    absence of male, 120, 122
    achievement, 120
    disintegration, 120
    illegitimacy in, 121–22
    instability, 130
    matricentrism, 120
    matrifocality in, 122–23
    Moynihan report, 121–22, 126

Afro-American family (*continued*)
    nuclear family in, 121
    role of women in, 120–23
    role segregation in, 122
    today, 120–30
Afro-American slave family, 116–19
Afro-American culture
    acculturated, 123
    externally adapted, 123
Afro-American history, 116–19
Afro-American leaders, goals of
    assimilation, 128–29
    power, 129
    separation, 129
Afro-American subculture, 115
Afro-Americans, 105
    ethnic identification of, 124–26
    occupational discrimination, 125–26
Age segregation, 306–11
Aging
    in contemporary U.S. family, 299–316
    in Hutterite society, 112
    marital relations in, 306
    residential decisions in, 306
    social networks in, 306
    socialization in, 304–06
American colonial family
    functional centrality in, 63–64
    institutional embeddedness in, 63–64
American colonial family life
    influence of European traditions, 59
American colonial society
    child's position in, 62

American colonial society
  (*continued*)
  family life in, 59–64
  formal education in, 63
  health care in, 63
  institutions in, 63
  power of female in, 61
  protection in, 63
  recreation in, 63
  religion in, 63
  role of mother, 62
  romantic love in, 60
American contemporary family
  adolescence in, 169–70, 172–74
  and love and mate selection, 203–30
  antecedents of, 55–76
  changes in, 64–75
  cultural forms of, 102
  divorce in, 70
  formation of nuclear family units, 66–67
  frameworks for study, 8–10
  historical developments in mate selection, 177–78
  household in, 18
  husband-wife power relationships in, 69–70
  internal changes, 68–69
  marital breakup, 70
  position of women in society, 71–72
  pre-colonial influences, 55–59
  premarital sex in, 176–200
  relation of change to industrialization, 65–66
  relation of nuclear family to external world, 72–73
  socialization in, 143-54
  subcultural models, 103
  summary and review, 349–53
American contemporary society
  changing sex codes, 67
  dating in, 67
  education in, 74
  health care in, 74
  institutional differentiation in, 74–75
  mate selection in, 67
  premarital behavior in, 67
American contemporary society
  (*continued*)
  protection in, 74
  recreation in, 74
  religion in, 74
American Indians
  incest taboos in, 30
  kin terms, 281
  socialization process in, 136–37
Amish, 107, 115
Anabaptist, 107
Andaman Islanders
  kin function, 279
Antecedents of the family, 10
Arab village, 19–20
  family structures in, 19
Arapesh, 135, 137
Arranged marriage, 58
  as type of mate selection, 176
Assimilation, 113–15
  of Afro-American subculture, 124
Authority in family, 24
Availability, permanent, 84–85
Avunculocal residence, 22

Back to Africa movement, 129
Behavioral autonomy
  in adolescence, 162
Bilateral descent, 22
  in United States, 22–23
Bilocality, 21
Black American family.
  See Afro-American family.
Black cultural style, 126
Black Muslims, 123, 129
Bride price, 17

Causes of love in U.S., 205, 206
Challenges to family
  analysis of, 320–28
  death, 341–43
  definition (perception of stressor), 327–28
  divorce, 331–41
  economics, and employment, 329–31
  expected or unexpected, 325
  external vs. internal origin, 325
  family structure in network, 326

Challenges to family (*continued*)
  illegitimacy, 328–29
  internal family organization, 326–27
Chicago school of sociology, 5
China, pre-Communist
  family in, 19
China, classical
  family in, 19
  household pattern of, 19
  kin functions, 278
Child-rearing
  developmental view, 153
  traditional view, 153
Chinese
  family, system of, 35–36
  destruction by state, 49–50
  historical perspective, 43–52
  influence of economy, 51
  influence of marriage on family structure, 47
  institutional and personnel embeddedness in, 36
  kinship organization in, 42ff.
  male relationships in, 48
  of pre-Communist China, 42
  parallels to American family, 52
  patrilineage in, 42
  size of, 46
  woman's role in, 49
  woman's status in, 48
Chivalry, 58
Choice of marriage partner, 204
Choice, open, 98
Choice, restricted, 98
Class endogamy
  in Protestant and Jewish groups, 210
College adolescent, 170–71
College student
  four types, 171
Communal organization, 108
Communication in marriage, 271–74
  positive value of, 272
Concentration camps, Nazi, 166
Conceptual frameworks
  as description, 8
  in family study, 8

Conflict with parents
  in adolescence, 167–70
Conscience, 138–39
  relation to cultural homogeneity or heterogeneity, 139
Controls on love, 203–04
  incest taboo, 204
  prohibition of homosexuality, 204
Cross-cultural applicability of disengagement theory, 301–3
Cross-cultural context
  family study in, 3
Cultural differences among blacks, 124
Cultural universals, 102

Darwinism, social, 4
Dating
  as courtship, 179
  as courtship continuum, 193–94
  as form of recreation, 180
  as form of socialization, 180
  as status placement, 180
  for ego needs, 180
  for selection of a marriage partner, 181
  general functions of, 180–81
  intergroup or heterogeneous, 185–86
  nature and functions of, 178–84
  parental influence in, 184–85
  problematic aspects of, 184–88
  role of females in, 182–83
Dating continuum, 178–80
  stages and specific functions of, 181–84
Death as challenge to family, 341–43
Decision-making
  in Hutterite family, 108
Descent
  definition, 22
Deterioration, intrapsychic, 238
Deterioration processes, 237–38, 239
Developmental view of child-rearing, 153
Deviation, order of, 102

Discipline
   in Hutterite family, 109
Discrimination
   against Afro-Americans, 125, 128
Disengagement theory, 300–04
   cross-cultural applicability, 301–03
   of Cumming and Henry, 301, 304
Disintegration of family, 92–93
   in Afro-Americans, 120
Division of labor, 85–93
   in old age, 312
   specialization, 87–91
Divorce, 13, 93
   as challenge to family, 331–41
   difficulty of, 88
Divorce
   in American contemporary family, 70, 331–41
   causes of, 335–37
   laws, 339–41
   prevalence of, 333–35
   significance and effects, 337–41
Dominance of middle-class style, 95
Dominant life roles
   in American contemporary society, 302–03
Double descent, 23
Double standard, 190–91, 197
Doukhobors, 107

Economic responsibility
   in Hutterite family, 112
Economics and employment as challenge to family, 329–31
Education
   in American contemporary family, 74
Ego struggle, 139–40
Emancipation of slaves
   effects on family, 117–19
Emancipation process in adolescence, 162–64

Embeddedness
   institutional, 11, 12
   personnel, 11, 12
Emotional autonomy in adolescence, 162
Endogamy, class, 210
Enlightened asceticism, 194
Equalitarianism, 24
Escalators, in marriage, 220
   commitment, 220
   habitualized escalator, 220
   identity needs, 220–21
   image of partner, 221
   value-activity involvement, 220
Ethnic group
   definition, 113
Ethnic homogamy, 210
Ethnic identification
   among Afro-Americans, 124–26
Ethnic subculture, 113–30
   family values in, 115
Evolutionary theory, 4
Exogamy taboos, 96
Extra-marital sex, 93

Family, American contemporary.
   See American contemporary family
Family
   as institution, 1
   as occupational group, 87
   as social segment, 87
   as source of discontent, 2
   as specialists, 87–91
   as unity of interacting personalities, 5
   as victim of social change, 2
   bonds in industrial society, 86
   definition, 13
   division of labor in.
      See division of labor
   historical view of, 1
   in folklore, 4
   in modern industrial society, 1
   in post-World War II Germany, 118–19
   in U.S.
      See American contemporary family
   jokes about, 2

Family (*continued*)
  lower-class model, 103–07
  middle-class model, 103–07
  origins of, 104–07
  radical view of, 2
  scientific facts about, 5
  study of, 1–13
Family challenges, analysis, 320–28
  See also challenges to family
Family in the U.S.
  future of, 348–59
Family of orientation, 277
Family response to change, 319–43
Family roles
  lower-class, 106
  middle-class, 105
Family structure, 15–33
  varieties of, 104–07
Family study
  a-historical approach, 9
  developmental framework, 9
  factual, 3
  history, 4
  institutional approach, 9
  interactional approach, 8
  interpretations, 3
  other frameworks, 10
  present functional, 7
  present sociological, 7
  problem-oriented, 5, 6
  reform-oriented, 6
  respectability of, 6
  scientific, 5
  scientific viewpoint of, 6
  situational approach, 9
  social criticism, 3
  sociological, 3
  social psychological approach, 8
  structure-functional approach, 8
  systematic, 4
  theory building, 8
  three periods in, 4–12
  trends in, 6
Family system, 10
  characteristics of, 96–100

Family, types of, 18
  three-generation extended, 18
Family units
  formation of, 95
  persistence of, 95
Family varieties, 15–33
  exemplified, 35–54
Family-kin culture, 10
Family-kin unit, 86, 88
Formal education
  in American colonies, 63
Fun morality, 195
Function of family, 10, 79–100
  affection, 84
  affectivity, 93–94
  companionship, 84, 88
  economic consumer, 94
  inconsistency of, 95
  loss of, 91–92
  primary relationships, 93–94
  refuge, 88
  reproduction, 81–82
  varieties, 95
Functional centrality, 80
  in American colonial family, 63

Gemein, 111
Generation gap, 2, 167–70
Gestapo, 116
Ghettoization, 125–26, 130
Goals of Afro-American leaders
  assimilation, 128–29
  power, 129
  separation, 129
Going steady, 181–82
Group marriage, 16
  See also monogamy, polyandry, polygamy, polygyny

Health care
  in American colonies, 63
  in American contemporary society, 74
Heterogeneous society, 136
Hindu family
  pattern of, 19
  structure of, 19
Historical processes
  in middle-class culture, 104
Historical view of family, 1

374 SUBJECT INDEX

Homogamy, ethnic, 210
   in mate selection, 208–11
   influence of salience on, 211
   racial, 208, 210, 224–30
      norms governing, 225–26
Homogeneous society, 136
Household arrangements, 18–21
Household, types of, 18–21
   blood ties (consanguineal), 18
   extended consanguineal, 18
Humanistic liberalism, 194
Humanistic radicalism, 194–95
Husband-wife power relations
   in American contemporary family, 69–70
Husband-wife relations
   in old age, 311–13
Hutterites, 107–12
Hutterite family
   adolescence in, 111
   discipline in, 109
   endogamy in, 109
   mate selection in, 111
   role differentiation in, 108
   role of women in, 112
   separation of sexes in, 111–12
   socialization in, 109–11
Hutterite society, 108–12, 115
   aging in, 112
   decision-making apparatus, 108
   economic responsibility in, 112
   education of children, 110
   role of men in, 112
   status in, 112

Ideal mate concept, 216–17
Ideal-typical continua, 96–100
Identification
   awareness, 141
   evaluation, 141
   incorporation, 141
   in socialization process, 140–42
   three steps, 141
Identity clarification
   in socialization, 137–38
Illegitimacy
   as challenge to family, 328–29
   in Afro-American family, 121–22

Incest motivation and structure, 31–32
Incest taboo, 26–30, 96
   among Arabs of Kurdistan, 32
   and theory of biological ill effects of inbreeding, 27
   bipolar theory of motivation, 30
   in U.S., 206–07
   origins, 27–28
   parent-offspring, 30–31
   relation to social solidarity (Fox and Young), 29–30
   structural confusion theory, 27
   theory of prohibition
      Freud, 29
      Lowie, 28
      Westermarck, 28
Industrialized society
   family in, 86
Inheritance
   definition, 22
In-law relations
   in U.S., 292–95
   sources of conflict, 293–94
Instability in Afro-American family, 130
Institution
   definition, 1
Institutional differentiation
   in American contemporary society, 74–75
Institutional embeddedness, 11, 12
   in American contemporary society, 73–74
Institutions
   in American colonies, 63
   kinds of, 11
Intermarriage
   laws, 226, 230
   racial.
      See Racial intermarriage
   religious, 208, 210–11

Kin distance, 285–86
   physical or residential, 285
   socio-emotional, 285
Kin-family systems, types of, 16
Kin functions, 278–80
   emotional ties, 280

Kin functions (*continued*)
　housing (residential proximity), 279
　in colonial America, 278–79
　obligatory, 279–80
Kin of orientation, 25, 277
Kin relations of the aged, 307–09
Kinship in U.S., 279–95
　adult sibling relations, 289–91
　categories, 288–95
　factors of conflict, 293–95
　in-law relations, 292–95
　parents and adult offspring, 288–89
　secondary kinship, 291–92
Kinship analysis, 281–88
Kinship network, 284, 286
Kinship relations, 277–95
Kinship system, 11, 80
Kinship units, functions of, 10
Kinsman, as person, 284–85
Kin terms, 281–84

Learning theory of socialization, 137
Literati (Chinese)
　family patterns of, 19
Loss of family functions, 91
Love, 95
　in U.S., 203–30
Lower-class family, 103–07
Lower-class socialization in U.S., 147–53

Marital conflict, in old age, 311
Marital predicaments, 269–71
　individualism vs. familism, 271
　internal vs. external commitment, 269–70
　permanent availability, 270
　planning and gratification, 270
　role differentiation, 269
Marriage
　abrupt transitions in, 235–36, 240
　adjustments in, 264–68
　as a process, 234–40
　changing roles in, 240–46
　communication in, 271–74

Marriage (*continued*)
　decision-making in, 259–62
　definition, 39
　equalitarianism in, 260, 262
　feminization of occupations, 246–47
　financial adjustment, 265–66
　gradual transitions in, 236–40
　husband-father role choices, 246–49
　husband-wife interaction, 259–64
　interactions and adjustments, 259–74
　motives of working wife, 261
　patterns in, 235
　positive value of communication in, 272
　role blurring in, 242–44
　role choice and conflict in, 244–46
　role consensus in, 251
　role differentiation in, 240–42, 262–64, 269
　role of father in, 248–49
　role of man in, 248–49, 264
　role of woman in, 249–50, 264
　role of working wife in, 250–51
　role specialization in, 263
　sexual adjustment in, 266–68
　socioadaptive aspects of personality in, 237–38
　status of working wife in, 252–54
　summary of, 268–74
　value of choice in, 272–74
　wife-mother role choices, 249–55
Marriage arrangements, types of, 16–18
　See also monogamy, polyandry, polygamy, polygyny
Marriage-family-household types
　three structural distinctions, 20–21
Mate selection
　arranged marriage, 176
　as process, 218–21
　empathic ability, 217–18
　filtering process, 218–21

Mate selection (*continued*)
  historical developments within U.S., 177–78
  homogamy in, 208–11
  in Hutterite family, 111
  in U.S., 67, 203–30
  negative factors, 206–11
  open choice in, 177–78
  other psychological factors in, 215–18
  parental image, 217
  positive factors in, 212–18
  restricted choice, 176–77
  types of, 176–78
  values in, 212–13
Mate selection continuum, 96–97
Matriarchal society, 24
Matricentrism in Afro-American family, 120
Matrifocality in Afro-American family, 122–23
Matrilineal descent, 22, 23
Matrilocality, 21
Mechanical solidarity, 86–88
Middle Ages
  effect upon American colonial family, 57
  family in, 56
  history of family in, 56
  nuclear family in, 56
Middle-class family, 103–07
Middle-class socialization
  in U.S., 147–53
Modern American family.
  See American contemporary family
Monogamy, origins of, 4, 17, 18
Moynihan report, 121–22, 126
Multiple marriage, 16
  See also group marriage
Mungdugumor, 135–36

National Council on Family Relations, 6, 7
  purpose, 7
Nayar
  family structure of, 36
  family system of, 35–36, 38
  marriage in, 36–38
Neolocality, 21

Normative household, delineation of, 19
Normative household unit, 18
Normative practices
  workability and value of, 42
Nuclear family, 15, 18–25, 89, 99, 121
  monogany of, 15, 18

Occupational group, family as, 87
Old age
  division of labor in, 312
  husband-wife relations, 311–13
  kin relations, 307–09
  marital conflict in, 311
  role changes in, 307–11
  social network and segregation, 306–11
  See also aging
Oneida Community, 107
Open choice, 98
  and mate selection, 177–78
Order of deviation, 102
Organic solidarity, 88
Orientation, family of, 25
Origins of family, 104–07

Papago Indians
  family structure, 40–41
  family system of, 35–36
  kin embeddedness in, 36
  kin functions, 278, 280
  kinship embeddedness, 40
  kinship organization, 40
  marriage, 41
  sororal polygyny, 42
Patriarchal and equalitarian patterns
  in U.S., 24
Patriarchy, 24
Patrilineage, 88
  and descent, 22
  and inheritance, 22
Permanent availability, 93
Personality adjustment
  relationship to family, 5
Personality integration, 142–43
  and interpersonal adjustment, 143

Personality integration (*continued*)
   and intrapersonal adjustment, 142–43
Personnel embeddedness, 11, 12, 99
   continuum of, 99
Pill, the, 193
Polygyny
   in African family, 117
   prevalence of, 17
Position of women in American contemporary society, 71–72
Premarital intercourse, 189
Premarital pregnancy, 335
Premarital relationships
   in U.S., 2, 176–200
Premarital sex
   as cultural alternative, 195–99
   and morality of American middle-class society, 196
   double standard in, 197
   in U.S., 2, 188–200
   value positions on, 193–95
Primary relationships, 88–91
Primogeniture, 28
Procreation, family of, 25
Propinquity, 207–08
Protection
   in American colonial society, 63
   in American contemporary society, 74
Protestant ethic, 104–07
Proximity, 207–08

Racial homogamy, 210, 224–30
   norms governing, 225–26
Racial intermarriage
   attractiveness-accessibility hypothesis, 228
   economic penalty hypothesis, 228–29
   motives for in U.S., 229–30
Racist attitudes, 128
Radicals
   attitude toward family, 2
Random liaisons, 98
Reform
   Chicago school's interest in, 5

Recreation
   in American colonial society, 63
   in American contemporary society, 74
Relationships
   primary, 88–91
   types of, 89–91
Religion
   in American colonial society, 63
   in American contemporary society, 74
Religious intermarriage, 208, 210–11
Religious subculture
   origins of, 107
Reproduction, 81–82
Residence, common, 15
Residential clustering, 21–22
Restricted choice, 98
   and mate selection, 176–77
Role choice continuum, 98–99
Role differentiation, 87, 105–06
   in adolescence, 165–66
   in Hutterite family, 108
   in marriage, 269
Role loss in old age, 301–02, 304
Roles in marriage, 234–55
Role segregation in Afro-American family, 122
Roles, traditional, 98
Romantic love
   effect of family structure in American colonial society, 60
   in U.S., 203–06
   origins, 58

Salience
   influence on homogamy, 211
Separatist societies, problems of, 112
Sex, extra-marital, 93
   premarital.
      See premarital sex
   relation to love, 203–04
Sex ratio and polygamy, 17
Sexual anarchy, 195
Shakers, 107
Simplification processes, 237
Single standard, 191–93

Slavery, 116–19
Social class endogamy, 209
Social Darwinism, 4
Social network of aged, 306–11
Socialization
    and adolescents, 172–74
    and identity clarification, 137–38
    as function of family, 105–06
    continuum of, 98
    definition, 134
Socialization in U.S., 143–54
    decisions of aged, 304–06
    discipline in, 149–50
    ego struggle, 145–46
    independence, 150–51
    interpersonal adjustment, 146
    intrapersonal adjustment, 146
    principles applied, 143–47
    principles of, 137–43
    psychoanalytic theory of, 137
Socialization process, 134–54
    conscience, 138–39
    ego struggle, 139–40
    identification, 140–42
    learning theory of, 137
    personality integration, 142–43
    psychoanalytic theory in, 137
    role-symbolic interaction theory, 137
Social segment, family as, 87
Sociology of the family, 5–12

Solidarity, mechanical, 86–87
Solidarity, organic, 88
Sororal polygyny
    among Papago Indians, 42
Status in Hutterite society, 112
Structural issues in family, 16
Structure of family, 10
Systematic theory building, 6

Traditional repressive asceticism, 194
Traditional view of child-rearing, 153
Types of descent, 22

Unilineal descent systems, 24
Universal family functions, 81–83
    reproduction, 81–82
    socialization, 82
    status placement, 82
Use of types
    as comparative constructs, 25
    as group identifications, 25
    as reference points on a continuum, 26
    in family structures, 25–26
    summary of, 26

Value autonomy in adolescence, 162
Value positions on premarital sex, 194–95

HQ535 .A56

a74322000016245c

WITHDRAWN
From Bertrand Library

DATE DUE

JUN 24 1981		
MAY 8 1983		
NOV 5 1986		
NOV 10 '87		
DEC 29 '87		
MAY 9 '89		
JUN 20 '95		
DEC 06 1996		
NOV 30 2001		
DEC 05 2006		